The Social Fabric

THE SOCIAL FABRIC

American Life from 1607 to the Civil War

Editors

JOHN H. CARY *Cleveland State University*

JULIUS WEINBERG *Cleveland State University*

LITTLE, BROWN AND COMPANY *Boston Toronto*

Picture research by Pembroke Herbert

Dedicated with love to

Kathryn Ditter Cary

and to Sean, Paul, Kenneth, and Carolyn

Preface

> I know histhry isn't thrue Hinnessy, because it ain't like what I see ivry day
> in Halsted Sthreet. If any wan comes along with a histhry iv Greece or Rome
> that'll show me th' people fightin', gettin' dhrunk, makin' love, gettin' mar-
> ried, owin' the grocery man an' bein' without hard-coal, I'll believe they was
> a Greece or Rome, but not befure.

The sentiment of Mr. Dooley, Finley Peter Dunne's comic Irish philosopher,
expresses the attitude of many people toward history. Young Americans,
especially, question the relevance of a history that deals only with politics,
diplomacy, governments, and famous leaders, and ignores the daily life of
average men and women. Two recent trends, however, are doing much to
remedy this neglect. One is increased popular interest in the forgotten mass
of men and women who tilled our fields, built our cities, and fought our
wars, but who achieved no particular fame and left very little record of their
lives and thought. The second development is the renewed concern of historians with social history.

This kind of history has more meaning for us, and touches our lives more
directly, than any other aspect of our past. In an age seeking "relevance"
nothing is more relevant than American social history. Each of us has direct
experience, or an intimate awareness, of being part of a family, of falling in
love and marrying, of poverty and pain, of suffering in war, of earning a living, of social oppression and reform. By understanding the social life of an
earlier age, we can gain an understanding of ourselves and of others, in
whatever time or place they lived.

This is an anthology of American social history for college history courses.
It began with our belief that college students would find more meaning in
the kind of history described by Mr. Dooley than in political, diplomatic,
or constitutional history. This and the companion volume of *The Social
Fabric*, which covers the period from 1865 to the present, touch upon marry-

ing and making love, fighting and getting drunk, owing the grocer, and going without heat. Covering the time from the earliest settlement of America to the Civil War, it contains descriptions of what it was like to cross the ocean in an immigrant ship and the Great Plains in a covered wagon, what marriage and the family were like in the eighteenth century and what sex was like in the nineteenth, what life was like for women workers in New England factories and for slaves on southern plantations, and how people behaved in a frontier revival meeting or in an austere Shaker community.

No single book can treat every aspect of our history, but these volumes examine American life in much of its diversity. There are essays on women as well as men; on Indians, blacks, and Mexicans as well as whites; and on the poor and the oppressed as well as the rich and the powerful. The sectional, class, racial, and religious differences among our heterogeneous people have created serious strains that at times threatened to tear the nation apart. But with all their diversity, the American people have also shared many common attitudes and traditions that provided a common social fabric to bind them together.

We have selected the readings from some of the most interesting writing on the American past. We have prefaced each reading with an introductory note, explaining the relation of the subject to broader developments in American history of the period. Each selection is also accompanied by an illustration, which provides a visual commentary on the topic under consideration. The study guide that follows the selection will help you review the special aspects of the reading, and may suggest issues for class discussion. The bibliographical note will help you find further material, should you wish to read more on the topic.

We hope that you will enjoy this sampling of American social history as much as we have enjoyed preparing it. In making the final selection from the many writings we might have used, we had the assistance of several of our own students, who gave us their judgments of the potential student interest in each. We express our appreciation to them, and especially to Jenny Chung, who provided secretarial and research assistance. Two editors at Little, Brown — Charles Christensen and Marian Abzug — encouraged us in this project, and the book owes much to their perceptive advice. Rab Bertelsen supervised the editorial and production work with great care and skill. The editors hope that both teachers and students will find this volume useful, and we welcome any suggestions that might improve it.

J.C.
J.W.

Contents

The Expansionist Urge   305

Animosity between Americans and Mexicans in the Southwest during and after the Mexican War.

From Carey McWilliams, *North from Mexico.*

Life in Wartime   321

The great bitterness and surprising compassion between Union and Confederate soldiers during the Civil War.

From Bell I. Wiley, *The Life of Johnny Reb.*

The Social Fabric

1 ORIGINS OF THE AMERICAN PEOPLE

The migration of peoples from Europe, Africa, and the Far East to the Western Hemisphere is one of the greatest stories in all of human history. Though the full force of immigration did not hit these shores until the nineteenth and twentieth centuries, the earliest age of exploration and settlement in the seventeenth and eighteenth centuries saw some of the most important developments in the history of the western world.

In 1600, the land we know as the United States was inhabited by at least 500,000 and perhaps as many as a million and a half Indians, thinly scattered in small tribes from the warlike Iroquois hunters of the Northeast to the pueblo-dwellers of the Southwest. These people, who had crossed from Asia to Alaska about 15,000 years earlier, had used the land and resources well. Killing only for food, traveling by water and forest paths, making their weapons and tools from stone, and using animal skins and bark for their shelters, they had left a beautiful, virgin landscape largely untouched.

By 1607, the first permanent settlement of Englishmen had been established at Jamestown, Virginia. The encounter of these two peoples, the one a hunting society that depended upon game and the other an agricultural people who cleared the forests for planting, was often tragic and sometimes brutal. By 1790, when the first census of the United States was taken, the Atlantic seaboard that the Indian had known was scarcely recognizable. Vast forest regions had been cleared, intercolonial roads were being built, the port towns were developing into bustling cities, and a growing number of adventurers were passing through the mountain gaps to settle the Ohio Valley. Excluding Indians, nearly four million men, women, and children of an extraordinary ethnic diversity lived in the new United States.

This section treats three of the earliest inhabitants of the New World — the American Indian, the African slave, and the English colonist. The first reading describes the life and culture of the Indian tribes that the English settlers first encountered. The second selection depicts the hardships of the voyage aboard an African slave ship, some of which were also suffered on the hundreds of small vessels that braved the rough North Atlantic to bring other settlers to the New World. The third reading describes one pattern of social organization that the colonists established — the New England town — which should be compared with the other forms, such as the southern county, that are described in your textbook or other course reading. Together, these first readings introduce us to three distinct racial groups — red, black, and white — whose conflicts and contributions go far to explain the special character of American society today.

"View of the Village of Secotan" by John White, c. 1584, showing an Indian settlement on the east coast. (Detail)

RUTH M. UNDERHILL

Indian Life and Culture

In order to understand the history of what is now the United States, one must first look to two remote cultures — the European world in the fifteenth century, in which the discovery of the Western Hemisphere was germinating, and the ancient Indian culture that existed on this side of the Atlantic. The red man has lived on this continent for at least 15,000 years and has been in contact with Europeans for nearly 500 years. Yet most Americans know little about Indian life and culture. The movie image of a treacherous savage and the trinket purchased at a souvenir shop have left the real character of the Indian as invisible to the white majority as the black man has been for 300 years.

Oliver La Farge has suggested that the Indian has always been unknown to his more recently arrived fellow countrymen, because of a number of myths that white men found convenient The earliest of these myths — picturing the Indian as a noble, uncorrupted child of nature — survived in distant Europe longer than it did in the British colonies. Here, the more convenient myth of the brutal, treacherous savage supplanted it, as settlers pushed inland and came into conflict with the Indian over land. Eventually, a third myth, that of a drunken, irresponsible dependent, became popular, as an industrialized America pushed the Indian tribes onto reservations.

Anthropologists and historians have been devoting serious attention to the American Indian since Lewis Henry Morgan published a path-breaking study of the Iroquois in 1851. Yet, much of the writing has necessarily been based on a record left by whites, has dealt mostly with Indian-white relations, and leaves the reader wondering what Indian life was like before the first

5

European contacts. Ruth M. Underhill, a distinguished anthropologist, wrote nearly twenty books on American Indians and resided on reservations for as many years while pursuing her studies. *Red Man's America* is one of the best general studies of American Indian societies from the northeastern Iroquois to the Pueblos of the Southwest. This chapter from her book gives us a sense of what life may have been like in the complex, civilized society of the southeastern tribes. Her descriptions of the training of boys for manhood, of attitudes toward war, and of other social institutions give one a sense of being in a prediscovery world. Underhill suggests that some southeastern Indians were influenced by the culture of "Nuclear America," a term that refers to the advanced civilizations that Indians established in Mexico, Central America, and the northeastern part of South America.

Along the streams in Mississippi, Alabama, and all the way up to Ohio, white pioneers used to plow up fine, thin pottery often in human and animal shapes which reminded students of wares from Nuclear America. There were copper plates and shell ornaments depicting warriors in feather mantles; there was cloth with painted designs. As these sites were excavated, it turned out that they were groups of pyramids, crude, perhaps, and made of earth rather than of decorated stone, but nevertheless a form of civic center.

Were the "Mound-builders" who left them a vanished race, even a white race? So went the first fantastic explanations, but it is now plain that the Indians in the Lower and Middle Mississippi area were the ancestors of Indians seen there in historic times and some of whom remain there today.

Their connection with Nuclear America is obvious and possible. The Caribbean Sea and its extension, the Gulf of Mexico, are practically encircled by a ring of warm, forested countries. It would be natural for slash-and-burn farmers in all this area to have worked out the same general arrangement of temples and public buildings in one spot, with the fields and dwelling huts in a wide circle around them. Perhaps the public buildings were placed on pyramids because of swampy land, but, the impressiveness of this style having once been established, many people might copy it. . . .

It would be interesting to know whether the life lived around these civic centers had anything in common with the organized government described

From chapter 3 of *Red Man's America* by Ruth M. Underhill. Copyright 1953 by The University of Chicago. All rights reserved. Reprinted by permission of the author and The University of Chicago Press.

in Yucatán, where the common people were practically serfs, the ruler holy, and human sacrifice a virtue. Certainly there are few signs of such a system among historic Indians, but we can point to one group, visited by the French from 1698 to 1732, who had a system decidedly different from the usual democracy of American Indians.

This group was the Natchez, living in Mississippi, near the site of the great Emerald Mound. . . . Their seven villages of thatched huts were ruled by an absolute monarch, known as Sun, who held such state that no one addressed him except from a distance with shouts and genuflections. When he went out, arrayed in feather mantle and feather crown, he was carried in a litter so that his feet did not touch the ground. He maintained a household of volunteer henchmen who hunted and worked for him and who were killed at his death along with his wife and any others who sought to be with him in the afterlife. When the French were in need of hunters or boatmen, they could always apply to Sun, who would call up as many men as he chose, allowing them no recompense. This may provide a hint as to how the heavy work of mound-building might have been done.

Sun had under him a number of officials, including a war chief and ceremonial officers. Four of these were the guardians of the temple, a wattle-and-daub building mounted on an eight-foot mound. Here a perpetual fire was kept burning, and in an inner room were spirit images and also the bones of former Suns, packed in cane baskets. Many a temple throughout the mound area may have had the same general plan.

The Natchez had a social system with well-defined classes, known as Suns, Nobles, Honored Men, and common people, whom the French called *Puants* or "Stinkards." We cannot be sure that the Natchez class divisions, with their peculiar revolving system of marriages to commoners, were practiced by other southeastern tribes. What we can suppose is that the Southeast was familiar with class titles and class privileges, a condition not usual except among organized people with enough surplus to incite rivalry. Other Natchez customs, echoed over and over again around the Caribbean, are the elevated temple, with its priests, its god-image, and its undying fire, and the war system, including special costumes and names for the warriors, torture of captives, and eating their flesh. More obvious still are items of material equipment — the litter, the bed, the feather cloak, and, of course, the temple mound.

The tribes of this chapter, although they show some traces of an elaborate equipment and organization, may have been late-comers to the area who did not share the full mound-builder culture. The Creek, or Muskogi, largest member of the group, state that they came in from the north when the country was already occupied. So, perhaps, did their relatives, the Chickasaw and Choctaw, all speaking a language known as Muskogean; the Cherokee, their neighbors, both in early southeastern days and after removal, spoke a related language, Iroquoian. They had perhaps separated from the famous

Iroquois of New York State during some early migration. These four show many differences, owing to resources and history, but we shall concentrate on the Creek, the only ones really well known.

The land occupied by these tribes was part of the almost unbroken forest which once stretched from the Mississippi to the Atlantic, threaded with rivers and providing a magnificent food supply. There were nuts, berries, roots, birds, fish, and beasts in such plenty that perhaps it was natural for the Indians not to spend too much time on agriculture. Fields around a Creek civic center usually constituted only 1 per cent of the arable land in the area.

Such work as was done, however, was thoroughly organized. In spring an appointed overseer went through the town blowing on a conchshell to summon all families to the fields. Each family had its own plot, and while the men worked, singing from one to the next, the women cooked the meal, and the day ended with games. Then came summer, when women did the hoeing, while children scared away birds and marauding animals. For harvest, the whole town was called out again, except that now each family reaped its own plot. Produce from the town plot went to the chief by way of both salary and taxes. A more democratic system than that described by Landa for the Maya but with a like flavor of planned organization!

The family plots, with their clusters of bark-covered dwellings, stretched along the creeks of Georgia and Alabama, whence the Indians got their English name. In some central open place was the "town," with its open plaza, the chief's house at one end, and the "great" or council house at the other. One of these, seen in the 1870's, would accommodate several hundred people. Near it was the summer gathering place, where seats were ranged in ranks around a quadrangle. There were a pole for torturing prisoners and a yard for playing the tribal game of chunky, or throwing poles after a rolling stone disk. Some such arrangement was kept long after the Creek moved across the Mississippi, and even the booths for a Baptist camp meeting still show the quadrangular arrangement. . . .

To picture the southeastern Indian, one must get rid of the popular image of a tall, blanketed figure, with long black braids and a sweeping feather headdress. The southeastern man went barefoot, in a breechclout of skin or cloth, and had nothing to decorate except his own body. On this he did elaborate work or had it done by an expert tattooer, with a garfish jaw and soot from the campfire. Each design was an official insigne, beginning with those allowed a youth when he first attained warrior age and then indicating further exploits. A full-fledged warrior, at a distance, might look as though he were wearing a figured skintight garment. His long black hair was pulled out with clamshell tweezers in all sorts of patterns, leaving the head bald on one side, or in front, or everywhere except for the topknot called a scalp lock and left as a challenge to the enemy to "come and get it." Nose and ears were decorated with huge pendants of shell, which were so popular that, in later days, whites made medals of silver and presented them to chiefs for this purpose. This elaborate decoration was for men. Women, having no war honors, were not tattooed. They wore a wrap-around skirt of cloth and, perhaps, some shell necklaces.

The Creek and, in fact, most all southeasterners, counted descent through the mother. This is a common arrangement with agricultural peoples over the world and was once thought to be the rule for all of them. However, the factors controlling human behavior are too varied for any fixed line of development. All the expert can say is that, since women were the first plant-gatherers and therefore the first planters, an agricultural tribe quite often allows its women to own the fields and perhaps the houses, taking in husbands to live with them. Women are not, however, the heads of families. Since the husbands are, quite often, transitory visitors, the position of family head is taken by the woman's brother. He comes away from his own family to discipline that of his sister, just as her husband goes to attend to his sister's family. It may sound complicated, but to those brought up to expect such an arrangement it works.

The mother-right families of the Southeast were usually organized in clans, groups which were, supposedly, descended from the same woman and who all thought of themselves as relatives, forbidden to intermarry. Each clan was named after some local animal, such as bear, deer, or beaver. Perhaps those "totems" were once treated with profound respect, but in the days we know of the relation had become shadowy. So had the tribal division into halves, or moieties, an arrangement which had more to do with government and public games than with family life.

Members of a number of clans might live in any town, and each had its local clan elder who took special responsibility for training the clan boys and guarding the clan morals. Creek training was stricter than that of many Indians, who rarely whip or punish their children and are shocked at the whites who do so. The clan elder saw that boys went out every morning to bathe in the creek which ran by every Creek village. Indeed, the whole population bathed, even breaking the ice in winter. As punishment for misdeeds, children had their arms and legs scratched with the sharp teeth of ever-ready garfish. Boys were often scratched for their own good to make them manly and to accustom them to the sight of blood. In such a case, the skin was first bathed with warm water. "Dry scratching," however, was a punishment meant to hurt. For really bad behavior unbecoming a future warrior, a boy might be beaten with canes — another use for that omnipresent material.

The regular road to success for a young man was war. For the gentle, for the poetic, for the would-be administrator or inventor, there was still no route to public respect but this. A youth before he had been on a war party was called by a "baby name." He sat in a special arbor at ceremonies and performed the most menial tasks. No wonder that the desire to be a great warrior seemed to every boy like a basic human instinct. What a joy and relief it was, at the age of fifteen or so, to follow the men of his first war party! Even if he achieved no killing, he could now have a new name. At the annual New Fire ceremony his clan elder would scratch him ceremonially, lecturing him well on his new status, and then the name would be called out before the assembled villagers. Now he might move to the arbor of the Little Warriors, but even here comrades would look askance upon him until he had brought home scalps or even limbs of enemies. This meant a new name and perhaps more tattooing and the right to wear certain paint and feathers. Occasionally, some youth of gentle nature found himself unable to face this strenuous life. Then he was permitted to don women's clothes and work with the women. No one reproached him, but, like a woman, he could not gain fame.

If he attained a war name in the normal way, a marriage would be ar- ranged for him with some industrious girl of another clan. The affair was conducted by the maternal relatives on both sides, and the young people were not consulted. Even the fathers had little to say, since this was a clan matter and the children belonged to their mother's clan, not to his. The person in charge was usually the maternal uncle, who would insist that the girl be well trained in pottery, weaving, and matmaking. Also she must be careful to keep away from men at the regular times when a supernatural power came upon her. The miracle which made a female capable of bearing children was, to most Indians, something to be feared as well as honored. They considered that a man who approached a woman at such times, ate what she cooked, or touched her belongings would lose his male strength. Therefore, southeastern women were secluded, both at menstruation and at pregnancy, a custom observed to the present day by some Cherokee and Choctaw.

The couple set up housekeeping in the wife's town, sometimes after a simple ceremony such as breaking a corn ear in two or planting two reeds. The Creek, like most Indians, considered marriage a secular and economic event, not under the domain of the spirits, as were the physical crises of birth, puberty, and death. They did allow a trial period, when the couple lived together until the next busk, or green-corn ceremony. At that time, when all debts were forgiven and the new year started, the trial marriage might be dissolved and different mates found.

This entry of the boy into a new family gave plenty of opportunities for friction, and the Creek, along with most southeasterners, used the remedy provided by other mother-right peoples in such a case — the mother-in-law taboo. This custom demands that the young man shall not speak to his mother-in-law and, in some tribes, not even see her. Thus quarrels about supremacy are avoided, and the two, sending ceremonious gifts to each other, regard their relationship as one of respect. With the Creek, the daughter- in-law is said also to have avoided her father-in-law, though, of course, she saw him less often. The whole custom was given up in later days. A man might have several wives if he could support them, but bringing a new woman into his wife's village was a ticklish matter, and her consent was required. If she needed a household helper, she might give it, but otherwise the new wife was visited in her own home, and her children belonged there. There were some elopements and infringements of the marriage rules, but the two clans who had made the alliance were severe on their young people. An unfaithful wife might have the tips of her nose and ears cut off, and her lover might be killed. Divorce, however, was possible with family consent.

Neither divorce nor death freed husband or wife from the marriage tie. The clan of the dead or abandoned spouse took care of the remaining one and saw that proper mourning was observed (one year for a man, four for a woman), and even talking with a person of the opposite sex during that time was adultery. Finally, the clan members provided a new mate from among their numbers, so that the alliance should not lapse. If this was impossible, they provided the widow or widower with new clothes and "set him free."

Southeasterners were elaborate in their mourning, the Creek even paying people to wail, long after the corpse had been interred with elaborate offerings, the house purified, and a new fire lighted there. The Choctaw and Natchez had a custom which suggests ancient burial mounds. They exposed a corpse until the flesh could be picked off by a Buzzard Man or Bone-picker and then placed in, with other skeletons, an earthen mound.

Souls of the dead traveled along the Milky Way, encountering numerous perils until the brave, who had faithfully followed Indian customs, reached the happy hunting ground. This primitive paradise, which had such appeal for whites, did not exist in the beliefs of all Indians, but the southeasterners seem really to have pictured it. Some even talked of its opposite, a sterile place which was the abode of cowards and lawbreakers.

The government of the Creek may seem informal to a modern white, but, compared with that of many Indian groups, it was well advanced in organization. Among historic Indians, only the Iroquois had gone further. Creek towns, when the whites first knew them in the early 1700's, were scattered over a huge expanse in the plateau country of present Alabama and Georgia. They did not all have the same traditions and ancestry or speak the same dialect. The small, compact group which called itself Muskogi told of arriving first in the country and settling down, with most of their towns in the northern part of the area. They became loosely known as the Upper Creeks. Other peoples, like the Hitchiti and the Alabama, drifted in, with the same general traditions but speaking slightly different languages. These got the name of Lower Creeks. The geographic division was not accurate, and the Creek themselves made another on the basis of descent. The old Muskogi group, no matter where located, called themselves the White people, while the others were the People of Alien Speech. All together they formed a loose alliance, recognizing each other as friends, sometimes sharing ceremonies, and looking to each other for help against enemies — not that they always got it.

A further division along administrative lines was growing up, though it never was thoroughly worked out. By this, the White People called themselves the People of Peace. Their towns were sanctuary for murderers and fleeing enemies. They never took the initiative in war, though they helped their allies when necessary. The People of Alien Speech, the Lower Creeks, were the War, or Red, towns who started wars and furnished no sanctuary. It sounds like a clear and interesting arrangement, but it was never completely workable, clans often gravitating somehow to the wrong side. One would like to know how efficient such an arrangement would have been if it had matured.

As it was, the static conditions of old Indian days did not enforce a tight organization. Each town was a little city-state, which joined the activities of either side only if convenient. Each had a *mico* whom the whites later called a king, and indeed, like the Natchez king, he was carried in a litter and wore a feather cloak. However, the Creek had no such reigning family as the Natchez. The king might be any suitable man chosen from some particular White clan. Other clans furnished his official entourage, consisting of a herald or public orator, an agricultural overseer, a feast manager, and perhaps several assistants. At public ceremonies these all had their places ranged according to rank in one of the four arbors, booths, or "beds." A special bed was usually reserved for the Beloved Men, whose very name is reminiscent of the Natchez castes. However, they were not a hereditary body but retired warriors with fine records who deliberated with the king before action was taken. Indians throughout the Southeast and, indeed, all over the country had councils something like this. However, we do not know of other southeasterners having so many officials as the Creek or making so much of rank.

In tranquil times the Creek council met with the king every day in the public square to talk over village affairs to see that everyone "walked the White path." The occasion was almost as much a religious as a civil one, and before it the whole company often purified themselves with an emetic. This "black drink," ceremonially mixed and handed around, was an infusion of *Ilex vomitoria* esteemed by all the tribes around the Gulf and known to the Cherokee as the "beloved tree."

Over against this civilian organization were the self-made men, the warriors, who had attained rank and title by their prowess. They usually had two "beds," one for the mature warriors and one for beginners. Since all men in the tribe were warriors, clan membership did not matter, but it is said that their leader, Big Warrior, must come from a Red clan. He was, in his way, a kind of priest, for he must have had visions promising spirit aid, and he was the custodian of the sacred war bundle, containing such sacred tokens from the spirits as birdskins and animal claws which gave supernatural help.

It was Big Warrior who initiated a war party if the family of some slain warrior were urging revenge or merely if the young bloods were thirsty for glory. He literally drummed up volunteers by marching around his house drumming. The men who gathered prepared themselves for the adventure by fasting and taking emetics for three days in Big Warrior's house. In the daytime they danced, each man using all his imagination to depict the scouting and killing he hoped to achieve. Finally, they smoked the pipe, which gave binding solemnity to any ceremony, as signatures do for modern whites. He "feelingly knew," thundered a Chickasaw war chief at such a time, that "their tomahawks were thirsty to drink the blood of their enemy and their trusty arrows impatient to be on the wing and lest delay should burn their hearts any longer, he gave them the cool, refreshing word: join the holy ark (the war bundle) and away to cut off the devoted enemy."

The Creek were one of the tribes who made much of close-in fighting with a club of hard wood, its knob sometimes spiked with a sharp point of stone or garfish teeth. Their rations were a few handfuls of parched corn per man, and this, mixed with water, would supply both food and drink. The party of thirty or more padded through the woods in single file, and some aver that they walked in one another's footsteps so none could know how many they were. Ahead walked the leader with the sacred bundle on his back. He never let it touch the ground, and at night, when he rested it on forked sticks, it must always point toward the enemy.

The attack was of the type used by modern commandos — a quick, destructive rush and then safe retirement. "They never face their enemies in open field," said [Mark] Catesby, "which they say is great folly in the English, but sulk from one covert to another," walking silently through the forests in order to surprise some sleeping town just before dawn. Throwing firebrands on the roofs of the thatched houses was an excellent commando tactic, then a shower of arrows on the escaping inhabitants, and, finally, some clubbing and scalping at close quarters. Scalps of women and children ranked as high as those of men, and, in fact, the Creek considered them more valuable, since they could not be had except by marching right into enemy country.

Scalps were not the only trophies. Like all the circum-Caribbean peoples, the southeasterners considered an arm, a leg, or a head just as good for proclaiming their achievement. Even better was a captive. The Creek did not make great use of slaves, as some other Indians did, and, if they took a few women and children or men who were not burned, these were usually adopted into the tribe. What they wanted was a warrior, in the prime of life, who could be tortured as a public spectacle. When such a man was tied to the slave post in the Creek square, he knew what was in store, and he was ready with his taunting death song. True, if he could escape to the house of the chief medicine man or to a White town, he would be safe. Still, this would have needed the connivance of some of the people, and, for them, this gruesome spectacle was one of the high points of the year, a release for emotions usually held in check. It was the women who took the chief part. Perhaps stabbing a victim with torches and cutting off parts of the body relieved the grief for their lost men which they could not assuage by active battle.

Southeasterners did not feast on the enemy's body as did the Aztec and a number of South American tribes. The victor, however, did sometimes eat the heart of a brave foe, in order to acquire his virtues. And fighting, though "a man's chief happiness," as the Cherokee said, was shot through with ceremony and always under the guidance of the spirits.

The torture scene had to wait until such warriors as had killed an enemy were freed of danger from his ghost. This attitude, well known in northern and western America, was unusual in the Southeast. The Creek, however, felt that ghosts, anxious to be avenged, would follow the war party home and, unless exorcised, would bring disease. Therefore the returned warriors retired to the house of their priestly leader to fast and take medicine for four days. After that came the victory celebration and honors for the war- riors. Those who could recount great achievements might receive such a title as Wild Man or Hardhearted Man, with special tattoo marks and with turbans of swan's feathers for the warriors and eagle feathers for the leader. That is, if the leader had been successful. Woe to him if the expedition had failed or if he had lost a man or two! Such bad judgment and disfavor of the spirits might be overlooked once, but, if it happened again, he would be deposed from his high position, even if he were Big Warrior, the great war chief, himself.

War was a business with the Civilized Tribes and, as such, a principal concern of the spirits. Even games, the "little brother of war," as the Cherokee called them, were undertaken only after fasting and with the help of medicine men. The tribal game, played with two netted racquets and a solid, hair-stuffed ball, was the southeastern version of lacrosse and probably its original. When played between two towns, it aroused as much excitement and involved as much betting as a modern college football game. It was rough enough to mean serious injury and, in fact, was instituted so that young men could distinguish themselves without risk of death in war.

Besides games, the Creek had the excitements of visiting and of trade. The southeasterners had regular trails running through the Gulf states — trails which have now become automobile highways. They could travel long distances by canoe with short portages or on foot, single file, through the forest. Whenever there was peace between tribes, little parties of men must have been always on the move. Seashells were brought from the coast to the inland region and copper from the Great Lakes. A crude kind of stool made in the West Indies appears now and then among the Creek or Cherokee. Here we have obviously the signs of contact, perhaps of long standing, and with north as well as south. The god-image in the temple is surely a southern trait. But the Five Tribes believed also in a number of spirits who often remind us of northern hunting tribes. These spirits were the plants and animals, which embodied for many Indians the mysterious force that seems to pervade all nature. Above them were spirits of the earth and the air, and beyond them all was Master of Breath, who had created man. This lofty conception is found among many eastern Indians, yet it is not equivalent to the white man's idea of God. Master of Breath had indeed given life, but he did not cherish and guard his people like the Jehovah of the Bible. Nor is he the master of the happy hunting ground, with some version of a devil ruling in hell. He is only one spirit among many, gifted with a special power. It behooves man to show respect to all spirits, making them small offerings at his meals and his hunt, observing the ceremonies which they dictated long ago, and obeying their laws.

Intermediaries between man and the spirits were of two kinds. One was the priest or doctor, the wise man trained in the rituals for curing disease, for bringing success in war, and for taking charge of the temple. Such a man had been through the long course of training with an older expert, but for some of the high offices it was necessary that he belong to a certain clan. He has a general relationship to the priests of Nuclear America, who also must learn their lore and receive their positions by appointment. Different from him was the inspired Knower, or shaman, who received his knowledge direct from the spirits. His is a type which we shall frequently meet among the simpler hunting peoples and which is often more complex. With most southeasterners the inspired shaman still had a function in foretelling events and in diagnosing disease.

This does not mean that he paid regard to symptoms, for, to most Indians, the outward form taken by disease had little significance. The important thing was its cause, whether in the breaking of some taboo, an evil dream, the anger of some offended spirit, or the malevolence of a human witch. If the cause were dealt with, the symptoms automatically disappeared. Hence the diagnostic functions of the Knower as one who must discover by trance or other form of divination what was causing the disease and therefore which expert could dispel it with his formula. With Creek and Cherokee, especially, the animals were frequent causes of disease. The Creek considered that each animal was lord over some ailment which it could cause or cure, depending on how it had been treated. The Cherokee, with even more logic, decided that the animals sent disease in revenge for being killed by the human race but that the plants, in mercy, provided the remedies. Formulas were known to the priest-doctors, to be used in combination with rubbing the patient or spurting medicine over him from mouth or tube, for the internal administration of remedies was not common. Thus the Creek, in curing headache, which was caused by mice, chanted the words:

> Gallop away, gallop away, gallop away!
> Red rat, red cloud.
> My head is hot, is roaring.

The Cherokee believed that the same ailment was caused by the Little People of the mountains. Their doctor chewed ginseng and spurted it over the patient, singsonging the hypnotic words:

> The men have just passed by, they have caused relief.
> The wizards have just passed by, they have caused relief.
> Relief has been rubbed. They have caused relief. Sharp.

Ailments caused by human witches might result in the loss of the soul, which was brought back by incantations. Or they could project a foreign object into the body, and this the doctor sucked out through a tube made of sawed-off bison bone. These witches were sometimes thought to be doctors gone wrong. A doctor whose ministrations often failed might be killed on suspicion of such practices, just as a war leader was deposed if not victorious. Southeasterners felt that spirit power, properly used, must always bring success.

Successful doctors, often chosen from special clans, took charge of the round of ceremonies by which the southeasterners kept the favor of the spirits. There were dances to celebrate the ripening of the various wild foods, but the ceremony which stood out above all others was that which celebrated the first eating in midsummer of green corn. The vanished Natchez had a feast of this sort most ceremoniously observed, and we can imagine that many of the Temple Mound people had done the same. All Five Tribes had something of the sort, while the Creek made this occasion, the busk, or *bosquito,* their New Year's festival, at which time each town was purified and set right with the spirits for the year. Aztec and Maya put out their fires every fifty-two years at the end of the Venus cycle and started afresh with a sacred fire from one of the temples. The Creek, like the Natchez, made no such elaborate calculation. Every year, in July, when the first corn was harvested, they swept their homes, put out the fires, and threw away the old dishes. New fire was made at the plaza, where the men sat fasting and purifying themselves with emetics. The Creek used a number of plants for this purpose, most frequently the *Cassine vomitoria*, which was revered by all the maritime tribes. For the solemn occasion, however, two emetics were mixed, each from a number of herbs. They were handed around with the ceremonial cry, "Yahola," and the writer, who has seen this observance, can testify that a man so purified spouted like a hydrant. Nevertheless, the men thus fasted and cleansed themselves for four days, while ranged in their arbors according to rank and listening to laws and admonitory speeches from the officials.

After the purification, new fire was made, and the women, coming to the forbidden holy ground, could light their torches and start home life anew. The new corn, from which everyone had abstained, even if he were reduced to a diet of berries, was now taken to the town granary, cooked like a sacramental feast, and eaten.

At this time all crimes were forgiven except that of murder. New laws were discussed by the council and called out by the crier from the chief's arbor. Boys were scratched and received their new names. Children were lectured by visiting uncles. There were nights of dancing outside the square, sometimes by men and sometimes by women. The celebration ended with a wild, tussling game, when men and women threw a baseball-sized missile at a skull or a carved bird atop a tall pole. Finally, the whole town marched to the nearby stream, men first, then women, then children. After a purifying bath, the ceremony was over and the town right for another year with its gods.

Cherokee and Seminole also took the black drink, and it was a custom among the Timucua in Florida. Some Oklahoma Creek still hold the ceremony, with a few of the midsummer dances, while the Seminole have even more. A favorite among these is the Snake Dance, performed for pleasure and known to whites as the "stomp dance." Here men and women, their hands on each other's shoulders, circle around a fire, the leader roaring out a line of song and the others responding antiphonally, ever louder and faster. Other ceremonies have lapsed unless they are part of a paid spectacle, to which whites are admitted, for most of the members of all the Five Tribes have been in Oklahoma for over a hundred years and are well on their way to assimilation into modern life.

STUDY GUIDE

1. How was society organized and governed among the southeastern tribes?

2. In what ways did the Indian family, and the roles of men, women, and children, differ from European and American patterns?

3. Considering Indian government, the Indian personality, and attitudes toward war and religion, how does the picture presented by Underhill differ from the myths that La Farge says Europeans held?

4. Consider where Underhill got her information for describing the southeastern Indians. What elements in her description might have come from Indian artifacts, archaeology, and Indian oral traditions, rather than from writings of whites?

BIBLIOGRAPHY

One should keep in mind that in this selection Underhill is portraying only one of many different Indian societies. Generally, we have tended to see Indian culture as a monolithic system and to ignore important differences among the various tribes. Many of us think of all Indians as wearing colorful headdresses, living in tepees, using horses and canoes for transportation, and depending upon the bow and arrow for their livelihood. Dress, housing, economy, marital customs, burial rites, and agricultural patterns varied widely in different regions. Your library may have some of the specialized studies of these aspects of Indian life or books on individual tribes through which you can extend your knowledge of these first Americans. The paperback edition of Underhill's book can be ordered from the University of Chicago Press, if you would like to know more about Indians in other parts of North America. The following are also excellent general studies (an asterisk after the title indicates that the book is available in paperback): Harold E. Driver, *The Indians of North America,** 2nd ed. (Chicago, 1969); William T. Hagan, *American Indians* * (Chicago, © 1961); Alvin M. Josephy, Jr., *The Indian Heritage of America* * (New York, 1968); and Clark Wissler, *Indians of the United States,** rev. ed. (Garden City, N.Y., 1966). Since the great conflict between the French and English for the North American continent centered on the northern colonies, the Iroquois and Algonquin peoples played an especially important role in eighteenth-century history. Anthony F. C. Wallace, *The Death and Rebirth of the Seneca* * (New York, 1970) is a fascinating study of one of the Iroquois tribes. Like Underhill's work, it draws upon both anthropological and historical studies.

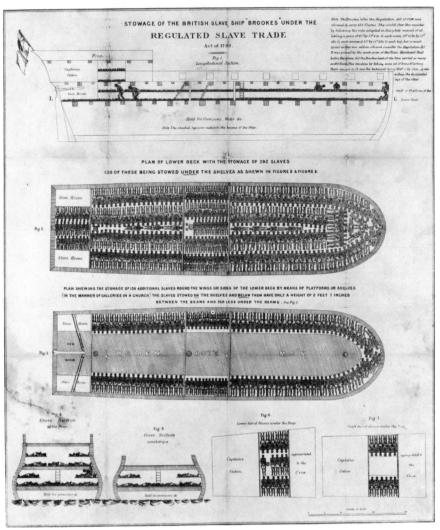

Diagrams of the slave ship Brookes, *1788. The science of stowing large numbers of blacks increased slave-trade profits.*

DANIEL P. MANNIX

MALCOLM COWLEY

Voyage from Africa

The attitude of British colonials — and later, of Americans — to blacks, who first landed at Jamestown in 1619, was as mythical as their view of the Indian. Influenced by sexual anxieties, economic self-interest, physical distinctions, and other factors, white men found it inconvenient, even impossible, to view the black man unemotionally.

The serious study of black history began well before 1900. As with Indian history, a number of circumstances limited such study, even by thoughtful scholars who tried to be objective and fair. Black Americans had left some written records and a substantial oral tradition, but most of the source material from which black history was written was left by whites — white newspaper reporters, white planters, and white travelers in the South. An equally important limitation was the fact that historians were most interested in those aspects of black history that shed light upon general American history. Thus, their attention was concentrated upon slavery. If one were interested in the period 1787–1850, one confronted slavery whether one studied the Constitution, agriculture, presidential and Congressional politics, westward expansion, or social reform.

Other aspects of Negro life and culture that were only marginally related to white concerns went unstudied. African influences upon American culture, black religion, slave marital and family patterns, even the impact of slavery on the American black's personality and psychology, received but scant attention. With the exception of slavery, black history before the cotton gin was not considered worthy of intensive study. The central stream of American social and cultural life clearly came from Europe, as had the ancestors of most Americans, and little note was taken of the very early origins of the Afro-American minority. School-children knew of the struggles aboard the Mayflower, but little of the conditions aboard the slave ship.

Yet a very large proportion of black Americans today can assume that their ancestors were in this country before 1800 — a larger proportion certainly than of white Americans. Most of them can also be certain that their ancestors came in chains. Like no other people, they were rugged pioneers who cherished freedom, suffering harrowing hardships involuntarily, helping to establish the foundations of American agriculture under the lash, and making the way easier for later generations who continued them in slavery. They resisted their oppression, frequently taking their own lives in the course of the infamous middle passage across the Atlantic Ocean. *Black Cargoes* by Daniel Mannix and Malcolm Cowley describes the notorious traffic in human beings from the capture and sale in Africa to the "breaking in" of slaves on New World plantations. The selection that follows gives us a vivid picture of the conditions aboard a slave ship — the quarters and food, the disease and filth, the brutality and boredom, and the courageous determination to gain freedom of a group of our forefathers who happened to be black.

There were two schools of thought among the Guinea captains, called the "loose-packers" and the "tight-packers." The former argued that by giving the slaves a little more room, with better food and a certain amount of liberty, they reduced the mortality among them and received a better price for each slave in the West Indies. The tight-packers answered that although the loss of life might be greater on each of their voyages, so too were the net receipts from a larger cargo. If many of the survivors were weak and emaciated, as was often the case, they could be fattened up in a West Indian slave yard before being offered for sale. The argument between the two schools continued as long as the trade itself, but for many years after 1750 the tight-packers were in the ascendant. So great was the profit on each slave landed alive in the West Indies that hardly a captain refrained from loading his vessel to her utmost capacity. The hold of a slaving vessel was usually about five feet high. That seemed like waste space to the Guinea merchants,

From *Black Cargoes: A History of the Atlantic Slave Trade* by Daniel P. Mannix and Malcolm Cowley. Copyright © 1962 by Daniel P. Mannix. Reprinted by permission of The Viking Press, Inc.

so they built a shelf or platform in the middle of it, extending six feet from each side of the vessel. When the bottom of the hold was completely covered with flesh, another row of slaves was packed on the platform. If there was as much as six feet of vertical space in the hold, a second platform might be installed above the first, sometimes leaving only twenty inches of headroom for the slaves; they could not sit upright during the whole voyage. The Reverend John Newton writes from personal observation:

> The cargo of a vessel of a hundred tons or a little more is calculated to purchase from 220 to 250 slaves. Their lodging rooms below the deck which are three (for the men, the boys and the women) besides a place for the sick, are sometimes more than five feet high and sometimes less; and this height is divided toward the middle for the slaves lie in two rows, one above the other, on each side of the ship, close to each other like books upon a shelf. I have known them so close that the shelf would not easily contain one more.
>
> The poor creatures, thus cramped, are likewise in irons for the most part which makes it difficult for them to turn or move or attempt to rise or to lie down without hurting themselves or each other. Every morning, perhaps, more instances than one are found of the living and the dead fastened together.

Dr. Falconbridge stated in his Parliamentary testimony that "he made the most of the room," in stowing the slaves, "and wedged them in. They had not so much room as a man in his coffin either in length or breadth. When he had to enter the slave deck, he took off his shoes to avoid crushing the slaves as he was forced to crawl over them." Taking off shoes on entering the hold seems to have been a widespread custom among surgeons. Falconbridge "had the marks on his feet where [the slaves] bit and pinched him." . . .

On the *Brookes,* which Captain Parrey considered to be typical, every man was allowed a space six feet long by sixteen inches wide (and usually about two feet, seven inches high); every woman, a space five feet, ten inches long by sixteen inches wide; every boy, five feet by fourteen inches; every girl, four feet, six inches by twelve inches. The *Brookes* was a vessel of 320 tons. By the law of 1788 it was permitted to carry 454 slaves, and the chart, which later became famous, showed how and where 451 of them could be stowed away. Captain Parrey failed to see how the captain could find room for three more. Nevertheless, Parliament was told by reliable witnesses, including Dr. Thomas Trotter, formerly surgeon of the *Brookes,* that before the new law was passed she had carried 600 slaves on one voyage and 609 on another. . . .

Those months when a slaver lay at anchor off the Guinea Coast, taking on her cargo, were the most dangerous stage of her triangular voyage. Not only was her crew exposed to African fevers and the revenge of angry natives; not only was there the chance of her being taken by pirates or by a hostile man-of-war; but also there was the constant threat of a slave mutiny. . . .

. . . James Barbot, Sr., of the *Albion-Frigate,* made the mistake of providing his slaves with knives so they could cut their meat. The slaves tore pieces of iron from the forecastle door, broke off their shackles, and killed the guard at the entrance to the hatchway. Before the mutiny was quelled, twenty-eight slaves either had been shot dead or had thrown themselves overboard. Bosman went through two mutinies. In the second of these the slaves would have mastered the ship had it not been aided by a French and an English vessel. About twenty slaves were killed. William Snelgrave survived more perils on the coast than any other Guinea captain of the early eighteenth century. Among the perils were three mutinies, one at Old Calabar, when there were four hundred slaves on his father's ship and only ten sailors not disabled by fever, and the other two on the Gold Coast. Both the Gold Coast mutinies were led by Coromantees, against hopeless odds. About the first of these he says:

> This Mutiny began at Midnight. . . . Two Men that stood Centry at the Forehatch way . . . permitted four [slaves] to go to that Place, but neglected to lay the Gratings again, as they should have done; whereupon four more Negroes came on Deck . . . and all eight fell on the two Centries who immediately called out for help. The Negroes endeavoured to get their Cutlaces from them, but the Lineyards (that is the Lines by which the Handles of the Cutlaces were fastened to the Men's Wrists) were so twisted in the Scuffle, that they could not get them off before we came to their Assistance. The Negroes perceiving several white Men coming towards them, with Arms in their Hands, quitted the Centries and jumped over the Ship's Side into the Sea. . . .
>
> After we had secured these People, I called the Linguists, and ordered them to bid the Men-Negroes between Decks be quiet; (for there was a great noise amongst them). On their being silent, I asked, "What had induced them to mutiny?" They answered, "I was a great Rogue to buy them, in order to carry them away from their own Country, and that they were resolved to regain their Liberty if possible." I replied, "That they had forfeited their Freedom before I bought them, either by Crimes or by being taken in War.". . . Then I observed to them, "That if they should gain their Point and escape to the Shore, it would be of no Advantage to them, because their Countrymen would catch them, and sell them to other Ships." This served my purpose, and they seemed to be convinced of their Fault. . . .

There are fairly detailed accounts of fifty-five mutinies on slavers from 1699 to 1845, not to mention passing references to more than a hundred others. The list of ships "cut off" by the natives — often in revenge for the kidnaping of freemen — is almost as long. On the record it does not seem that Africans submitted tamely to being carried across the Atlantic like chained beasts. . . .

As long as a vessel lay at anchor, the slaves could dream of seizing it. If they managed to kill the crew, as they did in perhaps one mutiny out of ten, they could cut the anchor cable and let the vessel drift ashore. That opportunity was lost as soon as the vessel put to sea. Ignorant of navigation, which they regarded as white man's magic, the slaves were at the mercy of the captain. They could still die, but not with any hope of regaining their freedom.

The captain, for his part, had finished the most dangerous leg of his triangular voyage. Now he had to face only the ordinary perils of the sea, most of which were covered by his owners' insurance against fire, shipwreck, pirates and rovers, letters of mart and counter-mart, barratry, jettison, and foreign men-of-war. Among the risks not covered by insurance, the greatest was that the cargo might be swept away by disease. The underwriters refused to issue such policies, arguing that they would expose the captain to an unholy temptation. If insured against disease among his slaves, he might take no precautions against it and might try to make his profit out of the insurance. . . .

On a canvas of heroic size, Thomas Stothard, Esq., of the Royal Academy, depicted "The Voyage of the Sable Venus from Angola to the West Indies." His painting is handsomely reproduced in the second volume of Bryan Edwards' *History of the West Indies,* where it appears beside a poem on the same allegorical subject by an unnamed Jamaican author, perhaps Edwards himself. In the painting the ship that carries the Sable Venus is an immense scallop shell, in which she sits upright on a velvet throne. . . .

Meanwhile the Sable Venus, if she was a living woman borne from Angola to the West Indies, was roaming the deck of a ship that stank of excrement, so that, as with any slaver, "You could smell it five miles down wind." She had been torn from her husband and her children, she had been branded on the left buttock, and she had been carried to the ship bound hand and foot, lying in the bilge at the bottom of a dugout canoe. Now she was the prey of the ship's officers, in danger of being flogged to death if she resisted them. Her reward if she yielded was a handful of beads or a sailor's kerchief to tie around her waist.

Here is how she and her shipmates spent the day.

If the weather was clear, they were brought on deck at eight o'clock in the morning. The men were attached by their leg irons to the great chain that ran along the bulwarks on both sides of the ship; the women and half-grown boys were allowed to wander at will. About nine o'clock the slaves were served their first meal of the day. If they were from the Windward Coast, the fare consisted of boiled rice, millet, or cornmeal, which might be cooked with a few lumps of salt beef abstracted from the sailors' rations. If they were from the Bight of Biafra, they were fed stewed yams, but the Congos and the Angolans preferred manioc or plantains. With the food they were all given half a pint of water served out in a pannikin.

After the morning meal came a joyless ceremony called "dancing the slaves." "Those who were in irons," says Dr. Thomas Trotter, surgeon of the *Brookes* in 1783, "were ordered to stand up and make what motions they could, leaving a passage for such as were out of irons to dance around the deck." Dancing was prescribed as a therapeutic measure, a specific against suicidal melancholy, and also against scurvy — although in the latter case it was a useless torture for men with swollen limbs. While sailors paraded the deck, each with a cat-o'-nine-tails in his right hand, the men slaves "jumped in their irons" until their ankles were bleeding flesh. . . .

While some of the sailors were dancing the slaves, others were sent below to scrape and swab out the sleeping rooms. It was a sickening task, and it was not well performed unless the captain imposed an iron discipline. James Barbot, Sr., was proud of the discipline maintained on the *Albion-Frigate*. "We were very nice," he says, "in keeping the places where the slaves lay clean and neat, appointing some of the ship's crew to do that office constantly and thrice a week we perfumed betwixt decks with a quantity of good vinegar in pails, and red-hot bullets in them, to expel the bad air, after the place had been well washed and scrubbed with brooms." Captain Hugh Crow, the last legal English slaver, was famous for his housekeeping. "I always took great pains," he says, "to promote the health and comfort of all on board, by proper diet, regularity, exercise, and cleanliness, for I considered that on keeping the ship clean and orderly, which was always my hobby, the success of our voyage mainly depended." Consistently he lost fewer slaves in the Middle Passage than the other captains, some of whom had the filth in the hold cleaned out only once a week. A few left their slaves to wallow in excrement during the whole Atlantic passage.

At three or four in the afternoon the slaves were fed their second meal, often a repetition of the first. Sometimes, instead of African food, they were given horse beans, the cheapest provender from Europe. The beans were boiled to a pulp, then covered with a mixture of palm oil, flour, water, and red pepper, which the sailors called "slabber sauce." Most of the slaves detested horse beans, especially if they were used to eating yams or manioc. Instead of eating the pulp, they would, unless carefully watched, pick it up by handfuls and throw it in each other's faces. That second meal was the end of their day. As soon as it was finished they were sent below, under the guard of sailors charged with stowing them away on their bare floors and platforms. The tallest men were placed amidships, where the vessel was widest; the shorter ones were tumbled into the stern. Usually there was only room for them to sleep on their sides, "spoon fashion." Captain William Littleton told Parliament that slaves in the ships on which he sailed might lie on their backs if they wished — "though perhaps," he conceded, "it might be difficult all at the same time." . . .

. . . The usual occasion for quarrels was their problem of reaching the latrines. These were inadequate and hard to find in the darkness of the crowded hold, especially by men who were ironed together in pairs.

In each of the apartments [says Dr. Falconbridge] are placed three or four large buckets, of a conical form, nearly two feet in diameter at the bottom and only one foot at the top and in depth about twenty-eight inches, to which, when necessary, the negroes have recourse. It often happens that those who are placed at a distance from the buckets, in endeavoring to get to them, tumble over their companions, in consequence of their being shackled. These accidents, although unavoidable, are productive of continual quarrels in which some of them are always bruised. In this situation, unable to proceed and prevented from going to the tubs, they desist from the attempt; and as the necessities of nature are not to be resisted, they ease themselves as they lie.

In squalls or rainy weather, the slaves were never brought on deck. They were served their two meals in the hold, where the air became too thick and poisonous to breathe. Says Dr. Falconbridge, "For the purpose of admitting fresh air, most of the ships in the slave-trade are provided, between the decks, with five or six air-ports on each side of the ship, of about six inches in length and four in breadth; in addition to which, some few ships, but not one in twenty, have what they denominate wind-sails." These were funnels made of canvas and so placed as to direct a current of air into the hold. "But whenever the sea is rough and the rain heavy," Falconbridge continues, "it becomes necessary to shut these and every other conveyance by which the air is admitted. . . . The negroes' rooms very soon become intolerably hot. The confined air, rendered noxious by the effluvia exhaled from their bodies and by being repeatedly breathed, soon produces fevers and fluxes which generally carry off great numbers of them."

Dr. Trotter says that when tarpaulins were thrown over the gratings, the slaves would cry, "Kickeraboo, kickeraboo, we are dying, we are dying." "I have known," says Henry Ellison, a sailor before the mast, "in the Middle Passage, in rains, slaves confined below for some time. I have frequently seen them faint through heat, the steam coming through the gratings, like a furnace." Falconbridge gives one instance of their sufferings.

Some wet and blowing weather [he says] having occasioned the port-holes to be shut and the grating to be covered, fluxes and fevers among the negroes ensued. While they were in this situation, I frequently went down among them till at length their rooms became so extremely hot as to be only bearable for a very short time. But the excessive heat was not the only thing that rendered their situation intolerable. The deck, that is, the floor of their rooms, was so covered with the blood and mucus which had proceeded from them in consequence of the flux, that it resembled a slaughter-house. . . . Numbers of the slaves having fainted they were carried upon deck where several of them died and the rest with great difficulty were restored. It had nearly proved fatal to me also. The climate was too warm to admit the wearing of any clothing but a shirt and that I had pulled off before I went down; notwithstanding which, by only continuing among them for about a quarter of an hour, I was so overcome with the heat, stench and foul air that I nearly fainted; and it was only with assistance that I could get on deck. The consequence was that I soon after fell sick of the same disorder from which I did not recover for several months.

Not surprisingly, the slaves often went mad. Falconbridge mentions a woman on the *Emilia* who had to be chained to the deck. She had lucid intervals, however, and during one of these she was sold to a planter in Jamaica. Men who went insane might be flogged to death, to make sure that they were not malingering. Some were simply clubbed on the head and thrown overboard.

While the slaves were on deck they had to be watched at all times to keep them from committing suicide. Says Captain Phillips of the *Hannibal*, "We had about 12 negroes did wilfully drown themselves, and others starv'd themselves to death; for," he explained, " 'tis their belief that when they die they return home to their own country and friends again." This belief was reported from various regions, at various periods of the trade, but it seems to have been especially prevalent among the Ibo of eastern Nigeria. In 1788, nearly a hundred years after the *Hannibal's* voyage, Ecroide Claxton was the surgeon who attended a shipload of Ibo. "Some of the slaves," he testified, "wished to die on an idea that they should then get back to their own country. The captain in order to obviate this idea, thought of an expedient viz. to cut off the heads of those who died intimating to them that if determined to go, they must return without heads. The slaves were accordingly brought up to witness the operation. One of them by a violent exertion got loose and flying to the place where the nettings had been unloosed in order to empty the tubs, he darted overboard. The ship brought to, a man was placed in the main chains to catch him which he perceiving, made signs which words cannot express expressive of his happiness in escaping. He then went down and was seen no more."

Dr. Isaac Wilson, a surgeon in the Royal Navy, made a Guinea voyage on the *Elizabeth* [of] Captain John Smith, who was said to be very humane. Nevertheless, Wilson was assigned the duty of whipping the slaves. "Even in the act of chastisement," Wilson says, "I have seen them look up at me with a smile, and, in their own language, say, 'presently we shall be no more.' " One woman on the *Elizabeth* found some rope yarn, which she tied to the armorer's vise; she fastened the other end round her neck and was found dead in the morning. On the *Brookes* when Thomas Trotter was her surgeon, there was a man who, after being accused of witchcraft, had been sold into slavery with his whole family. During his first night on shipboard he tried to cut his throat. Dr. Trotter sewed up the wound, but on the following night the man not only tore out the sutures but tried to cut his throat on the other side. From the ragged edges of the wound and the blood on his fingers, he seemed to have used his nails as the only available instrument. His hands were tied together after the second wound, but he then refused all food, and he died of hunger in eight or ten days.

"Upon the negroes refusing to take food," says Falconbridge, "I have seen coals of fire, glowing hot, put on a shovel and placed so near their lips as to scorch and burn them. And this has been accompanied with threats of forcing them to swallow the coals if they persisted in refusing to eat. This generally had the required effect"; but if the Negroes still refused, they were flogged day after day. Lest flogging prove ineffective, every Guineaman was provided with a special instrument called the "speculum oris," or mouth opener. It looked like a pair of dividers with notched legs and with a thumbscrew at the blunt end. The legs were closed and the notches were hammered between the slave's teeth. When the thumbscrew was tightened, the legs of the instrument separated, forcing open the slave's mouth; then food was poured into it through a funnel.

Even the speculum oris sometimes failed with a slave determined to die. Dr. Wilson reports another incident of his voyage on the *Elizabeth*, this one concerning a young man who had refused to eat for several days. Mild means were used to divert him from his resolution, "as well as promises," Wilson says, "that he should have anything he wished for; but still he refused to eat. He was then whipped with the cat but this also was ineffectual. He always kept his teeth so fast that it was impossible to get anything down. We then endeavored to introduce a Speculum Oris between his teeth but the points were too obtuse to enter and next tried a bolus knife but with the same effect. In this state he was for four or five days when he was brought up as dead to be thrown overboard. . . . I finding life still existing, repeated my endeavours though in vain and two days afterwards he was brought up again in the same state as before. . . . In his own tongue he asked for water which was given him. Upon this we began to have hopes of dissuading him from his design but he again shut his teeth as fast as ever and resolved to die and on the ninth day from his first refusal he died."

One deadly scourge of the Guinea cargoes was a phenomenon called "fixed melancholy." Even slaves who were well fed, treated with kindness, and kept under relatively sanitary conditions would often die one after another for no apparent reason; they simply had no wish to live. Fixed melancholy seems to have been especially rife among the Ibo and among the food-gathering tribes of the Gaboon, but no Negro nation was immune to it. Although the disease was noted from the earliest days of the trade, perhaps the best description of it was written by George Howe, an American medical student who shipped on an illegal slaver in 1859:

Notwithstanding their apparent good health [Howe says] each morning three or four dead would be found, brought upon deck, taken by the arms and heels, and tossed overboard as unceremoniously as an empty bottle. Of what did they die? And [why] always at night? In the barracoons it was known that if a Negro was not amused and kept in motion, he would mope, squat down with his chin on his knees and arms clasped about his legs and in a very short time die. Among civilized races it is thought almost impossible to hold one's breath until death follows. It is thought the African can do so.

They had no means of concealing anything and certainly did not kill each other. One of the duties of the slave-captains was when they found a slave sitting with knees up and head drooping, to start them up, run them about the deck, give them a small ration of rum, and divert them until in a normal condition.

It is impossible for a human being to hold his breath until he dies. Once he loses consciousness, his lungs fill with air and he recovers. The simplest explanation for the slaves' ability to "will themselves dead" is that they were in a state of shock as a result of their being carried through the terrifying surf into the totally unfamiliar surroundings of the ship. In certain conditions shock can be as fatal as physical injury. There may, however, be another explanation. The communal life of many tribes was so highly organized by a system of customs, relationships, taboos, and religious ceremonies that there was practically nothing a man or a woman could do that was not prescribed by tribal law. To separate an individual from this complex system of interrelationships and suddenly place him, naked and friendless, in a completely hostile environment was in some respects a greater shock than any amount of physical brutality. . . .

Along with their human cargoes, crowded, filthy, undernourished, and terrified out of the wish to live, the ships also carried an invisible cargo of microbes, bacilli, spirochetes, viruses, and intestinal worms from one continent to another; the Middle Passage was a crossroads and marketplace of diseases. From Europe came smallpox, measles (less deadly to Africans than to American Indians), gonorrhea, and syphilis (which last Columbus's sailors had carried from America to Europe). The African diseases were yellow fever (to which the natives were more resistant than white men), dengue, blackwater fever, and malaria (which was not specifically African, but which most of the slaves carried in their bloodstreams). If anopheles mosquitoes were present, malaria spread from the slaves through any new territories to which they were carried. Other African diseases were amoebic and various forms of bacillary dysentery (all known as "the bloody flux"), Guinea worms, hookworm (possibly African in origin, but soon endemic in the warmer parts of the New World), yaws, elephantiasis, and leprosy. . . .

Smallpox was feared more than other diseases, since the surgeons had no means of combating it until the end of the eighteenth century. One man with smallpox infected a whole vessel, unless — as sometimes happened — he was tossed overboard when the first scabs appeared. Captain Wilson of the *Briton* lost more than half his cargo of 375 slaves by not listening to his surgeon. It was the last slave brought on board who had the disease, says Henry Ellison, who made the voyage. "The doctor told Mr. Wilson it was the small-pox," Ellison continues. "He would not believe it, but said he would keep him, as he was a fine man. It soon broke out amongst the slaves. I have seen the platform one continued scab.

We hauled up eight or ten slaves dead of a morning. The flesh and skin peeled off their wrists when taken hold of, being entirely mortified." . . .

[Calms or storms along the equator constituted still another hazard for ships carrying slaves from Africa.] Ecroide Claxton's ship, the *Young Hero*, was one of [many] delayed for weeks before reaching the trade winds. "We were so streightened for provisions," he testified, "that if we had been ten more days at sea, we must either have eaten the slaves that died, or have made the living slaves *walk the plank*," a term, he explained, that was widely used by Guinea captains. There are no authenticated records of cannibalism in the Middle Passage, but there are many accounts of slaves killed for various reasons. English captains believed that French vessels carried poison in their medicine chests, "with which they can destroy their negroes in a calm, contagious sickness, or short provisions." They told the story of a Frenchman from Brest who had a long passage and had to poison his slaves; only twenty of them reached Haiti out of five hundred. Even the cruelest English captains regarded this practice as Latin, depraved, and uncovered by their insurance policies. In an emergency they simply jettisoned part of their cargo.

The most famous case involving jettisoned slaves was that of the *Zong* out of Liverpool, Luke Collingwood master. The *Zong* had left São Thomé on September 6, 1781, with a cargo of four hundred and forty slaves and a white crew of seventeen. There was sickness aboard during a slow passage; more than sixty Negroes died, with seven of the seamen, and many of the remaining slaves were so weakened by dysentery that it was a question whether they could be sold in Jamaica. On November 29, after they had already sighted land in the West Indies, Captain Collingwood called his officers together. He announced that there were only two hundred gallons of fresh water left in the casks, not enough for the remainder of the voyage. If the slaves died of thirst or illness, he explained, the loss would fall on the owners of the vessel; but if they were thrown into the sea it would be a legal jettison, covered by insurance. "It would not be so cruel to throw the poor sick wretches into the sea," he argued, "as to suffer them to linger out a few days under the disorders to which they were afflicted."

The mate, James Kelsal, demurred at first, saying there was "no present want of water to justify such a measure," but the captain outtalked him. To quote from a legal document, "The said Luke Collingwood picked, or caused to be picked out, from the cargo of the same ship, one hundred and thirty-three slaves, all or most of whom were sick or weak, and not likely to live; and ordered the crew by turns to throw them into the sea; which most inhuman order was cruelly complied with." A first "parcel," as the sailors called them, of fifty-four slaves went overboard that same day, November 29. A second parcel, this time of forty-two, followed them on December 1, still leaving thirty-six slaves out of those condemned to be jettisoned. (One man seems to have died from natural causes.) Also on December 1 there was a heavy rain and the sailors collected six casks of water, enough to carry the vessel into port. But Collingwood stuck to his plan, and the last parcel of condemned slaves was brought on deck a few days later. Twenty-six of them were handcuffed, then swung into the sea. The last ten refused to let the sailors come near them; instead they vaulted over the bulwarks and were drowned like the others. . . .

. . . On a few ships there was an epidemic of suicide at the last moment. Thus, when the *Prince of Orange* anchored at St. Kitts in 1737, more than a hundred Negro men jumped overboard. "Out of the whole," Captain Japhet Bird reported, "we lost 33 of as good Men Slaves as we had on board, who would not endeavour to save themselves, but resolv'd to die, and sunk directly down. Many more of them were taken up almost drown'd, some of them died since, but not the Owners Loss, they being sold before any Discovery was made of the Injury the Salt Water had done them. . . . This Misfortune was owing to one of their Countrymen, who came on board and in a joking manner told the Slaves that they were first to have their Eyes put out, and then to be eaten, with a great many other nonsensical Falsities."

These, however, were exceptional misfortunes, recounted as horror stories in the newspapers of the time. Usually the last two or three days of the Middle Passage were a comparatively happy period. All the slaves, or all but a few, might be released from their irons. When there was a remaining stock of provisions, the slaves were given bigger meals — to fatten them for market — and as much water as they could drink. Sometimes on the last day — if the ship was commanded by an easy-going captain — there was a sort of costume party on deck, with the women slaves dancing in the sailors' cast-off clothing. Then the captain was rowed ashore to arrange for the disposition of his cargo. . . .

There were horse traders' methods of hiding the presence of disease. Yaws, for example, could be concealed by a mixture of iron rust and gunpowder, a practice which Edward Long, the Jamaica historian, denounces as a "wicked fraud." Falconbridge tells of a Liverpool captain who "boasted of his having cheated some Jews by the following stratagem: A lot of slaves, afflicted with the flux, being about to be landed for sale, he directed the surgeon to stop the anus of each of them with oakum. . . . The Jews, when they examine them, oblige them to stand up, in order to see if there be any discharge; and when they do not perceive this appearance, they consider it as a symptom of recovery. In the present instance, such an appearance being prevented, the bargain was struck, and they were accordingly sold. But it was not long before a discovery ensued. The excruciating pain which the prevention of a discharge of such an acrimonious nature occasioned, not being [able] to be borne by the poor wretches, the temporary obstruction was removed, and the deluded purchasers were speedily convinced of the imposition."

The healthy slaves remaining after an auction were sold by "scramble," that is, at standard prices for each man, each woman, each boy, and each girl in the cargo. The prices were agreed upon with the purchasers, who then scrambled for their pick of the slaves. During his four voyages Falconbridge was present at a number of scrambles. "In the *Emilia*," he says, "at Jamaica, the ship was darkened with sails, and covered round. The men slaves were placed on the main deck, and the women on the quarter deck. The purchasers on shore were informed a gun would be fired when they were ready to open the sale. A great number of people came on board with tallies or cards in their hands, with their own names upon them, and rushed through the barricado door with the ferocity of brutes. Some had three or four handkerchiefs tied together, to encircle as many as they thought fit for their purpose." For the slaves, many of whom thought they were about to be eaten, it was the terrifying climax of a terrifying voyage. Another of Falconbridge's ships, the *Alexander*, sold its cargo by scramble in a slave yard at Grenada. The women, he says, were frightened out of their wits. Several of them climbed over the fence and ran about Saint George's town as if they were mad. In his second voyage, while lying in Kingston harbor, he saw a sale by scramble on board the *Tyral* [of] Captain Macdonald. Forty or fifty of the slaves jumped overboard — "all of which, however," Falconbridge told the House of Commons, "he believes were taken up again."

STUDY GUIDE

1. Some of the perils of the voyage across the Atlantic were similar in both the indentured servant "trade" from Europe and the slave "trade" from Africa. What afflictions and problems described by Mannix and Cowley would you expect to have been a part of the voyages from Europe? Which were unique in the slave trade?

2. The selection contains several quotations from Europeans who reacted with horror or at least compassion to what they witnessed. Why, then, did the trade continue for two centuries?

3. Can you find in the selection any evidence that Europeans questioned the morality of enslavement itself, or was it only the conditions and treatment of the slaves aboard ship that they questioned?

4. A part of a sensitive understanding of history is being able to imagine oneself in the position of other peoples, who may live in a completely different culture or who lived centuries ago. Try to imagine yourself as an enslaved African and as a European slave captain; explain how you would have felt, what you would have done, and what in your African or European background would have led you to think and act that way.

5. What instances can you think of in recent American history or in contemporary life that reveal the kind of callousness that results in considering other people as less than human?

BIBLIOGRAPHY

Other chapters of *Black Cargoes* are nearly as graphic as the selection reprinted here, but a number of recent works have modified the picture presented by Mannix and Cowley. Philip D. Curtin, *The Atlantic Slave Trade: A Census* * (Madison, Wis., 1969), contends that not nearly so many slaves came to North America as was formerly thought, and that the death rate among slaves was lower than earlier writers estimated, while the mortality of European crews was quite high.

The first chapter of John Blassingame's *The Slave Community: Plantation Life in the Ante-Bellum South* * (New York, 1972) discusses the voyage and the cultural shock of enslavement, as well as the question of African cultural survivals in the New World. Unlike most Europeans who came to the colonies, the African brought virtually no personal property with him — no jewelry, no utensils, no tools, no musical instruments, no clothes. He did, however, bring his values and traditions — his dances and music, his folklore and religion, his sense of family and personal relations. Since Melville J. Herskovits published his study of the subject, *The Myth of the Negro Past* (New York and London, 1941), scholars have devoted much energy to identifying African influences upon American Negro culture. Blassingame's opening chapter provides a good introduction to this subject.

Another important question is whether racism or slavery developed first in the British colonies. In the very early seventeenth century, Africans were treated as indentured servants who were freed after a number of years of service. Did English colonials, because of white racism, force Africans into slavery while allowing Europeans to continue in temporary servitude? Or was it the economic advantage of a wageless, hereditary labor force that led to enslavement, with racism following as a rationalization of white guilt? Anyone interested in this question should read Winthrop Jordan's lengthy study *White over Black: American Attitudes toward the Negro, 1550–1812* * (Chapel Hill, N.C., 1968).

The European nationalities that made up most of the population of the British colonies are treated in a literature too extensive to cite here. Your college library is likely to have some of the individual studies of the Germans, Scotch-Irish, and other groups that settled the New World. The origins, voyage, and New World condition of the European group that most closely paralleled the enslaved African is studied in Abbot E. Smith, *Colonists in Bondage: White Servitude and Convict Labor in America, 1607–1776* * (Chapel Hill, N.C., 1947).

A coverlet showing Greenfield Hill, Conn., c. 1800. (Detail)
A depiction in folk art of life in a New England town.

THOMAS J. WERTENBAKER

The New England Town

Two features of modern life are the extraordinary degree of organization of every aspect of human existence and the almost limitless regulation of our conduct and even our thought. Our jobs, our politics, our social and religious life, our education and recreation, even our birth and death, have been bureaucratized by various giant organizations. We have footprints taken at birth, identification numbers given as we enter the job force, and we cannot be buried without the ministrations of the undertakers' lobby. So dependent have we become, that most men have to pay others to cut down a tree in their own backyards, and a great many women would be helpless if they had to bake a loaf of bread or make their own clothes.

Our highly organized, industrial society has brought with it great advantages — convenience, a higher standard of living, and many others. But it has also undermined man's self-sufficiency and severely restricted his ability to determine his own fate. Increasingly, he has come to feel as helpless in trying to influence his union as in influencing corporations or government. Yet, when we glorify and romanticize the simple life and pleasures of an earlier age, we often ignore the problems such a society faced and fail to recognize that even in the earliest colonial settlements there was a degree of interdependence.

In the following selection from *The Puritan Oligarchy*, Professor Thomas J. Wertenbaker describes how New England pioneers transformed a wilderness into a settled community. Unlike the pattern of dispersed settlement in the South, which led to reliance on the county as the unit of local government, the pattern of communal settlement within a small area led New

Englanders to adapt the English town and manor to their needs.

The town, or township, coupled with the church, the family, and other traditional institutions of their agricultural background, served them well here, though these institutions necessarily underwent modifications on this side of the Atlantic. In England they had had cleared fields, long experience with crops and their cultivation, gristmills and sawmills near at hand, and accessibility to such essential craftsmen as blacksmiths. In America they faced endless forests, new crops and crop diseases, and a scarcity of professional craftsmen to assist them in building their houses, grinding their grain, and making their implements. What was true of their farming was equally true of their social life, their law and their public works, their places of worship and their marketing of goods. In each of these fields they brought a long and settled tradition with them, but they brought it to a new and quite unsettled world.

When the group of settlers had perfected their plans and received their instructions, they gathered their belongings around them, said goodbye to their friends and set out through the wilderness. To guide them along the forest trails they often had a trusted Indian. Trudging behind him came the men and women, driving before them the cows, sheep, swine and other domestic animals upon which they must in part depend for sustenance during the first year of the settlement; the children, together with household utensils and farm implements, in the crude carts that they had brought from England in separate parts and put together at the port.

It was with mixed emotions that they arrived at the site of their future home — dismay at the wildness of the country, the huge trees, the dense undergrowth, the lack of all facilities for civilized life; hope at the thought that the land was theirs, hundreds of acres of land, which their labor could convert into fields of waving Indian corn, or wheat or rye; sadness at the memory of England with its comfortable houses, its fertile farms, its villages and towns. But it was not a time for repining, for there was work to be done and without delay. . . .

. . . The first act of the freemen was to gather, perhaps in some open space in the woods, in order to elect a committee to decide upon the lo-

Reprinted by permission of Charles Scribner's Sons from *The Puritan Oligarchy* by Thomas Jefferson Wertenbaker. Copyright 1947 by Charles Scribner's Sons.

cation of the village, to plot its streets and lots, to supervise the surveying and to conduct the division of land. There must have been prolonged discussions as to where to place the village, since it was to be the center of religious, political and economic activities. If there were a body of navigable water at hand, some spot along its shores was usually chosen, so that transportation would be convenient and cheap. The village of Enfield was built on the east bank of the Connecticut; Cambridge, as near to the Charles as the marshy banks permitted; Milford, on the Mill and West rivers. In case navigable water was lacking, the village was usually laid out in the center of the town, so that as much of the surrounding arable, woodland and pasturage as possible would be within a short compass. It was of the utmost importance that the distance from residence to field be not too great for the owner to go out in the morning with his hoe or his ox team and return at the close of the work day.

In planning the village it was customary, if the lay of the land permitted, to have one long main street, with long, narrow home lots which abutted upon it on either side. The motorist who today passes through the quaint New England village with its old houses seldom realizes that the lots on which they are built formerly often stretched out behind for a mile or more. Thus the Enfield home lots, which had a frontage of 198 feet, were 1,920 feet in length. They constituted what must have seemed to their proprietors little farms in themselves, with ample space, not only for a residence, a barn, an orchard and a vegetable garden, but for fields of Indian corn or of English grain. In many cases the settlers contented themselves with their home lots for several years, before asking for additional land lying beyond.

In the distribution of lots, the settlers displayed a decided leaning toward economic democracy. There must be no aristocracy of wealth to vie with the aristocracy of religion, to dispute its authority and magnify the things of this world in comparison with the things of the next. In the words of Urian Oakes they hoped never to see the day when "houses and lands, lots and farms and outward accommodations are of more value . . . than the Gospel and Gospel ordinances. . . . Sure there were other and better things the People of God came hither for than the best spot of ground, the richest soil." So the leaders not only were very temperate in demanding land for themselves, but they would not permit others to monopolize the choice spots or to hold large areas for speculative purpose or to build up great estates. There should be no landed aristocracy in New England if they could prevent [it,] no Van Rensselaers, no Dulaneys, no "King" Carters.

Yet the Puritans did not carry economic democracy to the extreme of making every lot exactly equal in size and value so that no man would have any advantage over his neighbor. In Milford, for instance, they determined each man's share of the common land by "the rule of persons and estates," by which was understood the relative amount of a man's property and of his contributions to the undertaking, the size of his family and his powers of leadership. But inequalities were never carried to an extreme, and always great care was taken that injustice be done no man. In Enfield the Committee was empowered to determine "where and in what order men's lots and land" should lie; "the Committee laboring the best they can to suit and accommodate . . . and when a man lies bad in the first field to endeavor to mend him in the next."

Once the proud owner had taken possession of his home lot, he faced the arduous tasks, not only of erecting his house and barn, setting out his orchard and planting grain and vegetables, but of clearing away the trees and underbrush. In Enfield it was ordered "that every man cut up and clear the brush and bushes in the highway . . . all the breadth of his home lot from front of it for the one half of the highway or street." Time-consuming also, was the constructing of a fence around his lot to protect the precious crops from the depredations of cattle and swine. In some cases the fence was made of rails closely spaced, in others of paling. The Boston common was paled, each of forty-two persons erecting and keeping up his share.

Had one been able to fly over a New England village of three centuries ago, an interesting view would have presented itself. On either side of the main street were the houses of the freeholders, with the barns, the orchards and the gardens behind them. Here was the meeting-house, its simple lines and the absence of a steeple giving it more the appearance of a large residence than a church. Here was the gristmill, its fans spread to catch the breeze; here the schoolhouse; here the smithy; here the sawmill. Stretching out on all sides were the fields; the strips, planted some in Indian corn, some in wheat, some in rye, some in barley, giving the appearance of a crazy quilt. The broad bands of green on either bank of a small stream one recognized as the common pasture. And in the distance were the woods, awaiting the day when a new division would bring them under the axe.

The town imitated the manor, not only in its agricultural life, but in its economic semi-independence. It is true that the typical town was by no means completely cut off fom the rest of the world; it shipped out its surplus of Indian corn, wheat, rye, hides, etc., and received in return the finer grade of manufactured goods — clothing, firearms, household utensils, farm implements. But many of the articles of everyday use were made in the village itself by the local shoemaker, carpenter, cooper, weaver or blacksmith. There was no need to train artisans to serve the infant community, for there were many skilled workers among the immigrants. These men brought their tools with them and had only to begin in their new homes where they left off in the old. The "mystery" of their trade, as it was customary to call it, they passed on to their sons or to apprentices. . . .

In New England the social, as well as religious and political, unit was the village. The people of the little community knew each other's virtues, weaknesses, habits. Every woman in town could tell just how many gowns Goodwife Collins had in her chest, just how many dishes in her kitchen, how many feather beds she inherited from her father, shook her head when word went around that she had lost her temper when the cow kicked over the milk. And when she became ill it was the neighbors who sat beside her bed or did her chores for her. For the minister and congregation to admit one to the communion was an event of first importance to the villagers. The people passed each other on the street every day, they met several times a week for religious services, they stopped at the town pump to gossip or to pass the time of day, they saw each other at the mill or the smithy or at the shoemaker's shop. As in tidewater and piedmont Virginia and Maryland the key to social life was isolation, so in early New England it was concentration, but concentration chiefly in little units which themselves were isolated. . . .

The satisfaction which came with the ownership of land was tempered for the Puritans by the costliness of fencing it in. It was the custom to make the owner of every home lot responsible for the fence, and many were the regulations requiring it to be "good and sufficient" with five rails or "double rail and poles," etc. Yet it was frequently a strain upon "brotherly sweetness," when Deacon Smith's cows got into Master Jones' lot and trampled his wheat. Such a serious case might even come before the Selectmen. So it was a saving in labor as well as in tempers when it was ordered that for the common fields the whole, and not the lots of which it was composed, should be fenced. Of the common fence each man took his share both in its construction and maintenance. At Enfield the proprietors of each field met to "appoint men amongst themselves to see that each man's proportion of fence be done and made according to order." Should one dispute their decision or plead that they had assigned him a greater part than his just share, he could bring the matter before the Selectmen. It was a temptation to allow the fence to fall into disrepair at times, but once a rail was broken or a post began to rot, the negligent owner was certain to be called to account by the town fence viewers. . . .

The settlers were delighted to find that many of the fruits and vegetables, the seed of which they had brought with them, throve in the New England soil, and that they could make good use of others indigenous to the country. "Our turnips, parsnips and carrots are here both bigger and sweeter than is ordinary to be found in England," wrote Francis Higginson. "Here are stores of pumpions [pumpkins], cucumbers and other things of [what] nature I know not. Plenty of strawberries in their time, and penny-royal, winter savory, carvell and water-cresses, also leeks and onions." So every man laid out his garden in his home lot, perhaps back of his residence, and planted it with the pumpkins, beans, squashes, cabbages, turnips, onions, radishes, beets, spinach, and other vegetables which contributed so greatly to the health and enjoyment of his family.

Nearby was the orchard. "Our fruit trees prosper abundantly," John Josselyn reported. "Apple trees, pear trees, quince trees, cherry trees, plum trees, barberry trees. I have observed with admiration that the kernels on suckers planted produce as fair and good fruit, without grafting, as the tree from whence they were taken. The country is replenished with fair and large orchards." The apple tree especially prospered so greatly in New England soil that it became very important in the economy of the people and was a source not only of food but of drink as well. Especial inducements were held out for the erection of cider mills, and in Woodbury the town fathers went so far as to give permission to a certain Matthew Minor to set up one in the highway.

The English were prompt in making Indian corn their most important crop. No doubt they deemed it prudent to trust to a grain which had proved itself by experience, yielded more per acre than the European grains, gave a more uniform return, ripened early and was more hardy in resisting sudden changes of weather. A glimpse in the barn or perhaps in the loft of the typical settler would have revealed, side by side with a few bushels of oats or rye or wheat, a bountiful supply of maize, while a visit to his lots in the common fields would have shown acre after acre devoted to this staple. Yet the settlers were by no means negligent of the grain to which they and their fathers before them had been accustomed, bringing with them wheat, rye, oats and barley for a trial in the New England soil. When the first wheat crop proved a failure in the sandy soil of Plymouth, the Pilgrims were dismayed at the prospect of doing without English bread. But trials elsewhere proved more successful, so wheat soon attained an importance in the farm economy second only to that of Indian corn. Even when the blast visited New England to destroy whole fields of wheat and force the people to increase their acreage of rye, wheat continued an important part of the food supply. Barley was grown for beer, which was a standard drink, and oats for provender for horses. . . .

The settlers continued to use the agricultural implements which they had brought with them from England until they wore out, and then turned to the village blacksmith to fashion others just like them. Yankee inventiveness had not yet applied itself to producing machinery with which to plow, harrow, harvest and thresh, so that the work was done with infinite toil with the aid of hoes, scythes, spades and pitchforks. The Pilgrims had no plow for twelve years after their first landing, while in 1636, so it is stated, there were but thirty plows in all Massachusetts. Not infrequently a town would pay a bounty to a farmer to buy a plow on condition that he use it, not exclusively for his own needs, but for the community as a professional plowman. Crude contrivances these early plows were, whose wooden shares barely scratched the earth despite their four oxen and two drivers.

The settlers brought their cattle with them, for the Indians had none. The ocean voyage, when the animals were penned in a restricted space, where they were bruised and perhaps fatally injured by the tossing of the little vessels, often caused severe losses. If we may believe Captain John Smith, seventy of the two hundred cattle taken on board the Winthrop fleet of 1630 died on the way over. Yet the cattle increased rapidly in New England, so that in a few years all save the poorest family had one or more cows.

Though the arable land was divided among the individual owners, it was the custom to hold the pasture in common. A town meeting in Cambridge in March, 1679, ordered that "all the common land on the south side of the highway leading from Captain Cooke's mill to Watertown . . . be fenced in for a cow common for such as have cow rights recorded in the town book." The fence was to be "done with a stone wall, either a whole wall or a half wall and something of brush upon it and not be less than four foot high." To save the back-breaking labor of erecting walls such as this, the townsmen when possible availed themselves of necks of land, such as Great Neck in Dorchester, or the bend of a river, where the cattle would be confined in part by the water. . . .

If the village, with its home lots, its gardens and orchards, the grain fields, the cow commons, the meadows, formed the visible body of the town, so the congregation constituted its soul. To the settlers the spiritual side of their community was all-important. This it was which had led them into the wilderness, which shaped their characters and their thoughts, which determined the form of their social and economic life. So one of their first steps upon reaching the site of their new homes was to form themselves into a Church. This they did by assembling in some open space, perhaps a long-disused Indian cornfield, to enter into a solemn covenant with God.

The Pilgrims before them had formed such a covenant when they reverently repeated the one sentence: "We covenant with the Lord and with one another and do bind ourselves in the presence of God to walk together in all His ways, according as He is pleased to reveal Himself unto us in His blessed word of truth." The Northampton covenant was more detailed: "Disclaiming all confidence of, or any worthiness in, ourselves either to be in covenant with God or to partake of the least of His mercies, and also all strength of our own to help covenant with Him . . . by relying upon His tender mercy and gracious assistance of the Lord through Jesus Christ, we do promise and covenant in the presence of the Lord, the searcher of all hearts, and before the holy angels and this company, first and chiefly to cleave forever unto God with our whole hearts as our chief, best, yea and only good, and unto Jesus Christ as our only Savior, husband and Lord and only high priest, prophet and king. . . . We promise and engage to observe and maintain . . . all the holy institutions and ordinances which He hath appointed for His Church. . . . And as for this particular company and society of saints, we promise . . . that we will cleave one unto another in brotherly love and seek the best spiritual good each of other, by frequent exhortation, seasonable admonition and constant watchfulness according to the rules of the Gospel." . . .

The new congregation next proceeded to elect a minister. Had the settlers brought a minister with them it was nonetheless necessary to elect him, since they did not constitute a Church until they had made a covenant. Thus John Davenport, who led a company of Puritans to Quinnipiac to found the New Haven colony, was not elected pastor until his flock constituted themselves into a congregation some months after their arrival. The election at Salem in July, 1629, was preceded by "a solemn day of humiliation," after which the "company of believers . . . joined together in covenant," chose, by the votes of the male members, Endicott to be their minister.

The election of a minister was followed by the ordination. This, according to the *Platform of Church Discipline,* drawn up in 1646, was merely "the solemn putting a man into his place and office in the Church, whereunto he had right before by election; being like the installing of a magistrate in the commonwealth. . . . Ordination doth not constitute an officer, nor give him the essentials of his office." It was, however, a solemn ceremony, marked by prayer, preaching and the laying on of hands by the elders or by neighboring ministers. "Reverend Mr. Josiah Sherman was ordained pastor of the First Church for Woburn," Reverend Ebenezer Bridge wrote in his diary in 1755. "I began with Prayer. Reverend Mr. Dunbar preached of fellowship. It was a very large assembly." . . .

If the responsibilities of the minister were great, so was his authority, and bold indeed was the person who ignored his frowns or his admonitions. Not only might he become a black sheep, suspected and censured by the elders and the congregation, but he might suffer excommunication, with the loss of the privileges, political as well as religious, which were attached to Church membership. But it must not be forgotten that the minister was not only the moral censor and preceptor for his flock but their loving father as well. It has become too much the custom to regard him as a cold, unrelenting person, who forgot the frailties of the human body in his zeal to save the soul. One has only to become well acquainted with some of these men to discover under the outward cloak of ecclesiastical harshness the devoted husband, the kind father, the sympathetic pastor. But they did not think it kind to condone sin, to temporize with error, or to permit assaults upon what they firmly believed to be God's Church on earth. The men who were instrumental in sending innocent persons to the scaffold as witches or in subjecting the Quakers to cruel persecution acted from a strong sense of duty, were performing a most unpleasant task because they believed with all their hearts that they were carrying out the divine will.

Second to the minister in influence and power were the elders. Under the *Platform of Church Discipline,* the elders were "to open and shut the doors of God's house, by the admission of members approved by the Church, by ordination of officers chosen by the Church and by excommunication of notorious and obstinate offenders"; to call the congregation together, to serve as "guides and leaders," to "prevent and heal such offences in life or in doctrine as might corrupt the Church," to "feed the flock of God with a word of admonition," to "visit and pray over the sick brother." . . .

Discipline in the Church was every man's business. If Master Smith broke the Sabbath, it was the duty of his neighbors to reprove him; if Mistress Peters gossiped about her neighbors, it was certain to be reported to the elders. When one member committed an offense against another, the injured brother was to go to him privately to admonish him, and if this did not suffice, to return in the company of one or two others to renew the attempt. In case the offender still remained stubborn, the matter was brought to the attention of the elders, who were to place it before the Church. Should he now make a public penitent confession, he was declared "recovered and gained," otherwise he might be suspended from the fellowship of the Lord's Supper. Excommunication was reserved for exceptionally serious offenses such as heresy or blasphemy, for it was a severe punishment indeed. Not only was the congregation to refrain from communion with the culprit in spiritual matters, "but also from all familiar communion with him in civil things, further than the necessity of natural, domestical or civil relations do require, and are therefore to forbear to eat and drink with him, that he may be ashamed."

It was fundamental to the congregational conception of a true Church that none but saints be admitted. "By saints we understand such as have not only attained the knowledge of the principles of religion and are free from gross and open scandals, but also do, together with the profession of their faith and repentance, walk in blameless obedience to the Word, so that in charitable discretion they may be accounted saints by calling, though perhaps some or more of them be unsound and hypocrites inwardly." But should hypocrisy be discovered the persons concerned were to be cast out, since their example endangered the sanctity of others and "a little leaven leaveneth the whole lump." "Particular Churches ought to consist of saints and true believers on Christ," Increase Mather declared. "Nothing can be more fatal to the interest of religion than to constitute Churches of unsanctified members."

This high standard was a matter of grave concern to the people, not only because Church membership opened to them the doors to Heaven but also the doors to political freedom. As early as 1631 the General Court passed a law declaring that "to the end the body of the commons may be preserved of honest and good men . . . no man shall be admitted to the freedom of this body politic but such as are members of some of the Churches."

This drastic restriction upon the franchise has been praised by some historians, severely criticized by others. "Not birth, nor wealth, nor learning, nor skill in war was to confer the power, but personal character, goodness of the highest type," wrote J. G. Palfrey. Others have pointed out that to deny any voice in the government to good citizens merely because they were not in full harmony with the established Church was inconsistent with human rights and English traditions. Yet the Massachusetts leaders clung to the law as the cornerstone of their structure, even though it brought upon them the anger of the King and endangered their charter. . . .

Anyone desiring admission [to the Church] had first to satisfy the minister and the elders "and other able brethren" that he was duly qualified. This he must do in a series of conferences, in which he was interrogated upon his beliefs, his understanding of Church doctrines, his personal conduct and his willingness to join in the covenant. "I discourse with David Butterfield about coming into full communion," Reverend Ebenezer Bridge wrote in his diary. Thus the one sure means of enjoying Church fellowship, and also of gaining the right to vote in civil elections, was for the candidate to convince this small group of Church leaders that his life had been "subdued to some hope of godly conversation," and that he was in hearty sympathy with the established order. . . .

The Massachusetts Puritans were severely criticized in England and Scotland for refusing Church membership to so many persons. Thomas Lechford claimed that "here are such confessions and professions required of men and women both in private and public before they are admitted that three parts of the people of the country remain out of the Church." This John Cotton denied. "In the Churches within the Bay we may truly say that for the heads of families those that are admitted are far more in number than the other. . . . Those that are godly they are all admitted to some Church or other." However true this may have been in Cotton's day, the evidence tends to show that before the end of the century the freemen, who alone could vote for governor, deputies and magistrates, had become a minority in every town, while those who were not members of the Churches, but who were in sympathy with the established order, constituted a majority. A third group, consisting at first chiefly of servants and apprentices, but later recruited by newcomers and even the sons and grandsons of ardent Puritans, were hostile to the "theocracy." They it was who protested against their disfranchisement and fomented what Urian Oakes called "jealousies and fears in the minds of men concerning magistrates and ministers" and "false alarms of danger that the people may believe that religion and liberties are at stake and in danger to be lost."

The Puritan leaders made an effort to prevent the "unsanctified" groups from increasing in numbers, by restricting immigration. In 1636 the town of Boston ordered "that no townsmen shall entertain any strangers into their houses for above fourteen days, without leave from those that are appointed to order the town's business." Salem was even less hospitable, for there one Thomas Oliver was employed "to go from house to house about the town once a month to inquire what strangers do come to have privily thrust themselves into the town." To quicken his zeal, he was to be rewarded with the fines imposed on those who defied the ordinances against entertaining newcomers. In 1637 the colonial government itself took this matter in hand by enacting a law making it illegal for a town "to receive any stranger resorting thither with intent to reside" without the consent "of some one of the Council or of two other magistrates."

Despite these regulations the influx of strangers continued. He who succeeded in convincing the authorities that he was of good conduct and orthodox in faith might purchase land from an old inhabitant or he might receive a grant of a home lot from the town committee. He must, however, build upon it within a year, or perhaps two years, or forfeit his claim. Gradually the laws became less rigid, the enforcement less severe. The need for labor made it necessary for the town to admit servants, apprentices and journeymen, and common justice made it difficult to eject them after their terms had expired. The port towns attracted many sailors, some of whom were far indeed from being "saints"; English shipwrights came over in response to the demands of the shipyards; when a town was without a physician, or a blacksmith, or a miller, the Selectmen were not apt to be overscrupulous about religious requirements if one presented himself.

In the first days of the settlement, however, there were few inhabitants who were not freeholders and few freeholders who were not members of the Church. This gave a unity to the town which was gradually lost, but which, while it lasted, was the very cornerstone of the social, political and religious fabric. There was a clear distinction at all times between the congregation and the body politic, but this distinction was largely academic so long as the two bodies had an identic personnel. When the freemen assembled in the meeting-house for a town meeting they might, and usually did, concern themselves with religious as well as civic affairs.

It was the town meeting which determined the minister's salary, erected his house, levied tithes, built the meeting-house and allotted the seats in it. It could at one moment be considering the matter of the common fence around a grain field and the next, if it so chose, convert itself into the congregation without leaving the meeting room, and proceed to discipline wayward brothers or sisters, or elect a deacon, or receive a person to communion.

As the individual Church enjoyed a large degree of independence in ecclesiastical affairs, so the town meeting in local civic affairs was supreme. And like the Church, it drew its vigor as an institution in large part from the agricultural village, for the freemen, dwelling as they did in the shadow of the meeting-house, found it possible to constitute themselves a legislative body without the use of representatives. So, when they had been "warned" by the ringing of the bell or the cry of the watchman, they emerged from their houses, made their way down the street to the meeting-house, took their seats and at the order of the moderator proceeded with business. The election of the town officers was always a matter of great concern — the fence viewers, the treasurer, the field drivers, the hog reeves, the sealer of weights and measures, the town clerk, the constable, the tax assessors, the tithemen, the surveyors, the selectmen. Then Master Goodwin might rise and move that the meeting-house be reshingled, or that a bridge over the creek be repaired, or that a road be opened, or that a new division of arable be authorized, or that fifty acres of land be offered any wheelwright who would settle in the town. . . .

Thus did the English who came to New England found their Wilderness Zion. Although it was a unique experiment, for nothing like it existed in England, the blueprints had been made long before the exodus began. As Winthrop and Cotton and others were the builders, so [the English writers and clergymen] Ames, Parker, Baynes and before them Cartwright and Barrow and Browne were the architects. The semi-independence of congregations, the Church covenant, the fellowship of Churches, the synod, the close relationship of Church and State were not put into operation as afterthoughts; the Puritans came to America for the purpose of putting them into operation.

New England was not the extension of old England across the Atlantic, but rather an English conception which for the first time found its practical application. Even though the settlers brought with them the English language, English institutions, English architecture, continued to read English books, wear English clothes, use English implements, the structure of their society was essentially different from that of England. Nor did they constitute a cross section of the English people, since they came in large part from one part of the kingdom and from one religious group in that part.

They were separated from England, also, by the belief that they were God's chosen people, the especial object of His care and guidance, and that they had come to America in obedience to His direct command. "Hath God brought us into a wilderness and caused us to dwell alone and separated us for a peculiar people to Himself, that we should imitate the nations in their vanities?" asked Urian Oakes in rebuking the people for their "garish attire." "The ministers and Christians, by whom New England was first planted, were a chosen company of men," said Cotton Mather, "picked out of, perhaps, all the counties in England, and this by no human contrivance, but by a strange work of God upon the spirits of men that were, no ways, acquainted with one another — inspiring them as one man to secede into a wilderness, they knew not where." The synod of 1679 declared that "the ways of God towards this His people are in many respects like unto his dealings with Israel of old. It was a great and high undertaking of our fathers when they ventured themselves and their little ones upon the rude waves of the vast ocean, that so they might follow the Lord into this land."

This belief that God had set them apart for His special guidance and blessing pervaded every phase of New England religious and political life and gave to it a purpose and strength lacking in many societies. "In the wilderness we have dwelt in safety alone, being made the subjects of most peculiar mercies and privileges. . . . The Lord hath planted a vine, having cast out the heathen, prepared room for it and caused it to take deep root. . . . We must ascribe all these things, as unto the grace and abundant goodness of the Lord our God, so to His owning a religious design and interest." . . .

As Winthrop, Cotton, Norton, Shepard and the others viewed their Bible commonwealth, it must have seemed to them almost impregnable. Yet its disintegration began almost at once, and within half a century after the settlement of the Bay ministers were bewailing the degeneracy of the times, the laxity of the new generation, and the decay of religion. "He that remembers the good old spirit of those who followed God into this wilderness . . . cannot but easily discern a sad alteration," complained Urian Oakes in 1673. Among the many things of "solemn significance and awful import," in "the decaying and almost dying state of this poor country," only a few held open the door of hope.

Although Oakes and other ministers exaggerated the situation in their efforts to stay the forces of change, they were quite correct in pointing out that the old order was giving way to the new. The religious zeal of the first settlers was less apparent in the second and third generation; the ministers commanded less respect and love; the charter upon which such hopes had been based had been annulled; the unity of Church and State in the towns had been disrupted; despite all the efforts to exclude them, strangers had come in who were out of sympathy with the Church and the government; there were loud demands for the extension of the franchise; in Boston the organization of the Anglican congregation of King's Chapel bore testimony to the break which had been made in the wall of orthodoxy. Before the end of the seventeenth century, although the ideals of the founders still exercised a powerful influence upon the minds and hearts of the people, the experiment of a Bible commonwealth had definitely failed.

STUDY GUIDE

1. The New England agricultural community described by Wertenbaker has been characterized as "Yankee Communism" because of the relative equality and mutual cooperation of the townspeople. What evidence do you find in Wertenbaker's description that would support this characterization

— for example, in land distribution, cooperation in public works and agriculture, and the relative equality among townspeople in making town and church policy?

2. In what areas of town and church life can you detect a respect for authority and for class differences?

3. It would have been difficult, or impossible, in the early New England town for a single man or a separate family to be completely self-sufficient economically, socially, religiously, and in terms of essential services usually provided by government. In each of these categories of human existence, what common institutions and cooperative services did the New Englanders develop to meet their needs?

4. Today we think of a church as primarily a place of religious worship. Describe how the church in the New England town fulfilled the following additional functions: discipline and regulation of conduct in the community; service as a social institution; regulation of popular participation in government.

5. Generally, the initial group that founded a new town had common religious ideals, fairly close social connections, and common agricultural and governmental traditions. What factors contributed to the breaking down of this early unity of spirit and activities?

BIBLIOGRAPHY

The selection you have read is from one of three volumes Professor Wertenbaker wrote on the settling of America's three principal regions. The other two, in his trilogy entitled *The Founding of American Civilization,* are *The Middle Colonies* (New York, 1938) and *The Old South* (New York, 1942). For more than fifty years, following the example set by Herbert Baxter Adams in the late nineteenth century, historians have been investigating the English origins of colonial governmental institutions such as the town and county. Two general studies of the New England town from different angles are: Roy H. Akagi, *The Town Proprietors of the New England Colonies . . . , 1620–1770* (Philadelphia, 1924) and John F. Sly, *Town Government in Massachusetts, 1620–1930* (Cambridge, Mass. 1930).

More recently, historians have examined New England history through case studies of individual towns, trying to determine how the pattern in Sudbury, Dedham, and other towns was influenced by the area of England from which the settlers came, their conceptions of a holy commonwealth, the traditions of the English manor, and so forth. Among the many significant studies of individual towns, the following four are especially fine: Darrett B. Rutman, *Winthrop's Boston: Portrait of a Puritan Town, 1630–1649* * (Chapel Hill, N.C., 1965); Sumner C. Powell, *Puritan Village: The Formation of a New England Town* * (Middletown, Conn., 1963); Philip J. Greven, Jr., *Four Generations: Population, Land and Family in Colonial Andover, Massa-*

chusetts (Ithaca, N.Y., 1970); and Kenneth A. Lockridge, *A New England Town, The First Hundred Years: Dedham, Massachusetts, 1636–1736* * (New York, 1970).

Ola E. Winslow, *Meetinghouse Hill, 1630–1783* * (New York, 1952) is a study of the founding of a particular congregation and of the role of churches in Puritan society. William B. Weeden, *Economic and Social History of New England, 1620–1789*, 2 vols. (Boston and New York, 1890) is an older work that is quite comprehensive and worth looking into. An easier and, for the beginning student, a somewhat more interesting study is George F. Dow, *Everyday Life in the Massachusetts Bay Colony* (Boston, 1935). There are general surveys of the agriculture of the North and the South, but another book by Rutman that focuses directly on early New England is extremely interesting: *Husbandmen of Plymouth: Farms and Villages in the Old Colony, 1620–1692* (Boston, © 1967). If you like a biographical approach to history, the following two books are especially charming and reveal a good deal about the early colony of Massachusetts as well as the men who are studied: Samuel E. Morison, *Builders of the Bay Colony* * (Boston and New York, 1930) and Edmund S. Morgan, *The Puritan Dilemma: The Story of John Winthrop* * (Boston, 1958). James T. Adams, *The Founding of New England* * (Boston, © 1921) is much less sympathetic to the Puritans than most of the works mentioned. If Wertenbaker's work on the southern colonies is not available, another excellent work on that region is Wesley F. Craven, *The Southern Colonies in the Seventeenth Century, 1607–1689* * (Baton Rouge, La., 1949).

II COLONIAL SOCIETY

Each of the several races and nationalities that sought a new life in the British colonies brought their own traditions and social attitudes with them. People of English descent made up half of the total population, and the colonies were under the English government. Thus, the English influence was naturally predominant in shaping colonial institutions and social life. One must remember, however, that Africans and continental Europeans made up the other half of the population by the late eighteenth century. The language, customs, and culture of these peoples did much to modify English institutions and contributed significantly to the rich variety of American society.

The planting of new settlements in the American wilderness, begun at Jamestown in 1607, continued into the eighteenth century, Georgia being founded as the last of the colonies in 1732. By 1750, the new civilization had attained the characteristics of a mature social world. Colonial legislatures met in solemn session to make laws for the new land. The thousands of acres that had been cleared supported a flourishing agriculture, as the immigrants learned New-World ways of planting, fertilizing, and harvesting. The rude, lean-to huts of the earliest settlements had given way to sturdy houses built from the sawn lumber of the endless forests.

But it was the gradual and subtle modification of Old-World social values and practices that marked the true beginnings of a new society. By the middle of the eighteenth century, family life, education, and class distinctions were all beginning to take on a distinctive, American character.

Though we often think of the pioneers as hardy hunters, the first reading in this section presents the importance of women in colonial society. The significance of education in the minds of our colonial ancestors is seen in the fact that the settlers of Massachusetts Bay Colony founded Harvard College just six years after they landed on the barren shore of Boston Harbor. The second reading describes the remarkable growth of colleges in the eighteenth century, most of which were organized in patterns that were to influence American education through the nineteenth century. The Old-World attitudes toward class and social distinctions underwent greater modification on this side of the Atlantic than did family life and education. But the last reading concludes that, even in this area, American society could not entirely escape its European origins.

I AM NOT TWENTY

As thro' the grove the other day,
I rang'd so blythe and bonny.
Who should I meet upon the way
But my true love Johnny:
With eager hast,
He clasp'd my waist,
And kisses gave me plenty;
Tho I denyd
And thus replyd
Dear lad I am not twenty:

2
Whats that to me the shepherd cryd
You're old enough to marry,
Then come sweet lass and be my bride
No longer let us tarry.
But lets be gone

O'er yonder lawn
Where lads and lasses plenty,
Are fill'd with joy,
And kiss and toy,
Altho' they are not twenty.

3
I listend to his soothing tale
And gangd with him so rardy,
With song and pipe he did prevaill,
He won my wishes fairly:
O hes the lad
That makes me glad,
With kisses sweet and plenty;
So I declare
By all thats rare,
I'll wed, tho not quite twenty.

Sold whole sale by A. Doolittle N. Haven.

"I Am Not Twenty" by Horace Doolittle, 1804. Doolittle was twelve when he made this etching.

EDMUND S. MORGAN

Colonial Women

As children, most of us take marriage and the family very much for granted, as a part of the natural order of things. Eventually, we may come to wonder just how natural matrimony is, whether or not people are naturally monogamous, and whether marriage exists because of love or social necessity. Several factors account for the heightened skepticism about marriage in recent years. One, of course, is the rising divorce rate. Furthermore, the romantic conception of love and traditional views of the biological and emotional differences between the sexes have been seriously questioned.

Anthropology, biology, psychology, and other disciplines are contributing to a better understanding of the relationships of men and women and to a clearer perspective of marriage as a social institution. History may also be useful, since it can assist us in perceiving the common elements — as well as the changes that have taken place — in courtship and marriage across the ages.

As was the case with most colonial institutions, marital attitudes and practices in British America were heavily influenced by English and continental European customs. But in this sphere — as in their language, their government, and their class attitudes — the colonists found that what they had brought across the Atlantic slowly and subtly changed. Comparing American patterns with those of Europe in either the eighteenth or the twentieth century might lead one to think that the similarities in marriage and family life are greater than the differences. But in both periods, one can also see the development in this country of some special patterns of courtship and marriage. Indeed, there

were differences in attitude and practice between the colonial
South and New England, as well as between different classes of
people within a single region.

   In the following selection, Edmund S. Morgan writes of
courtship, marriage customs, and husband-wife relations in colonial Virginia. In the relative isolation of the rural society he
describes, marriage and the family may have had a much greater
importance in the lives of people than did schools, government,
or even religion. In contrast to Calvinistic New England, Virginia's
religious life was Anglican and lacking in vigor. This may have
softened the character of male-female relationships in that region,
or perhaps these relationships simply reflected the absence in
the South of that concern for discipline and authority we find
among many New England Puritans. Still another possibility is
that Morgan's portrayal of marriage in the South is somewhat
romanticized.

For most young people getting married was simple enough. The couple discovered one another in the usual ways, obtained the consent of their parents,
had the banns published in the parish church, and were married by the local
minister. They could forget their parents' consent — as far as the law was
concerned — if the girl was over sixteen and the boy was twenty-one, but of
course it was not good taste for children to proceed in these matters without
their parents' advice. Custom in Virginia demanded what in some of the
northern colonies the law required, that a man get the consent of a girl's
parents before he presumed to propose marriage. Marriage was not entirely
a private affair: it was family business, and the other members of a family
had a right to say something about who should be admitted to their circle.
However, the small farmers and artisans who made up the great majority of
the population of Virginia gave their children a broad freedom in these matters. A poor man with a large family could not expect to leave much to his
children when he died, nor could he afford to provide his daughter with a
dowry or his son with a marriage portion. His children would have to make
their way in the marriage mart as best they could; if they fell in love with
other boys and girls who owned as little property as themselves, no one
would be a loser by the match. It was a matter of courtesy and decency for
them to consult their parents, but where no great fortunes were at stake on

From *Virginians at Home* by Edmund S. Morgan. Copyright 1952 by Colonial Williamsburg, Inc., Williamsburg, Virginia. Reprinted by permission of Holt, Rinehart and Winston,
Inc.

either side there was little reason for parents to stand in the way of their children's wishes.

For the children of wealthier families, in Virginia as in every other part of the world, marriage was less simple. Boys and girls who could expect to come into an inheritance were not allowed to share their fortune with anyone who happened to please their fancy. They must take care to maintain and increase the portion allotted them. An eighteenth-century New Englander put the central problem of marriage eloquently if bluntly when he wrote that there was little to be said about marriage except this, that "if a man should be [so] unhapy [as] to dote upon a poore wench (tho' otherwise well enough) that would reduce him to necessity and visibly ruine his common comforts and reputation, and at the same time there should be recommended to him a goodly lass with aboundation of mony which would carry all before it, give him comfort, and inlarge his reputation and intrest, I would certainly, out of my sense of such advantage to my friend, advise him to leave the maid with a short hempen shirt, and take hold of that made of good bag holland." . . .

Since wisdom has never been the distinguishing mark of youth, the parents of families in the higher ranks of society frequently took an active part in planning their children's marriages. A man who had spent a lifetime in accumulating a fortune did not wish to see his son squander it on a maid with a short, hempen shirt, nor did he wish to see his daughter hand it over to a man who could not otherwise support her in a manner befitting her birth. Moreover, parents who had a position of dignity to maintain did not wish to be disgraced by connections with persons of ill fortune or ill repute. Sometimes parents arranged the whole business, with the children playing a comparatively passive role. More often, probably, a boy informed his father that some young lady had caught his fancy, whereupon the father, if he approved, would negotiate with the girl's parents. Thus Thomas Walker wrote to Colonel Bernard Moore:

Dear Sir: May 27th, 1764

   My son, Mr. John Walker, having informed me of his intention to pay his addresses to your daughter, Elizabeth, if he should be agreeable to yourself, lady and daughter, it may not be amiss to inform you what I feel myself able to afford for their support, in case of an union. My affairs are in an uncertain state, but I will promise one thousand pounds, to be paid in 1766, and the further sum of two thousand pounds I promise to give him; but the uncertainty of my present affairs prevents my fixing on a time of payment. The above sums are all to be in money or lands and other effects, at the option of my son, John Walker.

                                        I am Sir, your humble servant,

                                        THOMAS WALKER

Colonel Moore replied the next day:

Dear Sir: May 28, 1764

Your son, Mr. John Walker, applied to me for leave to make his addresses to my daughter, Elizabeth. I gave him leave, and told him at the same time that my affairs were in such a state that it was not in my power to pay him all the money this year that I intended to to give my daughter, provided he succeeded; but would give him five hundred pounds more as soon after as I could raise or get the money, which sums you may depend I will most punctually pay to him.

I am, sir, your obedient servant,

BERNARD MOORE

Probably not all negotiations were as smooth as these. Evidence from other colonies suggests that parents frequently bargained over the amounts to be given their children with all the enthusiasm they might have devoted to a horse trade. Samuel Sewall of Boston recorded in his laconic style an account of how he arranged his daughter's marriage with Joseph Gerrish: "Dine with Mr. Gerrish, son Gerrish, Mrs. Anne. Discourse with the Father about my Daughter Mary's Portion. I stood for making £550.doe: because now twas in six parts, the Land was not worth so much. He urg'd for £600. at last would split the £50. Finally Febr. 20. I agreed to charge the House-Rent, and Difference of Money, and make it up £600."

In Virginia as in New England there seems to have been a rule of thumb by which such bargaining was regulated: the girl's parents were expected to contribute about half of what the boy's parents did. Thus in 1705 Daniel Parke, a Virginian residing in London, wrote back to John Custis, whose son was courting Parke's daughter in Virginia:

Sir: I received yours relating to your son's desire of marrying my daughter, and your consent if I thought well of it. You may easily inform yourself that my daughter Frances will be heiress of all the land my father left which is not a little nor the worst. My personal estate is not very small in that country, and I have but two daughters, and there is no likelihood of my having any more, as matters are, I being obliged to be on one side of the ocean and my wife on the other. I do not know your young gentleman, nor have you or he thought fit to send an account of his real and personal effects; however, if my daughter likes him, I will give her upon her marriage with him, half as much as he can make it appear he is worth. . . .

. . . If a boy or girl were under age, it was possible to prevent a marriage, but even then a couple might elope and persuade some gullible minister that they were of age. Occasionally the patrons of the *Virginia Gazette* read advertisements like the one inserted by Benjamin Bowles on August 27, 1756:

Whereas *Sarah Holman,* a Niece of mine, under Age, and to whom I am Guardian, hath lately made an Elopement from me, and, as I believe, with an Intent to marry one *Snead* (alias *Crutchfield*) and as I think it will be greatly to her Disadvantage, this is to give Notice to all County-Court Clerks not to grant them Marriage License, and to all Ministers not to marry them by Publication of Banns. I not knowing what Part of the Colony they may resort to, to accomplish their Design, am obliged to make Use of this Method to prevent them.

Doubtless most boys and girls who had been brought up in the elegant manner were content to abide by the rules of the game and seek their mates among those who were as genteel — and as wealthy — as themselves. There were plenty of opportunities for the children of the first families to meet each other at the balls and entertainments which formed part of the high life of colonial Virginia. Probably many a match began in the formal banter which passed between couples engaged in the steps of a minuet or a country dance. The gentleman would pour out a string of extravagant compliments while the lady blushed and protested. Soon perhaps the gentleman would come visiting the lady at her father's plantation, and if his character and financial qualifications were in order, might eventually ask for her hand. At this point both he and the lady were obliged to follow a ritual which required considerable dramatic skill. Though everyone agreed that marriage must be a union of properly proportioned worldly fortunes, nevertheless convention demanded that the actual proposal take place in an atmosphere of almost religious formality. The lady must be approached with fear and trembling as a kind of saint, the lover prostrating himself either literally or figuratively before her, while she betrayed great surprise and distress at the whole idea of marriage and agreed to consider the proposition only after much protestation. . . .

The ladies occasionally objected to the conventions which demanded that they act without regard to their inner feelings. The *Virginia Gazette* on October 22, 1736, carried a set of verses entitled "The Lady's Complaint," in which the author deplored the greater freedom which custom gave to men.

> They plainly can their Thoughts disclose,
>   Whilst ours must burn within:
> We have got Tongues, and Eyes, in Vain,
>   And Truth from us is Sin.
>   . . .
> Then Equal Laws let Custom find,
>   And neither Sex oppress;
> More Freedom give to Womankind,
>   Or give to Mankind less.

Perhaps it was the author of these verses who a week later inserted this advertisement in the paper:

WHEREAS *a* Gentleman, *who, towards the latter End of the Summer, usually wore a Blue Camlet Coat lin'd with Red, and trim'd with Silver, a Silverlac'd Hat, and a Tupee Wig, has been often observ'd by* Miss Amoret, *to look very languishingly at her the said* Amoret, *and particularly one Night during the last Session of Assembly, at the Theatre, the said* Gentleman *ogled her in such a Manner, as shew'd him to be very far gone; the said* Miss Amoret *desires the* Gentleman *to take the first handsome Opportunity that offers, to explain himself on that Subject.*

N.B. She believes he has very pretty Teeth.

Such boldness was certainly bad taste, unless, as is quite likely, the advertisement was merely a printer's prank. In any case the ladies' complaints brought no change in custom. It was never leap year in colonial Virginia, and a self-respecting young woman of quality had to play out the role of aloof and unwilling goddess before she could gracefully take the part of a bride.

The wedding itself, when it finally occurred, was performed by the local minister according to the form prescribed in the Book of Common Prayer. It commonly took place at the home of the bride, usually in the afternoon. The friends of the bride prepared a handsome feast to follow the ceremony. There might also be a ball, and since balls frequently lasted for more than a single evening, the couple might have to put up with the wedding guests for several days.

The humbler people of Virginia, who had no time for the elaborate ritual of a genteel courtship, made as much of the wedding celebration as their wealthier neighbors did. In the frontier region known as the Valley, the German farmers who had come down from Pennsylvania used a wedding as the occasion for a frolic in which most of the community took part. In fact if neighbors or relations were not invited, they might take revenge by cropping the manes and tails of the horses of the wedding company while the festivities were in progress. Here, as in the Tidewater region, the wedding took place at the home of the bride. On the morning of the appointed day the friends of the groom, both male and female, assembled at the home of his father, in time to reach the home of the bride by noon. The whole party rode together with great hilarity until within a mile of their destination. Then at a given signal they raced to the bride's home at full gallop, the first to arrive winning "black Betty," a bottle of liquor.

The ceremonies took place at noon and were followed by a feast, during which the guests attempted to steal the bride's shoe. Four of the prettiest girls and four of the handsomest young men were appointed to defend her, each of them being presented with a beautifully embroidered white apron as a badge of office. Since these "waiters" had not only to defend the bride but also to serve the dinner, it was not impossible for a dexterous guest to succeed in stealing the shoe. If this happened the bride had to pay a forfeit of a bottle of wine and could not dance until she had done so.

The dancing, which began as soon as the dinner was over, lasted until morning. About nine or ten o'clock in the evening, when the music and dancing were in full swing, a party of young ladies quietly took the bride up a ladder to the loft and put her to bed. A delegation of young men then took the groom up. There followed a ceremony called throwing the stocking, in which the bridesmaids stood in turn at the foot of the bed, their backs toward it, and threw a rolled stocking over their shoulders at the bride. The groom's attendants did the same, aiming at the groom. The first to succeed in hitting the mark was supposed to be the next one married. Toward morning refreshments, including "black Betty," were sent up the ladder to the bridal pair. The festivities did not end with the morning but continued until the company were so exhausted that they needed as many days to recuperate as they had spent in reveling.

When the last of the guests had departed and the bride accompanied her husband to the home he had prepared for her, she had to face the hard work which marriage entailed. If her husband was a simple farmer, living remote from shops and stores and seeing very little money in the course of a year anyhow, her hands would have to make many of the things that another woman could purchase and do the things another woman could have done for her. She would have to spin cotton, flax, and wool, weave and knit them, sew, look after the hogs and poultry, milk the cows, make butter and cheese, bake bread, clean the house, and get the meals, besides bearing and rearing children. Sometimes she had to do part of her husband's work as well as her own. At hay and harvest time she would swing a scythe and help to gather in the grain; in the spring she might stand behind a plow, and in summer she would help to trim the weeds with a hoe. She and her family would have plenty to eat, but except for a wedding celebration or a house-raising or a harvesting bee, there would be little time for anything but work.

If she lived in the Valley, the wife of a hard-working German farmer, she would probably live to see the land prosper and in later life, after the Revolutionary troubles had passed, might at least enjoy security. If she lived on the southern frontier of Virginia, the region adjoining North Carolina, we may judge that her life was much harder. According to William Byrd, the women of this region got little help from their husbands in keeping the family alive. Byrd described the men as lazy and shiftless: "They make their Wives rise out of their Beds early in the Morning, at the same time that they lye and Snore, till the Sun has run one third of his course, and disperst all the unwholesome Damps. Then, after Stretching and Yawning for half an Hour, they light their Pipes, and, under the Protection of a cloud of Smoak, venture out into the open Air; tho' if it happens to be never so little cold, they quickly return Shivering into the Chimney corner. When the weather is mild, they stand leaning with both their arms upon the cornfield fence, and gravely consider whether they had best go and take a Small Heat at the Hough [Hoe]: but generally find reasons to put it off till another time. Thus they loiter away their Lives, like Solomon's Sluggard, with their Arms across, and at the winding up of the Year Scarcely have Bread to Eat." Byrd came across one family without even a roof on their house, so that whenever it rained, they had to take refuge in a haystack.

Life on a great plantation was never like this, but not even the greatest of Virginia matrons could boast the leisure of a woman comparably situated today. Though she might have all the servants she could ask for, most of them would be unwilling workers, indentured servants who looked forward only to the day when they would be free or slaves who had nothing to gain by their service. To manage a large mansion with such a crew was no small task in itself. It meant constant attention to see that the jobs assigned to every servant were completed. Getting a meal on the table was a major operation, for the housewife never knew how many mouths she must feed. Hospitality demanded that anyone who passed the plantation, whether friend or stranger, be invited to dine, and guests might stay for several days or even weeks. The Carter family at Nomini Hall consumed in one year 27,000 pounds of pork, 20 beeves, 550 bushels of wheat (to say nothing of corn, which was eaten exclusively by servants and slaves), 4 hogsheads of rum, and 150 gallons of brandy.

On special occasions, when the family gave a ball or entertainment for the neighboring planters, the preparations were on a grand scale, and the lady herself might work in the kitchen along with her helpers. Little Sally Fairfax recorded in her diary on December 26, 1771, that "mama made 6 mince pies, and 7 custards, 12 tarts, 1 chicking pye, and 4 pudings for the ball." There were doubtless many times when the mistress of a plantation felt that it was easier to do a job herself than entrust it to an irresponsible servant. [Philip] Fithian noted one evening after a visit to a neighboring plantation, that "When we returned about Candlelight, we found Mrs. Carter in the yard seeing to the Roosting of her Poultry." Mrs. Carter also managed the gardens which supplied her kitchen, and though there is no record in her particular case, it is known that on most plantations the lady of the house also took care of the sick, both white and colored.

Although her household duties required active hard work, the mistress of a plantation was obliged to maintain all the appearance of leisure. Fithian was much impressed with Mrs. Carter's grand manner. She was entirely accustomed, he said, to "the formality and Ceremony which we find commonly in high Life." Not only did she preside graciously over the dinner table, but she dressed with precise elegance. Fithian was perceptibly shocked one day, after he had been with the family for several months, by what he described as "a Phenomenon, Mrs. Carter without Stays!" Fashion demanded that ladies of Mrs. Carter's position be constantly enclosed in stays; not only that, but they must wear clothes which were clearly designed to hamper any sort of useful activity. This was the era of hoop petticoats, which made so simple a task as walking from one room to another a problem in navigation. At the time of Fithian's employment by the Carters, a memorable achievement of the clothes' designers was exhibited by an English governess who had just arrived on a neighboring plantation: Fithian describes with dismay the extent to which the latest fashion would cut the ladies off from the outside world: "Her *Stays* are suited to come up to the upper part of her shoulders, almost to her chin; and are swaithed round her as low as they can possibly be, allowing Her the liberty to walk at all: To be sure this is a vastly modest Dress!"

There were evidently compensations to being a farmer's wife. While Mrs. Carter sweltered in her stays in the Virginia summer, Molly, who worked beside her husband with a hoe, had at least the advantage of wearing only a linen shift and petticoat, with feet, hands, and arms bare.

The lady who graced the table of a Tidewater mansion and the housewife who cooked by the fire in a one-room cabin were equally subject to their husbands' authority. A single woman might own property, contract debts, sue and be sued in court, and run her own business, but a married woman, so far as the law was concerned, existed only in her husband. If he died before she did, she was entitled to a life interest in a third of his property, but during his lifetime he had the use of all her real property and absolute possession of all her personal property. He even owned the clothes on her back and might bequeath them in his will. Though he was not given power of life and death over her, he was entitled to beat her for any faults she exhibited. He had the right to order the lives of her children, even to the point of giving directions in his will for their management after his death. Her duty was submission to whatever he commanded. When William Byrd III, absent in the armed services, directed his wife to send her ailing baby to her mother-in-law at Westover, she replied submissively, "I am very sorry you have limited Poor, sweet Otway, so that he has but a short time to stay with me. . . . But Sir, your Orders must be obeyed whatever reluctance I find thereby." The force of convention was strong upon this point, so strong that it could even overcome religious prejudice. In 1708 Ann Walker, an Anglican married to a Quaker, objected in court to having her children educated as Quakers, but the Court, while acknowledging her own freedom to worship as she chose, instructed her not to interfere in any way with the instruction of her children, even forbidding her to expound any part of the scriptures to the children without her husband's consent. Such complete support for the husband's authority is all the more remarkable in view of the fact that the Anglican Church was the established church of Virginia, to which all the members of the court doubtless belonged.

In the face of all this testimony, it may be rash to suggest that eighteenth-century Virginia had as great a share of henpecked husbands as any other society. Yet one may venture a guess that women found ways to assert their power in spite of all the laws and conventions with which the men sought to protect themselves. One gets an inkling of this from the account by William Byrd II of a visit to one of his overseers on a remote plantation. Byrd found many things out of order and reprimanded the man for his neglect. "I also let him know," says Byrd, "that he was not only to Correct his own Errors, but likewise those of his Wife, since the power certainly belong'd to him, in

Vertue of his Conjugal Authority. He Scratcht his head at this last Admonition, from whence I inferred that the Gray Mare was the better Horse."

It is hard to know in how many families the gray mare was the better horse. In Byrd's own family it was often touch and go as to who should have the upper hand. On May 23, 1970, he wrote in his diary "I had a great quarrel with my wife, in which she was to blame altogether; however I made the first step to a reconciliation, to [which] she with much difficulty consented." Six weeks later he wrote, "In the afternoon my wife and I had a terrible quarrel about the things she had come in [that is, things she had had imported from London] but at length she submitted because she was in the wrong," and he added with insufferable smugness, "For my part I kept my temper very well." He did not say, however, whether Mrs. Byrd's purchases were sent back to England. On October 12, the same year, he noted that "After we were in bed my wife and I had a terrible quarrel about nothing, so that we both got out of bed and were above an hour before we could persuade one another to go to bed again." The next year on February 5, when the family was preparing to go to Williamsburg, there was another quarrel because Mrs. Byrd wished to pluck her eyebrows. "She threatened she would not go to Williamsburg if she might not pull them; I refused, however, and got the better of her, and maintained my authority." Byrd evidently regarded this as something of a triumph. In spite of all the restrictions which bound a woman to the will of her husband, it seems not unlikely that the colonial dame wielded as great a control over her husband as any modern wife does over hers.

There was, as a matter of fact, a good reason why women should have had something of an advantage over men in colonial Virginia: women were a scarce commodity. The first settlers of Virginia had been men, adventurers out to better their fortunes in the New World. Once the settlement was established women were sent over by the shipload in order to make wives for the colonists, and later immigrants included women as well as men. But in any colonization men are apt to predominate; they go first to prepare the way. By the eighteenth century most of the inhabitants of Virginia were of native birth, but there was always a stream of immigrants pouring into the land, and among these always a preponderance of men, so that throughout the colonial period there were never enough women to go around. Those men who had been left out in the marital game of musical chairs were constantly on the lookout for wives. A girl seldom had the opportunity to get beyond her teens before she married, and she might marry even earlier. William Byrd wrote to a friend in England that his daughter Evelyn, aged twenty, was "one of the most antick [antique] Virgins he knew of. And a widow, it would appear, scarcely had time to attend her husband's funeral before another suitor would be after her.

In view of this scarcity of women it would not be surprising if the Virginia wife managed to exert more authority in the household than custom and law allowed her. There are many examples in the records of wives who displayed an independence altogether out of keeping with what the etiquette books demanded. There was Sarah Harrison, who married Dr. James Blair, the founder of the College of William and Mary. At her wedding when the minister reached the part of the ceremony where she was supposed to promise obedience to her husband, she said "No obey," upon which, according to the only account of the wedding that has been preserved, the minister, a Mr. Smith, "refused to proceed and the second time she said No obey and then he refused again to proceed. The third time she said No Obey; yet the said Mr. Smith went on with the rest of the ceremony."

Another hot-tempered wife who refused to bow before her husband's superiority was Mrs. John Custis. She and her husband lived a hectic life at Arlington on the Eastern Shore, where they sometimes went for weeks without speaking to one another. On one occasion when they were out driving the husband proceeded to drive the carriage into Chesapeake Bay. When his wife asked him where he was going, he answered "To Hell, Madam," "Drive on," answered Mrs. Custis, "any place is better than Arlington." When he had carried his whim so far that the horses began to lose their footing, Mr. Custis turned toward shore again, saying to his wife, "I believe you would as lief meet the Devil himself, if I should drive to hell." "Quite true, Sir," she replied, "I know you so well I would not be afraid to go anywhere you would go." John Custis was sixty-four years old when his wife died, and seven years later, when he himself died, he had inscribed on his tomb:

> Beneath this Marble Tomb lies the Body
> of the *Hon. John Custis, Esq.*
>
> . . .
>
> Aged 71 Years, and yet lived but seven years,
> which was the space of time he kept
> a bachelor's home at Arlington
> on the Eastern Shore of Virginia.

A wife who found her husband unbearable could not hope to escape from him by a divorce, for there was no court in Virginia with authority to grant one. The courts did occasionally arrange legal separations, in which the husband was required to provide the wife with an independent maintenance, but the common remedy for an unbearable husband was to run away, either to another man or back to mother. The *Virginia Gazette* often carried advertisements inserted by irate husbands warning all merchants to grant no further credit to their eloped wives. Most of these advertisements give no clues as to why the wife had eloped, but occasionally a wife answered the advertisement with another which indicated that the fault was none of hers. When Filmer Moore announced the elopement of his wife, she countered with a notice which read:

As my Husband *Filmer Moore* has publickly said his Mother would sooner live in a hollow Tree than with me, and has removed me to my Father's House, with Promise to come and live with me until I could be better provided for (which I can prove by divers Witnesses) but since has falsified his Word, and has perfidiously absented, and kept himself from me these six Months, without any Provocation from me (*so that he has eloped from me, and not I from him*) I do here declare that I intend to remain in the Situation he has placed me until he does come and account for the undeserved scandalous Treatment which I have received at his Hands. And as he has forbid all Persons from crediting or entertaining me, I can prove this to be only Spite and ill Will; for I have not run him in Debt one Farthing, nor removed from my Station wherein I was placed by him.

Elizabeth Moore

In spite of such episodes there is no reason to suppose that colonial Virginia had more than its share of unhappy marriages, and it certainly had its share of happy ones. Among the letters from the eighteenth century which have been preserved are many which passed between husband and wife and which reveal as much warmth and tenderness as anyone could ask. Theodorick Bland, absent with the American armies in New Jersey in the winter of 1777, wrote back to his wife: "For God's sake, my dear, when you are writing, write of nothing but yourself, or at least exhaust that dear, ever dear subject, before you make a transition to another; tell me of your going to bed, of your rising, of the hour you breakfast, dine, sup, visit, tell me of anything, but leave me not in doubt about your health. . . . Fear not, my Patsy — yes, 'you will again feel your husband's lips flowing with love and affectionate warmth.' Heaven never means to separate two who love so well, so soon; & if it does, with what transport shall we meet in heaven?"

STUDY GUIDE

1. What differences were there between wealthy, upper-class women and lower-class women with respect to: the formalities of courtship and marriage; their lives after they were married?

2. What was the legal position of women in relation to their husbands? What factors — in actual daily relations — modified this legal position?

3. How might the position of a slave woman have differed from that of any white woman in such matters as her relationship with her husband, her control of children, her supervision of her household, her ability to preserve her self-respect?

4. How might the life of a woman in more settled areas, such as Boston or Philadelphia, have differed from that of a woman living in the rural, agricultural society depicted by Morgan?

5. In what ways has the position of women in American society changed substantially since the period described by Morgan, and in what ways has it remained basically the same?

BIBLIOGRAPHY

The other chapters of Professor Morgan's book, on childhood, servants and slaves, and houses and holidays, are as well written and informative as is the selection on marriage. A fuller work, with a great deal of fascinating detail, is Julia C. Spruill, *Women's Life and Work in the Southern Colonies* * (Chapel Hill, N.C., 1935). Another work by a woman historian, also written in the 1930s, which is not restricted to the southern colonies is Mary S. Benson, *Women in Eighteenth-Century America: A Study of Opinion and Social Usage* (New York, 1935). Morgan also wrote a work on family life in New England, presenting a somewhat different picture from his study of Virginia: *The Puritan Family: Religion and Domestic Relations in Seventeenth-Century New England,** rev. ed. (New York, © 1966); his chapter on husbands and wives is especially interesting. John Demos, *A Little Commonwealth: Family Life in Plymouth Colony* * (New York, 1970) is a fascinating study of nearly all aspects of family life — husband-wife and parent-child relationships, housing, furnishings, and the psychology of life in the seventeenth century.

The women's liberation movement of our time has led to the reprinting of many older works on women in America, but many of them are largely of antiquarian interest. Of the newer works, the most stimulating are polemical statements, psychological studies, and literary works; few of them are intensive historical studies. Historical works relating to the pre-Civil War women's rights movement are cited in the bibliography following the selection by Robert E. Riegel, "The Status of Women." A recent general study of women in American history is Page Smith, *Daughters of the Promised Land: Women in American History* (Boston, © 1970).

LAWS,

RELATING TO THE

MORAL CONDUCT, AND ORDERLY BEHAVIOUR,

OF THE

STUDENTS AND SCHOLARS

OF THE

University of Pennsylvania.

1.   None of the students or scholars, belonging to this seminary, shall make use of any indecent or immoral language: whether it consist in immodest expressions; in cursing and swearing; or in exclamations which introduce the name of GOD, without reverence, and without necessity.

2.   None of them shall, without a good and sufficient reason, be absent from school, or late in his attendance; more particularly at the time of prayers, and of the reading of the Holy Scriptures.

3.   Within the walls of the building, none of them shall appear with his hat on, in presence of any of the Professors or Tutors; or, in any place, fail to treat them with all the respect which the laws of good breeding require.

4.   There shall be no playing in the yard, or in the street, during the time in which the schools are assembled; nor, within the walls of the building, at any time: nor shall any boy cut or notch the furniture of the rooms; or draw any figures or characters on the walls; or tear, deface, or in any way injure, the books, or other property, belonging either to himself or others.

5.   When the schools are dismissed, whether in the morning or afternoon, the boys shall not remain in the yard, or in the neighbourhood of the building; but shall immediately disperse without noise or tumult, and return each to his respective home, so as to be at the disposal of his parents, or of those under whose care he is placed.

6.   The students of the Philosophical classes shall, each of them in succession, deliver an oration every morning in the Hall, immediately after prayers; the succession to begin with the senior class; and, in each of the two classes, to proceed in alphabetical order.

7.   In case of the transgression of any of the above laws, the transgressor, if he belong to either of the Philosophical classes, or be above the age of 14 years, shall, for each transgression, be subject to a fine, or suspension; and, if under that age, to the same penalty, or to corporal punishment, at the discretion of the Faculty. The fine, in no case, to exceed 25 cents.

8.   And if any student of the Philosophical classes, not prevented by sickness or other unavoidable necessity, shall twice successively neglect to appear in his turn, and pronounce his oration, as above directed; he shall be considered as guilty of a wilful disobedience to the laws of the institution; and shall be suspended, until, recourse being had to his parents or guardians, some competent security can be obtained for his more orderly behaviour in future.

Extract from the Minutes of the Board of Faculty.

WILLIAM ROGERS, *Secretary.*

September 19th, 1801.

Laws for students of the University of Pennsylvania, 1801.
Colleges have changed in many ways since colonial times.

BEVERLY McANEAR

College Life

In the 1960s, American universities were a source — some would say a haven — of much of the youthful revolt against society and at the same time a target of that revolt. Beginning with the Free Speech Movement and the protest against the impersonality of the multiversity at Berkeley, universities across the country were shaken by sit-in demonstrations, assaults on computer centers, charges of improper research on such things as biological warfare, and denunciations of university investments in war-industry corporations. Some changes did take place, and some of the changes have left a permanent mark upon the curriculum, admissions policies, and teaching practices of institutions of higher education. Yet the large, modern American university is a very different institution from the small liberal arts college of the eighteenth and early nineteenth centuries.

The colonial period in our educational history was largely ignored by writers on education in the first half of the twentieth century. Most such writers had great respect for our publicly supported system of secular education and tended to slight the private, religious colleges of the colonies. They also tended to think in terms of formal education in a school building and gave little consideration to the equally important informal education that is afforded by family, church, business, and a number of other social institutions. For younger children in the colonial period, the family and the master who took in a young apprentice were probably more important educationally than the brief time they spent in school.

Beyond the age of thirteen or fourteen, formal education became more important, though it must be remembered that training in a business house or aboard ship educated more young men than did colonial colleges. In the following selection, Beverly McAnear focuses on the formal institutions of higher education — the colleges of colonial America. In it we discover much about their origins, financing, student body and faculty, curriculum, and contributions that provides a striking contrast with the large universities of contemporary America.

In the year 1745 there were but three colleges in all of British North America. Yet by the beginning of the Revolution the virus that Ezra Stiles labeled "College Enthusiasm" had so widely infected the American colonists that seven new colleges had been firmly established; plans had been laid for three more which were to open during the Revolution; and at least six abortive projects had been undertaken by responsible people. Thus by 1776 every province and nearly every popular religious sect was planning and had arranged for financial backing for a school of its own. In addition to the older three — Harvard, Yale, and William and Mary — those actually giving instruction were: Dartmouth College in New Hampshire; the College of Rhode Island, now Brown University; King's College, from which Columbia University has descended; Queen's College, soon to bear the name of Rutgers; the College of New Jersey, destined to become Princeton University; the Academy and College of Philadelphia, still living as the University of Pennsylvania; and Newark Academy, ultimately to reappear as the University of Delaware.

This interest in the founding of colleges coincided with a growth of the spirit of rationalism that sought intellectual stimulation in sources other than theological — a spirit eagerly capitalized on by college promoters who urged the establishment of non-sectarian institutions. Sectarian discussion, such as the Old Light-New Light controversy, further spurred on the founding of colleges consecrated to the religious approach of the partisans. Finally, college founding was helped along by the years of prosperity after 1748, which made fund raising easier, and by the growth of civic and humanitarian spirit, which provided the stimulus. Between 1745 and 1765 most of the campaigns were organized by Yale graduates; after 1765 College of New Jersey men began to take the lead. Men educated in Great Britain and some who were not college men were also among the founders of the new colleges. Except for the role of Harvard graduates in the founding of Dart-

"College Founding in the American Colonies, 1745–1775" by Beverly McAnear. From *Mississippi Valley Historical Review*, Vol. XLII (June 1955). Reprinted by permission of The Organization of American Historians.

mouth and the part played by the College of Philadelphia in the establishment of Newark Academy, the graduates of the other American colleges did not figure prominently in the movement.

Regardless of their educational background, college promoters became interested in advancing higher education through affiliation either with a library company or with a church. Most organizers — and they were the most successful — were ministers interested in the advancement of their own sect. Clerical leaders campaigned for Dartmouth, Queen's, New Jersey, Newark, and, in their final stages of organization, for Rhode Island and King's. The reasons emphasized by clerics for establishing colleges were to educate ministers, to raise the level of general culture and morals through the influence of the clerical alumni, and to convert the Indians. They maintained that a college was a religious society whose basic and chief duty was to train its students to be religious and moral men. The study of nature was to be subservient to the inculcation of religion; the one was only a threshold to the other, and religious instruction therefore was to be emphasized. They freely promised toleration to all Protestant Trinitarian sects, but they demanded clerical administration and the dominance of one sect.

Those promoters identified with one of the library companies were usually laymen, often without much formal education. Colleges and libraries were at that time a natural conjunction of interests, for some of the library companies were originally designed as organizations which would not only circulate books but which would also provide popular lecture courses, particularly on scientific subjects. Men affiliated with libraries were concerned with the foundation of Rhode Island, King's, and Philadelphia, and with abortive proposals for colleges at Newport and Charleston. They argued that a college should properly be considered a civil society committed to the duty of training youths for service to the commonwealth, and the value of any type of training was to be measured according to its ultimate usefulness to the graduates in civil life. The best attribute of an educated man was an independent mind; free inquiry was therefore to be encouraged and religious instruction prohibited. To assure freedom, religious toleration and nonsectarianism were to be maintained, and even direct state control was proposed.

To their basic appeal for support each group of promoters added virtually the same arguments. College alumni would provide superior public servants, and the very presence of the college and its faculty would raise the cultural level of the province. The students' love of their native province would be protected against the alienation that might result from new attachments formed during their school years in distant parts, and thus the best minds of the colony would be saved for the service of their birthplace. Money would not flow out of the province to enrich the residents of college towns in other provinces. And, finally, a local school would provide a less expensive education for ambitious sons of residents. . . .

The building lot for the college was invariably provided by a public or semi-public organization in order to attract the college to its town. The difficulties that New Jersey College experienced in its attempts to secure a sizable sum in four different New Jersey villages indicate that the custom was not well established in the 1740's. But it caught on quickly, and Queen's was embarrassed by bids from New Brunswick, Tappan, and Hackensack, while Rhode Island felt obliged to hold an auction to terminate five months of competitive controversy.

As soon as money was available, a college hall, containing classrooms and a dormitory, was erected. To supervise construction, some colleges relied on artisans or amateur architects, but Rhode Island, New Jersey, and Philadelphia retained the services of the Philadelphia architect and builder, Robert Smith. The plans drawn by Smith and William Shippen, a physician and amateur architect of Philadelphia, were repeated elsewhere and virtually created in America the collegiate Georgian style. Essentially their design was an adaptation of that for King's College, Cambridge University. During the twenty-five years before the Revolution, five of these schools spent approximately £15,000 sterling for the erection or remodeling of buildings. "This they chose to do," President John Witherspoon of the College of New Jersey wrote, "though it wasted their Capital, as their great Intention was to make effectual Provision, not only for the careful Instruction, but for the regular Government of the Youth." A pretentious building was also desirable because it afforded publicity, and its inclusion of dormitory space and commons reduced student expenses.

The cost of the original hall invariably reduced the college to a state of near insolvency. Indeed, Philadelphia and Rhode Island invested in their buildings literally the last penny in the till. As a result, trustees tended to limit the materials for classroom demonstrations in physics, surveying, and astronomy. Thanks to the persistence of their presidents, however, by 1775 the scientific instruments of King's, New Jersey, and Philadelphia were equal to or better than those possessed by Harvard, Yale, and William and Mary. The other new colleges owned little or no scientific apparatus.

A greater handicap was the inadequacy of libraries. By the time of the Revolution, the Harvard library, with more than 4,000 volumes, was probably the largest college library in the colonies. Yale was not far behind, but William and Mary must have had less than 3,000. While Philadelphia, King's, and New Jersey, with perhaps 2,000 books each, made at least a respectable showing, library facilities at the other newly established institutions were either virtually or completely non-existent.

Nearly all the books in the libraries of the newer colleges had been presented: none customarily bought more than occasional titles. The only important purchases were three consignments for New Jersey, one of which was so costly that the trustees deemed it an extravagance and charged the bill to the president. To make matters more difficult, these libraries were largely the gifts of benevolent clergymen, and the weight of theology hung heavy upon them. "But few modern Authors, who have unquestionably some Advantages above the immortal ancient, adorn the Shelves," wrote a college official in 1760. "This Defect is most sensibly felt in the Study of Mathematics, and the Newtonian Philosophy." Philadelphia and New Jersey sought to remedy matters by assessing the students a library fee, but the income must have been small.

By the time the trustees of a college had built the hall and provided furniture, scientific equipment, and a library, they had invested approximately £5,000 — perhaps the equivalent of $350,000 today. By 1776 the physical properties of all the infant colleges probably represented the expenditure of something approaching £25,000 — an investment which produced virtually no income, since student rents could hardly have paid for maintenance.

In assembling a faculty, the trustees were apt to seek a president who had been trained in a British university, but since the necessary income was often lacking they were forced to be content with the product of an American college. The president bore the heaviest share of the burden of the school. He did a good part of the teaching and conducted the college's religious exercises. He was also the chief and sometimes the only administrative officer, and he was obliged to gather money and recruit students. To supplement his income, he often served as the pastor of a neighboring church. Such arrangements were discouraged by the trustees, however, and as the college grew more prosperous, pressure was placed on the president to confine himself to college affairs.

The other members of the faculty (seldom more than three) were usually younger men destined within a few years to be clergymen. Most were American trained, though Anglican schools secured some British-educated tutors. Lack of money prevented the hiring of a more stable, better-trained faculty, since almost any profession promised greater returns and better social status. The hardest position to fill was that of the science instructor. Few men with the necessary training were to be found in the colonies, and hence the post was often vacant. Each instructor normally was assigned a given class of students to whom he imparted knowledge on all subjects except the natural sciences. This arrangement demanded, however, that a faculty member undertake a considerable degree of specialization of subject matter, because the curricula emphasized given branches of learning in different years. . . .

Despite ardent campaigning, the enrollment in all these infant colleges was small. The opening class in any of them could hardly have been more than five to eight boys. Succeeding classes naturally increased enrollment, and the prosperous years of the early 1770's greatly aided recruitment. Even so, most of the newer schools prior to the Revolution had at best an attendance of only forty or fifty students. By all odds, the most successful was New Jersey, which grew to an enrollment of about one hundred. Yet, despite this rapid growth, New Jersey was still smaller than her older rivals, for after

1755 the student bodies of Harvard and Yale had often exceeded one hundred and fifty. Approximately four-sevenths of all college students of 1775 were enrolled in the three oldest institutions.

Upon appearance at college, the prospective student was required to pass an entrance examination, usually administered by the president. The requirements of the new colleges seem to have been copied from those of Yale; for Rhode Island, King's, and New Jersey the requirements were almost identical. Essentially, the test demanded ability to translate elementary Latin and Greek and a knowledge of arithmetic — this last being a contemporary innovation. It is doubtful that an applicant was ever sent home, though sometimes extra work was prescribed.

Many of the students admitted were mere boys. From 1750 to 1775 the median age of the entrants at Yale was only sixteen or seventeen; at Philadelphia it was sixteen; and at King's only fifteen. Eleven- and twelve-year-old freshmen were not unknown, and John Trumbull satisfied the Yale entrance examination at the age of seven years and five months. Because of the competition for students the colleges were in danger of becoming grammar schools. As a step toward remedying this difficulty, the governors of King's in 1774 ruled that after the admission of the class of 1778 entrance would be refused any applicant younger than fourteen "except upon account of extraordinary qualifications."

As a general rule, only freshmen were admitted. Though there were exceptions in every college, only Dartmouth, New Jersey, and possibly Philadelphia made a practice of admitting students to advanced standing. These boys had usually studied with a minister because such a training was less expensive than college residence. For admission to advanced standing, the college required payment of fees for the earlier years and passage of an entrance examination. The examination seems to have been largely a formality. Writing to a friend, one such candidate at New Jersey reported: "After examinations on the usual *authors,* when I and they, who were examined with me, received admission into the junior-class, we were told, that we should have been examined on the *Roman antiquities,* if it had not been forgotten." Witherspoon disliked the system and unsuccessfully sought to abolish it.

Rhode Island, King's, and New Jersey also patterned their curricula after the Yale model, a program that reflected the course of study developed in the English dissenting academies. Actually colleges, these institutions had broken away from complete concentration upon the classics and Aristotelianism and had instituted Newtonianism, social sciences, and modern languages. All four colleges required the same course of studies in the first two years: principally Latin, Greek, and Hebrew. That they assigned much more time to these subjects than did the English academies indicates an effort to repair the deficiencies of their matriculants who, compared to their English counterparts, were retarded about a year and a half. In the final two years, the American colleges emphasized natural sciences, mathematics, and metaphysics. President Samuel Johnson at King's apportioned three-fourths of the time of juniors and seniors to mathematics and the natural sciences, while Yale provided but one year, and Rhode Island and New Jersey considerably less than a year. To complete the studies for the senior year, Yale provided metaphysics and divinity, and New Jersey and Rhode Island oratory, composition, and almost certainly divinity. This difference in emphasis is partly explained by the desire of the dissenting colleges to train preachers and in part by the lack of scientific equipment and instructors. All devoted some time to logic, ethics, geography, and public speaking.

At Philadelphia a more independent approach to the curriculum was undertaken by President William Smith, who was influenced by Dr. Samuel Johnson, the great English writer, and by Robert Dodsley's *Preceptor*. Nonetheless, the subjects prescribed by Smith were much the same as those offered elsewhere, except that he placed much greater stress upon oratory and the social sciences and did not regularly offer courses on religion.

Between 1765 and 1775 the American institutions showed great capacity to adapt their curricula to trends appearing in the English academies. Stress was placed on English grammar and composition by requiring polished written translations and original products of the students' pens, and greater weight was placed on oratory. English literature, however, was never taught formally. Some schools began to offer modern foreign languages as electives, and with their growing popularity classes in Hebrew were deserted. Greater attention was also paid to history by Witherspoon at New Jersey and by President James Manning at Rhode Island, though, as was the case in England, apparently only ancient history was taught. In brief, during these thirty years the college moved to some degree from ancient to modern languages, from divinity to the social sciences, and from metaphysics to natural sciences. Only Dartmouth and King's seemed to find the older ideas the better. . . .

Classes began early and lasted through the day, punctuated by morning and evening prayers. Instruction was based upon recitations from and elaborations of textbooks, though the lecture method was used by some presidents in teaching the seniors. The college library was rarely used by undergraduates, and New Jersey claimed distinction for its policy of encouraging seniors to browse in the library. To stimulate scholarship, King's, New Jersey, and Philadelphia set up prizes to be awarded for excellence in specified subjects, and Manning wanted to adopt the plan at Rhode Island. But the system proved ineffective, and it was allowed to die.

Regular attendance, payment of fees, and proper deportment — or due regret for improper deportment — seemed almost invariably to yield a diploma on the scheduled day. "To the frequent scandal, as well of religion, as learning," wrote a contemporary critic, "a fellow may pass with credit through life, receive the honors of a liberal education, and be ad-

mitted to the right hand of fellowship among the ministers of the gospel.
. . . Except in one neighbouring province, ignorance wanders unmolested
at our colleges, examinations are dwindled to mere form and ceremony,
and after four years dozing there, no one is ever refused the honors of a
degree, on account of dulness and insufficiency." In 1756 there were 172
students enrolled at Yale, and all but seven eventually received degrees.
Elsewhere, virtually automatic progress by the student likewise seems to
have been the rule; only at King's and Philadelphia was the mortality
rate high. . . .

Most students lived in the college hall, two or three to a room or suite
of rooms. Meals were served in the college refectory, usually situated in the
basement of the college hall. The only important meal came at midday;
it consisted essentially of meat and potatoes. The evening meal was based
upon leftovers from noon, and breakfast brought only bread and butter.
While this community life was recommended by the college authorities,
many students preferred the more expensive but freer method of boarding
out in adjacent homes. Such freedom, however, sometimes created special
problems of discipline.

Relations between the faculty and the students seem to have been rea-
sonably good, although there were, of course, exceptions. Provost William
Smith, of Philadelphia, gained a reputation for harshness; Eleazer Whee-
lock, of Dartmouth, ruled with the care but without the indulgence of a
father; and Robert Harpur, the science instructor at King's, was hated
and tormented on general principles. But the newer colleges were free of
the student riots which occurred at Harvard and Yale. . . .

However valuable students found college life to be, their fathers regarded
the expense of maintenance with no little concern. During the years between 1746 and 1772 the charges of the College of New Jersey for room,
board, and tuition — £9 per year — were the lowest of any college. But
college fees gradually increased, and after 1772 an economical parent found
that the lowest bill, £12, was presented by the College of Rhode Island. The
highest annual charges made by any of the newer colleges were those of
King's — £18. And room, board, and tuition, of course, represented only
a fraction of a student's total expenses. Firewood, candles, and washing cost
£3 more; books and stationery, clothing and travel, and pocket money, too,
increased the cost. Thus in 1775 the lowest cost of educating a boy ranged
from £25 to £35 a year; it might easily amount to £55 or even more for
spendthrifts. But the highest expense in America was mild compared to
charges in England, where advanced education cost over £100 annually.

For colonial days these were large sums in terms of personal cash income.
An able carpenter with good employment earned about £50 a year; a captain in the royal army, £136; a college instructor, £100; and a good lawyer,
£500. Some relief was afforded by the extension of credit, and only too often
greater relief was gained by parents who defaulted payment of the indebtedness. A little money for needy students was raised through church collec-

tions and subscriptions by the Baptists at Rhode Island and the Presbyterians at New Jersey. But none of the infant colleges had annually appointed scholars, and it appears that only at Dartmouth did any number of students work to pay their expenses. Therefore, sooner or later, the father had to pay, and clearly only the well-to-do could easily afford to do so. Indeed, some contemporary commentators believed that only the sons of the wealthy should go to college.

The greatest problem faced by the college administrators was that of getting the money necessary to keep the college open, for students' fees paid only a small part of the cost of a boy's education. In their search for the requisite funds, promoters of the new colleges found that tapping the provincial treasury yielded only a trickle of cash. Harvard, Yale, and William and Mary all had been given both grants and annual subventions by their respective provincial governments or by the King. Among the newer colleges, only Dartmouth, King's, and Philadelphia were voted money from public treasuries, and King's alone was treated generously. None ever received an annual public subsidy, despite repeated applications.

Appeals to the general public by means of subscription lists and lotteries brought some funds, and occasional bequests added more; but the receipts from these sources were usually needed to meet recurring deficits. To gain capital for investment, efforts were made to raise funds in Europe and the West Indies. Between 1745 and 1775 the seven new colleges received well over £72,000 in gifts from thousands of people solicited by hundreds of well-wishers. Over the same period approximately two-sevenths of these funds were invested in income-producing endowment; about three-sevenths were used in meeting current operating expenses; and the remaining two-sevenths were absorbed in the erection of buildings. With the exception of King's, which was able to meet its running expenses with the income from its investments, all were operating on deficit budgets after 1770; and at the same time the raising of funds for colleges became increasingly difficult.

The most obvious effect of the work of the pioneer educators who were responsible for the establishment and operation of these newer colleges was the great increase in the number of college-trained men in the colonies. From 1715 through 1745 the three older colleges graduated about fourteen hundred men, but in the following thirty-one years over thirty-one hundred gained bachelors' degrees in British North America. Almost nine hundred of these degrees (28 per cent of the total number) were granted by the seven new colleges. These schools therefore were responsible for about half the increase of college-trained men during these decades.

Behind the growing interest in college attendance was increasing economic prosperity. Each advance in college enrollment followed by three or four years the initial point on a rise of the index of commodity prices. Mounting colonial wealth aided the establishment of colleges in provinces from which the older colleges had drawn few students. Probably over 90 per cent of the graduates of Harvard, Yale, and William and Mary came from eastern New Hampshire, Massachusetts, Connecticut, and Virginia. Rhode Island and the middle provinces were relatively fallow fields, and to the boys in those areas the younger colleges represented opportunity. Therefore, the advance in enrollment beginning in 1769 redounded to the advantage of the newer rather than the older colleges, and from 1769 through 1776 they graduated approximately 40 per cent of the bachelors of arts.

This sudden popular interest in a college degree brought repeated demands that college bills should not be so high as to exclude the sons of the less well-to-do. This insistence sprang in part from a belief that the duty of the college was to open the gates of opportunity to youths of merit regardless of their fathers' social and economic position. One of the college propagandists argued: "The great Inducement to Study and Application . . . is the Hope of a Reward adequate to the Expence, Labour and Pains, taken. In Countries where Liberty prevails, and where the Road is left open for the Son of the meanest Plebeian, to arrive at the highest Pitch of Honours and Preferments, there never will be wanting such Emulation, and of Course great Men. . . . Such at this Day, is Great Britain." Some extended the argument, maintaining that all classes of society needed some type of education beyond that of the common school.

These democratic concepts of education were being applied at the time to a class society which it was assumed educated men would buttress. Such efforts as were made to reduce the barrier of high cost came from the dissenting colleges. Groups of dissenters in England had long aided poor students financially, and the Baptists and Presbyterians in America followed the custom. Furthermore, ministers were badly needed in the colonies and usually they could be recruited only among the sons of farmers. A costly education, therefore, would handicap the Presbyterian and Baptist churches. Inevitably the administrators of dissenting colleges were forced to yield to pressure to keep their fees down, and hence their graduates included a goodly number of sons of artisans and farmers of modest means. Thus the requirements of religious sects gave effect to the demand for democratization of higher education.

One concern of this increased interest in higher education was the improvement of professional training. New Jersey was the first of the younger colleges to build a curriculum designed to train preachers, and it is not surprising, therefore, that about half of the pre-Revolutionary graduates of New Jersey entered the ministry. Rhode Island and Newark followed New Jersey's precedent, and President Smith at Philadelphia read lectures in divinity as a special course for candidates for the ministry. Through the influence of President Witherspoon, New Jersey was also the first of the new colleges to introduce formal graduate training in divinity, a program already long established at William and Mary.

Philadelphia in 1765 and King's in 1767 undertook to supply professional training in medicine, though on an undergraduate level. But physicians had a poor economic and social status, and so the medical schools were never overflowing with students. By 1776, Philadelphia had graduated but ten students and King's twelve. Perhaps it was as well, for one of the abler graduates of King's recommended in his thesis the prescription of a specific he had not the courage to administer.

This advance in educational standards also influenced the legal profession, and in 1756 the New York bar began to demand college work as a requisite for admission. By 1776 one-third of those entitled to plead before the provincial courts held the degree of bachelor of arts. Formal training in civil law, the common law, or municipal law was never undertaken in any colonial college, although King's, Philadelphia, and the advocates of the proposed college at Charleston all dreamed and planned for the establishment of such courses.

The colleges likewise raised the standards of secondary education. Throughout the period, criticism of the preparation of college matriculants was constant, and, in an effort to gain more satisfactory material, all the new colleges maintained their own grammar schools. These secondary schools were also essential to the colleges as "feeders" of matriculants. As the years passed, the number of independent grammar schools in the middle and southern provinces increased sharply, and the graduates of the newer colleges, particularly New Jersey, were in great demand as masters.

These college founders also made significant contributions to colonial interdependence. Hundreds of students crossed provincial boundaries to enroll in their alma maters. Half of Newark's enrollment came from provinces other than Delaware; 40 per cent of Philadelphia's from homes outside of Pennsylvania. New Jersey attracted men from North Carolina and Massachusetts. So heavy a migration was a significant change, for the three older colleges had drawn nearly all their students from relatively restricted areas. In the years immediately preceding the Revolution, students migrating northward were passed by northern-born graduates, particularly of Yale and New Jersey, moving to southern provinces. In Virginia and North Carolina, New Jersey men began a new cycle of college founding. Thus the younger colleges stimulated interprovincial migration of able men, trained in much the same intellectual pattern.

The history of higher education during these three decades, then, is dominated by the establishment of successful colleges and the development of promotional techniques. Each successive college was founded more easily and with better planning than its predecessors; problems were foreseen and precedents were available and accepted. Once opened, they carried on until subjected to military interference during the Revolution. These colleges significantly increased the cultural level of the population and raised the educational standards of the professions. The founders advanced the practice and idea of democratic higher education. They transplanted the essentials of the educational system of the English dissenting academies and saw the system take root; and virtually the entire task had been the accomplishment of men born and bred in America. They believed that they were strengthening the bonds of an empire in which America should be subsidiary, not subordinate, to England. From the beginning many had hoped the colleges would further the creation of cultural autonomy in America. In 1770, for example, Ezra Stiles tabulated the various degrees granted by the several American colleges and concluded: "Thus all the learned degrees are now conferred in the American Colleges as amply as in the European Colleges." As the colonial epoch closed, many Americans proudly felt that they had achieved educational self-reliance.

STUDY GUIDE

1. How does McAnear explain the founding of so many colleges in the British colonies between 1745 and 1775?

2. In the nineteenth century, a great many small colleges were founded by different religious denominations in the Midwest. What is the chief explanation for the recent expansion of state colleges and universities and the decline of the small, religious college?

3. What differences do you see between colleges in the colonial period and colleges in our own time with respect to: financial support, faculty, student body, and curriculum?

4. McAnear emphasizes two aims in college founding — preservation of religion and the development of an intelligent citizenry. Considering the membership of Boards of Trustees and of state agencies that provide the funds for colleges today, what might be some of their chief goals in supporting higher education?

5. Colonial colleges were frequently founded in association with churches or library companies, a fact that was reflected to some extent in their curricula. Think of examples from the later nineteenth and twentieth centuries of new curricula that have been introduced in direct response to new American institutions or interests — for example, big business, large-scale agriculture, science and technology, and government.

6. Describe how some of the patterns established by the colonial colleges continue to be influential in American education.

BIBLIOGRAPHY

There are some exceptions to the generalization, made in the introduction to this selection, that writers on educational history slight the colonial period and informal education. An early work, which takes a broader view and constitutes one of the most fascinating studies of colonial history, is Edward Eggleston, *The Transit of Civilization from England to America in the Seventeenth Century* (New York, 1901). In *Education in the Forming of American Society: Needs and Opportunities for Study* * (Chapel Hill, N.C., 1960), Bernard Bailyn points out some of the deficiencies of earlier writing on educational history and suggests some new directions for future study. The most ambitious work of this newer sort is Lawrence A. Cremin, *American Education: The Colonial Experience, 1607–1786* * (New York, 1970). Another general work that tells much about colonial colleges is Richard Hofstadter and Walter P. Metzger, *The Development of Academic Freedom in the United States* (New York, 1955). Shorter, but stimulating treatments may be found in Daniel J. Boorstin, *The Americans: The Colonial Experience* * (New York, © 1958), which is also informative on religion, law, science, and other subjects, and in the relevant chapters of Samuel E. Morison, *The Puritan Pronaos* (New York, 1936), which is titled *The Intellectual Life of Colonial New England* * in the paperback edition.

Morison also wrote several books on Harvard, including *Harvard College in the Seventeenth Century*, 2 vols. (Cambridge, Mass., 1936). Another readable history of a particular institution is Thomas J. Wertenbaker, *Princeton, 1746–1896* (Princeton, N.J., 1946). Education and colonial thought can also be studied through biographies of leading figures of the time; two excellent studies of educators are Edmund S. Morgan, *The Gentle Puritan: A Life of Ezra Stiles, 1727–1795* (New Haven, Conn., 1962) and Louis L. Tucker, *Puritan Protagonist: President Thomas Clap of Yale College* (Chapel Hill, N.C., 1962).

With respect to pre-collegiate education, historians have not yet reached agreement in judging the contribution of colonial America to our free public school system. Besides the work by Bailyn and the first book by Morison cited previously, Robert Middlekauff, *Ancients and Axioms: Secondary Education in Eighteenth-Century New England* (New Haven, Conn., 1963) should be read by anyone interested in secondary education. The books on New England family life by John Demos and Edmund S. Morgan (cited in the bibliography following the selection from Morgan, "Colonial Women") shed light upon the role of the family and the master-servant relationship in education. Though a great deal more work on colonial education is needed, the works mentioned here present a good picture of the contrasts, and the similarities, between colonial schools and colleges and those of the twentieth century.

"Mr. Peter Manigault and His Friends" by Louis Manigault, 1854, after an eighteenth-century sketch by George Roupell.

ARTHUR M. SCHLESINGER, SR.

Social Class

In our time, it is a truism that everyone in the United States, regardless of his real wealth or poverty, thinks of himself as being of the middle class. Just exactly how class-ridden our society is depends upon how one looks at it. Government statistics reveal extraordinary disparities between the wealthiest group in American society and those who are impoverished. A twenty-minute ride from Cleveland's Hough ghetto, which erupted in violence in 1966, to the palatial suburb of Shaker Heights, which for some years had the highest average income in the United States, provides graphic evidence of the class differences that still exist in our country. If, however, one considers the average income of American families or compares the standard of living here with ancient or medieval societies, one may conclude that our affluent society has been highly successful in affording a measure of comfort to its citizens and providing opportunities for rapid social mobility.

During the 1950s, a good many Americans tended to be oblivious to the inequalities in American life and rather self-congratulatory as to the accomplishments of the American economic system. Since historians frequently reflect the view of the times in which they write, it is not surprising that many of them who wrote during the fifties saw an open, middle-class society in our country's earlier history. Recent studies have suggested that there was considerable disparity in wealth between classes in the eighteenth century, and that in politics and other areas the lower classes deferred to their "betters."

The emphasis in the studies of the 1950s was upon the relative economic and political equality in the British colonies and the ease with which a poor man might make good. The outstanding study of class in early America by Jackson T. Main, concludes that class differences varied with the economic development of particular areas, and that there was more class mobility near the bottom of the scale than near the top. The chances were pretty good for a landless man to acquire a small farm, but few such men managed to rise to the upper-middle or upper class in wealth or social station.

Main's work was particularly impressive because he gathered a good deal of specific information about the income and property holdings of people in different occupations in all parts of the British colonies. The following selection by Arthur M. Schlesinger, Sr. emphasizes other aspects of class, especially the social badges of status, and he suggests that persons of every rank took class quite seriously. His description of colonial society raises the question of just how equalitarian our ancestors were, and it may lead one to reconsider aspects of class and social mobility in our own time.

For many years historical students have been so interested in discovering evidences of democracy in the colonial period that they have tended to distort the actual situation. This paper is an attempt to correct the balance.

The colonists unhesitatingly took for granted the concept of a graded society. It was the only kind they had known in Europe, and they had no thought of forgoing it in their new home. Indeed, they possessed a self-interested reason for retaining it. In this outpost of civilization it was man alone, not his ancestors, who counted. Even the humblest folk could hope to better their condition, for the equality of opportunity which they now had attained meant, as well, the opportunity to be unequal. The indentured servant, the apprentice, the common laborer, everyone in fact but the Negro bondsman, could expect to stand on his own feet and get on and up in the world.

Other factors, however, precluded a faithful duplicating of Europe's stratified order. As David Ramsay pointed out in his *History of the American Revolution* (1789), no remnants of the feudal age existed to thwart or hinder men's advancement. The occasional nobleman who went to America deserted his accustomed "splendor and amusements" only for temporary

"The Aristocracy in Colonial America" by Arthur M. Schlesinger, Sr. Reprinted from Massachusetts Historical Society, *Proceedings,* Vol. LXXIV (1962), by permission of the Society and Arthur M. Schlesinger, Jr.

exile, usually to cash in on a colonial proprietaryship or a royal governorship. Thomas Fairfax, settling in Virginia from England in 1747 at the age of fifty-four, was unique among the permanent comers in bearing so high a rank as baron, but he lived out the remaining thirty-four years of his life for the most part unobtrusively on his distant Shenandoah Valley estate. . . .

In the case of a few of the early colonies the English government sought by fiat to establish artificial class distinctions, but these efforts, occurring in the middle third of the seventeenth century, all came to grief. The London authorities, accustomed to titles of nobility at home, were blind to the very different conditions existing in the overseas wilderness. The people were sparse, strong-willed, and still scrambling for a living; the thought of a social strait jacket imposed from above outraged their mettlesome self-respect and, by the same sign, operated to deter prospective settlers. . . .

For the settlers to build a structured society on their own initiative and in their own interest was, however, quite another matter. This they proceeded to do in colony after colony as rapidly as time and circumstances permitted. In the case of Massachusetts, though, they did not have to wait. Not only did the founders themselves belong to Britain's rural and urban gentry but, as good Puritans, they considered their superior station divinely ordained. In the words of their first governor, John Winthrop, "God Almightie in his most holy and wise providence hath soe disposed of the Condicion of mankinde, as in all times some must be rich some poore, some highe and emminent in power and dignitie; others mean and in subieceion." Accordingly, the men so favored immediately assumed the key positions in government and society, sharing the honors with the foremost clergymen.

They overreached themselves, however, when they sought to legalize class differences in dress. Despite the heavy penalties for disobedience, ordinary people in this new land did not understand that they were to be permanently ordinary. To no avail did the legislature in 1651 express "utter detestation" that men "of meane condition, education and callings should take uppon them the garbe of gentlemen by the wearinge of gold or silver lace" and the like, and that "women of the same rank" should "wear silke or tiffany hoodes or scarfes." Both there and in Connecticut, which had somewhat similar regulations, the resistance to them was so stubborn that they were presently allowed to fall into disuse.

In all other respects, however, the aristocracy retained its primacy, and as the years went on, families with fortunes newly made on land or sea won admittance to the circle. The traveler Joseph Bennett wrote in 1740 of Boston, "both the ladies and gentlemen dress and appear as gay, in common, as courtiers in England on a coronation or birthday." And the author of *American Husbandry*, surveying the entire New England scene in 1775, reported that, though social demarcations were less conspicuous than abroad, "gentlemen's houses appear everywhere" and on the "many considerable land estates . . . the owners live much in the style of country gentlemen in England."

In New York, while the colony was still New Netherland, the Dutch West India Company had introduced a system of patroonships — immense tracts along the Hudson which the possessors were to cultivate with tenants bound to them by a semifeudal relationship. But only a few of the grants were actually made before the British took over in 1664, and of these Rensselaerswyck, in what is now Albany County, was the only one to work out well. The English governors in their turn followed the Dutch example to the extent of awarding enormous estates to favored individuals; and on this basis a privileged class evolved which divided political and social pre-eminence in the province with the leading merchants and lawyers of New York City.

Although the historical background in Pennsylvania was different, the outcome there, too, was the same. Despite the lowly antecedents of most of the Quaker settlers and their devotion to "plain living," an aristocracy of great landholders and merchant princes likewise arose. John Smith, an old-time Friend looking back from the year 1764, sadly depicted the change as it had come over Philadelphia. During the first twenty years, he said, as the members began to accumulate means, they commenced "in some degree conforming to the fashions of the World," and after another score of years, when "many of the Society were grown rich," vanities like "fine costly Garments" and "fashionable furniture" became usual. Indeed, the foremost families, not content with handsome urban residences, maintained in addition country estates as retreats from the intense heat of the Philadelphia summers.

But the Southern aristocracy attained the closest resemblance to the English landed gentry. There, in a predominantly rural economy, men on the make enjoyed the decisive advantage of an extensive servile class as well as of broad acres. There, also, to a degree unknown in the North, the Virginia patrician William Fitzhugh spoke for his class in avowing that his children had "better be never born than ill-bred." Josiah Quincy, Jr., visiting South Carolina in 1773, wrote that "The inhabitants may well be divided into opulent and lordly planters, poor and spiritless peasants and vile slaves." The Bostonian, however, overlooked the fact that, different from the other Southern provinces, the select circle in this particular one also included successful merchants, thanks to Charleston, the only important seaport south of Philadelphia. . . .

The English-appointed governor and his entourage in the provincial capital formed the apex of the social pyramid. These personages and their womenfolk emulated the pomp and circumstance of the royal court at home and furnished a pattern for the great landholders, mercantile princes, and the like who composed the native aristocracy. A beadroll of such families in the eighteenth century would include among others the Wentworths of

New Hampshire, the Bowdoins, Quincys, Hutchinsons, Olivers, Faneuils, and Hancocks of Massachusetts, the Redwoods, Browns, and Wantons of Rhode Island, the Trumbulls and Ingersolls of Connecticut, the De Lanceys, Schuylers, Van Rensselaers, Livingstons, and Coldens of New York, the Logans, Allens, Morrises, Willings, Pembertons, and Shippens of Pennsylvania and, in the plantation colonies, the Dulanys and Carrolls of Maryland, the Byrds, Randolphs, Carters, Masons, Pages, Fitzhughs, Harrisons, and Lees of Virginia, and the Rutledges, Pinckneys, Draytons, Laurenses, and Izards of South Carolina.

Families like these buttressed their position by matrimonial alliances both within and across provincial boundaries. To cite a few cases, the New Yorker John Franklin married Deborah Morris of Philadelphia, and her fellow townsman William Shippen wedded Alice Lee of the Old Dominion. The Allens of Philadelphia, the Redwoods of Newport, the New York De Lanceys, the Ervings of Boston, and the Izards of Charleston took mates in three or more colonies. The rare instances of gentlefolk marrying beneath their station scandalized their friends and kinsmen. To William Byrd II, for example, it was nothing short of a "tragical Story" when a wellborn Virginia girl in 1732 played "so senceless a Prank" as to marry her uncle's overseer, "a dirty Plebian."

By custom and official usage members of the gentry enjoyed the privilege of attaching certain honorific tags to their names. As in England, they alone could qualify as "Gentlemen," and they only had the right to the designations "Esquire" and "Master," although the latter term tended in ordinary speech to be pronounced "Mister." The common man, for his part, contentedly answered to "Goodman" — his day of being called "Mister" was yet to come. Equal consideration for class distinctions governed the allotment of pews in Congregational churches, where persons resisting their assignments were sometimes haled into court. And at Yale until 1767 and Harvard until 1772 even the order of reciting in class and the place of students in academic processions bore a relation to the social standing of their parents.

Not being to the manner born, most people aspiring to gentility had to learn from scratch how to act like their betters. Luckily manuals for the purpose lay at hand. The great majority were English importations, but to meet the rising demand colonial printers, as the years went by, put out their own editions. These treatises followed originals appearing in France and Italy, where since the age of chivalry the standards of approved behavior had been set for the whole of Europe. Among the writings most often listed in American booksellers' announcements and the inventories of private libraries were Henry Peacham's *The Compleat Gentleman* (1622), Richard Brathwaite's *The English Gentleman* (1630), Richard Allestree's *The Whole Duty of Man* (1660), and, for feminine guidance, Lord Halifax's *The Lady's New Year's Gift: or, Advice to a Daughter* (1688), the anonymous *Ladies Library* (1714), the *Friendly Instructor* (1745) by an unknown, and William Kenrick's *The Whole Duty of Woman; or, a Guide to the Female Sex from the Age of Sixteen to Sixty* (1761). Even the commonsensical Benjamin Franklin wrote his wife from London in 1758 that he wanted their daughter Sally to "read over and over again the *Whole Duty of Man*, and the *Lady's Library,*" and we know that George Washington as late as 1764 purchased an American reprint of the *Whole Duty of Man*.

These handbooks held up integrity, courage, justice, courtesy, and piety as the hallmarks of the gentleman, with modesty, chastity, tenderness, godliness, and the duty of submission to one's husband as the essentials of a gentlewoman. Wifely docility not only befitted the innate inferiority of the sex but attested lasting penance for the first woman's disobedience. If her yokefellow proved unfaithful, wrote Lord Halifax, she should "affect ignorance" of it; if he were a sot, she should rejoice that the fault offset her own many frailties; if he were "Cholerick and Ill-humour'd," she should avoid any "unwary Word" and soothe him with smiles and flattery; if he lacked intelligence, she should take comfort in the thought that "a wife often made a better Figure, for her Husband's making no great one." The writers, when treating behavior in company, instructed the ladies what to wear, how to arrange a dinner, what diversions were proper, and how to converse (with the admonition: "Women seldom have Materials to furnish a long Discourse. . . .").

Having discovered how to conduct themselves, the gentry further evidenced their status by the elegance of their attire. The pains they took to ape the latest court styles appear in their elaborate orders to English tailors and the loud complaints over the pattern or fit or color of the garments commissioned. George Washington, for one, cautioned his London agent, "Whatever goods you may send me, let them be fashionable, neat and good of their several kinds." According to the Englishman Daniel Neal in 1747, "there is no Fashion in London but in three or four Months is to be seen at Boston," and William Eddis after a few years in Annapolis wrote similarly in 1771 that he was "almost inclined to believe" that a new mode spread more rapidly among "polished and affluent" Americans than among "many opulent" Londoners.

Subject to the season's vagaries in matters of detail, gentlemen wore cocked hats, white ruffled silk shirts, and embroidered broadcloth frock coats, with knee breeches of fine texture and gorgeous hues, silk hose fastened with ornamental garters, and pumps displaying gold or silver buckles. Powdered wigs, an added adornment, began to lose favor about 1754, when George II discarded his, to be followed by the vogue of letting one's natural hair grow long and powdering it and queuing it behind or tying the tail in a small silk bag.

Gentlewomen on festive occasions tripped about on dainty high-heeled slippers in rustling gowns of imported brocade, bombazine, sarsenet, shal-

loon, damask, velvet, taffeta, and other expensive fabrics. They stiffened their
bodices with whalebone stays and stretched their skirts over great hoops of
the same material. They kept abreast of the latest English dress designs by
means of clothed dolls sent over from London, and shortly before the Revolution they had the additional help of engraved pictures. Indicative of the
irresistible sweep of style, the Yearly Meeting of Friends in 1726 at Philadelphia futilely decried the "immodest fashion of hooped petticoats" and such
improprieties as "bare necks" and "shoes trimmed with gaudy colors."

An object of special pride was milady's coiffure, a structure painstakingly
erected on a concealed crepe roller or cushion. In preparation for a ball or
party she would have her hair dressed the day before and perhaps sleep in a
chair that night to keep it in condition. For going about outdoors the first
families maintained their own equipages, stylish vehicles variously called
chaises, calashes, chairs, and landaus, or, still more grandly, they traveled in
coaches-and-four and berlins attended with liveried drivers and footmen.

The apparel of the simple folk similarly evinced their status. The men,
their hair short-cropped, typically wore caps, coarse linen shirts, leather
coats and aprons, homespun stockings, and cowhide shoes with either long
or short buckskin breeches, while the women's garments were of equal cheap-
ness and durability. The French Revolution in its impact on America was in
the years ahead to go far toward removing class differences in male attire,
but portents of what awaited revealed themselves in unexpected ways in the
events leading up to the rupture with Britain. Thus, to conceal their participation in the Stamp Act violence at Boston in August, 1765, "there were
fifty gentlemen actors in this scene," wrote Governor Francis Bernard, "dis-
guised with trousers and jackets on." Their motive was doubtless to escape
the possible legal consequences of their connivance, but it was probably just
a desire for sheer creature comfort which caused the South Carolina Assembly in 1769 to permit the members to forgo wigs and knee breeches in
order to transact committee business in caps and trousers — like "so many
unhappy persons ready for execution," objected a newspaper commentator.

For those on top of the heap the Anglican Church held a compelling attraction. Just as it was the allegiance of the upper class at home, so it was
that of the Crown officials sent to America. The dignified ritualism of the
Book of Common Prayer, with its setting of fine music, exerted an un-
doubted appeal, but the social prestige of membership probably formed the
greater magnet. At any rate hundreds of Congregationalists, Presbyterians,
Quakers, Lutherans, and others, as they moved upward in the world, forsook
the faith of their fathers for the more stylish communion.

Other evidences of snobbishness were even clearer. An English nobleman
passing through the colonies never failed to stir the social waters. Thus Lord
Adam Gordon, one of the few members of Parliament ever to visit America,
conquered all before him as he journeyed from Charleston to Boston in
1765; and Lord Charles Hope on a similar excursion in 1766 met with a like

reception. Four years later Sir William Draper crowned his New York stay by wedding Susannah De Lancey.

Two crucial moments in life — marriage and death — afforded special opportunities for ostentation. Weddings were celebrated with banqueting, innumerable toasts, and like festivities sometimes extending over several days. A funeral obliged the bereaved family to provide the assemblage with such souvenirs of the occasion as mourning gloves, scarves, and gold rings as well as quantities of food and drink. At the burial of John Grove of Surrey County, Virginia, in 1673, the liquor consumed equaled the cost of a thousand pounds of tobacco. Governor Jonathan Belcher of Massachusetts in 1736 distributed more than a thousand pairs of gloves in honor of his wife, but Peter Faneuil overtopped him two years later with three thousand at the services for his uncle Andrew. In addition, the grief-stricken friends would don appropriate attire for a further period at their own expense.

As this costly fashion seeped downward in society, it placed an excessive burden on families who, desiring to pay as great respect to their departed, could ill afford the outlay. To ease their plight the Yearly Meeting of Friends at Philadelphia in 1729 recommended to their co-religionists that "wine or other strong liquors" be furnished "but once." The Massachusetts legislature went so far in a series of statutes between 1721 and 1741 as to prohibit under heavy fine the "very extravagant" expense of gloves, scarves, rings, rum, or wine. But custom proved too stubborn; and no real change came about until the colonists, provoked by the Sugar Act of 1764 and its successors, saw a chance to strike back at Britain by disusing (among other things) the mourning materials they had hitherto imported.

Now public meetings from New Hampshire to Georgia urged "the new mode" on all who loved their country. The *Boston News-Letter,* March 9, 1769, observed with special gratification that the rich Charlestonian Christopher Gadsden had worn simple homespun at his wife's obsequies and that "The whole expence of her funeral, of the manufacture of England, did not amount to more than 3l. 10s our currency." At another South Carolina funeral the people in attendance spiritedly declined to accept the gifts which the family had provided. The First Continental Congress in 1774 climaxed these efforts by subjecting to boycott all persons who distributed scarves or went "into any further mourning-dress, than a black crape or ribbon on the arm or hat, for gentlemen, and a black ribbon and necklace for ladies." From this blow the practice never recovered.

One aspect of Old World patrician life, the *code duello,* the Americans did not achieve or even want to achieve. Perhaps because of their generally more humane disposition they instinctively recoiled from the settlement of disputes by personal combat. Though occasional duels took place during the century and a half, these typically involved royal officers on overseas assignment or recent comers not yet fully Americanized, unless perchance they partook of the shabby character of the encounter between the Charleston youth and a sea captain over what the *South-Carolina Gazette,* September 6, 1735, termed their "pretensions to the Favours of a certain sable Beauty."

The few affrays involving colonial aristocrats deeply shocked public sentiment and, if death resulted, provoked criminal prosecutions. What was apparently the earliest such affair cost the life of Dr. John Livingston of New York in 1715 at the hands of Governor Dongan's nephew Thomas, whom the court two days afterward found guilty of manslaughter. In 1728 occurred a sword fight between two Boston young men in which Henry Phillips killed Benjamin Woodbridge over differences not then or since revealed. Before the grand jury could bring in an indictment for murder (which it did a month later), the victor fled to France with the help of Peter Faneuil, a kinsman by marriage. Some years following, in 1770, Dr. John Haly of Charleston fatally shot Peter De Lancey, the deputy postmaster, in a duel in the candlelit parlor of a tavern. Though he, too, like Dongan, was convicted of manslaughter, he avoided the consequences through the pardon of the governor. In 1775 came the last instance, also between two South Carolinians, but this one differed markedly from the earlier clashes in that Henry Laurens, while willing to accept the challenge of John Grimké, declined as a matter of principle to fire on him. Happily he escaped unscathed. No one could have foreseen as the colonial period ended that the discredited practice would under altered circumstances find wide favor in the next generation.

The continuous recruitment of the top stratum of the community from beneath reveals sharply the basic aspect of colonial society: its fluidity, the incessant movement of people upward. The American aristocracy, however undemocratic when once it took form, was undeniably democratic in the method of its forming. The only class struggle in that far day was the struggle to climb out of a lower class into a higher one, for, as Nathaniel Ames put it in one of his almanacs,

> All Men are by Nature equal,
> But differ greatly in the sequel.

The self-made man thus began his career in America, to become in time a national folk hero. In the absence of England's officially prescribed ranks it was, above all, the acquisition of wealth which elevated a family to the social heights. Extensive land grants and other perquisites from the government, obtained perhaps through favoritism or fraud, might expedite the process. Further help could, and often did come, from lucrative marriages. Newspapers, with no thought of impropriety, would describe a bride as "a most amiable young Lady with a handsome Fortune," sometimes stating the amount, though, of course, the unions not infrequently joined couples already well-to-do. But, for the most part, it was industry and ability applied imaginatively to beckoning opportunities that ensured the outcome.

As early as 1656 John Hammond, a Briton who had spent many years among the Virginia and Maryland settlers, wrote that "some from being wool-hoppers and of as mean and meaner imployment in England have there grown great merchants, and attained to the most eminent advancements the Country afforded." And a century later, in 1765, the scholarly officeholder Cadwallader Colden similarly said of New York that "the most opulent families, in our own memory, have arisen from the lowest rank of the people." If a writer in the *Pennsylvania Evening-Post*, March 14, 1776, is to be credited, half the property in the city of Philadelphia belonged to "men whose fathers or grandfathers wore LEATHER APRONS." Indeed, Colden believed that "The only principle of Life propagated among the young People is to get Money, and Men are only esteemed according to . . . the Money they are possessed of." And even the pious *New-England Primer* taught:

> He that ne'er learns his A, B, C,
> For ever will a Blockhead be;
> But he that learns these Letters fair
> Shall have a Coach to take the Air.

Some examples of nobodies becoming somebodies will make the matter more concrete. Thus Henry Shrimpton, a London brazier, so expanded his interests and activities after settling in Boston in 1639 that when dying twenty-seven years later he left an estate of nearly £12,000, and with this nest egg his son Samuel (who in filial gratitude displayed a brass kettle on his "very stately house") succeeded before his death in 1698 in making himself the town's richest citizen. The Belcher family of Massachusetts progressed in three generations from the vocation of innkeeping at Cambridge to mercantile greatness in Boston and then to the officeholding eminence of grandson Jonathan, who served as royal governor of Massachusetts and New Hampshire from 1730 to 1741 and of New Jersey from 1747 to 1757.

In a like number of generations the Reverend John Hancock, an impecunious Lexington minister, apprenticed his son Thomas to a Boston bookseller; and Thomas, opening his own establishment in 1723 and later branching out into more profitable lines, amassed a fortune of £100,000 sterling, which at his demise in 1764 he willed to his nephew John, making him the Croesus of the patriot movement in Massachusetts. By the same token, Connecticut's Roger Sherman, another signer of the Declaration of Independence, started out as a shoemaker's apprentice and, after following the trade on his own for some years, turned to surveying, the law, and other fields which won him independent means.

In the Middle colonies Robert Livingston, son of a poor parson in Scotland and founder of the renowned New York clan, began his American career in 1673 at the age of twenty-one as town clerk in the frontier village of Albany and within another twenty-one years owned a princely domain of 160,000 acres. The great Manhattan merchant John Lamb, an associate of Livingston's descendants in Revolutionary days and general in the Continental army, was the American-born child of a Londoner who in 1724 had escaped hanging for burglary through commutation of his sentence to indentured service overseas.

Isaac Norris, the progenitor of the notable Pennsylvania family, arrived in Philadelphia from England in 1691 with a little more than £100 and in less than a quarter-century became the colony's principal landholder. George Taylor, coming as an indentured servant from Ireland in 1736, first worked at an iron furnace in Chester County, then, setting up in the trade with a partner, accumulated his ample means. He was another man of humble pedigree to sign the Declaration of Independence. The meteoric rise of Benjamin Franklin, the runaway apprentice from Boston, has become a legendary American success story.

Though the economic life of the Southern colonies differed markedly from that of the North, the outcome there too was the same. Thus the Irish-born Daniel Dulany, talented lawyer and political leader in early eighteenth-century Maryland, commenced his American years in 1703 as a penniless eighteen-year-old lad under indenture. In neighboring Virginia, John Carter, an English newcomer in 1649 of obscure antecedents, laid the material basis of one of that province's first families; his son Robert of Nomini Hall, known to his contemporaries as "King" Carter, owned some 300,000 acres, 700 slaves and over 2,000 horses and other livestock at the time of his decease in 1732. William Byrd, the forerunner of another Virginia dynasty, came from England in 1671 at the age of nineteen with the bequest of some land from an uncle, which he made the springboard for a great fortune in tobacco culture and trading before his death in 1704.

In South Carolina the Manigaults, Allstons, and Laurenses, among others, conformed to the familiar pattern. The first American Manigault, a French Huguenot emigré from London in 1695, originally tried farming, then made good at victualing and more remunerative ventures, and in 1729 he bequeathed an estate which his son Gabriel by the mid-eighteenth century built into the largest fortune in the province. By contrast, Jonathan Allston was "a gentleman of immense income, all of his own acquisition," according to Josiah Quincy, Jr., who visited his plantation in 1773. Henry Laurens, like the younger Manigault, owed the silver spoon in his mouth at birth to his father, in this case a Charleston saddler who had amassed riches in that and other undertakings.

But only a few Americans ever achieved the accolade of English noble rank, and this came about under circumstances so fortuitous as to make it the despair of other colonists. William Phips, who had risen from shepherd boy and shipwright's apprentice on the Maine frontier to prosper as a shipbuilder in Boston, was knighted in 1687 for raising in Haitian waters a Spanish galleon laden with £300,000 of treasure, of which the Crown awarded him £16,000 as well as his title. John Randolph, a distinguished Virginia lawyer and planter, obtained his knighthood in 1732 for his statesmanlike skill in negotiating certain differences between the London government and his colony. William Pepperrell, a business leader and landholder in Massachusetts and Maine, won the status of baronet in 1746 in return for commanding the victorious American forces against the French fortress of Louisbourg. A more dubious case was that of the well-to-do New Jersey officeholder William Alexander, who on the basis of tenuous evidence laid claim to being the sixth Earl of Stirling. Ignoring the rejection of his contention by a House of Lords committee in 1762, he continued to profess the title, and it was as Lord Stirling that he rendered valuable service to the American cause as a general in the War for Independence.

In a special category was the Cinderella-like story of Agnes Surriage. This comely, sixteen-year-old maiden, a barefoot servant in a Marblehead tavern in 1742, so captivated Charles Henry Frankland at first sight that the English-born revenue officer in Boston sent her to school at his own expense. Then he lived with her as his mistress in an elegant mansion he had built for her in Hopkinton. Even his inheritance of a baronetcy in no wise altered the relationship, but something that occurred while the couple were abroad in 1755 wrought the miracle, causing Sir Henry at long last to make Agnes his wife. According to tradition it was her daring rescue of him during the Lisbon earthquake. Boston society, hitherto scandalized, now forgot her past and as Lady Frankland received her with open arms. Warm-hearted by nature, she had by all accounts become through the years a person of cultivation and charm. Her unusual tale has fascinated numerous chroniclers, including Oliver Wendell Holmes, who recounted it in ballad form in *Songs in Many Keys* (1865).

Governor Francis Bernard of Massachusetts, seeing in the creation of an American peerage an opportunity to "give strength and stability" to supporters of Britain, urged the proposal on the Ministry in 1764 soon after the difficulties with the colonists arose. "Although *America*," he conceded, "is not now (and probably will not be for many years to come) ripe enough for an hereditary *Nobility*; yet it is now capable of a *Nobility* for life." Indeed, in men like Thomas Hutchinson, Philip Livingston, Franklin, and Henry Laurens (to name no others) the colonies possessed personages who by Old World standards could qualify for even heritable rank. But whatever fate might have befallen the scheme if it had been put forward and adopted earlier, it could hardly have succeeded at so late a juncture. With the colonists already fearful of British designs on other counts, anybody who accepted an honorific dignity at this stage would have forfeited all public esteem. He would have marked himself indelibly as one who had sold out to the government. But the matter never came to a test, for the Ministry quietly shelved the suggestion.

By 1776 the colonial aristocracy had endured for more than a century and a half in the oldest regions, for over a century in others, and had sunk deep roots elsewhere. With the passage of time it had consolidated its position and constantly replenished its vitality with transfusions of new blood. Its members had not, moreover, used their station exclusively for self-aggrandizement and outward show but, as a class, had considered themselves trustees for the common good, identifying their welfare with that of the community at large. In the case of the Southern gentry the need to superintend the lives of hosts of slaves served to heighten this sense of stewardship, making them feel as fit to rule as were the guardians to whom Plato had entrusted his republic.

In all the colonies men of quality occupied responsible posts in every sphere of official activity: the executive department, the provincial and local lawmaking branches, the armed forces, the judiciary. True, the alternative would have been to allow ill-prepared and possibly rash underlings to seize the reins, but the deeper reason lay in the conviction that only the rich and wellborn possessed the required wisdom and capacity. In no less degree they provided the cultural leadership. They not only exemplified for all to see the refinements of living, but they set standards of tasteful architecture and well-kept grounds and through their patronage enabled portrait painters to pursue their calling. In like fashion they assembled the best private libraries and afforded their sons superior intellectual advantages. And from their largess came the principal benefactions to religion and education, to charity and projects of community improvement.

Nor did their role in any of these respects excite resentment among the mass of the population. Men in every walk of life not only accepted the concept of a layered society, but believed in its rightness. The clergy preached it; all classes practiced it. Whatever might be the shortcomings of the English aristocracy — and colonial editors repeated from the London press lurid accounts of its immoralities and profligacy — the American variety was no privileged group living off the unearned increment of ancestral reputations. They, by and large, had mounted the heights through shrewdness and ability and had stayed there by the continued exercise of those faculties. The ordinary citizen deemed it only proper to accord them deference. Very rarely did their real or alleged abuses of authority provoke popular opposition, and such occasions seldom lasted long.

The quarrel with the mother country had nothing to do with the stratified character of British society, only with the objectionable policies of certain individuals in positions of power. Not even the fiery Tom Paine condemned it in his tract *Common Sense* when blasting the titular head of the system as "the royal brute." Nor did the framers of the Declaration of Independence do so later that year. Though they proclaimed that all men are created equal, they merely rebuked their brethren at home for suffering George to act a "tyrant" toward his American subjects.

To be sure, in the events foreshadowing this final crisis the colonial gentry betrayed divided sympathies, notably in New York and Pennsylvania, some siding ardently with Britain or at least seeking to prevent an irreparable break. But the well-informed Thomas McKean, himself a Signer, stated in retrospect that almost two-thirds of the country's "influential characters" — that is, the overwhelming majority — had favored the American cause.

The heritage of a common history and culture bound the upper-class patriots to the homeland no less than it did the loyalist minority; but, unlike the latter, they had developed a passionate attachment to colonial self-government, a fierce jealousy of any encroachments on the authority which they had so long and capably wielded. Besides, the new taxation and trade legislation, falling heaviest on the well-to-do, supplied a clear economic motive which was intensified by the conviction that, if the present enactments went unchallenged, worse ones would follow. The phenomenal progress of the colonies during the many years that London had permitted them virtual autonomy thoroughly justified in their minds implacable resistance to the ministerial innovations.

To counteract the measures, however, they required the support of the humbler elements; but this they were accustomed to enjoy. Sometimes to their alarm these allies threatened the orderly course of opposition by gratuitously resorting to riot and violence, but the men of quality were invariably able to regain control. In recogniton of their role the Continental Congress, when the war broke out, unanimously chose a Virginia aristocrat as commander in chief of the armed forces, and in due course a grateful Republic named him its first President. The revolt against upper-class dominance was to come in later times.

STUDY GUIDE

1. Who constituted the aristocracy in colonial America, and how could they be distinguished by dress, manners, and the titles by which they were addressed?

2. How did the colonial class structure differ from European societies of the time with respect to: the role of achievement and inheritance in attaining upper-class status; the relation of wealth to social standing; the degree of mobility between classes?

3. What evidence does Schlesinger provide that an aristocracy in fact existed in colonial America? What evidence can you think of in contemporary America that class differences still exist? Think in terms of social, economic, educational, cultural, and language differences, and explain why you think these factors should or should not be the basis of class status.

4. In describing cases of individuals and families rising from "leather aprons" to "powdered wigs," Schlesinger frequently mentions land and trade as the important factors in their ascent. What factors are especially important for upward mobility in our time?

BIBLIOGRAPHY

Most historians who have studied class in the colonial period have been concerned with economic status or the relation of class to politics, rather than with the social aspects that Schlesinger describes. Robert E. and B. Katherine Brown have written a number of books and articles in which they emphasize the widespread distribution of property and the resulting political equality of colonial society. Other historians have placed more emphasis upon evidence that colonials deferred to their social and political "betters," as does Charles S. Sydnor in a charming book on the Virginia aristocracy, *Gentlemen Freeholders: Political Practices in Washington's Virginia* (Chapel Hill, N.C., 1952), which in the paperback edition is entitled *American Revolutionaries in the Making.** A volume that deals with the thought and aspirations of the Virginia planters is Louis B. Wright, *The First Gentlemen of Virginia: Intellectual Qualities of the Early Colonial Ruling Class* * (San Marino, Cal., 1940). Carl Bridenbaugh's works on colonial social history were quite influential in suggesting areas for study, and his books often touch upon class and status. Two short, fascinating volumes by him — the second coauthored with his wife, Jessica — are *Myths and Realities: Societies of the Colonial South* * (Baton Rouge, La., 1952), which studies three social worlds of the colonial South, and *Rebels and Gentlemen: Philadelphia in the Age of Franklin* * (New York, 1942).

The most precise study of economic class and social mobility in colonial America as a whole is Jackson T. Main, *The Social Structure of Revolutionary America* * (Princeton, N.J., 1965). James T. Adams, *Provincial Society, 1690–1763* (New York, 1927) is an older, more impressionistic study of colonial society, while Dixon Wecter, *The Saga of American Society: A Record of Social Aspirations, 1607–1937* (New York, 1937) covers "high society" in the longer period indicated in the title. Two general works of considerable interest that treat social history on the eve of the Revolution are Richard Hofstadter, *America at 1750: A Social Portrait* * (New York, © 1971) and Arthur M. Schlesinger, Sr., *The Birth of the Nation: A Portrait of the American People on the Eve of Independence* (New York, 1969).

III   A NEW NATION

The last quarter of the eighteenth century is a remarkable period in American history. During these twenty-five years, the nation achieved its independence from England, wrote new constitutions for nearly every state, adopted a federal constitution and established a government that was truly national in its operation, and enunciated political ideas that became so deeply embedded in the national consciousness that they are referred to as the American Credo. Perhaps the most remarkable thing about these years is that they began in such scarring social discord that more than 100,000 citizens fled the country; yet the century ended in a political and social harmony that we today might envy. Though the war that was fought here from 1775 to 1783 was a war for independence from Britain, the divisions within colonial society were so intense that towns and families were split apart. The harmony achieved by 1800 was partly owing to the fact that so many Loyalists had left the United States. There were still divisions in American society, but at his inauguration on March 4, 1801, President Thomas Jefferson discerned a political unity in America that rose above such names as Federalist and Republican.

The treatment of Loyalists, and sometimes of Patriots in British hands, during the American Revolution demonstrated how deep and intense the animosities were. Tarring and feathering, riding on a rail, and throwing dung on porches were but a few of the punishments meted out in the first American civil war. The first reading in this section gives a graphic description of these and other reprisals against Loyalists of the period. Paradoxically, the same period saw a rising sense of social concern for the more unfortunate in American society. Beginning during the Revolution, a humanitarian sentiment evolved among the American people that led in many cases to substantial improvements in the lot of the enslaved, the poor, and the unfortunate. The second reading describes the reform spirit of the late eighteenth century. The final reading paints a portrait of the United States in the year 1800. As the new century opened, the American people were beginning to feel like a nation, and a small but mature society had passed well beyond the stage of settlement and colony. The diverse groups, classes, and sections of the infant country seemed to have enough in common to promise the development of a single American society.

*"The Bostonians Paying the Excise-Man" by Philip Dawe, 1774,
shows the punishment of John Malcolm.*

WALLACE BROWN

Social War

One of the most elusive goals of the historian, and of the human mind in general, is objectivity. In our time, most historians recognize that, try as they may to avoid it, some prejudice and human values are bound to creep into their thought and into the history they write. One illustration of this is in the difference in treatment that history accords to the winners and losers in any revolution. Rebels who fail don't get a very good press from historians, since their society is likely to denounce the revolutionary leaders as traitors or madmen. If the revolution succeeds, the same men may be celebrated as patriots and statesmen, while the ruling group that is overthrown is castigated as oppressive or corrupt.

Between 1765 and 1775, British colonial society developed some serious internal divisions and antagonisms. Upon the outbreak of war, provinces, towns, and families were split, and brother fought brother with all the hatred that civil war can engender. By 1783, more than 100,000 people were driven out of the colonies; farms and businesses of Loyalists were confiscated, and thousands of these British adherents were intimidated and mistreated. Many of them had been distinguished contributors to colonial society — governors, judges, ministers, farmers, craftsmen, and laborers. Had the British won the war, the names of Thomas Hutchinson, Joseph Galloway, William Franklin, and Jonathan Boucher would today be as celebrated as are John Adams, Thomas Jefferson, Patrick Henry, and John Hancock.

One question worth pondering is what American society may have lost by the exile of the Loyalists and the victory of the Patriot cause. A substantial reservoir of political talent and experience certainly evaporated, but among the many who cast their lot for independence was an extraordinary number of men of talent to take the Loyalists' places. More difficult to judge is the loss to American thought and culture. A number of Loyalists were able or distinguished scientists, artists, writers, and religious leaders who made their contributions in Canada or Europe rather than here. More important than such individuals was the effect of the break upon American political and constitutional thought, which — it has been argued — suffered the loss of a valid conservative tradition with the exile of the Loyalists.

Another question that has interested historians since the Revolution began is just what a Tory or Loyalist was. The simplest definition is that he was one who remained loyal to England. This raises the question of why they were loyal, whereas immediate neighbors of similar background and position became revolutionary leaders. Many answers to this question have been offered — that it was one's religion that made the difference, or one's wealth, age, occupation, national origins, or temperament. Yet for all the Loyalists who were influenced by such factors, there were at least as many men of the same class who chose the Patriot side.

Wallace Brown, a contemporary student of these questions, has made use of statistical techniques to try to determine the percentage of Loyalists of different occupations, religions, and so forth. Since the statistical parts of his studies are based on fragmentary records, they have been criticized by some historians. However, his book *The Good Americans,* from which the following selection is taken, is a general study of Loyalism that is less dependent upon statistics than his earlier work. Chapter 5 of *The Good Americans* presents a vivid account of the suffering that Loyalists endured during the American War for Independence. If few groups have since been subjected to such direct violence, the persecution of the Loyalists nonetheless reminds one of the fate of many another unpopular minority in later American history. And it should make us cautious about accepting only a "winner's" view of historical losers.

In November, 1777, the Continental Congress recommended the confiscation of Loyalist estates, a suggestion already made by Thomas Paine, and in some places already acted upon. All states finally amerced, taxed, or confiscated much Loyalist property, and in addition New York and South Carolina taxed Loyalist property in order to compensate robbery victims. Some towns simply raffled off Tory property. Patriot officers requisitioned horses and supplies from Loyalists rather than Whigs, and, of course, there was much old-fashioned looting, particularly of the property of exiles. Like Henry VIII's dissolution of the monasteries, the disbursement of Loyalist property created a vested interest in revolution. Also, the device of trying partially to finance the war with traitors' wealth was naturally very popular, if of limited success.

Although the majority of active Loyalists suffered much loss of property, some attempted by various subterfuges to preserve their estates quite apart from having a wife or third party act as purchaser. One scheme was to make over one's property, or make a sham sale, to a sympathetic, moderate friend who had escaped suspicion.

Much commoner was the device used by exiles of leaving their wives or relatives behind in order to keep a foot in both camps. For example, Benjamin Pickman fled from Salem, Massachusetts, in 1775, but left his wife behind to look after their property, to which he returned ten years later. Some brothers may even have chosen opposite sides for such a reason. As the British claims commissioners commented on one split family, "it is possible that this may be a shabby family Compact . . . to preserve the property whether Great Britain or America prevailed."

The overall severity of the various laws against the Loyalists has been estimated as follows:

"Harshest" — New York, South Carolina.
"Harsh" — Massachusetts, New Jersey, Pennsylvania.
"Light" — Rhode Island, Connecticut, Virginia, North Carolina.
"Lightest" — New Hampshire, Delaware, Maryland, Georgia.

With some exceptions, notably Georgia, laws were harshest in states where Loyalists were most powerful, and as the war progressed, the purpose of the laws changed from conversion to "revenge and hate." Similarly, enforcement varied and was usually severest where danger was greatest and civil war bitterest.

A prominent Southern Tory reported that in Virginia, where the Loyalists were weak and little problem, the property of those who joined the British army went to their wives and children "on the Spot . . . as if the Father was dead," and he noted that his own wife "had never been molested but on the contrary treated with the utmost Kindness and Respect." Other Loyalists described being turned off their property with only the clothes on their backs.

But perhaps more typical was the fate of the Chandler family of Worcester, Massachusetts. Colonel John Chandler, a very prominent citizen of distinguished Massachusetts pedigree, dubbed "Tory John" and later in England the "Honest Refugee," fled from Boston with the British army to become a permanent, proscribed exile. For over two years his wife and family continued to enjoy their property undisturbed, until the Worcester Committee of Correspondence began a process that resulted in the confiscation of all but a third of their real and personal property, which third was reserved for Mrs. Chandler's use as long as she remained in the United States. Her husband did not return (he was forbidden to by an act of October, 1778), and on her death special legislation was needed to secure her property for her children.

A myriad of particularities could play a part in determining the extent of persecution. A well-liked or respected Tory (and there were a few such) might well escape, as might someone whose skills were especially valued, for example, a doctor. Influential but quiet Loyalists were more apt to avoid penalties than those of lower social standing or those more vociferous in their beliefs.

The zeal of the patriots could be extremely capricious and, as always with witch-hunts, frequently ridiculous and heavy-handed. One citizen was accosted for naming his dog "Tory," the implication being that a Tory was forced to lead a dog's life. In 1776 at Stratford, Connecticut, an Episcopal minister was brought before the local committee because he had officiated at a baptism where the child was named Thomas Gage. The committee viewed the action as a "designed insult" and censured the cleric. In the same state Zephaniah Beardslee reported that he was "very much abused" for naming his daughter Charlotte, after the queen. It may be noted that Beardslee, apparently a very serious Loyalist, had also been found drinking the king's health. The frequent persecution of Tories for this activity, however, is not as picayune as it seems, because toasts presuppose groups in taverns and the chance of Loyalist plots and associations. Thus, Abraham Cuyler held a gathering in Albany, New York, in June, 1776, that featured drinking and the singing of "God Save the King." At last the enraged Whig citizens crashed the party and carried the royal merrymakers off to jail. . . .

The results of Loyalism might simply be social ostracism — being sent to Coventry — as, for instance, happened to James Allen, who noted in his diary for February 17, 1777: "I never knew how painful it is to be secluded from the free conversation of one's friends"; and to George Watson, a mandamus councillor, when he entered a church at Plymouth, Massachusetts, and "a great number of the principal inhabitants left." Or it might mean serious loss of services, as when the blacksmiths of Worcester County, Massachusetts, refused to work for any Loyalists, their employees, or their dependents; or an economic boycott, as in Connecticut, where the local committee forbade "all Persons whatever viz. Merchants Mechanicks Millers and Butchers and Co. from supplying . . . John Sayre or Family with any manner of Thing whatever." Lawyers, teachers, doctors, apothecaries, and others often lost their customers and hence their livelihoods. Mathew Robinson, a Newport trader, from the first branded as "a Rank Torey," suffered several indignities, including the pulling down of his fences by a "multitude . . . under colour of laying out a Highway" and climaxing in 1781 when, after *"a New England Saint"* charged that Robinson "drank the King's Health, and damn'd the Congress and call'd them damn'd Rebels and Presbyterians," he was imprisoned by the rebels without examination, this being even "against their own Bill of Rights."

In many areas — for example, New York — the Loyalists were allowed to sell their property before departing, but such hurried, desperate sales were unlikely to net a fair price, and the result amounted to confiscation.

All wars and revolutions cause great mental strain and suffering, most of which goes unmeasured. The history of the Revolutionary era is liberally punctuated with stories of Loyalists who succumbed to melancholia, became mad, died, or committed suicide.

Alexander Harvey, a Charleston lawyer, wound up in a private English madhouse, having been "driven to Distraction" by his experiences as a Loyalist; George Miller, a North Carolina merchant whose fright had conquered his Loyalist principles, was thrown "into Convulsions" by the strain of serving in the American militia; Peter Harrison's death came after the shock of Lexington, and with it America lost its greatest colonial architect; several Loyalists, including the wife of William Franklin, simply died of "a Broken Heart"; the widow of Dr. Robert Gibbs of South Carolina recounted that the prospect of the loss of his property "so preyed upon his Spirits" that he died. Andrew Miller, of Halifax, North Carolina, was estranged from all his friends by his Loyalism, which literally killed him; others chose suicide — Millington Lockwood of Connecticut was wounded in the head, lost his reason, and drowned himself, while some years later, in London, after years of fruitless waiting for compensation, an unnamed, ruined Loyalist shot himself in despair, blaming an ungrateful country.

Although Americans at the time of the Revolution would clearly have found it odd, today one of the sharpest historical debates is over the question of how far the American Revolution was a *real* revolution. Even those historians who, noting the social dislocation, argue that the American Revolution was rather like the French Revolution stress the absence of the Terror. Mass executions there were not, a guillotine there was not, yet atrocities and terror there most certainly were. It is fitting that in the beginning the rebels "hoisted the Red Flag or Flag of Defence."

Leaving aside civil-war aspects such as the execution and maltreatment of prisoners and the burning of towns (by both sides: for example, the Americans fired Norfolk and Portsmouth; the British, Falmouth and Fairfield), we can cite a great range of fates that awaited the

Loyalists; they were catalogued by "Papinian" as tarring and feathering, rail riding,

> . . . chaining men together by the dozens, and driving them, like herds of cattle, into distant provinces, flinging them into loathsome jails, confiscating their estates, shooting them in swamps and woods as suspected Tories, hanging them after a mock trial; and all this because they would not abjure their rightful Sovereign, and bear arms against him.

Tarring and feathering (pine tar and goose feathers) became the classic Whig treatment of the Tories, and the British Government believed there was "no better proof of Loyalty" than suffering this punishment. A famous instance of it occurred in Boston on January 25, 1774, and is worth recounting in some detail.

At about eight o'clock in the evening a club-wielding mob milled along Cross Street. Their objective was John Malcolm, a distinguished but hot-tempered veteran of the French and Indian War, a native Bostonian, an ex-overseas merchant turned royal customs official, and a highly unpopular man for many reasons connected with both his personality (he was inordinately quarrelsome) and his job.

His recent arrival in Boston had been preceded by the unpopular news that in 1771 he had helped the governor of North Carolina against those reputedly Whiggish rebels known as the Regulators and that in October, 1773, he had officiously seized a brigantine at Falmouth (now Portland), Maine. Malcolm waited, ready and armed, behind barred doors. Undeterred, the mob raised ladders, broke an upstairs window, captured their prey, dragged him onto a sled, and pulled him along King Street to the Customs House, or Butcher's House, as it was popularly known, where the spectators gave three mighty cheers.

Although it was "one of the severest cold nights" of the winter, so cold that both Boston Harbor and even the very ink as it touched paper had frozen hard, the wretched man was put in a cart, stripped "to buff and breeches," and dealt the punishment of tarring and feathering, which American patriots were soon to convert into a major spectator sport. Malcolm, self-styled "Single Knight of the Tarr," as opposed to English Knights of the Garter, had already suffered the same indignity the year before for his conduct at Falmouth. He later claimed to be the first in America tarred for loyalty.

A contemporary description gives a good idea of how Malcolm and many others were treated:

> The following is the Recipe for an effectual Operation. "First strip a Person naked, then heat the Tar until it is thin, and pour it upon the naked Flesh, or rub it over with a Tar Brush, *quantum sufficit*. After which, sprinkle decently upon the Tar, whilst it is yet warm, as many Feathers as will stick to it. Then hold a lighted Candle to the Feathers, and try to set it all on Fire; if it

will burn so much the better. But as the Experiment is often made in cold Weather; it will not then succeed — take also an Halter and put it round the Person's Neck, and then cart him the Rounds."

Malcolm, flogged and otherwise molested at intervals, was paraded around various crowded streets with his neck in a halter and was finally taken to the Liberty Tree, where he refused to resign his royal office or to curse Thomas Hutchinson, the hated governor of Massachusetts.

The crowd then set off for the gallows on Boston Neck. On the way Malcolm gasped an affirmative when one of his tormentors asked if he was thirsty and was given a bowl of strong tea and ordered to drink the king's health. Malcolm was next told to drink the queen's health; then two more quarts of tea were produced with the command to drink to the health of the Prince of Wales.

"Make haste, you have nine more healths to drink," shouted one of the mob.

"For God's sake, Gentlemen, be merciful, I'm ready to burst; if I drink a drop more, I shall die," Malcolm implored.

"Suppose you do, you die in a good cause, and it is as well to be drowned as hanged," was the reply.

The nine healths, beginning with the "Bishop of Osnabrug," were forced down the victim's throat. Malcolm "turned pale, shook his Head, and instantly filled the Bowl which he had just emptied."

"What, are you sick of the royal family?"

"No, my stomach nauseates the tea; it rises at it like poison."

"And yet you rascal, your whole fraternity at the Custom House would drench us with this poison, and we are to have our throats cut if it will not stay upon our stomachs."

At the gallows the noose was placed in position around Malcolm's neck and he was threatened with hanging, but he still refused to submit, whereupon he was "basted" with a rope for a while, and finally, on pain of losing his ears, he gave in and cursed the governor. The stubborn, brave man was further carted around the town, made to repeat various humiliating oaths, and finally deposited back at his home just before midnight, half frozen, an arm dislocated, and, as he said, "in a most mizerable setuation Deprived of his senses." Five days later, bedridden and "terribly bruised," he dictated a complaint to Governor Hutchinson, which his injuries obliged him to sign with an X.

The frost and tar caused an infection that made his skin peel extensively. However, he was careful to preserve a piece of skin with the tar and feathers still adhering (the stuff was the very devil to get off), which he carried to England as proof of his sufferings when, somewhat recovered, he set sail on May 2, 1774, to try to gain compensation for his loyalty.

Another Tory punishment that became traditional was the gruesome riding on a rail that sometimes followed tarring and feathering, but was severe enough in itself. It consisted of jogging the victim roughly along on "a sharp rail" between his legs. The painful effect of these "grand Toory Rides," as a contemporary called them, can readily be imagined. Seth Seely, a Connecticut farmer, was brought before the local committee in 1776 and for signing a declaration to support the king's laws was "put on a Rail carried on mens Shoulders thro the Streets, then put into the Stocks and besmeared with Eggs and was robbed of money for the Entertainment of the Company."

Persecution of the Loyalists came in many forms. In 1778 prisoners in Vermont were made to tread a road through the snow in the Green Mountains. The wife of Edward Brinley was pregnant and waiting out her confinement at Roxbury, Massachusetts, accompanied by "a guard of Rebels always in her room, who treated her with great rudeness and indecency, exposing her to the view of their banditti, as a sight 'See a tory woman' and striped her and her Children of all their Linens and Cloths." Peter Guire, of Connecticut, was branded on the forehead with the letters G. R. (George Rex). Samuel Jarvis, also of Connecticut, related that the following treatment made his whole family very ill:

That your Memorialist for his Attachment to constitutional Government was taken with his Wife and Famely, consisting of three Daughters and one little Son by a Mob of daring and unfeeling Rebels from his Dwelling House in the dead of Night Striped of everything, put on board Whale Boats and Landed on Long Island in the Month of August last about 2 oClock in the Morning Oblieging them to wade almost to their Middles in the Water.

Probably the best-known mobbing in Philadelphia was that of Dr. John Kearsley, whose widow finally submitted a claim to the commissioners. Kearsley, a leading physician, pill manufacturer, and horse dealer, was a pugnacious American with strong Loyalist views. He was seized by a mob in September, 1775, and had his hand bayoneted; then he was carried through the streets to the tune of "Rogue's March." Sabine reports that he took off his wig with his injured hand and, "swinging it around his head, huzzaed louder and longer than his persecutors." This display of spirit notwithstanding, he nearly died following this treatment, according to his widow. His house was later ransacked, he was arrested, and he finally died in jail.

Atrocious punishments of Loyalists were sometimes carried out by local authorities in semilegal fashion — it was noted that the tarring and feathering of a New York victim in 1775 "was conducted with that regularity and decorum that ought to be observed in all publick punishments." But just as often mobs, drumhead courts, and all the horrors of vigilante policing were found. Indeed it is possible that the term "lynch law" derives from Charles Lynch, a Bedford County, Virginia, justice of the peace who became renowned for his drastic, cruel action against neighboring Tories.

The number of Loyalists subjected to cruel, often extra-legal, punishments can only be estimated, and likewise the number of those murdered or executed "legally" will never be known, but no one familiar with the sources — Whig newspapers are full of accounts of executions — can doubt that it is substantial, although the statement by a New York Loyalist that the rebels "made a practice of hanging people up on a slight pretence" is no doubt an exaggeration. Probably only fear of reprisals kept numbers from being much larger than they were. The carrying out of the supreme penalty was usually reserved for some overt aid to the British such as spying, piloting ships, guiding troops to the attack, recruiting, counterfeiting.

One of the most notorious executions of a Loyalist was that of John Roberts, a native-born Pennsylvania Quaker, who had aided the British occupying forces in Philadelphia and rather foolhardily had not departed with them. His trial was in 1778, and even many Whigs petitioned the authorities for a pardon, but in vain. A contemporary described the situation thus:

> Roberts' wife, with ten children, went to Congress, threw themselves on their knees and supplicated mercy, but in vain. His behaviour at the gallows did honor to human nature. He told his audience that his conscience acquitted him of guilt; that he suffered for doing his duty to his Sovereign; that his blood would one day be demanded at their hands; and then turning to his children, charged and exhorted them to remember his principles, for which he died, and to adhere to them while they had breath. This is the substance of his speech; after which he suffered with the resolution of a Roman.

In 1792 the state of Pennsylvania restored Roberts' confiscated estate to his widow, Jane, a belated act of justice, for it seems Roberts had been a scapegoat, only one among so very many who had cooperated with the British. Roberts' behavior would doubtless have made him a remembered hero had he suffered for the other side. Similarly, in Connecticut, Moses Dunbar was tried and hanged for accepting a British commission and recruiting troops at about the same time that Nathan Hale suffered the same penalty. Connecticut honors Hale but forgets **Dunbar**. One of the more bizarre executions was reported by the *Boston Gazette* for November 3, 1777, under the date line Fishkill: "Last Thursday, one Taylor, a spy was hanged at Hurley, who was detected with a letter to Burgoyne, which he had swallowed in a silver ball, but by the assistance of a tartar emetic he discharged the same."

But perhaps more moving across the years than accounts of atrocities are the more pedestrian misfortunes of war. Women in particular are always the great sufferers, being separated from their husbands and sons, living in constant dread of bereavement. In 1780 Mary Donnelly petitioned the British authorities in New York for relief. Her husband had been serving on board a privateer when "about seven months ago as my youngest Child lay expireing in my Arms an account came of the Vessil being lost in a Storm." Mrs. Donnelly was now destitute, "frequently being affraid to open my Eyes on the Daylight least I should hear my infant cry for Bread and not have it in my power to relieve him. The first meal I had eat for three days at one time was a morsel of dry bread and a lump of ice."

On June 6, 1783, Phebe Ward, of East Chester, wrote to her husband Edmund, a native of the province of New York:

Kind Husband

I am sorry to acquant you that our farme is sold. . . .

thay said if I did not quitt posesion that thay had aright to take any thing on the farme or in the house to pay the Cost of a law sute and imprisen me I have sufered most Every thing but death it self in your long absens pray Grant me spedy Releaf or God only knows what will be com of me and my frendsles Children

thay say my posesion was nothing youre husband has forfeted his estate by Joining the British Enemy with a free and vollentary will and thereby was forfeted to the Stat and sold

All at present from your cind and Loveing Wife

phebe Ward
pray send me spedeay anser.

One of the most pathetic stories of all concerns Filer Dibblee, a native-born lawyer, and his family. In August, 1776, they fled from Stamford to Long Island, but a few months later the rebels turned Dibblee's wife and five children "naked into the Streets," having stolen the very clothes from their backs as well has having plundered the house. The family fled to New York City, where Dibblee obtained sufficient credit to settle at Oyster Bay, Long Island, but in 1778 the rebels plundered the family a second time and carried Dibblee as prisoner to Connecticut, where he remained imprisoned six months until exchanged. With further credit the family established themselves at Westhills, Long Island, where they were "plundered and stripped" a third time; then came a move to Hempstead, Long Island, and in 1780 a fourth ravaging. Dibblee now, for the first time, applied for relief from the commander in chief and received about one hundred dollars. In 1783 the whole family moved to St. John, New Brunswick, where they managed to survive a rough winter in a log cabin, but Dibblee's "fortitude gave way" at the prospect of imprisonment for his considerable indebtedness and the fate his family would suffer as a consequence. The result was that he "grew Melancholy, which soon deprived him of his Reason, and for months could not be left by himself," and finally in March, 1784, "whilst the Famely were at Tea, Mr. Dibblee walked back and forth in the Room, seemingly much composed: but unobserved he took a Razor from the Closet, threw himself on the bed, drew the Curtains, and cut his own throat."

Shortly afterward the Dibblee house was accidentally burned to the ground, was then rebuilt by the heroic widow, only to be accidentally razed again the same year by an Indian servant girl.

It is not surprising that imprisonment and escape loom large in Loyalist annals. The most celebrated prison was in Connecticut at the Simsbury (now East Granby) copper mines, where the ruins still afford a dramatic prospect. The isolated and strongly Whig back country of Connecticut was considered a good spot to incarcerate important Loyalists from all over the Northern colonies, and the mines, converted into a prison in 1773, were ideal. The "Catacomb of Loyalty," to quote Thomas Anburey, or the "woeful mansion," to quote an inmate, contained cells forty yards below the surface, into which "the prisoners are let down by a windlass into the dismal cavern, through a hole, which answers the purpose of conveying their food and air, as to light, it scarcely reaches them." The mere threat of the "Mines" could make a Loyalist conform. One prisoner regarded being sent there as a "Shocking Sentence (Worse than Death)." The mines received such celebrated Loyalists as Mayor Mathews of New York and William Franklin, who wrote of his "long and horrible confinement" and was described on his release as "considerably reduced in Flesh."

In May, 1781, there was a mass breakout. The leaders of the escape, Ebenezer Hathaway and Thomas Smith, arrived in New York some weeks later, and their alleged experiences were reported by Rivington's newspaper. Hathaway and Smith recalled that they had originally been captured on a privateer, sentenced, and marched the seventy-four miles from Hartford to Simsbury. The entrance to the dungeon was a heavily barred trap door that had to be raised

> by means of a tackle, whilst the hinges grated as they turned upon their hooks, and opened the jaws and mouths of what they call Hell, into which they descended by means of a ladder about six feet more, which led to a large iron grate or hatchway, locked down over a shaft about three feet diameter, sunk through the solid rock. . . . They bid adieu to this world,

and went down thirty-eight feet more by ladder "when they came to what is called the landing; then marching shelf by shelf, till descending about thirty or forty feet more they came to a platform of boards laid under foot, with a few more put over head to carry off the water, which keeps continually dropping." There they lived for twenty nights with the other prisoners, using "pots of charcoal to dispel the foul air" through a ventilation hole bored from the surface until the opportunity to escape came when they were allowed up into the kitchen to prepare food and rushed and captured the guards.

Some colorful Connecticut escapes in other places are also recorded. Nathan Barnum avoided appearing for trial in 1780 by inoculating himself with smallpox, whereupon he was "sent to the Hospital, where he was chained to the Floor to prevent his Escape, he found Means to bribe one of the Nurses, who not only brought him a File to cut off his Irons, but amused the Centinal, placed over him while he effected it. . . ."

Samuel Jarvis and his brother got out of prison "by the assistance of Friends who had privately procured some Women's apparel which they Dressed themselves in, and by that means made their escape through the Rebel Army." James Robertson asserted that while he was in jail at Albany, the British attacked and set the building on fire, whereupon, unable to walk, he managed to crawl into a bed of cabbages "and chewing them to prevent being suffocated" was found three days later badly burnt.

There was even a series of Tory hiding places between New York and Canada, rather in the fashion of the "Underground Railroad" of the pre-Civil War days.

The treatment of imprisoned Loyalists ranged over the widest possible spectrum. Simsbury was notoriously the worst prison, almost the Andersonville of the time. Many Loyalists suffered close confinement in much pleasanter conditions; others merely underwent house arrest; others were only prevented from traveling; some were on parole and, if banished to some remote part of America, were boarded with reluctant Whigs. Some worked in the normal way by day and simply spent the night in jail. In 1776 Thomas Vernon, a fanatically early riser, was removed, with three other prominent Rhode Island Loyalists, from Newport to Glocester, in the northern part of the state, because he had refused the test oath. The foursome's journey and their few months' stay in Glocester were pleasant and gentlemanly, almost Pickwickian. The friends walked and admired the countryside, ate, drank, and conversed well in the local inn where they lived; they planted beans, killed snakes, trapped squirrels, fished, played Quadrille (a card game); they were very well treated by the ladies of the house and by neighboring females. Their chief complaints were the lack of books, some local abhorrence of Tories, particularly by the men (their landlord said "the town was very uneasy" at their being there), a few fleas, tedium from the lack of friends and family, and some stealing of their food by their far from genial host. . . .

The Whigs suffered as the Tories did — legal persecution, mob action, imprisonment (the British prison ships were particularly horrible and gave rise to effective propagandist literature), and all the excesses of civil war. Adrian C. Leiby, the historian of the Hackensack Valley, for example, reports that there was barely a Whig family there that had not lost someone to a Tory raiding party. There is at least one recorded tarring and feathering of a Whig by British troops — of one Thomas Ditson, Jr., in Boston in March, 1775. In June, 1779, the *Virginia Gazette* reported the murder of a Whig captain by a party of Tories whom he had discovered robbing his house. A sentinel wounded him with a gunshot; then, after taking all the horses from the stables, the Tories pursued the captain into the house, where he was lying on a bed, and

> immediately thrust their bayonets into his body several times, continuing the barbarity while they heard a groan; and lest life might still be remaining in him, they cut both his arms with a knife in the most inhuman manner. The villain who shot him, had been his neighbour and companion from his youth.

The victim lived another two days.

STUDY GUIDE

1. Be prepared to discuss the following quotation from Sir John Harington, who lived two centuries before the American Revolution:

    Treason doth never prosper; what's the reason?
    Why, if it prosper, none dare call it treason.

    Evaluate Harington's epigram with respect to Loyalists and Patriots in the War for Independence; and second, explain why the favorable historical reputation of the losing Civil War general Robert E. Lee is an exception to this dictum.

2. Summarize the various devices used to punish the Loyalists — both in their persons and in their property. What was the relation between official policy by state governments and actual treatment of Loyalists by neighbors and townsfolk?

3. Does the picture presented in this chapter modify your view of the American Patriots? If so, how?

4. Is there any evidence here that would support the view that the Revolution was a civil war between different groups of colonials, as well as a war for independence from England?

BIBLIOGRAPHY

As suggested in the introduction to this selection, the Loyalists have not received very sympathetic treatment from American historians. Even more important than this is that they have generally been ignored. It was not until 1974, for example, that an extended biography of the distinguished Massachusetts Loyalist Thomas Hutchinson was finally published. Aside from the works of a few early scholars such as Claude Van Tyne, the serious study of Loyalism is a very recent phenomenon. A growing number of historians in the last two decades have devoted their attention to these forgotten Americans, most notably William H. Nelson, in *The American Tory* * (Oxford, Eng., 1961); Wallace Brown, in *The King's Friends: The Composition and Motives of the American Loyalist Claimants* (Providence, R.I., 1966); Paul H. Smith, who describes the military involvement of the Loyalists in *Loyalists and Redcoats: A Study in British Revolutionary Policy* * (Chapel Hill, N.C., © 1964); and Mary B. Norton, in *The British-Americans: The Loyalist Exiles in England, 1774–1789* (Boston, 1972). An earlier work that attempts to identify the character of the Tory mind and psychology is Leonard W. Labaree, *Conservatism in Early American History* * (New York, 1948).

Anyone who is interested in the antagonisms in British colonial society can find a comprehensive survey in Elisha P. Douglass, *Rebels and Democrats: The Struggle for Equal Political Rights and Majority Rule during the American Revolution* * (Chapel Hill, N.C., 1955). Since 1950, however, many historians have argued that this was simply a war for independence, rather than an internal social revolution, and have suggested that eighteenth-century colonial society was characterized by broad consensus rather than conflict. This view has been argued in studies of individual colonies, in studies of revolutionary ideology, and in studies of the consequences of the Revolution. For some years the views of Edmund S. Morgan, Daniel Boorstin, Robert E. Brown, and other scholars were so widely accepted that a general consensus as to the conservative nature of the American Revolution seemed in the offing. More recently, this view has been challenged by a group of younger historians, frequently identified as the "New Left." In a series of articles, Jesse Lemisch and Staughton Lynd, among others, have argued that conflict did in fact exist in the revolutionary period, and that the laboring men of urban areas were as important as farmers in the uprising.

The views concerning the causes and character of the American Revolution are so varied and the important books so numerous that they cannot be mentioned here. The bibliographies of most textbooks will refer you to the more important studies, or you can find a good bibliography, with selections from various historical writings, in Robert F. Berkhofer, Jr., *The American Revolution: The Critical Issues* * (Boston, © 1971).

The first sermon at the Philadelphia City Prison, sponsored by the Philadelphia Society for Distressed Prisoners in 1787.

MERRILL JENSEN

American Humanitarianism

Many people assume that revolutions are necessarily forward-looking and progressive in their ideology. In fact, many revolutions in the pre-industrial period of Western history have been against change, and in no period is there any certainty about whether a particular revolution will bring about generally beneficial changes in a society or will become repressive. One reason for this is that people cannot always predict the course that the best-laid plans may take; revolutionary leaders may have one thing in mind, but something very different may result.

The historian J. Franklin Jameson has suggested that, whether it was deliberately planned or not, the American Revolution led to substantial changes in American society and institutions — changes that he thought were significant enough to constitute a revolution comparable to such a great upheaval as the French Revolution. Jameson's arguments have been widely disputed, and many historians today believe that what happened between 1775 and 1783 was nothing more than a war of national independence from England. They suggest that the real revolution had taken place in the hundred years before the war began, that it consisted of the development of a distinctive American civilization, and that the Revolutionary War was but a final sundering of the ties of two very different peoples.

Merrill Jensen has written extensively on the revolutionary period and believes that while the Revolution was not revolutionary in intent, it turned out to be revolutionary in result. In the following selection, he studies social changes that took place between the beginning of the war and the end of the century. Some of the reforms he discusses may have been a direct result of the Revolution, but others had gained acceptance years before in the general spirit of the Enlightenment. All of them owed a good deal of their force to a new feeling that was developing, the concern for other human beings that we call humanitarianism.

The social problems of the eighteenth century stemmed not so much from corrupt government or rapacious economic interests as from simple neglect and insensitivity. Until then, the holding of people in slavery, the imprisonment of persons for debt, the shackling of the insane, and the extensive use of execution and bodily mutilation as punishments were not regarded by most people as either unusual or abhorrent. On both sides of the Atlantic in the eighteenth century, a number of sensitive men such as John Howard, John Woolman, Anthony Benezet, and Phillippe Pinel questioned such practices and provided a social philosophy directed toward a more humane world. In the period of which Jensen writes, this new spirit, and the impulse of the Revolution itself, led to the founding of a multitude of societies to aid immigrants, shipwrecked sailors, and even persons suffering from suspended animation. Education, medicine, law, and a host of other fields benefited from the intellectual quickening and the moral involvement that characterized the American people in the 1780s.

The political upheaval and change that was an integral part of the American Revolution made possible other changes in American society: changes that were sometimes an answer to ancient grievances, and sometimes a response to new conditions. The deep-rooted antagonism to established churches was expressed in the revolutionary constitutions and in laws disestablishing or removing the special privileges of established churches. Negro slavery, long hateful to some, was attacked anew as inconsistent with the idealism of the Revolution, and several states (invariably where slavery was unimportant) abolished slavery and the slave trade. The criminal codes, long as merciless as England's, were revised in the direction of humaneness. Prison reform was advocated and conditions were improved. The engrossment of the land was not stopped but the abolition of laws of entail and primogeniture did away with one legal foundation for great land holdings. British Crown lands and confiscated estates of

Loyalists fell to the individual states and in turn were sold and granted, usually in smaller lots. In a measure, this contributed to the democratization of land holding, as did the opening up of the vast national domain west of the Appalachians.

On the practical side, Americans now got together as they had never done before in creating societies for social and economic improvement, digging canals, building bridges, and improving roads. They founded newspapers and magazines at a rate undreamed of before the war. All these and many more activities were a reflection of the new spirit and the new opportunities which were the result of the successful outcome of the American Revolution. . . .

. . . Negro slavery had long been opposed in the colonies. The Quakers had delivered the first protests against it. The independent small farmers in the South objected to a labor system with which they found it difficult to compete. Many planters such as William Byrd II, Thomas Jefferson, and others, objected to slavery although their way of life was in large part founded on it. Clergymen like George Whitfield preached against it and found support among the back countrymen. The equalitarian ideals of the Revolution itself caused more than one man to question their reality when faced with the fact of human bondage. Freedom from Britain made it possible to act, for the British government had consistently supported slavery and the slave trade. In the decade just before the Revolution several of the colonies, including some in the South, made serious efforts to stop the trade, only to have all legislation vetoed in London. At the beginning of the war only Georgia and South Carolina were in favor of the slave trade, and in every colony there were believers in the abolition of slavery.

Within a few years after 1775, either in constitutions or in legislation, the new states acted against slavery. Within a decade all the states except Georgia and South Carolina had passed some form of legislation to stop the slave trade. Freeing the slaves was much more difficult except in those states where there were very few of them. Vermont abolished slavery in her Constitution of 1777. In 1780 the Massachusetts Constitution declared that all men were born equal and endowed with freedom. It was at once argued that this part of the bill of rights freed all the slaves held in the state, and the state supreme court agreed. New Hampshire followed this lead in its Constitution of 1784. Other states such as Connecticut, Pennsylvania, and Rhode Island passed acts for piecemeal abolition. There was no unanimity, however, even in New England. A writer calling himself "Not Adams" declared that ever since "that class of people called Negroes" began to imbibe the idea they were not slaves, they have been coming to Boston. This made it harder for the poor inhabitants of the town to make a living. No Negroes should be allowed in Boston, he said, except such as had been born there.

The concern with slavery led to the creation of many organizations which were the forerunners of the abolitionist societies of a later age. The first abolitionist society in America was organized in 1774. As with most Philadelphia societies during his lifetime, [Benjamin] Franklin was president. Pennsylvania passed a law for the gradual abolition of slavery in 1780. This was largely the work of George Bryan, one of the democratic leaders in the state, and one of slavery's most tireless opponents. The law was evaded and when the Society re-emerged in 1784, it made prosecution of such evasion its main business. It was instrumental in having the law revised and for years was an active force in the abolition movement. By 1800 Pennsylvania had less than 2,000 slaves left, as a result of her gradual emancipation law and of the watchful vigilance of the Society.

In New York the "Society for the Promotion of the Manumission of Slaves and Protecting such of them that have been or may be Liberated" was organized in 1785 with John Jay, a slaveholder, as president, and Alexander Hamilton, as secretary. There was strong anti-Negro feeling in New York where a good many slaves had always been held, and the Society was unable to secure passage of a bill for gradual abolition. It kept up its agitation, however. In 1788 it agreed that its members would boycott all auction masters who sold slaves and to give business only to those who "shall uniformly refrain from a practice so disgraceful and so shocking to humanity." It likewise concerned itself with building a school for the children of free Negroes. But despite all its efforts there were more than 20,000 slaves in the state in 1790.

The well-publicized activities of the Philadelphia and New York societies led to the formation of others, usually with names as top-heavy. One was organized in Delaware in 1788, and between then and 1794 others were organized in Rhode Island, Connecticut, New Jersey, Maryland, and Virginia. Maryland had a very active movement for gradual abolition. A writer in Maryland declared that slavery was inconsistent with the principles of the Revolution and he pointed to the horrors of slavery in the South.

There was important opposition to slavery in the South during and after the Revolution. Washington, Jefferson, Madison, and Patrick Henry all hoped that slavery could be ended in some fashion. They were in a minority, although Virginia did pass laws making it easier to free slaves. Farther to the south there was bitter opposition to the idea of abolition and to any restriction on the slave trade. Tolerance soon disappeared from Virginia as well, and the law making it easy to free slaves was repealed and petitions for abolition were ignored. Economics and idealism met head on and the former won an easy victory.

Still another institution that was a source of both labor supply and immigration to America was the system of indentured servitude. Tens of thousands had come to the new world in this way, and although it had offered them opportunity to escape from the evil of poverty in Europe, their lot as "servants" was not a happy one. Very few people either during or after the Revolution, except the German societies, seem to have shown much concern over these people or the improvement of their lot. In New York an effort was made to get a group of citizens to liberate a shipload of white servants by paying their passage, taking in return small deductions from wages. It was argued that while immigration was necessary, the traffic in white people was contrary to the idea of liberty and to the feelings of many citizens. However, the only laws passed during the 1780's were simply to clarify their status rather than to change it, and the system did not die out for decades.

Americans were far more deeply concerned about their fellow men who lost their freedom through crime and debt. The accounts of the treatment of law breakers, the violence with which they were punished, and the jails into which they were thrown, have about them a nightmarish quality difficult to realize. This was as true in Europe as in America, and such conditions there brought about investigations and demands for reform which found their counterpart in America. The list of acts for which one could be punished was long and the penalties brutal. Death was common for robbery, forgery, housebreaking, and counterfeiting. In Pennsylvania in 1783, five men were put to death for one robbery. Two years later, a man in Massachusetts who made fifty counterfeit dollars was set in the pillory, taken to the gallows where he stood with a rope around his neck for a time, whipped twenty stripes, had his left arm cut off, and finally was sentenced to three years' hard labor. Actually this was an improvement (from the public if not his point of view) for the usual punishment had been death.

There was a sharp demand for reform of the laws of Pennsylvania. William Penn at the beginning of the colony had drawn up a humane code but it had been vetoed by the British government. For a time the legislature had stuck to Penn's ideas but eventually it gave in and followed the English code. The Constitution of 1776 demanded a revision, but the death penalty for such crimes as robbery was not repealed for ten years. The demand did not stop with this law. Men like Dr. Benjamin Rush and William Bradford continued to propagandize for more humane criminal laws. Year in and year out, they wrote and spoke against capital punishment with such effectiveness that in 1794 Pennsylvania made a sweeping revision of her whole code, retaining the death penalty only for wilful murder. This code was to be a model for other American states for years to come.

One other side of the law in its relation to the individual gave concern to Americans. No "tank" in a twentieth century American city, however bad, can equal the horrors of an eighteenth century "gaol." All ages, all varieties of criminals, and both sexes were crowded together in filthy, often unheated jails. Food was poor at its best and at its worst, rotten. Jailers were of the lowest kind and made money robbing the inmates of their clothing and selling liquor to those who had means to buy. So bad was the jail in Philadelphia, said a grand jury in 1787, that it had become "a desirable place for the more wicked and polluted of both sexes." Investigations during the 1780's revealed conditions that were horrifying to some people. The infamous Newgate prison in Connecticut was established by thrifty Connecticut legislators. It was an old copper mine in which men lived in conditions that only a fevered imagination can visualize.

Conditions in Philadelphia were so bad that they led to the formation of the "Philadelphia Society for Assisting Distressed Prisoners" in 1776. The Society bought covered wheelbarrows which it sent through the streets daily carrying a sign "Victuals for the prisoners." British occupation put an end to the Society but in 1787 "The Society for Alleviating the Miseries of Public Prisons" was organized. In it were men such as Dr. Benjamin Rush, Tench Coxe, and Bishop William White of the Episcopal Church, who was its president for forty years. This Society investigated the prisons and made suggestions for their improvement. It proposed that the sale of liquor be stopped, that men and women be separated, that rooms be washed with lime, and many other things.

The jailers naturally opposed interference with their prerogatives. They objected to inspections: they said the criminals were too desperate. Once when Bishop White visited the jail, the chief jailer put on a show. He started by asking the visitors to give him their valuables for safekeeping. The prisoners were lined up in the common room facing loaded cannon beside which men stood ready to fire. The prisoners, unfortunately for the chief jailer's purpose, were so struck by the proceedings that they were quiet and polite while the good bishop questioned them. The Society did much to bring about the adoption of the new penal code. When regular prison inspectors were created by law in 1790, most of them came from its membership.

Prison reform in New York took a different turn. There it was concerned with those imprisoned for debt. No people in eighteenth-century society were more luckless than those imprisoned for debt, and they were an astonishingly large part of the jail population. The idea of imprisonment for debt seems completely irrational in an age which has different notions of what is reasonable, but it seemed logical enough in the "age of reason." People were put in jail for small sums. In Boston, for instance, a woman was jailed for four months for failing to pay a fine of sixpence. No one ever explained how a debtor in jail was better able to pay his debts than a debtor out of jail and at work. But more and more people were questioning the sense of it all, particularly for people whose debts were small, and they demanded legislation to free debtors from jail sentences. In New York the "Society for the Relief of Distressed Debtors" was organized. Its twenty-four members were required to see that jailed debtors got food, fuel, and clothing to lighten the burdens of their stay in jail. Despite such activity and newspaper comment on the idiocy of the practice, dominant opinion for some years to come was that of the creditors who could see no fallacy in jailing a man when he failed to pay his debts.

The organization of societies for the abolition of slavery, the improvement of jails, and of the lot of debtors, was not an isolated phenomenon in the years after the war. Immigrant aid societies had been organized in most colonial towns by Scotch, Welsh, Irish, English, and German immigrants to take care of those who followed them. Library societies were formed in Philadelphia, New York, Providence, and Charleston, and in smaller towns before the middle of the eighteenth century. Marine societies were organized in New England and other towns.

All told, some thirty-odd such societies were organized during the colonial era, most of them in the four urban centers of Philadelphia, New York, Boston, and Charleston. Philadelphia had at least eleven, Charleston eight, New York six, and Boston three or four. Most of these societies were small and exclusive and concerned more with social affairs than with practical ones, but they were a focus for humanitarian ideals and intellectual interests. Most of them suspended activity at the outbreak of the war, but before it was over they began to revive and new societies began to appear, five of them in Boston alone. Between 1783 and 1786, eleven pre-revolutionary societies got going again and no less than eighteen new ones were formed. Between 1786 and 1789 fourteen more new societies were formed and most of the rest of the pre-revolutionary ones were reorganized. This was extraordinary activity: more societies were organized between 1776 and 1789 than in the whole colonial period. They were much more active; their meetings were more regular; and their influence spread wider and wider as in the case of the abolition and prison reform groups.

Perhaps the most intriguing of the new societies were the "humane" societies: one in Boston and one in Philadelphia. Their main concern was the rescue of those suffering from "suspended animation": that is, those who appeared to be dead but actually were not. The primary cause of "suspended animation" was drowning, but hanging, sunstroke, lightning, drinking laudanum, drinking cold water when overheated, and so on, were also recognized as causes.

These societies drafted first aid rules, published them in American papers, and posted them in likely spots. They offered rewards for lives saved. They provided special lifesaving equipment and stored it at wharves and taverns near the waterfront. Such equipment included bellows for inflating and deflating the lungs, drags, hooks, and medicines. An extraordinary device, long a favorite with the Massachusetts Humane Society, was the "fumigator," an instrument for pumping tobacco smoke into the rectum of a person supposed to be drowned. In addition, the Massachusetts Society erected huts at spots along the coast where shipwrecks were likely. These were stocked with food and firewood and proved useful, although prowlers soon broke in and ate the food and used the wood.

The marine societies cooperated closely with the humane societies during the 1780's. These organizations had appeared before the Revolution and had operated continuously. They were organizations of seamen, and particularly of pilots who were much concerned, not only with their present but their future. As early as 1786 it was proposed to build a hospital for disabled seamen in Boston and to place it under the direction of the marine society in that town. The marine society likewise worked with the humane society in the building of huts for the shipwrecked. In Philadelphia there were two organizations: the "Society for the Relief of Poor and Distressed Masters of Ships, Their Widows and Children," and the "Society for the Relief of Widows of Decayed Pilots." In 1788 the legislature provided that the latter society should receive a quarter of the tonnage duties paid by shipowners.

Societies for specifically charitable purposes were organized as well. One of the first was the "Massachusetts Charitable Society" which had roots before the war but was not incorporated until March 1780. It was religious in spirit but professed to be nonsectarian for it declared that "charity is a principle that no particular persuasion can monopolize. . . ." It was interested in general charities and tried to raise money for a girls' school. A Black Friar's Society was organized in New York for both charitable and social purposes. In Philadelphia a "Corporation for the relief and employment of the poor" was organized. An "Amicable Society" was organized in Richmond for the purpose of relieving strangers in distress. As early as 1769 Charleston had a "Fellowship Society" which gathered funds, half for "the deplorable maniac" and the other half for the education of children.

The beginnings of temperance organizations are also to be found, and this alone, if nothing else, is adequate testimony to the optimism of a period in which the per capita consumption of liquor was enough to win the admiration of all other ages. Dr. Benjamin Rush, one of the most optimistic of joiners, declared in 1788 that now that traffic in slaves was over in Pennsylvania, his next task would be the correction of abuses of liquor. The next year a temperance society was actually organized in Litchfield, Connecticut, where the forty members agreed not to use liquor in their business and to serve only beer and cider to workingmen.

The immigrant aid societies were only partly humanitarian in purpose. They were also social clubs for immigrant groups. Inevitably they were political as well, for leading politicians in towns like Philadelphia made a point of belonging to all the groups, whatever the politicians' own origins might be. With few exceptions their activities were convivial. A French traveler in describing an initiation to the Irish Society of Philadelphia said that they were "initiated by the ceremony of an exterior application of a whole bottle of claret poured upon the head, and a generous libation to liberty and good living, of as many as the votary could carry off." The chief exceptions were the societies organized by Germans in Philadelphia, New York, Charleston, and Baltimore. There were few social or political leaders among them and they had a pietistic streak that led some of them to forbid meetings in taverns. In Philadelphia the society demanded a bureau for the registration of German immigrants and the legislature set one up in 1785. For years thereafter it was manned by members of the society. They visited vessels coming into port to see that immigrants had not been mistreated; they got jobs for immigrants; they provided legal aid for indentured servants. They were concerned also with charity and education. They set up German language grammar schools and founded a library. They established scholarships to send poor German boys to the University of Pennsylvania and during the 1780's supported fifteen scholars in that school. . . .

At the same time there was a rapid development of medical societies which had both humanitarian and scientific interests. The first ones were organized during the 1760's in New Jersey and Connecticut and were concerned primarily with establishing standards for medical practice. But in medicine, as in so many other things, Philadelphia was the center. The Philadelphia Hospital was founded in 1751. The American Medical Society was organized in 1773. Medical education began in 1765 when the College of Philadelphia, at the urging of Dr. John Morgan, began formal instruction in medicine. King's College in New York started medical training in 1767. Meanwhile, more and more American doctors were being educated in Europe, particularly at Edinburgh University. Between 1758 and 1788 no less than sixty-three Americans were graduated from it. The Revolution itself gave doctors an opportunity to "practice" as they never had before and, as Ramsay pointed out in his history, they learned more in one day on the battlefield than in months at home.

After the war Philadelphia continued to be a center of medical activity. The "Society for inoculating the Poor Gratis" had been organized in 1774 by doctors and others and was providing free vaccinations for all who applied at the state house. It disappeared during the war but in 1787 the dispensary was providing free medicine for the poor. During that year Brissot de Warville said that it had treated 1,647 people at a cost of £200. During the 1780's the College of Physicians was formed. It met for discussion of medical research and took an active interest in improving public health in such matters as street cleaning, quarantines, and in the creation of a "contagious" hospital.

The doctors of Boston organized the Massachusetts Medical Society in 1781. It was interested in standardizing fees but also in medical research. It founded a library in 1782 and by the 1790's was publishing research papers. It was soon in competition with the new medical school which Harvard established. Harvard announced the appointment of three professors of medicine in the fall of 1783. A curriculum was outlined, and the whole story was sent forth to the newspapers of the United States and was printed in many of them. Harvard and the Medical Society engaged in a bitter struggle over the examination and licensing of doctors to practice, but the competition seems not to have hurt either institution.

But great difficulties were encountered everywhere by medical schools in getting "materials" for training purposes. Adequate medical training called for the dissection of bodies, but the populace looked upon this as sacrilege. Antagonism developed until, in New York, it led to the "doctors' riots" of 1788 in which the militia was called out and several people were killed. While great advances were made in medicine, even greater distances were yet to be traveled. As always, popular opinion and much medical opinion was opposed to the "radicals." Barbers, druggists, and dentists were "doctors" and still practiced on the citizenry and the citizenry still found quacks more appealing than scientists. A certain Reverend W. M'Kee announced that at last he had found the cure for cancer. He got testimonials for his product which he had tried on the helpless denizens of the Philadelphia almshouse. Not only would it cure cancer but ulcers, scurvy, ringworm, and other dread afflictions. It was such charlatanry that led Dr. Lemuel Hopkins to write his biting ode to a man killed by a cancer quack:

> Here lies a fool flat on his back,
> The victim of a cancer quack;
> Who lost his money and his life,
> By plaster, caustic, and by knife.
> The case was this — a pimple rose,
> South-east a little of his nose,
> Which daily reddened and grew bigger,
> As too much drinking gave it vigor.
> A score of gossips soon ensure
> Full threescore different modes of cure;
> But yet the full-fed pimple still
> Defined all petticoated skill;
> When fortune led him to peruse
> A hand-bill in the weekly news,
> Signed by six fools of different sorts,
> All cured of cancers made of warts;
> Who recommend, with due submission,
> This cancer-monger as magician. . . .
> Go, readers, gentle, eke and simple,
> If you have wart, or corn, or pimple,
> To quack infallible apply;
> Here's room enough for you to lie.
> His skill triumphant still prevails,
> For death's a cure that never fails.

The Revolution had devastating effects on many established schools. School after school was abandoned, colleges were "purged" of those tainted with Loyalist sentiments, their endowments were ruined, and their student bodies decimated. Yet at the same time many revolutionary leaders were much concerned with the development of an educated people. Five of the new state constitutions declared that the state was responsible for education. John Adams said in his "Thoughts on Government" that "laws for the liberal education of youth, especially of the lower class of people, are so extremely wise and useful, that, to a humane and generous mind, no expense for this purpose would be thought extravagant." Jefferson, believing in education as an indispensable basis for democracy, tried to establish a public school system in Virginia with his "Bill for the More General Diffusion of Knowledge," but could not get it passed. New winds blew through old halls when, under Jefferson's prodding, the College of William and Mary set up chairs of law and modern languages. Once the war was over, men like Jefferson, John Adams, Benjamin Rush, and, as we have seen, Noah Webster, preached the idea of public education. Various states, including New York, Georgia, and North Carolina, set up university organizations, at least on paper. Private academies were being founded in every state as well as private colleges, some of them with public support. In 1786 the *Massachusetts Centinel* applauded the "encouragement of literature, and diffusion of knowledge" in the southern states and cited the money and land given by the Pennsylvania legislature to Dickinson College, and the lands given for schools by North and South Carolina and Georgia. Elaborate plans for a public school system in Pennsylvania were set forth to the readers of the *Pennsylvania Gazette*. . . .

In this survey of the varied activities of Americans in the first years of independence one can realize something of the enthusiasm with which the citizens of the new nation worked at altering the pattern of society they had inherited from colonial times. It is true that much of what they did had earlier roots, but their achievements are also the result of a new freedom of choice and of a delight in national independence. This enthusiasm bolstered native optimism and furnished the motive power for new deeds in years to come.

STUDY GUIDE

1. Summarize the changes made in the revolutionary period in the following areas: slavery and the slave trade; indentured servitude; criminal law and prisons. Be precise as to the regions or states in which the greatest changes took place.

2. What factors in the eighteenth century do you suppose led people to depend on private societies, rather than government, to effect reforms in the various fields discussed? Did their ideas as to the proper functions of government influence their thinking?

3. Based on your general knowledge of later American history, would you say that most reforms have been brought about by constitutional amendments that gave the government new powers to regulate economic and social affairs, or because of changes in the social attitudes of citizens?

4. How are the following institutions in our society financially supported and regulated today: immigrant assistance; poor relief; the practice of medicine; animal protection; education? What is the role in each of these fields of the national government, state and local government, and private groups?

5. Based on your knowledge of American history as a whole, what relation do you see between major periods of reform and the following factors: the party that is in power; economic depression; periods of war?

BIBLIOGRAPHY

The decade of the 1780s is bounded at the beginning by the American Revolution and at the end by the writing of the United States Constitution and the inauguration of the new government. This may explain why the social history of the time has been slighted, as compared with the political history of the Confederation. In an extremely influential work published in 1888, John Fiske dubbed the decade "the critical period," suggesting that times were so bad that the survival of the new nation hung in the balance. Merrill Jensen is the leading scholar who has challenged Fiske's view, and while Jensen's own position on the character of the Confederation has also been questioned, he makes a persuasive case that the period witnessed substantial accomplishments in social reform. An equally enlightening view of the changes of the revolutionary period is presented in chapter 6 of Bernard Bailyn's *The Ideological Origins of the American Revolution* * (Cambridge, Mass., © 1967). Bailyn, however, sees less class conflict in American society than does Jensen; a similar view is expressed by Benjamin F. Wright in *Consensus and Continuity, 1776–1787* * (New York, 1967), a short essay on attitudes toward government in the period.

The argument that economic conflict was the basis of the dispute over the Constitution of 1787 was most strikingly presented in a highly controversial work by Charles A. Beard, *An Economic Interpretation of the Constitution of the United States* * (New York, 1913). The most serious questions about Beard's work have been raised by Forrest McDonald in his *We the People: The Economic Origins of the Constitution* * (Chicago, © 1958). In *The Anti-Federalists: Critics of the Constitution, 1781–1788* * (Chapel Hill, N.C., 1961), Jackson T. Main presents a somewhat different economic interpretation of the Constitution, suggesting that the conflict over that document was between commercial and noncommercial regions. Important as these and several other works on the Constitution are in understanding the Confederation period, they provide only a limited view since they deal only with political and economic history.

For the social history of the period, one must turn to either regional studies or to works on specialized subjects. Carl Bridenbaugh's *Cities in Revolt: Urban Life in America, 1743–1776* * (New York, 1955) contributes much to an understanding of the revolutionary period, as does the cultural history by Max Savelle, *Seeds of Liberty: The Genius of the American Mind* * (New York, © 1948). Evarts B. Greene, *The Revolutionary Generation, 1763–1790* *

(New York, 1943) is a general work in the series *A History of American Life,* edited by Arthur M. Schlesinger and Dixon R. Fox. More recently, Professor Daniel J. Boorstin has written a broad social history of the American people, the first two volumes of which are useful in understanding the United States in the late eighteenth and early nineteenth centuries: *The Americans: The Colonial Experience* * (New York, © 1958) and *The Americans: The National Experience* * (New York, 1965). James T. Adams, *New England in the Republic, 1776–1850* (Boston, © 1926) and Thomas P. Abernethy, *The South in the New Nation, 1789–1819* (Baton Rouge, La., 1961) are regional histories on the periods indicated in the titles. There are a number of articles, and some books, on charity, penal reform, and other movements mentioned by Jensen; one of the best full-length studies is Sydney V. James, *A People Among Peoples: Quaker Benevolence in Eighteenth-Century America* (Cambridge, Mass., 1963).

"Fourth of July Celebration" by John Krimmel, 1818, shows the hearty good humor and patriotism of young America. (Detail)

HENRY ADAMS

America in 1800

In 1893 the Wisconsin historian Frederick Jackson Turner wrote a short paper on American history and culture that was to have an influence upon historical writing and social thought for the next half-century. Entitled "The Significance of the Frontier in American History," it argued that too much emphasis had been placed upon our European origins and their influence upon American civilization. Turner claimed that the European heritage of ideas and institutions that the colonists had brought here had, of necessity, been greatly modified in the New-World environment. Living in a new land, with different flora and fauna, different problems of transportation and housing, and facing an untamed wilderness, the European found that the old ways did not always work. Every aspect of his life — agriculture, politics, language, religion, and social life — changed as he encountered the American frontier. Turner suggested that the frontier was an important cause of our early wars and a crucial force in the development of social and political democracy in the New World.

A number of eighteenth- and early nineteenth-century observers of the American scene had noted some special characteristics of Americans well before Turner wrote. One French writer considered the American a "new man," who was a model for the European. Writers have described a vast range of characteristics as being typically American — idealism, pragmatism, hospitality, violence, inventiveness, poverty of spirit, generosity, loquacity, boorishness, to name only a few. There are many reasons why different observers have seen Americans in different ways. One is that the customs, politics, and even the character of a people may change, and later writers may be viewing a nation substantially different from the one seen by those who wrote a century before. Equally important is the personal perspective of the observer, which depends on such things as whether he had a generally conservative or progressive outlook, whether he was a foreign traveler here for a few months or a native American, and, if American, whether he was a Yankee or a Southerner.

Henry Adams was a New England descendant of two presidents, and he wrote a multivolume history of the United States during Thomas Jefferson's presidency. The first of his volumes is a classic description of America at the opening of the nineteenth century. In chapter 2, Adams describes the American character and social life of the time. The nation had been independent from England for only a quarter of a century in 1800, and English influences upon American life were to continue for many years. But there was evidence, even before the American Revolution, that a distinctively American culture and outlook was developing.

Though Americans in 1800 might continue to read English books and imitate English manners, substantial changes were becoming apparent, especially in the development of popular attitudes and the American character. The country, of course, was remarkably diverse, as indicated by such coexisting stereotypes as the shrewd New England Yankee, the hard-working and pietistic German farmer of Pennsylvania, and the leisured southern gentleman. In view of the differences, the question has been raised as to whether or not there really was a single "American" character, in the sense that one can discern a French, Italian, or Spanish character. Adams believed that there was, but he also wrote separate chapters on the regional differences of New England, the South, and the Middle Atlantic states. While his portrait of the American character describes people who lived at the opening of the nineteenth century, certain features of it are relevant to an understanding of Americans in the 1970s.

The growth of character, social and national — the formation of men's minds — more interesting than any territorial or industrial growth, defied the tests of censuses and surveys. No people could be expected, least of all when in infancy, to understand the intricacies of its own character, and

From *History of the United States of America during the First Administration of Thomas Jefferson*, Vol. I, by Henry Adams. Published by Charles Scribner's Sons.

rarely has a foreigner been gifted with insight to explain what natives did not comprehend. Only with diffidence could the best-informed Americans venture, in 1800, to generalize on the subject of their own national habits of life and thought. Of all American travellers President Dwight [Timothy Dwight, President of Yale] was the most experienced; yet his four volumes of travels were remarkable for no trait more uniform than their reticence in regard to the United States. Clear and emphatic wherever New England was in discussion, Dwight claimed no knowledge of other regions. Where so good a judge professed ignorance, other observers were likely to mislead; and Frenchmen like Liancourt, Englishmen like Weld, or Germans like Bülow, were almost equally worthless authorities on a subject which none understood. The newspapers of the time were little more trustworthy than the books of travel, and hardly so well written. The literature of a higher kind was chiefly limited to New England, New York, and Pennsylvania. From materials so poor no precision of result could be expected. A few customs, more or less local; a few prejudices, more or less popular; a few traits of thought, suggesting habits of mind — must form the entire material for a study more important than that of politics or economics.

The standard of comfort had much to do with the standard of character; and in the United States, except among the slaves, the laboring class enjoyed an ample supply of the necessaries of life. In this respect, as in some others, they claimed superiority over the laboring class in Europe, and the claim would have been still stronger had they shown more skill in using the abundance that surrounded them. The Duc de Liancourt, among foreigners the best and kindest observer, made this remark on the mode of life he saw in Pennsylvania:

> There is a contrast of cleanliness with its opposite which to a stranger is very remarkable. The people of the country are as astonished' that one should object to sleeping two or three in the same bed and in dirty sheets, or to drink from the same dirty glass after half a score of others, as to see one neglect to wash one's hands and face of a morning. Whiskey diluted with water is the ordinary country drink. There is no settler, however poor, whose family does not take coffee or chocolate for breakfast, and always a little salt meat; at dinner, salt meat, or salt fish, and eggs; at supper again salt meat and coffee. This is also the common regime of the taverns.

An amusing, though quite untrustworthy Englishman named Ashe, who invented an American journey in 1806, described the fare of a Kentucky cabin:

> The dinner consisted of a large piece of salt bacon, a dish of hominy, and a tureen of squirrel broth. I dined entirely on the last dish, which I found incomparably good, and the meat equal to the most delicate chicken. The Kentuckian eat nothing but bacon, which indeed is the favorite diet of all the inhabitants of the State, and drank nothing but whiskey, which soon made him more than two-thirds drunk. In this last practice he is also supported by

the public habit. In a country, then, where bacon and spirits form the favorite summer repast, it cannot be just to attribute entirely the causes of infirmity to the climate. No people on earth live with less regard to regimen. They eat salt meat three times a day, seldom or never have any vegetables, and drink ardent spirits from morning till night. They have not only an aversion to fresh meat, but a vulgar prejudice that it is unwholesome. The truth is, their stomachs are depraved by burning liquors, and they have no appetite for anything but what is high-flavored and strongly impregnated by salt. . . .

One of the traits to which Liancourt alluded marked more distinctly the stage of social development. By day or by night, privacy was out of the question. Not only must all men travel in the same coach, dine at the same table, at the same time, on the same fare, but even their beds were in common, without distinction of persons. Innkeepers would not understand that a different arrangement was possible. When the English traveller Weld reached Elkton, on the main road from Philadelphia to Baltimore, he asked the landlord what accommodation he had. "Don't trouble yourself about that," was the reply; "I have no less than eleven beds in one room alone." This primitive habit extended over the whole country from Massachusetts to Georgia, and no American seemed to revolt against the tyranny of innkeepers.

"At New York I was lodged with two others, in a back room on the ground floor," wrote, in 1796, the Philadelphian whose complaints have already been mentioned. "What can be the reason for that vulgar, hoggish custom, common in America, of squeezing three, six, or eight beds into one room?"

Nevertheless, the Americans were on the whole more neat than their critics allowed. "You have not seen the Americans," was [William] Cobbett's reply, in 1819, to such charges; "you have not seen the nice, clean, neat houses of the farmers of Long Island, in New England, in the Quaker counties of Pennsylvania; you have seen nothing but the smoke-dried ultra-montanians." Yet Cobbett drew a sharp contrast between the laborer's neat cottage familiar to him in Surrey and Hampshire, and the "shell of boards" which the American occupied, "all around him as barren as a sea-beach." He added, too, that "the example of neatness was wanting"; no one taught it by showing its charm. Felix de Beaujour, otherwise not an enthusiastic American, paid a warm compliment to the country in this single respect, although he seemed to have the cities chiefly in mind:

> American neatness must possess some very attractive quality, since it seduces every traveller; and there is no one of them who, in returning to his own country, does not wish to meet again there that air of ease and neatness which rejoiced his sight during his stay in the United States.

Almost every traveller discussed the question whether the Americans were a temperate people, or whether they drank more than the English. Temperate they certainly were not, when judged by a modern standard. Every one acknowledged that in the South and West drinking was occasionally excessive; but even in Pennsylvania and New England the universal taste for drams proved habits by no means strict. Every grown man took his noon toddy as a matter of course; and although few were seen publicly drunk, many were habitually affected by liquor. The earliest temperance movement, ten or twelve years later, was said to have had its source in the scandal caused by the occasional intoxication of ministers at their regular meetings. Cobbett thought drinking the national disease; at all hours of the day, he said, young men, "even little boys, at or under twelve years of age, go into stores and tip off their drams." The mere comparison with England proved that the evil was great, for the English and Scotch were among the largest consumers of beer and alcohol on the globe.

In other respects besides sobriety American manners and morals were subjects of much dispute, and if judged by the diatribes of travellers like Thomas Moore and H. W. Bülow, were below the level of Europe. Of all classes of statistics, moral statistics were least apt to be preserved. Even in England, social vices could be gauged only by the records of criminal and divorce courts; in America, police was wanting and a divorce suit almost, if not quite, unknown. Apart from some coarseness, society must have been pure; and the coarseness was mostly an English inheritance. Among New Englanders, Chief-Justice Parsons was the model of judicial, social, and religious propriety; yet Parsons, in 1808, presented to a lady a copy of "Tom Jones," with a letter calling attention to the adventures of Molly Seagrim and the usefulness of describing vice. Among the social sketches in the "Portfolio" were many allusions to the coarseness of Philadelphia society, and the manners common to tea-parties. "I heard from married ladies," said a writer in February, 1803, "whose station as mothers demanded from them a guarded conduct — from young ladies, whose age forbids the audience of such conversation, and who using it modesty must disclaim — indecent allusions, indelicate expressions, and even at times immoral innuendoes. A loud laugh or a coarse exclamation followed each of these, and the young ladies generally went through the form of raising their fans to their faces."

Yet public and private records might be searched long, before they revealed evidence of misconduct such as filled the press and formed one of the commonest topics of conversation in the society of England and France. Almost every American family, however respectable, could show some victim to intemperance among its men, but few were mortified by a public scandal due to its women.

If the absence of positive evidence did not prove American society to be as pure as its simple and primitive condition implied, the same conclusion would be reached by observing the earnestness with which critics collected every charge that could be brought against it and by noting the substance of the whole. Tried by this test, the society of 1800 was often coarse and sometimes brutal, but, except for intemperance, was moral. Indeed, its chief offence, in the eyes of Europeans, was dullness. The amusements of a people were commonly a fair sign of social development, and the Americans were only beginning to amuse themselves. The cities were small and few in number, and the diversions were such as cost little and required but elementary knowledge. In New England, although the theatre had gained a firm foothold in Boston, Puritan feelings still forbade the running of horses. [President Dwight wrote:]

> The principal amusements of the inhabitants . . . are visiting, dancing, music, conversation, walking, riding, sailing, shooting at a mark, draughts, chess, and unhappily, in some of the larger towns, cards and dramatic exhibitions. A considerable amusement is also furnished in many places by the examination and exhibitions of the superior schools; and a more considerable one by the public exhibitions of colleges. Our countrymen also fish and hunt. Journeys taken for pleasure are very numerous, and are a very favorite object. Boys and young men play at foot-ball, cricket, quoits, and at many other sports of an athletic cast, and in the winter are peculiarly fond of skating. Riding in a sleigh, or sledge, is also a favorite diversion in New England.

President Dwight was sincere in his belief that college commencements and sleigh-riding satisfied the wants of his people; he looked upon whist as an unhappy dissipation, and upon the theatre as immoral. He had no occasion to condemn horse-racing, for no race-course was to be found in New England. . . .

. . . The rough-and-tumble fight [described by many writers as the most shocking characteristic of Virginia society] differed from the ordinary prize-fight, or boxing-match, by the absence of rules. Neither kicking, tearing, biting, nor gouging was forbidden by the law of the ring. Brutal as the practice was, it was neither new nor exclusively Virginian. The English travellers who described it as American barbarism might have seen the same sight in Yorkshire at the same date. The rough-and-tumble fight was English in origin, and was brought to Virginia and the Carolinas in early days, whence it spread to the Ohio and Mississippi. The habit attracted general notice because of its brutality in a society that showed few brutal instincts. Friendly foreigners like Liancourt were honestly shocked by it; others showed somewhat too plainly their pleasure at finding a vicious habit which they could consider a natural product of democratic society. Perhaps the description written by Thomas Ashe showed best not only the ferocity of the fight but also the antipathies of the writer, for Ashe had something of the artist in his touch, and he felt no love for Americans. The scene was at Wheeling. A Kentuckian and a Virginian were the combatants.

> Bulk and bone were in favor of the Kentuckian; science and craft in that of the Virginian. The former promised himself victory from his power; the latter from his science. Very few rounds had taken place or fatal blows given, before the Virginian contracted his whole form, drew up his arms to his face, with his hands nearly closed in a concave by the fingers being bent to the full extension of the flexors, and summoning up all his energy for one act of despera-

tion, pitched himself into the bosom of his opponent. Before the effects of this could be ascertained, the sky was rent by the shouts of the multitude; and I could learn that the Virginian had expressed as much beauty and skill in his retraction and bound, as if he had been bred in a menagerie and practised action and attitude among panthers and wolves. The shock received by the Kentuckian, and the want of breath, brought him instantly to the ground. The Virginian never lost his hold. Like those bats of the South who never quit the subject on which they fasten till they taste blood, he kept his knees in his enemy's body; fixing his claws in his hair and his thumbs on his eyes, gave them an instantaneous start from their sockets. The sufferer roared aloud, but uttered no complaint. The citizens again shouted with joy. . . .

Border society was not refined, but among its vices, as its virtues, few were permanent, and little idea could be drawn of the character that would at last emerge. The Mississippi boatman and the squatter on Indian lands were perhaps the most distinctly American types then existing, as far removed from the Old World as though Europe were a dream. Their language and imagination showed contact with Indians. A traveller on the levee at Natchez, in 1808, overheard a quarrel in a flatboat near by:

> "I am a man; I am a horse; I am a team," cried one voice; "I can whip any man in all Kentucky, by God!" "I am an alligator," cried the other; "half man, half horse; can whip any man on the Mississippi, by God!" "I am a man," shouted the first; "have the best horse, best dog, best gun, and handsomest wife in all Kentucky, by God!" "I am a Mississippi snapping-turtle," rejoined the second; "have bear's claws, alligator's teeth, and the devil's tail; can whip *any* man, by God!"

And on this usual formula of defiance the two fire-eaters began their fight, biting, gouging, and tearing. Foreigners were deeply impressed by barbarism such as this, and orderly emigrants from New England and Pennsylvania avoided contact with Southern drinkers and fighters; but even then they knew that with a new generation such traits must disappear, and that little could be judged of popular character from the habits of frontiersmen. Perhaps such vices deserved more attention when found in the older communities, but even there they were rather survivals of English low-life than products of a new soil, and they were given too much consequence in the tales of foreign travellers.

This was not the only instance where foreigners were struck by what they considered popular traits, which natives rarely noticed. Idle curiosity was commonly represented as universal, especially in the Southern settler who knew no other form of conversation. [Wrote Weld:]

> Frequently have I been stopped by one of them, . . . and without further preface asked where I was from, if I was acquainted with any news, where bound to, and finally my name. "Stop, Mister! why, I guess now you be coming from the new State?" "No, sir." "Why, then, I guess as how you be coming from Kentuck?" "No, sir." "Oh, why, then, pray now where might you be

coming from?" "From the low country." "Why, you must have heard all the news, then; pray now, Mister, what might the price of bacon be in those parts?" "Upon my word, my friend, I can't inform you." "Ay, ay; I see, Mister, you be'ent one of us. Pray now, Mister, what might your name be?"

Almost every writer spoke with annoyance of the inquisitorial habits of New England and the impertinence of American curiosity. Complaints so common could hardly have lacked foundation, yet the Americans as a people were never loquacious, but inclined to be somewhat reserved, and they could not recognize the accuracy of the description. President Dwight repeatedly expressed astonishment at the charge, and asserted that in his large experience it had no foundation. Forty years later, Charles Dickens found complaint with Americans for taciturnity. Equally strange to modern experience were the continual complaints in books of travel that loungers and loafers, idlers of every description, infested the taverns, and annoyed respectable travellers both native and foreign. Idling seemed to be considered a popular vice, and was commonly associated with tippling. So completely did the practice disappear in the course of another generation that it could scarcely be recalled as offensive; but in truth less work was done by the average man in 1800 than in aftertimes, for there was actually less work to do. "Good country this for lazy fellows," wrote Wilson from Kentucky; "they plant corn, turn their pigs into the woods, and in the autumn feed upon corn and pork. They lounge about the rest of the year." The roar of the steam-engine had never been heard in the land, and the carrier's wagon was three weeks between Philadelphia and Pittsburg. What need for haste when days counted for so little? Why not lounge about the tavern when life had no better amusement to offer? Why mind one's own business when one's business would take care of itself?

Yet however idle the American sometimes appeared, and however large the class of tavern loafers may have actually been, the true American was active and industrious. No immigrant came to America for ease or idleness. If an English farmer bought land near New York, Philadelphia, or Baltimore, and made the most of his small capital, he found that while he could earn more money than in Surrey or Devonshire, he worked harder and suffered greater discomforts. The climate was trying; fever was common; the crops ran new risks from strange insects, drought, and violent weather; the weeds were annoying; the flies and mosquitoes tormented him and his cattle; laborers were scarce and indifferent; the slow and magisterial ways of England, where everything was made easy, must be exchanged for quick and energetic action; the farmer's own eye must see to every detail, his own hand must hold the plough and the scythe. . . . New settlers suffered many of the ills that would have afflicted an army marching and fighting in a country of dense forest and swamp, with one sore misery besides — that whatever trials the men endured, the burden bore most heavily upon the women and children. The chances of being shot or scalped by Indians was hardly worth considering when compared with the certainty of malarial fever, or the strange disease called milk-sickness, or the still more depressing home-sickness, or the misery of nervous prostration, which wore out generation after generation of women and children on the frontiers, and left a tragedy in every log cabin. Not for love of ease did men plunge into the wilderness. Few laborers of the Old World endured a harder lot, coarser fare, or anxieties and responsibilities greater than those of the Western emigrant. Not merely because he enjoyed the luxury of salt pork, whiskey, or even coffee three times a day did the American laborer claim superiority over the European. . . .

If any prediction could be risked, an observer might have been warranted in suspecting that the popular character was likely to be conservative, for as yet this trait was most marked, at least in the older societies of New England, Pennsylvania, and Virginia. Great as were the material obstacles in the path of the United States, the greatest obstacle of all was in the human mind. Down to the close of the eighteenth century no change had occurred in the world which warranted practical men in assuming that great changes were to come. Afterward, as time passed, and as science developed man's capacity to control nature's forces, old-fashioned conservatism vanished from society, reappearing occasionally, like the stripes on a mule, only to prove its former existence; but during the eighteenth century the progress of America, except in political paths, had been less rapid than ardent reformers wished, and the reaction which followed the French Revolution made it seem even slower than it was. . . .

This conservative habit of mind was more harmful in America than in other communities, because Americans needed more than older societies the activity which could alone partly compensate for the relative feebleness of their means compared with the magnitude of their task. Some instances of sluggishness, common to Europe and America, were hardly credible. For more than ten years in England the steam-engines of Watt had been working, in common and successful use, causing a revolution in industry that threatened to drain the world for England's advantage; yet Europe during a generation left England undisturbed to enjoy the monopoly of steam. France and Germany were England's rivals in commerce and manufactures, and required steam for self-defence; while the United States were commercial allies of England, and needed steam neither for mines nor manufactures, but their need was still extreme. Every American knew that if steam could be successfully applied to navigation, it must produce an immediate increase of wealth, besides an ultimate settlement of the most serious material and political difficulties of the Union. Had both the national and State Governments devoted millions of money to this object, and had the citizens wasted, if necessary, every dollar in their slowly filling pockets to attain it, they would have done no more than the occasion warranted, even had they failed; but failure was not to be feared, for they had with their own eyes seen the experiment tried, and they did not dispute its success. For America this question had been settled as early as 1789, when John Fitch— a mechanic, without education or wealth, but with the energy of genius — invented engine and paddles of his own, with so much success that during a whole summer Philadelphians watched his ferryboat plying daily against the river current. No one denied that his boat was rapidly, steadily, and regularly moved against wind and tide, with as much certainty and convenience as could be expected in a first experiment; yet Fitch's company failed. He could raise no more money; the public refused to use his boat or to help him build a better; they did not want it, would not believe in it, and broke his heart by their contempt. Fitch struggled against failure, and invented another boat moved by a screw. The Eastern public still proving indifferent, he wandered to Kentucky, to try his fortune on the Western waters. Disappointed there, as in Philadelphia and New York, he made a deliberate attempt to end his life by drink; but the process proving too slow, he saved twelve opium pills from the physician's prescription, and was found one morning dead.

Fitch's death took place in an obscure Kentucky inn, three years before Jefferson, the philosopher president, entered the White House. Had Fitch been the only inventor thus neglected, his peculiarities and the defects of his steamboat might account for his failure; but he did not stand alone. At the same moment Philadelphia contained another inventor, Oliver Evans, a man so ingenious as to be often called the American Watt. He, too, invented a locomotive steam-engine which he longed to bring into common use. The great services actually rendered by this extraordinary man were not a tithe of those he would gladly have performed, had he found support and encouragement; but his success was not even so great as that of Fitch, and he stood aside while Livingston and Fulton, by their greater resources and influence, forced the steamboat on a sceptical public.

While the inventors were thus ready, and while State legislatures were offering mischievous monopolies for this invention, which required only some few thousand dollars of ready money, the Philosophical Society of Rotterdam wrote to the American Philosophical Society at Philadelphia, requesting to know what improvements had been made in the United States in the construction of steam-engines. The subject was referred to Benjamin H. Latrobe, the most eminent engineer in America, and his Report, presented to the Society in May, 1803, published in the Transactions, and transmitted abroad, showed the reasoning on which conservatism rested:

> During the general lassitude of mechanical exertion which succeeded the American Revolution, . . . the utility of steam-engines appears to have been forgotten; but the subject afterward started into very general notice in a form

in which it could not possibly be attended with much success. A sort of mania began to prevail, which indeed has not yet entirely subsided, for impelling boats by steam-engines. . . . For a short time a passage-boat, rowed by a steam-engine, was established between Bordentown and Philadelphia, but it was soon laid aside. . . . There are indeed general objections to the use of the steam-engine for impelling boats, from which no particular mode of application can be free. These are, first, the weight of the engine and of the fuel; second, the large space it occupies; third, the tendency of its action to rack the vessel and render it leaky; fourth, the expense of maintenance; fifth, the irregularity of its motion and the motion of the water in the boiler and cistern, and of the fuel-vessel in rough water; sixth, the difficulty arising from the liability of the paddles or oars to break if light, and from the weight, if made strong. Nor have I ever heard of an instance, verified by other testimony than that of the inventor, of a speedy and agreeable voyage having been performed in a steamboat of any construction. I am well aware that there are still many very respectable and ingenious men who consider the application of the steam-engine to the purpose of navigation as highly important and as very practicable, especially on the rapid waters of the Mississippi, and who would feel themselves almost offended at the expression of an opposite opinion. And perhaps some of the objections against it may be obviated. That founded on the expense and weight of the fuel may not for some years exist in the Mississippi, where there is a redundance of wood on the banks; but the cutting and loading will be almost as great an evil.

Within four years the steamboat was running, and Latrobe was its warmest friend. The dispute was a contest of temperaments, a divergence between minds, rather than a question of science; and a few visionaries such as those to whom Latrobe alluded — men like Chancellor Livingston, Joel Barlow, John Stevens, Samuel L. Mitchill, and Robert Fulton — dragged society forward. What but scepticism could be expected among a people thus asked to adopt the steamboat, when as yet the ordinary atmospheric steam-engine, such as had been in use in Europe for a hundred years, was practically unknown to them, and the engines of Watt were a fable? Latrobe's Report further said that in the spring of 1803, when he wrote, five steam-engines were at work in the United States — one lately set up by the Manhattan Water Company in New York to supply the city with water; another in New York for sawing timber; two in Philadelphia, belonging to the city, for supplying water and running a rolling and slitting mill; and one at Boston employed in some manufacture. All but one of these were probably constructed after 1800, and Latrobe neglected to say whether they belonged to the old Newcomen type, or to Watt's manufacture, or to American invention; but he added that the chief American improvement on the steam-engine had been the construction of a wooden boiler, which developed sufficient power to work the Philadelphia pump at the rate of twelve strokes, of six feet, per minute. Twelve strokes a minute, or one stroke every five seconds, though not a surprising power, might have answered its purpose, had not the wooden boiler, as Latrobe admitted, quickly decomposed, and steam-leaks appeared at every bolt-hole.

If so eminent and so intelligent a man as Latrobe, who had but recently emigrated in the prime of life from England, knew little about Watt, and nothing about Oliver Evans, whose experience would have been well worth communicating to any philosophical society in Europe, the more ignorant and unscientific public could not feel faith in a force of which they knew nothing at all. For nearly two centuries the Americans had struggled on foot or horseback over roads not much better than trails, or had floated down rushing streams in open boats momentarily in danger of sinking or upsetting. They had at length, in the Eastern and Middle States, reached the point of constructing turnpikes and canals. Into these undertakings they put sums of money relatively large, for the investment seemed safe and the profits certain. Steam as a locomotive power was still a visionary idea, beyond their experience, contrary to European precedent, and exposed to a thousand risks. They regarded it as a delusion.

About three years after Latrobe wrote his Report on the steam-engine, Robert Fulton began to build the boat which settled forever the value of steam as a locomotive power. According to Fulton's well-known account of his own experience, he suffered almost as keenly as Fitch, twenty years before, under the want of popular sympathy. [He said, according to Judge Story's report:]

> When I was building my first steamboat at New York, . . . the project was viewed by the public either with indifference or with contempt as a visionary scheme. My friends indeed were civil, but they were shy. They listened with patience to my explanations, but with a settled cast of incredulity upon their countenances. I felt the full force of the lamentation of the poet —
>
> > "Truths would you teach, or save a sinking land,
> > All fear, none aid you, and few understand."
>
> As I had occasion to pass daily to and from the building-yard while my boat was in progress, I have often loitered unknown near the idle groups of strangers gathering in little circles, and heard various inquiries as to the object of this new vehicle. The language was uniformly that of scorn, or sneer, or ridicule. The loud laugh often rose at my expense; the dry jest; the wise calculation of losses and expenditures; the dull but endless repetition of the Fulton Folly. Never did a single encouraging remark, a bright hope, or a warm wish cross my path.

Possibly Fulton and Fitch, like other inventors, may have exaggerated the public apathy and contempt; but whatever was the precise force of the innovating spirit, conservatism possessed the world by right. Experience forced on men's minds the conviction that what had ever been must ever be. At the close of the eighteenth century nothing had occurred which warranted the belief that even the material difficulties of America could be removed. Radicals as extreme as Thomas Jefferson and Albert Gallatin were contented with avowing no higher aim than that America should reproduce the simpler forms of European republican society without European vices; and even this their opponents thought visionary. The United States had thus far made a single great step in advance of the Old World — they had agreed to try the experiment of embracing half a continent in one republican system; but so little were they disposed to feel confidence in their success, that Jefferson himself did not look on this American idea as vital; he would not stake the future on so new an invention. "Whether we remain in one confederacy," he wrote in 1804, "or form into Atlantic and Mississippi confederations, I believe not very important to the happiness of either part." Even over his liberal mind history cast a spell so strong, that he thought the solitary American experiment of political confederation "not very important" beyond the Alleghenies.

The task of overcoming popular inertia in a democratic society was new, and seemed to offer peculiar difficulties. Without a scientific class to lead the way, and without a wealthy class to provide the means of experiment, the people of the United States were still required, by the nature of their problems, to become a speculating and scientific nation. They could do little without changing their old habit of mind, and without learning to love novelty for novelty's sake. Hitherto their timidity in using money had been proportioned to the scantiness of their means. Henceforward they were under every inducement to risk great stakes and frequent losses in order to win occasionally a thousand fold. In the colonial state they had naturally accepted old processes as the best, and European experience as final authority. As an independent people, with half a continent to civilize, they could not afford to waste time in following European examples, but must devise new processes of their own. A world which assumed that what had been must be, could not be scientific; yet in order to make the Americans a successful people, they must be roused to feel the necessity of scientific training. Until they were satisfied that knowledge was money, they would not insist upon high education; nor until they saw with their own eyes stones turned into gold, and vapor into cattle and corn, would they learn the meaning of science.

STUDY GUIDE

1. Summarize Adams's view of each of the following American characteristics: attitude toward privacy; coarseness and brutality; idleness or industriousness.

2. What evidence does Adams give that Americans were basically conservative in this period? Considering politics, religion, and social customs, what evidence might be given that Americans were progressive and innovative?

3. Early in his essay, Adams suggests that "the standard of comfort had much to do with the standard of character." Explain how the relatively satisfactory standard of living of white Americans may have influenced their character.

4. Adams quotes an exchange of words preceding a fight aboard a flatboat recorded by a Natchez traveler in 1808. What is there in the language and the attitudes expressed that would be quite unlike an account of an argument between two Frenchmen or Italians in the streets of Paris or Rome?

5. Be prepared to discuss the abiding influence of regionalism in our country today, and the extent to which there is a single American character. What modern developments in American life have tended to make regional differences in language, customs, politics, and the like less pronounced than they were in the 1800s?

6. Describe the characteristics of contemporary Americans with respect to: violence; conservatism; attitudes toward hard work; attitudes toward privacy.

BIBLIOGRAPHY

The study of the "American character" has been a favorite preoccupation of Americans and foreign travelers alike. Since the classic, early-nineteenth-century portraits of the American by Harriet Martineau, Frances Trollope, Alexis de Tocqueville, and Charles Dickens — all of whom came from Europe to visit and travel here — there have been numerous writers on both sides of the Atlantic who have made an effort to fathom the patterns of thought and behavior of our people.

The emphasis on the frontier as the predominant force in shaping the institutions and values of the American people will be found in the writings of Frederick Jackson Turner: *The Frontier in American History* * (New York, © 1920); *The Significance of Sections in American History* (New York, © 1932); and *The Early Writings of Frederick Jackson Turner*, comp. by Everett E. Edwards (Madison, Wis., 1938). In an essay on "American Democracy and the Frontier" in the *Yale Review*, Vol. XX (Dec. 1930) Benjamin F. Wright, Jr., challenges Turner's contention that the West was the source of the American democratic impulse. Henry Nash Smith, in *Virgin Land: The American West as Symbol and Myth* * (Cambridge, Mass., 1950), suggests that Turner romanticized and exaggerated the significance of a frontier that was rapidly disappearing.

A number of volumes on the American character tend to concentrate on particular traits we exhibit as a nation — and in some instances at a particular point in our history. In *People of Plenty: Economic Abundance and the American Character* * (Chicago, 1954), David M. Potter describes the culture and the values of our nation as products of abundance; while the Englishman Geoffrey Gorer, in *The American People: A Study in National Character* * (New York, 1948) portrays us as rebels against authority. On the other hand, David Riesman, with Reuel Denny and Nathan Glazer, in *The Lonely Crowd: A Study of the Changing American Character* (New Haven, Conn., 1951), describes Americans as a nation of conformists; and Daniel J. Boorstin in three separate books — *The Americans: The Colonial Experience* * (New York, © 1958), *The Americans: The National Experience* * (New York, 1965), and *The Genius of American Politics* * (Chicago, 1953) — depicts the American people as singularly pragmatic and innovative. A survey of virtually all the literature on the subject will be found in Michael McGiffert, *The Character of Americans: A Book of Readings* * (Homewood, Ill., 1970).

IV DEMOCRACY AND SOCIAL CHANGE

One of the questions frequently asked of historians is how close an approximation there is between their reconstruction of the past and the past as it really was. In our own time, we seldom think of being a part of an "age," and are scarcely aware of the "patterns of development" that later historians may detect. With the perspective of time, historians may see an earlier decade or century as a revolutionary period, a time of economic imperialism, an age of reform, a renaissance, or a period of cultural decay. Any such characterization of a period is somewhat artificial. It ignores many contradictory developments of the time, and with still further perspective, later historians often come to doubt the evaluation of earlier writers.

The last decade of the eighteenth and the first quarter of the nineteenth century are generally regarded as a period of centralization and nationalism. Following the adoption of the Constitution in 1788, the Federalist period of Washington, Hamilton, and Adams was characterized by the strengthening of the national government in both domestic and foreign affairs and the development of national interests quite distinct from those of European powers. The nationalistic thrust was continued under the Virginian presidents from Jefferson to Monroe, though support for a domestic program along these lines was stronger in Congress than in the executive mansion.

The second quarter of the nineteenth century has proved to be more difficult to characterize. Historians have long emphasized the democratic features of American society in the "Age of Jackson." Constitutions were revised, the suffrage widened, and Jackson himself — in the reconstruction of historians, at least — stood as proof that the simple frontier farmer and working man could rise to the highest office in the land. This view of the Age of Jackson is supported by the first reading in this section, which describes a democratization of American religious life that began at the very end of the eighteenth century and continued to stir American society for many decades. The second reading, however, raises questions about the characterization of this period as democratic and suggests that much contradictory evidence from the social history of the time has been ignored. The 1830s have also been seen as a decade of extraordinary social ferment, giving rise to the first great reform movement in American history. Women were entering new professions and were deeply involved in such reforms as abolitionism. The third reading describes various attitudes toward women in the early nineteenth century. The last reading, on utopian communes, describes the attempts of one particular group, the Shakers, to create the perfect society. As you complete the readings in this section, you might reflect on whether or not such a term as the "Age of Democracy" or the "Age of Reform" accurately reflects what really happened in the years from 1830 to 1850.

"Sing-Sing Camp Meeting" by Joseph B. Smith, 1838. (Detail)
One of the faithful is "treeing the devil."

CHARLES A. JOHNSON

Religious Democracy

Religious organizations, like most institutions, reflect the social forces of their particular society and time. Even such a world-wide organization as the Roman Catholic Church has differed in doctrine and rites of worship in different countries, and most churches that survive a century or more undergo subtle changes. American Protestantism has been substantially transformed since it was first brought to these shores, and few of the changes have been so profound as those that came about in the first half of the nineteenth century.

Both New England Calvinism and the pietistic religions of Pennsylvania were brought to the colonies by small, tightly knit groups of devout believers. But the churches soon faced the question of whether or not to modify their doctrines and soften their requirements in order to retain the membership of later generations who held the beliefs less intensely and found the worship less satisfying. By the early 1700s, many people felt that the churches had compromised too much, and they responded enthusiastically to the first "Great Awakening," a religious revival movement that attracted many followers in the 1730s. The second major revival movement, which began about 1800, had its roots in a society that seemed to be increasingly secular and among a people who found a highly rational religion emotionally barren. Yet the remarkable religious awakening that swept across the country at the beginning of the nineteenth century was quite different from the earlier revival and had a much longer-range impact upon American Protestantism.

Theologically, one of the characteristics of the Second Great Awakening was the new emphasis upon Jesus, rather than upon

God the Father or the remote Creator of the Deists, an emphasis that has dominated Protestant thought and worship ever since. Preaching the salvation of all men, Protestant churches in the early nineteenth century outgrew the boundaries of a single colony or state and developed broad, national denominations. Between 1800 and 1850, Protestantism also assumed a new sense of mission and destiny, as did the American secular philosophy of the period. Bible, tract, and missionary societies were formed to carry the Word to the unsettled West, and each denomination established a multitude of colleges to provide a Christian education for the young.

Many of these developments took place after the most emotional revivalism had subsided. Yet the whole first half of the century witnessed a strong element of religious emotionalism and democratization, as evidenced in the founding of several new faiths. Spiritualism, Mormonism, and Adventism all had distinctive appeals, but like the revival itself, they succeeded because they found a people who were receptive to an emotional religious experience. Evidence of the revival was seen in the eastern states even before 1800, but the frenzy took its most distinctive form in the frontier communities farther west. Kentucky camp meetings were awesome in the crowds they drew and the religious exercises that characterized them. In the following selection, Charles A. Johnson gives a composite portrait of such meetings.

The setting of the early Kentucky camp meeting was "nature's temple" — the forest clearing. Just one step removed from the cabin meeting place, frontier encampments "offered nothing by way of worshipful environment save the natural beauty of a grove of trees on a sloping green." This very lack of artificiality gave the open-air revival its great religious power, a power that was never more explosively demonstrated than during the era of the Second Great Awakening (1800–1805).

The first encampments were cleared areas of the forest close to meetinghouses which in their turn served the several functions of worship centers, refuges for prostate mourners, and lodging places for visiting clergymen. Since frontier churches were frequently located near waterways, it was only natural that camp sites were chosen near springs or

From chapter 3 of *The Frontier Camp Meeting* by Charles A. Johnson. Reprinted by permission of Southern Methodist University Press.

creeks and if possible on navigable rivers. Hence the distinctive names of the encampments of the Great Revival — "Muddy River," "Drake's Creek," "Red River," and "Cabin Creek." Aside from its aesthetic appeal, the chosen site had to provide drinking water, dry ground, shade, pasturage for the horses, and timber for tentpoles and firewood.

These desirable locations were not hard to find in the newly settled regions, and men with ax and sledge could quickly convert a two- to four-acre tract of forest land into an encampment. There was hectic activity as the prospective worshipers arrived at the spot, a week before or just prior to meeting time. Underbrush was cleared away, trees were felled, and preparations were made for a tent city.

Through the years encampments adhered to three general patterns: the rectangular, horseshoe, and circular forms. The last-named was by far the most popular. Regardless of shape, tents formed the outer shell which enclosed the core of the camp meeting, the open-air auditorium. After a few years' experience, sponsors in the West urged that a supervisor be appointed to inform incoming wagoners of the encampment plan, so that much of the milling about on the first meeting day could be avoided.

Circular rows or streets of tents were irregularly arranged following the contour of the land on the edge of the area of cleared ground, with walks between. Camp meeting veteran Jesse Lee described the living facilities utilized in 1809:

> The land is cleared . . . to hold as many tents as will be erected, we then have the front of the tents on a line on each side, and at each end. Back of the tents we have a place cleared for the carriages to stand . . . so that every tent may have a carriage belonging to it in a convenient position. Just back of the carriages we have the horses tied and fed. Before the tents we generally have the fires for cooking, and to help in giving light at night to see who are walking about (if more convenient), fires are placed behind the tents.

The number of temporary camp structures that rose as if by magic varied with the stage of settlement in the community involved. There might be twenty or as many as two hundred tents, of various materials and sizes. Some were made of sail or cotton cloth "hung upon poles in the shape of a roof of a house." Others were strictly homemade affairs, fashioned from two or three old quilts or coverlets sewn together. Even several sheets tacked together served the purpose; wealthier folk might make a home out of a bolt of muslin. "Bush arbors" erected beside covered wagons or carriages served some as temporary housing. A few even had wooden shelters with clapboard roofs. These were the "log tents," although cloth ones were more usual.

The backwoods camp meeting differed from its eastern imitator in size as well as in the number of tents. Encampments of the East, although very similar in design to those of the frontier, were established on a grander and more pretentious scale. While some eastern shelters housed but a single group, a great number were large enough for many families. Perhaps twenty to fifty and even a hundred individuals found shelter under a single canvas. Mammoth tents were typical here. Likewise the eastern campers' furnishings included many of the comforts of home. The pioneer, by contrast, was lucky to have any piece of rude furniture. His bed might be of straw, or a makeshift one of poles and blankets. Indeed, many at the Great Revival camp meetings slept on the ground, rolled up in blankets, when the homes of neighbors and the meetinghouse were full.

Preachers shared the same simple accommodations as the worshipers. Bishop William McKendree's quarters at the initial encampment in the Missouri Territory were "made by sewing the preacher's saddle blankets together and spreading them over a pole supported by forks in the ground like soldiers' tents." One end of the tent was closed with green boughs, while the other was left open, with a fire in front of it. Bedding arrangements were often as primitive. At one eastern campground six ministers slept in a huge bed made up of overlapping blankets, ingeniously arranged.

The main physical feature of any camp meeting landscape east or west was the pulpit. Once a site was cleared, this was set up at one or both ends of the natural amphitheater, facing the parallel rows of seats. These stands were supplemented by fallen logs or wagon beds, from which ministers spellbound groups of listeners. Some of the pulpits were merely upraised platforms on stilts; others were sturdy, two-level affairs, often roofed to keep out the elements. Possibly ten feet square, the platforms were commodious enough to hold not only the speaker but also the several exhorters and ministers who were awaiting their turns to speak. Many were large enough to accommodate a dozen people. By standing in an elevated position four to eight feet higher than the milling crowds, a preacher had a better chance of being seen and heard. Competing attractions gave the flighty a chance to wander from one orator to another, and the din and disorder gave even certain "sons of thunder" trouble.

If the minister proved to be a pulpit thumper, members of the audience who seated themselves directly below the scaffold occupied a hazardous position. The Reverend James B. Finley recalled that more than once a front seat occupant was "suddenly aroused by the fall of a pitcher of water, or the big Bible upon the cranium." Seats for the audience, where they existed, were merely felled logs cross-laid, or planks supported by tree stumps. The bark was dressed and the top adzed off to make them as comfortable as possible. This crude arrangement was not only the result of necessity; it was also consonant with John Wesley's rule concerning church seating: "Let there be no pews, and *no backs* to the seats." Also in accordance with the founder's wishes, the open-air auditorium was carefully divided, the women located on the right and the men on the left. On some campgrounds a rail fence or wooden partition emphasized this demarkation of the sexes.

In both slaveholding and nonslaveholding regions, the Negroes were allowed to set up their own camps behind the preacher's rostrum. Because of the close proximity, their services often merged with those of the whites, adding no little to the general confusion and emotional excitement. The Negro housing area, with its crazy-quilt tents after the fashion of Joseph's coat, was a picturesque affair. As the camp meeting matured, the Negro camp section was sometimes separated from that of the whites by a plank partition. This barrier was torn down on the final meeting day when the two peoples joined together in a song festival and "marching ceremony."

Illumination for the evening services presented no problem to the resourceful campers. At first, the lighting was provided by candles and pine knot torches affixed to preaching stands, trees, or other convenient places. Jesse Lee, writing of the first campgrounds, recalled seeing one hundred and twenty candles burning at the same time. When campfires were located in front of the tents, they also helped light up the worship area. Gradually, fire stands known as "fire altars" came into regular use. These stands were erected in the four corners of the auditorium and consisted of earthen-covered platforms on upraised tripods some six feet high. Bark, twigs, or "pine wood fires" burned on top of a layer of earth and sod. Later, oil lamps were utilized. At night the glare of the campfire, the flickering candles and torches, and the blazing fire altars all added an eerie touch to the colorful services.

The communion table set up at the initial woodland meeting in Missouri in 1809 was doubtless similar to those used during the Kentucky Revival. That sacramental table consisted of a "puncheon" split from a log, smoothed on the upper side, and laid on crossties supported by four forks placed in the ground. The whole was covered with a sheet, "for there were no table-cloths then."

Usually no provisions were made for inclement weather; at the first Kentucky meetings enthusiasts worshiped out of doors in the midst of violent rainstorms. A few people could huddle in cloth or log shelters, but the western camp meeting was not noted for its comforts. The worshipers at the Goshen, Illinois, encampment of 1807 must have been surprised to find a large arbor in the form of an L erected there, an arbor spacious enough to cover seven hundred people. In the East, by contrast, most campgrounds were dominated by huge tents that afforded privacy for prayer in good weather and shelter in bad weather. Kentucky accommodations in 1800 were crude but sufficient, and the pioneer settler did not complain. He had journeyed to the camp meeting expecting no great physical comforts; he had come to see for himself this religious marvel that was transforming men's lives.

The Second Great Awakening was the era of the gigantic camp meeting — the "General Camp Meeting" — where the unusual was the usual, where Presbyterian, Methodist, and Baptist ministers worked side by side, where the crowds were numbered in the hundreds and frequently the thousands, and where scores were swept into mass hysteria by the frenzied proceedings. These joint meetings were of two types, the "Sacramental" and the "Union" meeting, the former being so named because of the celebration of the Lord's Supper. When the time arrived for this ceremony Baptist leaders withdrew and the Methodists and Presbyterians conducted joint communion services. It was at the Union encampments, however, that the three denominations worshiped together most successfully. About these early meetings [James] McGready could write glowingly that "bigotry and prejudice have received a death wound. . . . Presbyterians and Methodists love one another."

Among the Methodists, William McKendree looms large in the story of the "General Camp Meeting." He was assisted by a host of other traveling preachers, including William Burke, John Sale, Benjamin Lakin, and Henry Smith. McKendree had become enthusiastic over the camp meeting while an itinerant and district supervisor in southern Kentucky. In 1801 he overcame his denominational prejudice to co-operate with certain Presbyterian leaders who were pioneering the innovation. Joint committees were set up, empowered to make camp regulations and appoint speakers for the outdoor sacraments. It was evident that enthusiasm for a new technique and the excitement of leading great numbers to the Lord were bringing about close co-operation among frontier preachers of differing denominations. The future of interdenominational harmony looked bright as the camp meeting enjoyed its first tumultuous surge.

During his union arrangement with the Presbyterians McKendree temporarily suspended the Methodist class meetings, the "love feasts," and the regular operations of the itinerant system. By 1802 the highly successful General Camp Meetings of Methodists and Presbyterians (and sometimes Baptists) were well known. Yet rumbles of discontent with the practice were heard late in the very first year, indicating that the spirit of partisanship was still strong.

William Burke, speaking for the Methodists, complained bitterly that Presbyterians "were pressing in their invitations" to the sacramental gatherings but refused to support his denomination's open-air quarterly meetings, because of other appointments they had to meet. While the rivals of Methodism remained away from encampments on Friday, Saturday, and Sunday, continued Burke,

> on Monday we generally saw some of their ministers in the congregation, but having our plans filled up for that day we consequently paid no attention to them; for we were fully satisfied that they only wanted the Methodists to shake the bush, and they would catch the birds. My advice to our official members

in quarterly meetings was, to quietly withdraw from their meetings, and mind our own business. They did so.

Actually, the co-operative arrangement did last several years longer, although the union grew weaker and weaker, terminating in the last year of the Great Revival, 1804.

Attracted by the forest revival's novelty, families of every Protestant faith mingled at these Great Revival encampments. Reports of the frenzied services had caused some to think the world was coming to an end; others anticipated a dreadful calamity about to befall the young country as a judgment of God on an impious people; still others saw meetings as "the work of the devil who had been unchained for a season . . . to deceive the ministers of religion and the very elect themselves." The byways were alive with settlers, and the numbers in attendance were almost unbelievable. It seemed as if the entire population were hitting the camp meeting trail. Writing in the 1840's, Presbyterian Robert Davidson reflected upon the revival's lure:

> The laborer quitted his task; Age snatched his crutch; Youth forgot his pastime; the plow was left in the furrow; the deer enjoyed a respite upon the mountains; business of all kinds was suspended; dwelling houses were deserted; whole neighborhoods were emptied; bold hunters and sober matrons, young women and maidens, and little children, flocked to the common center of attraction; every difficulty was surmounted, every risk ventured to be present at the camp-meeting.

Participants in the 1800 and 1801 Kentucky and Tennessee camp meetings have insisted that the crowds numbered from three to twenty thousand at various times, according to the density of population in the neighboring territory. Although seemingly fantastic, these figures are borne out by more than one account. "Many thousands" met at Desha's Creek in August, 1800, to fall "like corn before a storm of wind." At the Cabin Creek Union Meeting in May, 1801, twenty thousand worshipers congregated; Point Pleasant had four thousand in attendance; and Indian Creek had ten thousand.

Perhaps equally significant was the great number of frontier preachers who turned their siege guns on the campers. Peter Cartwright said the number of churchmen of different denominations who joined forces at any one of these woodland Bethels in Kentucky, Tennessee, and the Carolinas might reach "ten, twenty, and sometimes thirty." They preached, harangued, exhorted, and prayed "night and day, four or five days together," and often for a week or more.

The immensity of the throng impressed a newcomer to a Cumberland Revival camp meeting — a "scene of confusion that could scarce be put into human language." There were not enough ministers present to keep the crowds seated or attentive; spectators walked about talking, laughing, smoking, and gesticulating during the services. Free of the restraint of a formal meetinghouse, the people indulged in complete emotional freedom and frequently reverted to herd behavior. If a particular sermon or song excited them, they cried, shouted, groaned, or repeated the spoken phrases over and over again in increasing tempo.

> There would be an unusual outcry; some bursting forth into loud ejaculations of prayer, or thanksgiving, for the truth; . . . others flying to their careless friends, with tears of compassion; beseeching them to turn to the Lord; some struck with terror, and hastening through the crowd to make their escape, or pulling away their relations; others . . . fainting and swooning away.

Preachers often found it impossible to maintain order when they themselves were physically exhausted from straining their voices so that thousands could hear them. At communion services their labors were intensified. The Reverend John Lyle, a Presbyterian, thought he was going to faint or die from the exertion of delivering the "action" sermon to about eight thousand at a Paint Creek meeting in 1801, "yet notwithstanding spoke above an hour."

Competing with the preacher most of the day were the typical background noises — outbursts from the audience, sermons being delivered from other stands, and the offerings of praying and singing circles and groups. Largely unplanned, the service routine was most often spontaneous. At two separate stands, said one itinerant,

> we had preaching alternately through the day. . . . Each public service was followed by a prayer meeting which was not to be broken off to make way for preaching, but the trumpet was sounded at the other stand, whither all who wished to hear preaching were wont to repair.

The Reverend John Lyle reported that ten, twenty, and sometimes the majority of people under conviction offered up individual prayers simultaneously. Since this was a social as well as a religious occasion, whiskey had to be available to ease the parched throats of the participants. The "dissolute and irreligious were frequently more numerous than the serious minded," and to cater to their tastes, barrels of whiskey were hidden in the bushes to be retailed by the cupful later. Preacher Richard McNemar commented on the dregs of frontier society that took this opportunity to heckle and carouse. Even harsher judgment was expressed by Methodist historian Nathan Bangs:

> It is admitted that in such vast multitudes, assembled in the open air, under circumstances of such peculiar excitement, and many of them not well instructed in science or morals, there must have been some disorder, some mingling of human passions not sanctified by grace, and some words and gesticulations not in accordance with strict religious decorum. Every action, therefore, and everything which was said and done [at these camp meetings], I am by no means careful to defend or pledged to justify.

Immoral practices were frequent enough at these encampments to be commented upon by the camp leaders. Such immorality is not surprising when the mixed character of the pioneer audiences is taken into account. Certainly, the precedent-shattering size of the crowds and the emotional hysteria of the services did nothing to weaken such tendencies. Preacher Lyle, a sharp critic of the revival, stated that acts of immorality took place on the grounds under cover of darkness, or in the neighboring forest. He candidly told the facts of the situation concerning his own congregation. Some of the women who were the most persistent victims of the "falling exercise" were the ones prone to forget the edict of virtue. Thus "Becca Bell, who often fell, is now big with child to a wicked trifling school master of the name of Brown who says he'll be damned to hell if he ever marries her." Several other of Lyle's female parishioners "got careless," including "Polly Moffitt who was with child to Petty and died miserably in child bed." A preventive measure of indeterminate value was the "night watch" set up at the Sugar Ridge, Kentucky, camp meeting of August, 1802. This consisted of two men who patrolled the grounds and checked the meetinghouse to prevent any irregularities.

Often setting the pattern of emotionalism was the camp preacher, himself overcome by the excitement and by his own success as a soul-saver. William McGee "would sometimes exhort after the sermons, standing on the floor, or sitting, or lying in the dust, his eyes streaming, and his heart so full that he could only ejaculate 'Jesus, Jesus.'" A Methodist minister claimed that Presbyterian leaders, not being accustomed to such noise and shouting, were particularly susceptible when they yielded to their emotions and "went into great excess, and downright wildness." When preaching had ended, the service was frequently carried on by the audience — men, women, and even little children — who exhorted one another, prayed, wept, and even preached. One tale is told of a seven-year-old child who "sat on the shoulders of a man and preached til she sank exhausted on the bearer's head." There was scarcely a moment when activity was not going on, whether staged by the minister or by his congregation. "When the shout of the King was in the camp" evening worship frequently extended until dawn. Old men who knew they could not spend the night awake brought "great coats" to keep themselves warm and took short naps on the ground with the sleeping children under the shelter of the trees while the worship surged around them.

The doctrines advanced during the Great Revival consisted of the preaching of universal redemption, free and full salvation, justification by faith, regeneration by the Holy Ghost, and the joy of a living religion. Often, the method used to convey this message created bedlam. A settler of sin-soaked habits was overwhelmed by electrifying tirades. The celebrated Presbyterian revivalist, James McGready, deliberately used strong language in classifying the erring members present. Blasphemers would be dragged by the fiends of Hell into the "liquid, boiling waves" only to fall to the "deepest cavern in the flaming abyss." With the shrieks and yells encompassing him, the listener could well believe Judgment Day was upon him at that very moment, and that he himself, found lacking, was at the mouth of Hell. Such frightening preaching amidst eerie surroundings mowed the weary and overwrought sinners down in sheaves.

Less violent methods were also effectively used to bring about conversion. Songs such as "Hark My Friend That Solemn Toll" and "Pray Cast a Look Upon That Bier" reminded the sinners sadly of the universal end of man. The refrain of one song by John A. Granade, a contemporary camp meeting song writer, was aimed directly at the wavering:

> Think on what the Saviour bore,
>   In the gloomy garden,
> Sweating blood at every pore
>   To procure thy pardon;
> See him stretch'd upon the wood,
>   Bleeding, grieving, crying,
> Suff'ring all the wrath of God,
>   Groaning, gasping, dying!
>
> 'Tis done! the dreadful debt is paid,
>   The great atonement now is made;
> Sinners on me your guilt is laid,
>   For you I spilt my blood.

The first response of the crowds to the novel encampment conditions and the high-tension services was improvised and diverse. Later, these first responses tended to become stereotyped and to be repeated in every meeting. Most of the disorder and at least a part of the physical excitement came under leader control as the camp meeting developed. These first camp meetings were tumultuous almost beyond comprehension, and the effect upon the participants was in proportion. It was almost impossible for the worshipers not to feel that something great and extraordinary — that is, the active participation of the Lord — was going on.

The record of "acrobatic Christianity" at the Kentucky and Tennessee revivals is the more understandable when viewed against the backdrop of the awe-inspiring evening worship, where candlelight and campfires lit the shadowy scene, and where impassioned exhortations, prayers, and spirituals contributed to the extreme excitement of the "awakened sinners." From this high-voltage atmosphere burst forth many strange things. Five hundred or more would shout aloud "the high praises of God at once," and the "cries of the distressed . . . the rejoicing of those that were delivered from their sins of bondage" would rend the air. Women, particularly, would be affected. Some in the "transport of their feelings" hugged and kissed everyone in their vicinity. As Methodist leader John McGee described the "Ridge" meeting of August, 1800:

> The nights were truly awful; the camp ground was well illuminated; the people were differently exercised all over the ground, some exhorting, some shouting, some praying, and some crying for mercy, while others lay as dead men on the ground.

Terror, distress, and despair seemed to overcome some congregations. Saints and sinners, young and old, white and Negro would, "with a piercing scream, fall like a log on the floor, earth, or mud, and appear as dead."

Along with the shouting, the "falling exercise" was the most common of all forms of bodily excitement. According to one participant, the "falling down of multitudes, and their crying out . . . happened under the singing of Watt's Psalms and Hymns, more frequently than under the preaching of the word." When six or more hymns were sung simultaneously by different groups at a Providence, Kentucky, revival in 1801, there were accompanying violent motions of the body. Women in their frantic agitations sometimes "unconsciously tore open their bosoms and assumed indelicate attitudes." Those falling would be affected in varying degrees:

> Sometimes, when unable to stand or sit, they have the use of their hands, and can converse with perfect composure. In other cases, they are unable to speak, the pulse becomes weak, and they draw a difficult breath about once a minute; in some instances their extremities become cold, and pulsation, breathing and all the signs of life, forsake them for nearly an hour. Persons who have been in this situation have uniformly avowed, that they felt no bodily pain; that they had the entire use of their reason and reflection, and when recovered, they could relate everything that had been said or done near them.

When the "fallers" had recovered, they often arose shouting, "Praise God!" Soon those saved broke forth in a volley of exhortation. Some had seen visions, heard unspeakable words, smelled fragrant odors, and had "a delightful singing in the breast." The Reverend George Baxter reported that the first persons who lost consciousness at the Cane Ridge revival were a source of amazement for some of the Presbyterians in the audience, but after a little time "the falling down became so familiar as to excite no disturbance." In the summer of 1801, a Fleming Creek encampment had one hundred fallers, a Point Pleasant camp meeting two hundred and fifty, and at Indian Creek eight hundred persons were reported struck down. When the falling reached such alarming proportions, to prevent those stricken from "being trodden under foot by the multitude, they were collected together and laid out in order, on two squares of the meeting house, til a considerable part of the floor was covered."

Some were struck down at the camp meeting after exhibiting symptoms of "deepest impressions" and the shedding of tears; others fell on their way home, or while working in the fields. The Reverend John Lyle was more concerned about the aftereffects of this manifestations. He feared they would become habitual: "The oftener they fall they will more easily fall again, and will become at length the sport of lesser passions." A case in point was Henry McDanal's wife, who had "swooned away" for two successive days at an 1801 encampment, "and since she came home has fallen again and again and still feels guilt and misery." Lyle's application of a "vial of hartshorn" to the fallen was without success in any case. The lancet was equally ineffective, although used to such an extent that according to one excited camper, the Gasper River meeting place "was crowded with bleeding bodies like a battlefield."

In many cases toughs and scoffers fell at the services "as suddenly as if struck by lightening," sometimes at the very moment when they were cursing the revival. One unbeliever tried to prove that the fallers were shamming, and so prodded them with a nail on a stick, but to no avail. He had boasted that he would not fall, and so got liquored up, thinking that would pacify his feelings. In a short time, however, he too was struck down, and when able to speak "acknowledged himself a great sinner, and hoped for pardon through Christ."

If the seizure was not so sudden, different manifestations might occur before exhaustion set in. Numerous leaders of the Kentucky Revival, including Stone, Baxter, Finley, McNemar, and Lyle, have described versions of nervous affection, in addition to falling — jerking, rolling, dancing, running, singing, laughing, and barking. The "jerking exercise" seemed to be the most common reaction to the stimulus offered at the Kentucky and Tennessee meetings, and the one that spread most rapidly through a congregation. Even preachers were not immune. The Reverend Samuel Doak insisted he was occasionally the subject of that bodily exercise for more than twenty years. The jerks varied in some degree from person to person:

> Sometimes the subject of the jerks would be affected in some one member of the body, and sometimes in the whole system. When the head alone was affected, it would be jerked backward and forward, or from side to side, so quickly that the features of the face could not be distinguished. When the whole system was affected, I have seen the person stand in one place, and jerk backward and forward in quick succession, their heads nearly touching the floor behind and after. . . . I have inquired of those thus affected. They could not account for it; but some have told me that those were among the happiest seasons of their lives. I have seen some wicked persons thus affected, and all the time cursing the jerks, while they were thrown to the earth with a violence. Though so awful to behold, I do not remember that any of the thousands I have seen ever sustained an injury in body. This was as strange as the exercise itself.

Peter Cartwright recollected that he had seen more than five hundred persons jerking at one time at Great Revival encampments. It would excite his "risibilities" to see the ornately dressed gentlemen's and young ladies' "fine bonnets, caps, and combs fly; and so sudden would be the jerking of the head that their long loose hair would crack almost as loud as a wagoner's whip." If one eccentric reporter is to be believed, some camp leaders in anticipation of this exercise cut saplings breast high to support the jerkers, who "kicked up the earth as a horse stamping flies."

Then there was the "rolling exercise." Starting with a violent jerk that threw the person down, it doubled him up and rolled him over and over like a wheel or ball. According to a Great Revival minister, "this was considered very debasing and mortifying, especially if the person was taken in this manner through the mud and sullied therewith from head to foot."

More socially acceptable was the "dancing exercise." This movement began with the jerking of the legs and feet and proceeded to assume the characteristics of a dance, as the person affected "continued to move forward and backward in the same track or alley til nature seemed exhausted." Spectators seemed to think this was "heavenly." Some insisted that "there was nothing in it like levity, nor calculated to excite levity in beholders."

The "running exercise" was merely an attempt to escape the nervous affections. If any person tried to resist, the jerks would become more severe. One rowdy, feeling the jerks coming on, tried to escape to the bordering woods and fortify himself with some liquor, but the bottle was knocked from his hands and broken on a seedling. At this he became so enraged that he cursed and raved, but "at length he fetched a very violent jerk, snapped his neck, and soon expired, with his mouth full of cursing and bitterness." This fatality is the only one on record attributed to the jerks.

To preacher Stone the most unaccountable phenomenon was the "singing exercise." The subject, with a happy countenance, "would sing most melodiously, not from the mouth or nose, but entirely in the breast, the sounds issuing thence. . . . It was most heavenly. None could ever be tired of hearing it." Equally indescribable to Stone was the "laughing exercise." He stated that it happened frequently but only to the devout worshipers. Paradoxically, this loud hearty laughter indulged in by a few individuals was not infectious, but produced solemnity in saints and sinners. Other chroniclers called it the "holy laugh," but referred to it as a form of hysteria that gripped audiences most frequently after 1803.

The "barking exercise" was intimately related to jerking. It seemed that the disorder passed from the nerves and muscles to the mind. Men fancied themselves dogs, "went down on all fours and barked til they grew hoarse. It was reportedly no uncommon sight to behold numbers of them gathered about a tree, barking, yelping, 'treeing the devil.' " Preacher Stone discounted this dog delusion, preferring to believe that the grunts or barks resulted from the suddenness of the jerks. The name of the exercise apparently originated when an old Presbyterian clergyman in eastern Tennessee got the jerks and grasped a tree for support. Some punster who found him in that position reported he had found the minister barking up a tree.

The most fabulous of all Great Revival camp meetings, the one which seemed to incorporate and enlarge upon every excess of the previous revivals, was Cane Ridge. A "General Camp Meeting," the Cane Ridge sacramental services were staged some seven miles from Paris in Bourbon County, Kentucky. This camp meeting began on August 6, 1801, and continued for six long days. From Friday to Wednesday the frenzied worship continued night and day without intermission "either in public or private exercise of devotion." Even heavy showers failed to scatter the audience. Although it was held under joint sponsorship, Cane Ridge seems to have been largely the work of the Presbyterian Reverend Barton W. Stone, a farmer-preacher. Another churchman of the same faith reported that he attended along with "eighteen Presbyterian ministers, and Baptist and Methodist preachers," although he could not recall the exact number of the latter two groups.

Cane Ridge is important not only as a turning point in the history of the camp meeting but as a phenomenon of the Second Great Awakening. In many ways atypical, it has been the model many critics have used to create their lurid pictures of the outdoor revival. Cane Ridge was, in all probability, the most disorderly, the most hysterical, and the largest revival ever held in early-day America.

Attendance estimates of Cane Ridge range from ten to twenty-five thousand, with most authorities placing the number somewhere between the two figures. Eager participants had boasted that "many had come from Ohio"— probably from the Miami River Valley. While every shade of religious opinion was represented, there were many visitors whose religious convictions were nebulous. Tumult and disorder were inevitable when a heterogeneous group of such large proportions assembled, especially since the occasions for social companionship were so rare on the frontier.

If there is no agreement among participants as to the exact number that attended Cane Ridge, neither is there unity of opinion as to its place in history. Peter Cartwright insisted that Cane Ridge marked "the first camp-meeting ever held in the United States, and here our camp-meetings took their rise." The "Kentucky Boy" was not alone in this opinion. Confusing the issue was William Burke, Methodist participant at Cane Ridge. He insisted that this sacramental occasion was no camp meeting at all. While it was true that there were carriages and wagons on the grounds, "not a single tent was to be found, neither was any such thing as a camp meeting, heard of at that time." Burke himself had the only true tent, one he made on the spot out of poles and papaw bushes.

The Cane Ridge services, if they can be dignified by that name, almost defy description. A visitor to the Sunday sessions reported four different groups meeting simultaneously at various crude speaker's stands about a hundred yards apart. One of the rostrums contained a colored exhorter addressing his race. Another contemporary described the continuous preaching and exhorting. The attractions that caught his eye were the many "small [prayer] circles of ten or twelve," close together where "all engaged in singing Watts's and Hart's hymns." At the same time a minister would step upon a stump or a log and would attract as many as could collect around him. William Burke's technique is a case in point. He mounted a log and

> commenced reading a hymn with an audible voice, and by the time we concluded singing and praying we had around us, standing on their feet, by fair calculation ten thousand people. I gave out my text in the following words: "For we must all stand before the judgment seat of Christ," and before I concluded my voice was not to be heard for the groans of the distressed and the shouts of triumph. . . . Here I remained Sunday night, and Monday and Monday night; and during that time there was not a single moment's cessation, but the work went on.

Peter Cartwright said that at times there were more than a thousand shouting at once, creating such a volume of noise that the sound carried for miles. The overwhelming impact of this deafening uproar and contagious bodily excitement has been depicted by James B. Finley, who was then, according to his own appraisal, somewhat of a free thinker in religious matters.

> The noise was like the roar of Niagara. The vast sea of human beings seemed to be agitated as if by a storm. I counted seven ministers, all preaching at one time, some on stumps, others in wagons, and one . . . was standing on a tree which had, in falling, lodged against . . . another. Some of the people were singing, others praying, some crying for mercy in the most piteous accents, while others were shouting most vociferously. While witnessing these scenes, a peculiarly-strange sensation, such as I had never felt before, came over me. My heart beat tumultuously, my knees trembled, my lip quivered, and I felt as though I must fall to the ground. A strange supernatural power seemed to pervade the entire mass of mind there collected. . . . Soon after I left and went into the woods, and there I strove to rally and man up my courage.
>
> After some time I returned to the scene of excitement, the waves of which, if possible, had risen still higher. The same awfulness of feeling came over me. I stepped up on to a log, where I could have a better view of the surging sea of humanity. The scene that then presented itself to my mind was indescribable. At one time I saw at least five hundred swept down in a moment, as if a battery of a thousand guns had been opened upon them, and then immediately followed shrieks and shouts that rent the very heavens. . . . I fled for the woods a second time, and wished I had staid at home.

Probably the most intense excitement at Cane Ridge was experienced when the Sunday sacrament was served to some eight hundred to eleven hundred Presbyterian communicants and an indeterminate number of Methodists. Then the delivery of the impassioned sermons and exhortations prior to the sacrament resulted in some breath-taking spectacles. One preacher commented on the "one hundred persons of all classes, the learned and the unlearned, at once on the ground crying for mercy of all ages from eight to sixty years"; another reported that "undue excitement of animal feeling" resulted in at least one thousand persons' being swept into the falling exercise. The old campaigner, James Crawford, perhaps the "most reliable" of the Presbyterian frontier preachers, conscientiously counted the fallers and gave the higher figure of three thousand. A regular system of caring for the afflicted was in force. When a person was struck down he was carried out of the congregation, and then some minister or exhorter prayed with him against the background of a hymn "suitable to the occasion."

At this largest of all encampments the greatest number of sexual irregularities occurred. After the Saturday evening worship, for instance, six men were found lying under a preaching stand with a woman of easy virtue. The following evening a couple were caught in the act of adultery. James B. Finley, present at Cane Ridge, observed that while the religious services were going on, "all manner of wickedness was going on without." "Men," he continued, "furious with the effects of the maddening bowl would outrage all decency by their conduct." Camp sponsors declared that such carnal actions of "unclean persons" were deliberately aimed at bringing the religious revival into disrepute. Thus they discussed plans for supervision — having the stands watched and placing elders in the meetinghouse to make certain of the separation of the sexes in the sleeping arrangements.

There is no means of weighing the seriousness of the impression that Cane Ridge made upon the hearts and nervous systems of its thousands of participants. Certainly thousands were deeply moved. The number of those who professed conversion was estimated somewhere between one thousand and two thousand. The healing touch of revivalism was apparent on every hand. Among the happy converts were many men destined to be vigorous champions of the Christian life. James B. Finley, the celebrated circuit rider, dated his conversion from his troubled state of mind while a Cane Ridge visitor.

But what of the Kentucky Revival as a whole? Whether the majority of the conversions were lasting is problematical. Yet one contemporary historian, evaluating the movement in 1809, wrote:

The effects of these camp meetings were of a mixed nature. They were doubtless attended for improper purposes by a few licentious persons and by others with a view of obtaining a handle to ridicule all religion. . . . The free intercourse of all ages and sexes under cover of night and the woods was not without its temptations. It is also to be feared that they gave rise to false notions of religion by laying too much stress on bodily exercises, and substituting them in the place of moral virtues or inward piety. These are too often considered as evidences of a change of heart and affections, though they neither proved or disproved anything of the kind. After each deduction is made of these several accounts, it must be acknowledged that the good result-ing from the camp meeting greatly preponderated over the evil. They roused that indifference to the future destiny of man which is too common, and gave rise to much serious thoughtfullness on subjects confessedly of the most in-teresting nature.

Visible proof of the effectiveness of Great Revival camp meetings is of-fered also by the tremendous growth in church membership of those churches which used them. In Kentucky alone, between 1800 and 1803, the Baptists gained ten thousand members, and the Methodists about an equal number. The Presbyterians also added large numbers to their congregations during these years, although later evangelical schisms were responsible for the Presbyterian church's losing ground in the West. During the period in question the Methodists enjoyed an average increase of two thousand mem-bers a year, which necessitated a rapid division and redivision in church territories, districts, and circuits.

The 1801 Bourbon County meeting at Cane Ridge not only helped mul-tiply church membership but also gave a powerful impetus to the revival itself. Richard McNemar declared that "the work breaking out in North Carolina resulted from people who had been to Cane Ridge." As the move-ment continued, the charting of its progress became increasingly difficult, as it spread out in ever-widening circles. A concurrent revival in the East, although mainly restricted to indoor "protracted meetings," made it appear that the "heavenly fire" from Kentucky had spread in almost every direction.

By the year 1803 the religious excitement had caught on in the Western Reserve District of Ohio, had spread back into western Georgia, North Caro-lina, and thence to South Carolina, and was strong in other parts of the East. An ardent advocate of the camp meeting, the Reverend Henry Smith, staged one in Virginia while serving on the Winchester Circuit in 1803 — this at a time when his constituents insisted: "It may do in the West, but it won't do here." From Virginia the outdoor revival spread through neigh-boring Maryland, Delaware, Pennsylvania, and New York, and fanned out into Massachusetts, Connecticut, Vermont, and New Hampshire. The camp meeting even caught on in certain sections of Canada. When settlers moved forward into the Mississippi Territory the open-air revival soon followed. In a short while evangelical Christianity blanketed the entire nation and found in the camp meeting its favorite method.

STUDY GUIDE

1. What might have led ministers living in such sparsely settled states as Ohio and Kentucky to cooperate with preachers of different faiths in "Union" camp meetings? What factors led to the breakdown of coop-eration?

2. Considering the lives of the people in these areas, what might have contributed to their massive participation in camp meetings and to the exaggerated responses they displayed? What evidence does Johnson provide that the occasion might have been as much social as religious?

3. Different observers have given different explanations of religious exercises such as falling and barking. What arguments can you develop to support each of the following explanations: (a) the exercises represent a strong religious response by people who could not attend worship regularly; (b) the exercises provide people who have lived in social isolation for an extended period with a means of "letting off steam"; (c) the exercises are a result of poor diet, poor health, and exhaustion produced by the camp meeting environment?

4. Consider the reform movements of the 1830s, such as abolitionism and women's rights, and then think about the words of the Civil War song "Battle Hymn of the Republic." Is it legitimate to suggest that the sense of mission and the emotional urgency of Protestantism in this period shaped these other aspects of American life? Or was the character of American religious life simply a reflection of a broader sense of missionary zeal and destiny among all of the American people in that period?

BIBLIOGRAPHY

There are a number of works on religion in the West and the great religious revival of the nineteenth century. One of the most prolific writers on American religious history was William W. Sweet, who wrote *Revivalism in America: Its Origin, Growth and Decline* * (New York, 1944) and also edited four volumes of writings entitled *Religion on the American Frontier* (New York and Chicago, 1931–1946). Ranking with Johnson's work as one of the most interesting books on the revival is Bernard A. Weisberger, *They Gathered at the River: The Story of the Great Revivalists and Their Impact upon Religion in America* * (Boston, 1958). William G. McLoughlin, Jr., *Modern Revivalism: Charles Grandison Finney to Billy Graham* (New York, 1959) is a delightful series of sketches of revivalists from the early nineteenth to the mid-twentieth century. Among special studies on certain regions or aspects of revivalism, two of the best are Timothy L. Smith, *Revivalism and Social Reform in Mid-Nineteenth Century America* (New York, 1957) and Whitney R. Cross, *The Burned-Over District* * (Ithaca, N.Y., 1950), which concerns the revival spirit in New York State.

Besides the studies of individual denominations, there are several general books on American Protestantism. Winthrop S. Hudson, *American Protestantism* * (Chicago, 1961) is a general survey which provides an excellent introduction to the subject. Another book by Hudson, *Religion in America* * (New York, 1965), is also worth reading, as are the works of two distinguished scholars — H. Richard Niebuhr, *The Kingdom of God in America* * (Chicago, 1937) and Sidney E. Mead, *The Lively Experiment: The Shaping of Christianity in America* (New York, 1963).

There are two basic introductions to Catholicism and Judaism in the United States, the bibliographies of which contain references to many other works: John T. Ellis, *American Catholicism,* 2nd ed. * (Chicago, 1969) and Nathan Glazer, *American Judaism* * (Chicago, 1957). Alice Felt Tyler's *Freedom's Ferment: Phases of American Social History to 1860* * (Minneapolis, Minn., 1944) describes some of the many smaller sects and new religions that arose in the early nineteenth century. Many of the special works on those subjects lack objectivity, but two good works on the Mormons are Thomas F. O'Dea, *The Mormons* * (Chicago, 1957) and Fawn M. Brodie, *No Man Knows My History: The Life of Joseph Smith, the Mormon Prophet* (New York, 1945).

The most comprehensive book on the religious history of American blacks was published more than fifty years ago: Carter G. Woodson, *The History of the Negro Church* (Washington, D.C., © 1921). Shorter studies include E. Franklin Frazier, *The Negro Church in America* (New York, © 1963) and chapter 42 of the newest general survey of American religious history, Sydney E. Ahlstrom, *A Religious History of the American People* (New Haven, Conn., and London, Eng., © 1972).

"The Dinner Party" by Henry Sargent, 1821. This luxury contrasts with the alleged equality of "the Age of the Common Man."

EDWARD PESSEN

Inequality in American Life

The decade of the 1830s, long known as the Age of the Common Man, was one of the first great periods of reform in the United States. Major constitutional and political changes intended to extend the suffrage and democratize politics were undertaken. The women's rights movement was begun, serious attempts at labor organization were made, the antislavery crusade gained new support, and much was done to improve the condition of the unfortunate and to assist the handicapped. Yet Edward Pessen, in the following selection, questions just how equalitarian the Age of the Common Man was, and he suggests that neither the political nor the social democracy was as real as some accounts might lead one to believe.

 In terms of surface appearances and underlying realities, American life in our own time affords striking parallels to this period, which is also called the Age of Jackson. With the recent lowering of the voting age to eighteen, the suffrage has been extended to more people than in any previous period of American history. The years from 1950 to 1970 also seemed to be marked by an extraordinary affluence and material well-being among the American people. Never had there been so many government agencies working with so much money to improve educational opportunities, alleviate poverty, and prevent abuses and discrimination against minorities, consumers, and other groups. Despite all these advances, increasing criticism and doubts about American life were voiced. Some questioned the reality of governmental concern and its responsiveness to the average citizen. Others criticized the huge profits made by giant corporations while many Americans were living in desperate poverty. The irre-

sponsibility of businesses in polluting the environment, the unbelievable conditions of migrant farm workers, and the miles of
ghetto areas led many to question how democratic, equalitarian,
and humane American society was.

Judging a country's political democracy, social equalitarianism, or standard of living poses many difficult questions. When
we speak, for example, of democracy, do we mean simply the
right to vote, or can a government based on a broad suffrage still
be quite unresponsive and controlled by special interests? Is social equality determined simply by an absence of hereditary position, by attitudes toward class, by wealth, or by social mobility?
Is a country's economic justice to be judged by equality of opportunity or by the standard of living it provides for everyone,
even for those who — because they are handicapped, unskilled,
or psychologically unemployable — cannot take advantage of the
opportunity to earn a good living? By carefully considering Pessen's critique of Jacksonian America, one may achieve some perspective on the accomplishments, and the failures, of the United
States in providing a good life for citizens today.

From May 11, 1831, to February 20, 1832, two young French aristocrats
visited this country, commissioned by their government to study the American prison system. Among the results of their brief visit was a valuable account they wrote of American penitentiaries that came out in 1833. They
observed a good deal more than prisons, however. In 1835 the more thoughtful of the two visitors, Alexis de Tocqueville, published the first part of
Democracy in America, one of the most brilliant and penetrating studies
of a civilization ever written. Surely it is among the most influential, as well,
for from that day to our own the period it described has been known as the
Age of the Common Man, in perfect accord with Tocqueville's own evaluation of it. Fashions in the interpretation of Jacksonian politics or banking
or labor may come and go, but the reputation of its society or social developments remains fixed, resistant to the ravages of time and changing custom.
Now, as then, the second quarter of the 19th century is known as the era
when Tom, Dick, and Harry came into their own.

The belief has prevailed that if the United States was not altogether a
classless society, it was the nearest thing to one that was conceivable. With

Adapted with permission from Pessen, *Jacksonian America* (Homewood, Ill.; The Dorsey
Press, © 1969), chapter 3.

the exception of the unfortunate Negroes, the Indians and perhaps the recently arrived Irish immigrants, Americans overwhelmingly belonged to the middle class. While wealth and poverty existed here, both extremes were atypical and likely to be ephemeral. . . .

One of the important foundations of the belief in the era's social democracy is its reputation for sweeping political reforms. The view is well known. New western states brought with them into the union democratic constitutions. In the older eastern states the overthrow of property requirements for voting, the installation of a popular system for choosing presidential electors, the discarding of the caucus system for making nominations, meant the removal of obstacles thwarting the common man's control of government. The spoils system, particularly Jackson's own rationale for it, stressing as it did the ordinary citizen's ability to perform the tasks of government, was further evidence that politically as in other ways the age belonged to the common man. For that matter, the rise of Andrew Jackson and the other "new men" who came to the fore after the end of the Virginia Dynasty was widely regarded as the ascension of self-made common men — albeit men of unusual ability and determination — to the highest levels of government. That humble origins — actual or alleged — were all the rage in the era of "Tippecanoe and Tyler too," was a sign that the people would no longer settle for leadership by an elite. Tom, Dick, and Harry insisted on leaders in their own image. That some of these notions are sheer myth does not detract from their influence. They remain embedded in the nation's memory of its political past as a dramatic reminder of the rise of the common man.

Another reason for the era's reputation is simply that there is much evidence for it. Foreign visitors were amazed at the material well-being evidently enjoyed by most if not all Americans. The sympathetic Michel Chevalier who, like his young predecessors, had been sent here by the French government in 1834 — in his case to study American public works — became so fascinated with this society that he extended his stay to two years. According to him, the "one thing in the United States that strikes a stranger is the appearance of general ease in the condition of the people of this country." He found no paupers — "at least not in the northern and western states." He observed with some enthusiasm that in New York City, "every man was warmly clad . . . every woman had her cloak and bonnet of the latest Paris fashion." The eminent Sir Charles Lyell, touring the country a few years after the Panic of 1837, reported that he had "met with no beggars, witnessed no signs of want but everywhere the most unequivocal proofs of prosperity.". . .

The glad tidings were also discerned by Americans, Edward Everett detecting an exuberant prosperity in the nation's cities; William Dean Howells' father recalling that the typical farm folk of the Ohio Valley during the era may have lived plainly but "they usually had enough to eat." Ordinary farm folk began in the early decades of the century to use or bring into their homes articles and implements earlier enjoyed only by the well-to-do, commodities serviceable in function if lacking in decorative detail. Gourmets might be discomfited at its quality but as has been seen there was universal agreement that the quantity of food was more than ample. In fact, fastidious Americans and foreigners alike were somewhat repelled by the mammoth helpings of meat, fowl, dairy products, cakes, and beverages devoured by Americans of all descriptions, at hotels, boarding houses, or other public places. That the nation's reputation in the culinary arts was a low one was yet one more example that in this as in other respects, standards were based not on the desires of the sophisticated but on the wants of commoners.

James Fenimore Cooper and the eminent New Yorker, Philip Hone, agreed that the deterioration they noted in the quality of American life was an unhappy manifestation of the levelling tendencies that marked the era. Visitors found Americans noticeably sensitive and what they were most touchy about was any word, sign, or gesture remotely suggesting that any American was not as good as any other human being on the face of the globe. The conspicuous slouching done by Americans at every variety of public place — to the dismay of fastidious visitors — seemed only one more expression of the common man's influence on manners, not to mention his contempt for the niceties he evidently identified with an aristocratic society. Visitors were also startled at the social democracy of a society in which "a coarse familiarity is assumed by the grossest and the lowest in their intercourse with the highest and most refined." In this country of easy, endless handshaking — which so complicated the assignment of those observers who were trying to fix the social standing of particular Americans — prisoners were even observed shaking hands with a warden. And in what other society could "any man's son . . . become the equal of any other man's son?" Egalitarian ideals also influenced art and science. Painters now found their most precious themes in the most commonplace subjects, while in medicine, the attempt to restrict medical practice to the licensed or trained was rudely challenged as a species of monopoly by what Richard Shryock has called Jacksonian Democrats proclaiming "their inalienable rights to life, liberty and quackery."

European visitors to Jacksonian America were particularly influential in fostering the impression of its egalitarianism. In view of the very great role played by the visitors in establishing the prevailing image of Jacksonian equality, it is useful — even at the risk of being repetitive — to examine closely the special problems they faced as analysts of American society. . . .

All of the visitors had foibles. The predilections of the more gifted commentators are of special consequence in view of their greater influence. Mrs. [Frances] Trollope . . . was frankly unhappy with the American people. Francis Grund, on the other hand, was a cheerful and excellent reporter, whose enthusiastic admiration for democracy and Democrats led him to give short shrift to their opponents. Miss Harriet Martineau was indefatigable and omnipresent, brimming over with perhaps too much confidence in her powers of understanding, a steady and sensible observer beyond doubt, though inclined to wear rose-colored glasses. Captain Marryat, one of the most widely read of the visitors, was prone to exaggeration and even worse, managed to involve himself in situations so embarrassing, even ridiculous, during the course of his stay, that one wonders about his judgment. At one point he had the bad judgment of being in bed with a married woman and the worse luck of having her husband hiding under it. Chevalier, like his more famous countryman, was prone to indulge his sociological bent, producing some striking generalizations, nuggets of capsuled abstraction that are stimulating in the extreme, if somewhat disquieting for the frailness of their documentation. (Did *every* New York woman actually wear the latest Parisian fashions?) Every one of these observers tried honestly and fairly to report the truth, but the fact remains that their commentary is at least as much a Rorschach into their own mentality as it is a reliable report on American society. . . .

Another important similarity in the European commentators was this: whether friendly or hostile to America, they all had a tendency to exaggerate the democratic or egalitarian features of American society. Doctrinaire conservatives and antidemocrats, sincerely scornful of the misguided system that subordinated the gifted to the misfits, had no compunctions about attributing all manner of democratic excess to the United States. Since this country was regarded by so many English liberals and reformers as the hope of the future, visiting Tories believed that they scored points against their political enemies at home by stressing the weakest and most sordid parts of the American system. And to dedicated conservatives what was weaker and more sordid than a chaotic society without ranks, with no barriers protecting the better sort from the worse, with "a coarse familiarity" shown by the lower orders toward their superiors? A society without respect for tradition or order, lacking a class capable of imposing standards and values worthy of respect? Warmhearted English friends of the common man, on the other hand, hoped to strengthen the cause of democracy at home by emphasizing its happy effects on the "fabled republic." . . .

The burden of my argument to this point is that the Jacksonian era's reputation for egalitarianism, to the extent that it is based on the observations of contemporary, particularly foreign, observers, does not rest on a firm foundation. When the other bases of its reputation are examined critically, they also turn out to be less than solid. . . .

A strong case can be made . . . that not equality but disparity of condition was the rule in Jacksonian America. It was manifested above all in the nation's cities which were becoming increasingly important in an era marked by a great urban expansion. Old cities grew at an unprecedented rate while new ones were built seemingly overnight. Rochester was not the only city in which tree stumps could be found in the cellars of the buildings that had been put up around them. In the west, too, cities became increasingly important, attracting large amounts of speculative capital, providing their classic economic functions for their hinterlands, and acting as a magnet to settlers, many of whom "came across the mountains in search of promising towns as well as good land." Turner's frontier, as Richard C. Wade has shown, also included Cincinnati, Lexington, Pittsburgh, St. Louis, and Louisville.

The housing of the urban rich, as a case in point, set them apart from the great majority of town dwellers. In western cities choice locations were preempted by the well-to-do; "other people moved to less desirable areas." In the east, observers commented on the "genteel dwelling houses [of the rich]," made of fine stone or brick, with white marble increasingly used for doorsteps, window sills, lintels, and entire first stories. Pure silver ornaments and "costly European importations [that] decorated the homes of the rich" led one almost abject admirer of this country to concede that there was something in such refinements "very unlike republican simplicity."

Working people lived very differently. According to Mathew Carey, the wealthy philanthropist, working-class families in Philadelphia were squeezed together, 55 families to a tenement, lacking "the accommodation of a privy for their use." Their houses, according to a recent study, "were strung along, side to side as boxcars . . . obscured from the street view. . . ." Their tenants typically had one room per family, living "huddled to the rear . . . victims of a parsimonious building policy which meant crowding, noise, inadequate sanitation, lack of facilities for rubbish removal." The fresh water newly pumped from the Schuylkill — and which was so admired by many European travelers — went into the homes of the wealthy but not to the working classes. According to the labor press, the major cities of the nation abounded with dismal alleys, "the abodes of the miserable objects of grinding poverty." Andrew Jackson and Nicholas Biddle, on the other hand, could repair to the "Hermitage," outside of Nashville, or "Andalusia," near Philadelphia, similar in their opulence for all the political differences of their owners.

Glaring disparities were not confined to housing alone. If beggars were not readily apparent on the streets, they could be discerned in less public places. Bell had seen "scores of destitute homeless wretches lying on bulks or under the sheds about the markets of New York and Philadelphia." Fellow travelers claimed they saw as much poverty here as elsewhere. Statistical studies confirmed the rising rates of pauperism and of those too poor to pay a minimal tax. Nor does the evidence indicate that membership in these forlorn groups was swelled by the dramatic failure of eminent men. Rather some poor men became poorer. Imprisonment for debt was also on the rise, in some cities evidently accounting for the majority of men in jail. This abuse was shortly to be outlawed, in large part because its negative effects were felt by businessmen as well as by the poor. In the Jacksonian era, however, its main victims were men who owed debts of $20 or less. Abject poverty was not the characteristic lot of Americans who were not wealthy, but neither was it a negligible problem. One labor newspaper edited by the respected George Henry Evans — who was to become "the heart and soul" of the land reform movement of the 1840's — estimated that in Boston in 1834 more than 5,000 persons were "aided annually as paupers." The reliable Edward Abdy reported that not only was pauperism increasing in the nation's major cities, but that "there . . . [was] little reason to hope it . . . [could] be checked by the judicious application of charity."

The great bulk of Americans living in towns and cities were neither paupers nor debtors facing imprisonment. They were for the most part artisans or mechanics, to a lesser extent small business people and less than wealthy professionals. If they did not live in penury, the nation's journeymen lived and worked under conditions of extreme difficulty, far removed indeed from the "general equality of condition" mentioned by visitors who merely glanced their way. For the better part of the period, artisans put in a working day that rivalled the farmers' sunup to sundown. The spectre of unemployment haunted them, particularly in the cold weather months of short working days. And when they did work, artisans were paid in a paper currency that invariably was not worth its face value. They had little to fall back on when their shops closed down. In the decade of inflation that preceded the Panic of 1837, workers discovered that their wages did not keep up with runaway prices. The depression that came on the heels of the Panic kept perhaps one-third of the working classes unemployed for long periods in the early 1840's. Quite apart from the depression years, labor fared poorly during the Jacksonian era. Most modern studies indicate that real wages stood still during an otherwise exuberant economic surge in the 1830's, at best approximating what they had been at the turn of the century. . . .

. . . Wages of farm hands and farm labor were even lower than those earned by urban workers. Impressionistic evidence, in the form of diaries and journals left by moderately successful independent farm families in different sections of the country, suggests the monotony, the hard work and the generally poor quality of life enjoyed by the nation's yeomanry during the era. Thomas Coffin's family in New Hampshire worked hard, lived frugally and had little leisure. Ridding the farm of vermin constituted an amusement or form of recreation for the young. A large farm that was regarded as "fairly well improved," located on one of the "better developed farm communities" in Iredell County, North Carolina, characteristically eked out a living, its "produce yielding only a small return for the work involved, while prices of necessities bought were high." Living conditions were indeed discouraging to men who found that their incomes from sales frequently only balanced their purchases. American farmers in the antebellum period were also convinced that their status was low. The "agrarian myth" that romanticized rural life was either unknown to most farmers or disbelieved by them. . . .

It was not only radical labor leaders who charged that real equality did not exist in the United States. The point was also made by conservative Americans of the highest standing. John Quincy Adams had told Tocqueville that while in the north there was "a great equality before the law, . . . it ceases absolutely in the habits of life. There are upper classes and working classes." In Philadelphia Tocqueville had been advised by an eminent attorney, "there is more social equality with you at home [in France] than with us. Here . . . wealth gives a decided pre-eminence." Peter Duponceau confirmed Adams' point "that equality exists only on the street. Money creates extreme inequalities in society." But such comments seem to have made little impression on a mind that was busy creating theories based on very different assumptions. Some years later James Fenimore Cooper would assert that in the United States "inequality . . . [existed] and in some respects, with stronger features than it is usual to meet with in the rest of christendom." Thomas Hamilton would not go so far: the United States was no worse than Britain in this regard. But it was nonsense to call this country the land of equality merely because it lacked a "privileged order." Chevalier, too, impressed as he was by the absence here of aristocratic titles or an idle rich, concluded that great inequalities in income were becoming more and more the rule, dividing society as forcefully as name and land did in Europe. Even Mrs. Trollope, who had been willing to concede an equality of condition for which she had no admiration, came to the conclusion that the American poor were "kept in a state of irritation by feeling that their boasted equality is a falsehood." For all the absence of aristocratic distinctions in this country, it enjoyed only a "fictitious equality."

The case for egalitarianism is a subtle one, depending on a number of propositions that have nothing to do with wealth as such. But its underlying axiom, alleging the slightness of disparities in material condition, does not come off too well. The American rich lived a most distinctive life of relative comfort and splendor that differed dramatically, not only from the lives of the poor, but from the experience of the great majority of ordinary citizens. True, the rich were few in number. Moses Beach's list of New York City's rich men, the Boston list of the most heavily taxed, Philadelphia's roster of wealthy citizens, contained closer to 1 percent than 5 of their cities' populations. But that is precisely the case in most societies marked by inequality. Were the rich more typical, yeasayers could quite rightly make much of the great amount of room at the top available in the egalitarian society they admire.

The egalitarian theory is also based on certain assumptions concerning social class and its role. It does not deny the existence of classes but rather stresses the ease of movement between them. The term "class" has been variously defined, of course. Sociologists have come to no agreement: one school emphasizing wealth and income; another, occupation; another, family; another, such intangibles as prestige and standing; another, style of life; another, religion and nationality; Miss Nancy Mitford recently redirected attention to the importance of speech; while eclectics have combined some or all of these plus other attributes to fashion their concept of class. In this discussion, the term will assume a group that is distinguished from others mainly by its members' means of making a living, the costliness and quality of the life they command, and the comparative influence and prestige they enjoy.

E. Digby Baltzell has sensibly written that "leadership and some form of stratification are inherent in all human social organization." When we leave the drawing board or the realm of the purely theoretical, there are no classless societies, certainly not in the civilized world. The important questions concerning a society have to do not with whether classes exist, but with the extent of class differences, the relative ease of access to the most favored class, and the degree of power and influence wielded by the latter. Where differences are slight, upward mobility is great, and power is with the middling orders, the society can properly be adjudged socially democratic. Jacksonian society, of course, enjoys just such a reputation.

The case for social fluidity, as might have been expected, was put most forcefully by Tocqueville. "In America," he wrote, "most of the rich men were formerly poor." It is a striking idea, of profound importance, not least because for later periods in American history it does not seem to be true. Stephan Thernstrom's recent study of working people in the Massachusetts town of Newburyport, for the period 1850 to 1880, shows that while parents were pleased at the rise to more prestigious working-class occupations that was made by some of their sons, no dramatic movement to the top took place. Earlier studies of the social backgrounds of rich men of the late 19th and 20th centuries, disclosed that, for the most part, they were sons of men of unusual wealth, prestige, education, favored religious denomination and other attributes of high rank. If Tocqueville was right, then the Jacksonian era stands alone for the 19th century. He may yet turn out to be right, but unfortunately his assertions are based not on substantial evidence, but rather on his own deductions, largely from what one informant told him concerning the disappearance of the law of entail in this country.

Alexandra McCoy's recent study of Wayne County, Michigan, for the latter part of the Jacksonian era, defines mobility as "the achievement of wealth by men of lower class origins" and finds very little evidence of the phenomenon. The economic elite of that important area were not self-made men. Like the successful men of a half century later, shown by William Miller and his students to be fortunate sons of wealthy fathers, Wayne County's rich seem to have "enjoyed an advantaged early environment to enable them to start a business in the west." Plebeians could not afford the five or six thousand dollars required. If the wealthy were born of the rich, they also tended to remain in that closed circle. "Those [in Wayne County] who were at the top in 1844 tended to stay there. Only one took a fall." The eminent modern historian, Oscar Handlin, long ago disclosed that Boston in the 1830's and 1840's "offered few opportunities to those who lacked the twin advantages of birth and capital." Boston was not unique. . . .

Richard Wade has shown that even in the youthful cities of the West, at the beginning of the era, merchants made up a distinctively wealthy and socially prominent group. "Their wives belonged to the same clubs, their children went to the same schools, and they participated in the same amusements and recreations." They lived in their own districts, physically separated from others; "by 1830, social lines could be plotted on a map of the city." They went to great pains to match the lavish living of the older upper classes of the eastern cities, succeeding to a large degree. Many of them lived in "villas." Expensive furniture, overloaded tables, fancy dress for dinner, extravagant entertainment, elegant carriages, ornate cotillions led by dancing masters imported from the East, characterized merchant life in the "frontier towns." Wade notes dryly that in the first decades of the 19th century, "local boosters talked a great deal about egalitarianism in the West, but urban practice belied the theory. Social lines developed very quickly and although never drawn as tightly as in Eastern cities, they denoted meaningful distinctions." Vigne found "an aristocracy in every city of the Union; and perhaps as many as four or five different sects or circles, notwithstanding their boasted equality of condition.". . .

The egalitarian theory is in part based on the belief that the common man dominated Jacksonian politics. Popular suffrage meant to Tocqueville, the "sovereignty of the people. . . . The people reign in the American political world," he wrote, "as the Deity does in the universe." Chevalier called America a "popular despotism." By this theory of politics, near oligarchies which regularly send 95 percent or better of their citizenry to the polls are actually ruled by their voters. It is not necessary to subscribe to an ultra-realist view of politics to detect the naïveté in such an analysis.

In Jacksonian America, the common man's possession of the suffrage subjected him to much flattery by political leaders, for it is quite true that his votes decided whether this or that one would take office. (Tocqueville, who was no great admirer of the common man, hoped that direct elections would be increasingly replaced by indirect ones, thus minimizing the dangers of the manhood suffrage.) In his brilliant book of two decades ago, Arthur M. Schlesinger, Jr., synthesized, updated, and gave new life to a traditional interpretation which held that since the party battles of the era were fought over great social and economic principles, the common man's choice of Jackson over his enemies was fraught with crucial political significance and was as well a demonstration of popular power. That is not the view, however, of many of the excellent studies of the past 20 years. They tell a tale of major parties during the Jacksonian era, which, for all the difference in their political rhetoric, were more like than unlike, not least in the extent to which their basic structures and policymaking apparatus were controlled by unusually wealthy men.

How much power could the common man exercise when there was little real choice left open to him by the parties that counted? In the states, small groups of insiders had a tight control over nominations and policymaking, with popular influence more nominal than real. Whether in New York or Mississippi, Pennsylvania or South Carolina, Michigan or New Jersey, Massachusetts or Florida, Tennessee or Ohio, Democratic leaders, more often than not, were speculators, editors, lawyers, the "land office crowd," coming from the "wealthier elements in the society," typically of the same economic background as their Whig opponents. For that matter, Andrew Jackson himself, not to mention the men who launched him in presidential politics, was uncommonly wealthy. As Robert V. Remini has noted, "it cost a great deal of money to enter politics." Jackson may have spoken in ringing terms of the common man's right to high office, as well as his ability to perform its tasks, but in point of fact Jackson, like his "aristocratic" predecessors, filled Cabinet and high civil service posts with men who possessed unusual wealth and social eminence. This is not to say that the era's leaders dealt with political issues primarily in terms of class interest. Rich men no more than poor live by bread alone. It is not farfetched, however, to interpret the lack of real issues on the national level in the decade of the 1820's, or the ambiguity of issues in the subsequent decades of the Jacksonian era, as due in part to the backgrounds of the era's leaders.

Wealth exerted political power most directly on the local level. At a time when local boards of government typically received small salaries or none at all, wealthy merchants sat in the seats of municipal power, determining policies and expenditures. The way of life of the town dweller was significantly affected by upper-class decisions to build wharves or expensive market houses rather than improve the night watch or drain pools. Robert Dahl's recent study of New Haven politics underscores these points. In that small eastern city, prior to 1842, "public office was almost the exclusive prerogative of the patrician families. . . . Wealth, social position and education" were the main determinants of patrician status. During this period, according to Dahl, control over such a factor as wealth enabled the individual who enjoyed it to "be better off in almost every other resource" — such as "social standing and control over office." The prime beneficiaries of this "cumulative inequality" were the old merchant elite. A revolution of sorts was to take place in 1842 with the election of a wealthy manufacturer to the office of mayor, ushering "in a period during which wealthy entrepreneurs dominated public life almost without interruption for more than half a century." I am not sure whether the Jacksonian era was still in force when new wealth replaced older in the City Hall of New Haven, but in the one case as in the other, working people and so-called "ethnic groups" made up nothing better than a passive electorate. Until well after the middle of the 19th century, the city's aldermen continued to be composed almost entirely of wealthy professionals and businessmen in the entrepreneurial as during the patrician phase of their city's political evolution. Nor was

New Haven atypical. Elite upper classes controlled mayors' offices and municipal councils or boards of aldermen in New York City and Boston as well as in Detroit and the cities of the South and West for most of the era.

The Jacksonian era witnessed no breakdown of a class society in America. If anything, class lines hardened, distinctions widened, tensions increased. Wade noted that while, with the passage of time, "new families entered the circle [of the merchant elite] and older ones fell out," there was also a "heightened . . . sense of separateness, . . . the circle itself becoming tighter and more distinct." Communities already stratified "found lines sharpened, class division deepened," as they grew in size and as their economies became more specialized. The wealthiest merchants, according to the testimony of their own diaries and of travelers' accounts, became even more class conscious. Their children had absorbed so well the lesson of social exclusiveness that, if anything, they "moved in an even more insulated circle than their parents." In eastern cities it has also been noted that social stratification intensified during the Jacksonian era.

Has the time not come, then, to discard the label, the Era of the Common Man? Like its companion designation, the Age of Egalitarianism, it has rested on questionable assumptions. Struck by surface examples of popular influence or by the absence of aristocratic titles in America, we have jumped to unwarranted conclusions. The absence of a caste system has been interpreted as though it denoted the absence of a class system. It is true that, theoretically, individuals could move freely up the social ladder, actually doing so if they had the talent and good fortune. But these restless men on the make should not be confused with the bulk of the nation's workingmen or small farmers. An expanding capitalistic society everywhere dips into the less privileged strata to provide some of the manpower it requires for entrepreneurial leadership. There is no evidence, however, that during the Jacksonian era the poor made dramatic movement up the social ladder in greater numbers than they made the move westward to Turner's frontier and its alleged safety valve.

The belief that the era was dominated by the common man has rested on political assumptions that have been pretty well demolished. That white men without property had won the right to vote, even before Andrew Jackson stood for the presidency, is something that every politician knew. Shrewd men in politics, therefore, paid lip service to the common man, managing to explain their own origins, their careers, and their political beliefs in terms that were highly flattering to Tom, Dick, and Harry. Though Jackson spoke of turning high office over to ordinary men, he did not do so. The men surrounding the Old General, like those who ran his party on the state level, were decidedly uncommon or wealthy. Common men there were in abundance. That pragmatists in high places addressed them artfully, however, is less proof that the common man held power than that skillful politicians knew how to delude him into believing that he did.

An age is not ordinarily named after its most typical members, regardless of their real power. For if it were, almost every age would have to be known as the era of the ordinary man. Whatever it might have been, the era named after Andrew Jackson was neither an age of egalitarianism nor of the common man.

STUDY GUIDE

1. What special problems does Pessen find in the writings of European observers of the American scene? In what ways might the comments of European observers be more enlightening about American life and politics than those of Americans themselves?

2. Summarize Pessen's evaluation of each of the following aspects of America in the Jacksonian period: the extent to which political reforms achieved a real political democracy; the material well-being of the people as a whole; the reality of social equalitarianism.

3. What evidence does he give for his evaluation of each of those aspects of American life? Does the evidence seem well-balanced, representing different regions of the nation, both farm and city, and a balanced group of observers?

4. More specifically, what evidence does he use in evaluating the following: urban housing; poverty; farmers; the rich; class differences and class mobility; the common man's influence upon politics?

5. How would you evaluate conditions in this country today with respect to: farm life; urban housing; standard of living; class differences and class mobility; the average man's influence upon government. What evidence can you think of to support your evaluation? To what extent is your evaluation based on personal feelings, rather than evidence?

BIBLIOGRAPHY

Pessen is just one of many recent historians who have challenged the conclusions of earlier writers that Jacksonian America was characterized by equalitarianism. This earlier view can be found in the works of several historians, including Carl Russell Fish, *The Rise of the Common Man, 1830–1850* (New York, 1927) and the extremely influential book by Arthur M. Schlesinger, Jr., *The Age of Jackson* * (Boston, 1945), which argues that eastern workingmen gave strong support to Jackson.

The newer view taken by Pessen is expressed in a number of state and regional studies, in some biographies of leading figures, and in special studies in such fields as labor and banking history. Richard C. Wade, *The Urban Frontier: The Rise of Western Cities, 1790–1830* (Cambridge, Mass., 1959) analyzes American society and economic life from the angle of western urban history. Perhaps the most influential state study is the one done by Lee Benson, *The Concept of Jacksonian Democracy: New York as a Test Case* * (Princeton, N.J., 1961), a work that utilizes new methods to examine various social elements in the politics of the period. Another work on the same state is Douglas T. Miller, *Jacksonian Aristocracy: Class and Democracy in New York, 1830–1860* (New York, 1967).

The questions posed concerning the Jacksonian period — like most other problems in American history — can be approached in a variety of ways. The studies of the 1960s and 1970s have tended to emphasize economic history and a new kind of social history that employs demographic analysis to study American society in the 1830s. In the 1950s, however, historians were especially captivated by the study of ideas. John W. Ward, *Andrew Jackson: Symbol for an Age* * (New York, 1955) is a delightful study utilizing this approach, while Marvin Meyers, *The Jacksonian Persuasion: Politics and Belief* * (Stanford, Cal., 1957) is a more difficult but valuable work in intellectual history. Aside from Benson's work, one of the most influential of the demographic studies is Stephan Thernstrom, *Poverty and Progress: Social Mobility in a Nineteenth Century City* * (Cambridge, Mass., 1964). It covers a longer period than the Age of Jackson, but it is extremely revealing with respect to the "common man," who is often overlooked in historical study. Thernstrom's work is also relevant to a number of subjects besides social mobility, particularly immigration history. If you are interested in Jackson himself and the politics that revolved around him, two very readable short books by Robert V. Remini provide a good introduction: *Andrew Jackson* * (New York, 1966) and *The Election of Andrew Jackson* * (Philadelphia, © 1963). Glyndon G. Van Deusen, *The Jacksonian Era, 1828–1848* * (New York, 1959) is a general, one-volume study of the entire period.

"The Polka" by Pinkerton, Wagner, and McGiugan, 1844, shows female propriety and fashion in the early nineteenth century.

ROBERT E. RIEGEL

The Status of Women

The reform crusade of the 1830s, to aid the handicapped and unfortunate, was undertaken largely by committed individuals and
private humanitarian societies, rather than by the national government. In this and succeeding decades, women were especially
active in the various reform organizations. Dorothea Dix traveled
thousands of miles investigating the care of the insane and peti-
tioning legislatures for improved facilities. Angelina Grimké filled
a Boston theater as she preached against slavery, while Harriet
Beecher Stowe wrote her emotionally appealing *Uncle Tom's
Cabin* and actively assisted runaway slaves.

Some of the women of the period extended their concerns
to areas such as the antislavery crusade after they had become
aroused by the discrimination they experienced as women. Many
others first began working in abolition and humanitarian reform
movements and turned their attention to the women's rights crusade only after discovering that their "meddling" in these areas
evoked taunts, threats, and disparagement of women in public
affairs. Their reforms ranged from dress styles that afforded more
freedom to equality in marriage, law, and employment. Women
entered industry, journalism, medicine, teaching, and other areas.
Both women's colleges and co-educational institutions were
founded before the Civil War to afford educational opportunities
to women, and some changes were made in state laws on property holding, marital rights, and the like.

Yet, throughout the nineteenth century the majority of
American women continued to see their roles as that of wives
and mothers. They remained on the pedestal described by Robert
Riegel, and there is little evidence of substantial changes in either

male or female attitudes toward women during this period, despite the Declaration of Women's Independence that issued from a national women's convention in 1848. Women did not achieve the right to vote until World War I, and women's liberationists of the 1970s have contended that such legal changes are largely meaningless because of the continuation of discriminatory social attitudes toward the roles of men and women.

In the following selection, Riegel describes the position of women in the 1830s. Much of the selection describes the artificial ideal that women were expected to personify, but he also discusses the reality of daily life and the demands for change that were beginning to be voiced.

"American women are the prettiest in the whole world," rhapsodized a long succession of devotees to female beauty, but not without dissenters who reported pasty faces, sloping shoulders, "their busts not sufficiently developed," and "Devilish Big Feet." Only the most churlish curmudgeon could denounce them as *"All* deformed & unhealthy looking." Such male observations were based presumably on only the upper tier of the feminine form, since prevailing fashions shrouded the lower two-thirds in almost complete mystery.

The ideal of womanly beauty was youth, freshness, pallor, and languor. Most poetically beautiful to the age was a young and innocent maiden who faded into an early consumptive grave before experience had robbed her of her innocence. Languid pallor indicated little sun and less exercise. A true lady might make beds and sweep floors, but other bodily activity should be little more than a short, unhurried stroll. The most vigorous sport permitted a woman "conformably with the preservation of her feminine character for grace and delicacy" was horseback riding, and even in this sport several New York women almost caused a riot by riding without corsets. Youth and freshness meant an age of less than thirty, since lack of exercise, overwork, frequent childbearing, and improper food and clothing caused women to become drawn and haggard early, quite different from the interesting delicacy considered so attractive in young girls.

Women's clothes were designed for beauty rather than for comfort or health. The prime mark of gentility was the small waist produced by the current armor of cloth and whalebone. A favorite technique was for the lady to tie her corset strings to a bedpost, expel her breath, and walk as far away as

From *Young America: 1830–1840* by Robert E. Riegel. Copyright 1949 by the University of Oklahoma Press.

possible. The results were considered esthetically pleasing, but were anathema to a legion of reformers, who fulminated against these "libels upon the great Creator's most wonderful contrivance, the human frame." Scathing denunciations were widely printed, being particularly virulent in the medical and educational journals; the women's magazines raised more feeble outcry. . . .

An American woman was well dressed — whether the leisured rich or the Irish maid on her day off. Silks, up-to-the-minute hats, fine gloves, elegant parasols, and lace veils were exclusive to no one class. Parisian styles were watched eagerly by city dressmakers, who were copied by country seamstresses and by women who made their own clothes, for "the French mode dominates in the United States."

A formal evening dress aped the hourglass. It might be made of any rich material such as silk, crepe, satin, or fine muslin, and be any color of the rainbow. Above the constricted waist was a tight bodice which displayed large areas of the "neck" — a modest description of the part of the anatomy which necessarily emerged plentifully for public inspection. Necklines might be square or V-shaped or straight, so that the entire shoulders emerged. Early in the decade, sleeves were leg-of-mutton, flared with whalebone, buckram, or even down pillows. Later the tight French sleeves made the wearer of an old dress uncomfortably aware of the inflated bags on her arms.

Compensating the abbreviated bodice was a voluminous skirt which hung between the shoetops and the floor. The slight bustle used late in the decade was practically lost in the draperies. The material saved in the bodice appeared in skirt decorations — flounces, ruffles, fringes, painted figures, and embroidery. Most striking were the velvet bands in contrasting colors and decorated with yards of embroidery. And then there was the "Lace — lace — lace, wherever it can be stuck on. The gowns have lace trimmings and falls — spencers, shawls, caps, bonnets, handkerchiefs; all have lace."

Milady's dress needed little foundation above the waist and a great deal below. Underwear consisted of vest and drawers of fine cambric, muslin, or wool. Then, of course, came the corset and corset cover, followed by flocks of petticoats — flannel in the winter and muslin or other lighter cloth in the summer. Stockings were of wool, cotton, or open-work silk in any color, but white was preferred. They were visible only with a strong wind, a high coach step, or some unfortunate accident. Everyday shoes were of black leather and high, but a party brought forth low-heeled slippers or sandals, often fastened with ribbons across the ankles. The color was optional, but was usually black or white, and the common materials were satin, morocco, or kid. High-heeled shoes came into vogue late in the decade. . . .

Lower in the economic scale, party clothes were similar to those of the wealthy, but common garments were much more utilitarian. A farmer's wife with seven children hardly wore an organdy dress and an embroidered silk apron for making tallow candles and scrubbing the floor. Homemade linsey-woolsey garments might be deficient in style, but they were long on wear; while shoes, stockings, and other accessories might be omitted most of the year. At the very bottom of the economic scale, the Negro slave wore the poorest possible material made like a long bag, open at each end and tied in the middle. . . .

[Whatever her social class,] a girl was impressed with her female distinctiveness from birth. A little girl was cautioned not to be as boisterous as a little boy, but to be sober and sedate and helpful. She received special training, pursued special occupations, and wore feminine clothes. Although physical sex differences were not mentioned in polite society and lectures and books on sex were considered indecent, the average girl did not need her mother or a doctor to give her a long-delayed statement of the "facts of life." As a member of a large family and surrounded by farm animals, she was not dependent on vague and flowery references to bees and flowers, or on the leering remarks of dubious friends. She not only knew how life was produced, but had witnessed the process.

The girl's first half-dozen years were spent at home learning the necessary household arts. Then, if her father could spare the money, she went to school — possibly more than her brothers, since her work at home was less necessary. At twelve to fourteen she finished her common-school education, and then helped her mother or got a job until she was married. A few girls from prosperous families went to finishing school or seminary to absorb French, music, deportment, fancy sewing, painting, and other aids to social success and to luring a husband. After marriage, a young lady might use these accomplishments — perhaps — to amuse herself and her friends.

Americans believed overwhelmingly that coeducation was morally dangerous and that the male mysteries of the classics and mathematics could not be undertaken by women without injury to their delicate natures. The traditionalists insisted that "making puddings and nursing babies . . . must be attended by one sex or the other, and of what use can algebra and other abstruse matters be to a woman in her present state?" The opposition countered by asking the utility of French and of painting on china, but without making many conversions to its radical doctrine. . . .

No young miss, whether at home with her mother, working in a Lowell mill, or embracing the social whirl, forgot that her main business was the acquisition of a husband. By accepted fiction man was the pursuer, but in fact woman utilized every feminine wile to encourage pursuit and to expedite capture. A girl unmarried by her mid-twenties was well advanced toward an unlovely spinsterhood in which she soon lost her looks, her social importance, and her economic security.

Every girl believed romantically in love at first sight for the "one man," but probably the usual fact was an almost imperceptible ripening of a long friendship. "I found myself clinging to his interests, distressed by his long absences. I found on analyzing my regard for him that I loved him." And then the long and deep conversations: "He has made an exposition of his character to me. So simple. So pure. So just what Jesus loved. We talk little of heaven, but are already deep in schemes for our future independence and comfort." Then the long letters and the appeals for still longer: "Let me follow you some day, from the moment you open your eyes . . . till sleep closes the eyes I love so well."

Ideally, young love was confined to deep conversations, long letters, or the treasuring of a scented glove or a precious lock of hair. In actual fact, hugging, kissing, and other caresses expressed strong inward urges and seemed unobjectionable to all but the most prudish. Not infrequently, however, youthful ardor exceeded the most tolerant standards, and the young lady found herself on the road to maternity — whereupon her young man usually did the "right thing" and married her. Cynics noted that an unreasonably large proportion of "premature" babies were the first born.

The more religious and conscientious lover was greatly perturbed lest human love replace or supersede the love of God and therefore be sinful. A very able man declared his love thus: "I know it will surprise and even amaze you, Angelina, when I say to you as I now do, that for a long time, *you have had my whole heart."* But then conscience forced him to add: *"Not supremely.* Grace has restrained me from that extreme. I *do* love the Lord our righteousness *better* than I love *you.* And it is *because* I love Him *better* that I love you *as* I do."

Angelina proved not surprised by the declaration and returned the love, but she had her own religious troubles: "One thing I want to ask you, My Dear Brother. Ought God to be *all in all* to us *on earth?* I tho't so, and am frightened to find *He is not,* that is, I feel something else is necessary to my happiness. I laid awake thinking why it was that my heart longed and panted and reached after you as it does. Why my Saviour and my God is not enough to *satisfy* me. Am I sinning, am I ungrateful, *am I an* IDOLATOR?"

An engagement ended normally in either a church or a home wedding, where the word "obey" was frequently omitted from the bride's vows. The usual wedding was celebrated in the evening and followed by a reception or a supper. Then the happy pair might take a wedding trip, although more frequently the bride and groom went directly to their new home, where, after a reasonable period for settling down, they received their friends.

Once married, the girl put aside the frivolity of youth, "just as if she entered a convent, except however that it is not taken ill that she have children." Gaiety and charm were presumably turned to common sense, self-control, industry, economy, piety, affection, and love for home. The wife was merged in her husband, a change symbolized by the taking of his name. He acquired her property, had exclusive use of her person, and could inflict moderate physical chastisement.

The wife was expected to love, cherish, counsel, and obey her husband.

"As the vine which has long twisted its graceful foliage around the oak, and been lifted by it into sunshine, will, when the hardy plant has been rifted by the thunderbolt, cling around it with its caressing tendrils, and bind up its shattered bough; so it is beautifully ordered by Providence, that woman who is the mere dependent and ornament of man in his happier hours, should be his stay and solace when smitten with sudden calamity, winding herself into the rugged recesses of his nature, tenderly supporting the drooping head, and binding up the broken heart."

The wife should be completely absorbed in her husband. "Even when exhausted nature sinks to brief repose, forgetfulness is denied. Even in sleep she seems awake to the one great object of her care. She starts and rises from her slumbers, raises her drooping head, watches with dreamy eyes the face she loves, then sinks again to rest, to start with every chime or clock, or distant sound, that formerly had passed unheard, or only served as lullaby to her sweet sleep."

The theory that a wife obeyed her husband, honored him, bore his children, and ministered to all his wants was not always in accord with the facts. Sometimes she was a bad cook, a poor housekeeper, and an empty-headed fool. Sometimes it was the husband who did the pampering, with the wife domineering and shrewish, or dissatisfied and querulous. At other times the couple lived in a hotel or rooming house to avoid the very duties that the wife supposedly gloried in performing. In other words, husbands and wives acted quite humanly and naturally.

Sex conduct inside marriage must remain partly shrouded in mystery. The double bed, the nightgown and nightshirt, and the cold room seem to suggest frequent sex expression. But there were several deterrents. Both husband and wife worked hard, and dropped into bed dead tired. Furthermore, they had been impressed that frequent intercourse was not only sinful but physically debilitating; the healthiest man or woman was presumably the virgin. And, of course, such an ecstatic pleasure must obviously be a sin.

Marriage should be consummated, according to the moralists, with a sense of piety and responsibility rather than with those "innumerable, horrible, unspeakable, earthly, sensual and devilish distortions of married life." Ideal marriage was the mating of immortal souls and should be far above the earthy degradation of physical passion. But by this time the purist had overshot his mark, so he backed down to the extent of admitting intercourse to be proper for the begetting of children, which presumably meant not over once a year. He was slightly consoled by the belief that sex relations would not be so attractive to married people as to unmarried, since excitement was much greater if a stranger were involved.

Marital intercourse was also limited by the deeply rooted conviction that no nice woman had strong physical desires. She was merely the receptacle for male passion, and wife and husband would both have been shocked if the wife had shown exuberance. Such demonstrations were reserved for prostitutes. This attitude must have damped sexual displays. Then, too, the husband felt it was both sinful and physically dangerous if he made demands on his wife during pregnancy or shortly after parturition. The average wife was almost always in one or the other condition.

A final hazard was the frequency with which marital relations ended in pregnancy. Many a couple tried to limit its progeny by abstaining from intercourse — frequently a losing fight which produced only mental and physical tension. Contraceptives were little known, of dubious effectiveness, and anathematized by religious and medical leaders as "conjugal onanism." Their use brought a heavy feeling of guilt which was unalleviated by success.

Sex morals apparently were not good, even though adultery was rare. Prostitution was commonplace, and nonprofessional moral lapses had the eloquent testimony of the number of unmarried mothers. Rape was frequent, if the newspapers are to be believed. Masturbation seems to have been widespread in spite of the shock and horror tactics used to combat it; people tried, somewhat unsuccessfully, to believe that it was rare among boys and nonexistent among girls. Homosexuality was not mentioned publicly, but consider the writer (male) who bemoans the stiffness and formality of his correspondent (also male): "And often when the gushings of my soul have prompted me to throw my arms around your neck and kiss you, I have violently quelled these impulses and affected a *manly bearing*." However, he continues, in imagination "your stern voice startles me from my maiden dreams!" Other abnormalities sometimes emerged, as when a Brooklyn pastor in 1844 admitted fondling ten young girls too intimately and showing them his sex organs; of course, he blamed the devil.

Almost as important to the wife as her husband were her children, whom she often bore so regularly that her spouse became "somewhat restiff under these multiplying blessings." The only trial worse than having too many children was having none, which provoked jests about the vigor of the couple, particularly the virility of the man.

Young children, according to the storybooks, learned their basic religious and philosophic truths at their mother's knee. "Our moral and political institutions depend, for their purity and permanence, on that simplicity and singleness of purpose, which are generally imbibed at the mother's knee." Actually, the young finishing-school product, married at sixteen and a mother by seventeen, was hardly qualified for such instruction, while the harassed mother of half a dozen had her hands full in feeding and clothing her offspring. There were flaws in the current conviction of the sanctity and divine inspiration of motherhood. . . .

Woman's place in society was related to her physical disabilities. She was smaller and weaker, even though men sometimes forgot this fact in hiring laundresses and scrub women. She was subject to special ills, including pregnancy, parturition, and lactation, which occupied a large proportion of a married woman's time. The obvious corollary was that she should have duties that could be performed in the home, and this standard was maintained even when the woman was not married. She was expected to accept these limitations with resignation, since they had resulted from Eve's sin in leading Adam astray.

Physical sex differences implied to most people equivalent mental differences, even though a small but vocal minority insisted that the sexes were inherently equal in ability, and that apparent inequalities represented only differences in training. The usual dogma was that women's minds were inferior. "The intellect of woman bears the same relation to that of man as her physical organization; — it is inferior in power, and different in kind."

Arguments concerning total brain power implied no disagreement in what was held to be the obvious truth, that women inherently had distinctive mental and emotional traits. These were stated many times, with variations. "Man is strong, woman is beautiful; man is daring and confident, woman is diffident and unassuming; man is great in action, woman in suffering; man shines abroad, woman at home; man talks to convince, woman to persuade and please; man has a rugged heart, woman a soft and tender one; man prevents misery, woman relieves it; man has science, woman taste; man has judgment, woman sensibility; man is a being of justice, woman of mercy."

Prime virtues for a woman were faith, simplicity, goodness, and self-sacrifice. She should be tender, affectionate, frail, sentimental, pious, loving, humanitarian, decorous, meek, gentle, submissive, humble, and pure: "By a glance she will draw a deep and just conclusion. . . . While she trusts her instinct she is seldom deceived, and she is generally lost when she begins to reason." Above all, the woman should love, trust, and honor God — even more than she did her husband — since "religion with them is a sentiment, which like love, rejects all doubt, and suffers no analyzing process to disturb and cool its confiding faith."

Woman's crowning virtue — supposedly innate — was her modesty. This modesty included not only personal fastidiousness but also a withdrawal from the hurly-burly, rough contacts of the marketplace. "Retired within the sacred precincts of her own abode, she is preserved from the destroying taint of excessive intercourse with the world . . . and her heart is untainted by the dire temptations of strife with her fellows."

Intense modesty could be called prudery, and one lady remarked: "I hope the charge will always remain a true one." In polite company, no undergarment was ever mentioned, although this prohibition did not extend to the printed page or even to the lecture. Delicate females hesitated to discuss their symptoms with their doctors. Medical handbooks suggested the doctor cut short any visit to a lady's bedroom, make any intimate suggestions through a nurse or elderly female relative, and make a real examination only in case of great necessity, and then under a sheet in a darkened room. A proposal to dissect a female body was considered improper, and in the South would have brought a challenge from the nearest male relative. Even a phrenological examination of the head was considered a trifle indelicate, and ladies were praised for refusing to thus compromise their modesty.

For some reason the female form was considered increasingly immoral as one moved south. Polite society referred to the neck when it meant the breast, and to the breast when it meant the abdomen — a stomachache was thereupon a pain in the breast. Sea bathing was suspect because, even with woolen dresses and petticoats, the wet clothes outlined the lower extremities. No one spoke openly of a "leg," which was the most taboo word in the language. "If you are not ashamed of having legs you ought to be — at least, we are in this country, and never mention or give the slightest token of having such things, except by wearing very short petticoats, which we don't consider objectionable." The leg complex was carried to inanimate objects, as "a square pianoforte with four *limbs*." Rumor had it that the most refined female academies covered such "limbs" with little trousers ending in lace frills.

Exaggerated modesty had its anomalies. Décolletés were very low. Advertising was rather frank. Physical-education lectures, with skeletons and anatomical drawings, were delivered to mixed audiences. A gentleman caller finding the lady sewing on a chemise would make sly remarks which would receive polite evasions, but no one was fooled. Both sexes knew the "facts of life," and each knew that the other knew. . . .

American women, it must be admitted sadly, did not always embody the ideals which the philosophers of both sexes praised. Complete daintiness, with a strong mixture of religious contemplation, was hardly possible for the average wife with half a dozen children under foot as she slaved at cooking, cleaning, sewing, and tending a garden. When the father came home, she was hardly prepared to radiate peace, sympathy, and loving kindness. Her nearest approach to the ideal came on Sunday, when she dressed in her best and took the children to church. Her unmarried sister, caring for someone else's children, should at least have acquired Christian fortitude; actually, she tended to become waspish.

Even herculean efforts to attain the proper feminine virtues did not always bring praise. When a diligent woman carried needlebook, thread, thimble, and pincushion with her in making a call, she was berated over "the slavery to which fashion has reduced them." When she went to church, she was accused of primary interest in showing her new clothes, which was vanity, or of overidealizing her minister, which was derogatory to her husband. When she joined a society to evangelize the Chinese, reform prostitutes, or furnish clothes for paupers, she was told that her real purpose was gossip. When she held the inevitable ladies' charity fair, she was told that she was blackmailing men into paying fancy prices for useless knickknacks.

Almost no secular amusement was free from criticism. Even the simplest party generated undesirable excitement and late hours. The theater presented displays of illicit passions and crimes to the degradation of the pure female. Novel reading was at least wasteful of time, and probably dangerous morally. Lectures and debates were doubtful amusements for impressionable womanhood, with even the galleries of Congress suspect. No matter what women did, or failed to do, someone was displeased.

The husbandless woman faced even greater difficulties, for where could an occupation be found that would not unduly tax her lesser intellect and delicate physique? Where could she preserve her sensitive nature from the dulling contacts of competitive business, and her modesty from the rude and even lewd remarks of the sterner sex? Certainly not in an executive job, any kind of selling, or any occupation in which men and women must work side by side. Yet even women had to eat fairly regularly. They could do laundry or scrubbing, work as seamstresses, dressmakers, milliners, or boardinghouse keepers. All these occupations called for long hours, hard work, and small pay. In industry, woman could traditionally enter printing, textiles, shoes, food, and tobacco products, even though they worked beside men. In justification it was pleaded that these had been home industries earlier — a plea not entirely true. The truth was that men were not sufficiently entrenched in these industries to repel the feminine invasion.

If women worked, then current ideology insisted that conditions approach those of the home, where feminine virtues flourished best. Girl textile workers were herded into synthetic homes. Home industries, such as making stockings, shirts, hats, trousers, and dresses, were widely approved in spite of starvation wages. An abortive effort was made to discover other similar jobs which would not injure feminine delicacy. The radical suggestion to raise the wages of women was rejected because of the supposed operation of some vague but powerful natural law which would then end the occupations and leave the women penniless.

Hard work and low pay encouraged many women to adopt their oldest profession, prostitution. But thereby good theory was endangered, for "No woman ever voluntarily surrendered the blessings of a fair name. The sensitive plant shrinks not more instinctively from the touch, than the nature of woman from defilement." The obvious conclusion was that a prostitute had originally been seduced, raped, or tricked into a fraudulent marriage — probably through youthful innocence.

Estimates of the number of prostitutes varied, with New York being credited with anywhere from one to ten thousand. The existence of many brothels was made evident by their prodigal output of shootings and stabbings. Most publicized was the case of the prostitute, Helen Jewett, who was found beaten to death in April, 1836. Bloody tracks led over a back fence, and a known visitor of the previous night, R. P. Robinson, had whitewash on his coat, and owned the murder axe. At the trial, the defendant proved to be a good-looking and well-connected lad of nineteen, while the witnesses for the prosecution were prostitutes. Robinson never took the stand, and the jury pronounced him "not guilty" within fifteen minutes.

The clientele of a brothel consisted mainly of bachelors, particularly sailors and young bloods of fashion, but one spot check showed at least one-third to be married men. Such patrons may have had sick or absent wives, but there is also the possibility that a repressed wife with a feeling of sin could not compete with the sophisticated prostitute. The fact that many men frequented brothels was an open secret — but still a secret, since men did not boast of their amours.

Prostitution was often considered a necessary evil that provided an outlet for men's passions, so that they would not contaminate pure womanhood; the "bad" woman preserved the virtue of the "good." Laws against prostitution were unenforced, and the police undoubtedly received protection money. Periodically a few madams and girls were haled into court to keep them impressed with police power. In New York they were charged as vagrants and confined with other females in large rooms at "the college of vice at Bellevue," where they did effective missionary work.

The evil of prostitution attracted its due proportion of reformers, who curiously enough exhibited no interest in the economic condition of women or in modifying current moral concepts. Prostitutes were approached with moral exhortation. Men were urged to be more "pure" — to avoid late hours, fashionable parties, plays, novels, and other titillating excitements — to work hard, and to live simply. "Good" women were implored to shun libertines and to eschew such evils as low-necked dresses and waltzing, which aroused men's lowest passions and inspired them to visit prostitutes.

Female moral-reform societies often did little more than provide opportunities for ladies to discuss subjects that otherwise were taboo. The following extract from one annual report suggests that the ladies rolled sex over their tongues with lingering relish: "Though we have not been called upon to mourn the fall of any members of our society, yet some circumstances lead us to apprehend that there have been recent outrages upon the cause of moral purity within the bounds of our congregation."

The usual method of attack in fighting prostitution was to enlist the aid of a male Magdalen Society, whose members preached to the fallen women and sometimes established homes for those desiring regeneration. The theory was that the unfortunate women were more sinned against than sinning, and that innate female purity would respond joyously to a religious appeal if the process of degeneration had not gone too far. Unfortunately the results were slight. Few answered the appeals, and the majority who entered homes eventually lapsed again into their old ways. . . .

In spite of the general agreement on the proper place of women in society, changes were coming. A few men and women were conscious rebels from the traditional standards, but more important were the contributions of thousands of women who had no conscious desire for change. A girl working in a textile mill accepted wholeheartedly the ideal of woman as a wife and mother, functioning in the sanctity of her home, and yet she was a symbol of a changing economy that was making the old ideas obsolete. . . .

Women were welcome in religious and moral reform movements, and furnished a high proportion of the workers for such worthy causes as missions, abolition, and temperance, but once more troubles arose. The ladies began, immodestly, to be interested in holding offices in the movements. Furthermore, they soon realized that political action was vital, as in the abolition movement, and that to be effective, they could not work entirely through their husbands and brothers. Consequently they began to speak publicly — at first to audiences of their own sex and then to mixed audiences.

Women on the lecture platform stung the traditionalists into full cry, since these "female exhibitions in publick" violated all current ideas of woman as a modest and retiring creature, confined to the sanctity of her home. A group of Massachusetts ministers expressed the widespread horror when they excoriated "the mistaken conduct of those who encouraged females to bear an obtrusive and ostentatious part in measures of reform, and countenance any of that sex who so far forget themselves as to itinerate in the character of public lecturers or teachers." The height of horror was reserved for Fanny Wright as she presented sexual and religious radicalism to mixed audiences; such conduct was practically blasphemy.

Some women even attempted to invade the pulpit to give their messages. "A woman properly educated, and with feelings suitable to her sex, would as soon be caught pitching quoits or engaged in a game of nine-pins, as be seen in the pulpit; and womanhood is as lovely in one place as the other." The force of this magnificent sarcasm is somewhat lost on a later generation that accepts both female speaking and female sports.

The slashing criticism received by women for overstepping masculine prerogatives in their crusade for moral reform served to make some of them unpleasantly conscious of their inferior status. Able abolition leaders such as Sarah and Angelina Grimké and Abby Kelly became sex conscious and began to fight for women's rights. Again one heard of taxation without representation, and that governments derive their just powers only from the consent of the governed. Women objected to being classified with children, Negroes, the insane, and the criminal, and even questioned the omniscience of the male sex. Treason was abroad in the land as the females held they were not properly represented by husbands, brothers, and sons. The Women's Seneca Falls Declaration of Independence was less than a decade away.

Feministic radicals left most Americans with conflicting emotions of irritation, amusement, and bewilderment, for did not a woman already have all the best of life — a protected existence, a better seat at the theater, and the adoration of men? A woman solved the paradox neatly: "Many silly things have been written, and are now written, concerning the equality of the sexes, but that true and perfect companionship, which gives both man and woman complete freedom *in* their places, without a reckless desire to go out of them, is as yet imperfectly understood. 'In the future' it will be perceived that all this discussion about relative superiority, is as idle as a controversy to determine which is most important to the world, the light of the sun, or the warmth of the sun."

Arguments over the place of women immediately involved the marital relationship, since obviously not all marriages had been made in Heaven. The conservatives talked of human failures in effort. The liberals supported more rights for wives, such as control over their own property. The radicals talked of easier divorce. Theophilos R. Gates wanted complete freedom of divorce, while Abner Kneeland added state care for children. John Humphrey Noyes experimented with "male continence" and group marriage. Joseph Smith Jr. embraced polygamy for the Mormons.

One of the radicals, Robert Dale Owen, who aimed at complete sex equality with institutional care for children, insisted that current sex practices were the core of the troubles. He wrote: "Nothing short of control over the reproductive, it appears to me, can relieve women from sexual slavery. If they must be, on all occasions, nuns or mothers — mothers, too, perhaps of a dozen children — they are & will remain slaves; they suffer and will suffer, grievously, both physically & mentally. I cannot conceive equality between the sexes, except with the recommendation contained in the M. P. as a foundation stone."

The "M. P." to which Owen referred was his little book *Moral Physiology, or, a Brief and Plain Treatise on the Population Question* (1830), which had the distinction — dubious at the time — of being the first American book to describe and approve contraceptive methods, and the second in the world. The English-born Owen was a man of varied interests, which may explain why the book was hastily done and inadequate. Of the three contraceptive methods described, preference was given the poorest — that mentioned in Genesis. Owen argued the sex act was normal and desirable, holding that people not only would not and could not refrain, but should not. Only by contraceptives could the overly large family, with its strain on the pocketbook of the father and the health of the mother, be averted. The advantages claimed were largely personal.

Owen's book might have been more significant if it had not been overshadowed by another, *Fruits of Philosophy, or, the private companion of young married people,* written by a young American doctor, Charles Knowlton. Knowlton's interest was a direct result of his background as hypochondriacal boy, penniless medical student, doctor with few patients, and husband with a growing family and no funds. Seeking to solve his own troubles, he investigated contraceptives, and then wrote down his results; a few patients were enthusiastic over the manuscript, so in 1832 he had it published.

Knowlton argued for contraceptives on both personal and social grounds. In social terms, contraception would avoid the overcrowding envisaged by Malthus and hence avert the necessity of vice, war, famine, and disease on a large scale. In personal terms, the proper spacing of children would improve the wife's health and the family's finances. The alternative of abstention was both physically undesirable and practically impossible, leading only to the evils of masturbation and the resort to prostitutes. With knowledge of contraceptives, young lovers could marry and thus enhance the happiness and morality of the community. Knowlton then described the sex organs and their functions, although with some errors, and gave instruction in several contraceptive methods.

These two books were greeted with profound silence by the American press, which probably was shocked. The one exception was a comment by the *Boston Medical Journal* on the Knowlton book: "We think . . . the less that is known about it by the public at large, the better it will be for the morals of the community." Knowlton got into jail, but Owen did not. Probably the objections and prosecutions would have been greater if the books had appeared a few years later, after Victorian morality had become really dominant.

The distribution of the books is difficult to estimate. Possibly fifteen to twenty thousand were sold within the decade, but the number of readers was undoubtedly greater. One can imagine a wife reading surreptitiously at night after the children were in bed, hiding the book behind the mantel clock, and then next day slipping it under her apron to carry to her next-door neighbor. Possibly constant circulation is the reason few copies of either book remain. Of course an alternate possibility is that a later generation considered the matter too vile to be allowed to exist.

The influence of the books is also difficult to estimate. The American birth rate fell throughout the nineteenth century, with a specially large drop between 1840 and 1850, if the census figures are reliable. After a period of obscurity, both books were revived in the late eighteen seventies, and there seems to have been an exceptionally large decline in the birth rate between 1880 and 1890. These juxtapositions may have been entirely accidental, but they certainly were at least a remarkable coincidence.

The family, as one of the most basic of human institutions, changes slowly and reluctantly. A ten-year period is too short for even a minor revolution, and yet the American family was obviously in a period of transition between 1830 and 1840. Its functions were declining. The activities of the old self-sufficient farming family were being eroded by the tide of manufacturing and transportation. The single-product factory helped produce the single-product farm, with its increased dependence on the outside world, as well as more city families in which the father worked outside the home and the mother acted more and more as a purchasing agent.

Women became increasingly independent as their labors became less and as greater opportunity beckoned from the new mills. Each feminine mill worker was one more woman who could survive without male support, no matter how little she desired her new independence. Inevitably women came to be drawn into social, religious, literary, and political activities, and here they began to feel the impress of their inferior status and to become more interested in their "rights."

These changes were all accentuated by the increasing use of contraceptives. Smaller families were less fitted for diversified farming. Homes could be smaller, and apartments became practical. Fewer children meant more time for each child, and less financial strain; also, it meant easier divorce. Fewer children also brought more free time to the wife, with hours and energy for new play and work; increasingly she could leave the house to shop and to gossip, to hear lectures, to attend plays, and to participate in meetings to advance abolition, suffrage, and other reforms. The family was in the throes of a revolution. A brave new world was being born.

STUDY GUIDE

1. Describe the behavior, dress, and education of a "true lady." What do these reveal about the period's idea of a woman's mind and sensibilities? What changes in behavior and the like did the reformers advocate?

2. What was the role of women in marriage? What changes do you see in the early nineteenth-century conceptions from the earlier period described by Edmund Morgan in his essay on colonial Virginia?

3. Hypocrisy may be too simple an explanation for the disparity between the prudish sexual attitudes and the widespread prostitution. What role might the following have played in this situation: anxiety about intimacy with one's wife; religious concerns; social attitudes toward married and unmarried women? What differences are there in sexual practices and sexual attitudes today as compared to the period Riegel describes?

4. Riegel describes the distinctive mental and emotional characteristics that were ascribed to men and women. How might these reflect the economic and social needs of the early nineteenth century? How have industrialization and mechanization of the home modified these conceptions of men and women?

5. What differences do you see in the goals and techniques of the women's rights movement of the early nineteenth century and the women's liberation movement of our time? How do you explain the necessity for a women's liberation movement in the 1970s in view of the fact that women's suffrage was attained in 1920?

BIBLIOGRAPHY

The women's reform movement of the early nineteenth century can be fully understood only in the context of the general spirit of reform of that period. Two good studies of reform in its various manifestations are Alice F. Tyler,

Freedom's Ferment: Phases of American Social History to 1860 * (Minneapolis, Minn., 1944) and Clifford S. Griffin, *The Ferment of Reform, 1830–1860* * (New York, 1967). There are separate works dealing with the peace crusade, temperance, prison reform, aid to the mentally ill, and, of course, a huge literature on the antislavery movement. E. Douglas Branch, *The Sentimental Years, 1836–1860* * (New York, 1934) is an amusing, well-written account of the fads and foibles of the time.

Mary R. Beard, *Woman as Force in History: A Study in Traditions and Realities* (New York, 1946) is still worth reading, though more specific studies have appeared after it. Alma Lutz, *Crusade for Freedom: Women of the Antislavery Movement* (Boston, 1968) describes the role women played in abolitionism. Lutz has also written biographies of two of the leading women's rights leaders, *Created Equal: A Biography of Elizabeth Cady Stanton, 1815–1902* (New York, 1940) and *Susan B. Anthony: Rebel, Crusader, Humanitarian* (Boston, 1959).

Anne F. Scott, *The Southern Lady: From Pedestal to Politics, 1830–1930* (Chicago, 1970) is a recent work on the romanticized idea of southern womanhood. There are several general works on women in American society, with special reference to women's rights, including: Eleanor Flexner, *Century of Struggle: The Woman's Rights Movement in the United States* (Cambridge, Mass., 1959); Robert E. Riegel, *American Feminists* (Lawrence, Kan., 1963); William L. O'Neill, *Everyone Was Brave: The Rise and Fall of Feminism in America* * (Chicago, 1969); Andrew Sinclair, *The Better Half: The Emancipation of the American Woman* * (New York, 1965); and the interesting article by Barbara Welter, "The Cult of True Womanhood, 1820–1860," *American Quarterly*, Vol. XVIII (1966), pp. 151–174. The history of black women has been accorded even less attention than that of white women. Gerda Lerner includes them in her short work *The Woman in American History* (Reading, Mass., 1971) and has published a separate book of readings, *Black Women in White America: A Documentary History* (New York, 1972).

A recent, charming, general study of women in American history is Page Smith, *Daughters of the Promised Land: Women in American History* (Boston, 1970). Jean E. Friedman and William G. Shade, *Our American Sisters: Women in American Life and Thought* (Boston, 1973) is a collection of articles on women's history, while Aileen S. Kraditor, ed., *Up from the Pedestal: Selected Writings of American Feminism* (Chicago, 1968) is a collection of writings from contemporaries of the women's rights movement.

Shaker Community, Inc., Hancock, Mass.

"A Tree of Love, a Tree of Life," 1857, suggests the close relation of faith and community life in Shaker society.

EDWARD D. ANDREWS

Utopian Communes

One of the most unusual developments of the counter-culture of the 1960s was the establishment of hundreds of communes across the United States. Ranging from a few people buying a farm they planned to work together to much larger groups with a distinctive philosophy of life, these experiments in living revealed a disenchantment with the larger, competitive society and emphasized the sharing and brotherhood of an "extended family."

This was by no means the first movement of this sort in American history. The first settlers of several of the colonies had been members of small, tightly knit groups that stressed a strong sense of mutual responsibility among the members. The same spirit had sometimes characterized new communities on the frontier as Americans moved west. Such religious sects as the Mormons and Moravians had displayed a similar unity of spirit and purpose. The clearest parallel to the communes of the 1960s can be found in the many groups in the 1830s that established small settlements in the Northeast and Midwest in an attempt to create a perfect community as an example for society as a whole.

Some of the communities were formed by European immigrants, such as the Rappites of western Pennsylvania, and some were based on social philosophies of European origin. Others were natively American, such as the Brook Farm community in Massachusetts. Some were religiously oriented; others were socialistic. They embodied a wide range of beliefs including vegetarianism, free love, celibacy, and the abolition of money. So varied were they, that there was no such thing as a typical community that would give one an idea of life in any of the others.

Yet there were common impulses and common beliefs behind the founding of most of them. One, of course, was a dissatisfaction with the state of society. There was also a widespread belief that it was possible to establish a perfect social order among a small group of people. What constituted perfection differed from one group to another; some thought it was to be found in the common ownership of property, while others believed it would only be achieved by coming into a perfect kingdom ordained by Christ. Finally, most of these groups believed that if a perfect community could be created on a small scale, with thirty or one hundred people, it would serve as a model that could be extended to the entire society.

The Shakers, founded by Mother Ann Lee, were one of several religious groups that adhered to the rule of celibacy in their communities and thus died out for lack of new recruits. Like many of the religious minorities of the early nineteenth century, the Shakers were millennialists, who believed in the second coming of Christ as the answer to the world's problems. In their case, they felt that Mother Ann was the female embodiment of the second coming, and that the millenium was already here — in the small Shaker communities in which they lived. In his book *The People Called Shakers*, Edward D. Andrews explains the theology and worship of the Shakers and also describes the daily life and human relations in a celibate, religious community that hoped to create a perfect order for American society.

Chief among the factors affecting all Shaker life was the unique relationship existing between brethren and sisters. The application, under the same roof, of the seemingly irreconcilable theories of equality and separation set the movement apart from other communal-religious institutions and aroused, more than any other characteristic of the church, skeptical comment and barbed abuse. Every reliable source, however, indicates that the dividing line was held. One sex was always conscious of the presence and support of the other. But to pass that invisible boundary was to invite both bondage of soul and communal disfavor.

Convictions concerning a fundamental tenet of the order, of course, aided the adjustment: for the rule of celibacy was a selective agent, attracting not only those who believed in the principle on doctrinal grounds, but those

Excerpts from *The People Called Shakers* by Edward Deming Andrews. Oxford University Press, 1953.

others, chiefly women, who were drawn in because of their desire to escape from marital difficulties and broken homes. For persons oppressed by poverty and economic ills the Shaker community, like the cloister, offered the opportunity for a renewal of life in useful service, in which case the rule was accepted as a condition of security. Once the rule was accepted, the Shakers underwent a thorough course of instruction. The work of God, they were told, proceeded by a spiritual union and relation between male and female. If, in the course of the period of probation, the cross seemed repellent, they were free to withdraw or remain in an "out family." On the other hand, should they wish to travel on to the junior and senior order, they did so in full realization of what it entailed. If husband and wife entered together, they were usually assigned to separate families. . . .

. . . [Joseph] Meacham's basic law — that "no male or female shall support, or have a private union or correspondence together, neither shall they touch each other unnecessarily" — was also supported, in time, by detailed "separation acts" and ordinances for the "purity of the mind." It was "contrary to the gift," for instance, for a brother to pass a sister on the stairs, for a brother to go into a sister's room without knocking, for a sister to go to a brother's shop alone, for brethren to shake hands with the sisters and give them presents, and so on.

Surveillance was facilitated by the smallness of the family and the lack of privacy. From two to six individuals shared each sleeping or retiring room, the day's routine was organized, and most of the work was done in groups. In meeting, . . . the ministry could supervise proceedings through shuttered apertures; and at Pleasant Hill, two watchtowers on the roof of the dwelling served a similar purpose during the day. The Millennial Laws stated that if anyone knew of any transgression, he or she was morally obligated to reveal it to the elders, "otherwise they participate in the guilt." Under such conditions an atmosphere of mutual suspicion was almost inevitable; the feeling that one was being spied upon during every hour of the day and night was bound to deprive the individual of dignity and self-respect.

The most noteworthy device for regulating sex relations, however, was a constructive one. As the church was being organized, Meacham realized that "correspondence" was unavoidable, that brethren and sisters must consult on temporalities, that social solidarity could not rest on negative grounds. Since they "*would* have a union together," he testified, "if they had not a spiritual union, they would have a carnal." His corrective was the "union meeting," which for over seventy years, from 1793 on, played an important role in Shaker domestic life. These gatherings usually took place two evenings a week and twice on Sundays. A group of four to ten members of each sex met in a brethren's retiring room, where they sat facing each other in rows about five feet apart. (If girls and boys were present, they were placed beside their elders or by themselves in ranks in the rear.) Then, for a stated period, one hour on week nights and one or two on the Sabbath, each member of the group conversed freely and openly with the person opposite him on some familiar or suitable subject; or the occasion might be turned into a singing meeting. The pairs had been carefully matched, on the basis of age and "condition of travel," by the elders. No one was worthy to attend if he or she harbored any ill-feeling toward another.

The conversation — "simple, sometimes facetious, rarely profound" — was limited, for sacred, literary, and certain secular topics were all prohibited. Some visitors, like [A. J.] Macdonald, found the meetings dull. Nevertheless the time seemed to have been agreeably passed; the company had their own world to talk about, with zest and unrestraint if they wished; "gentle laughter and mild amusement" were not unknown; and in the early years smoking was customary. The union meetings, in fact, belied the common assumption that the Shakers were an austere folk, though discipline varied with the family or community and was likely to be more strict in the Church Order. Self-restraint and sobriety, however, never excluded simple joys. One observer comments on "the amenity of their intercourse [which was] much less restricted than is generally supposed." Another noticed that they were "disposed to be merry and enjoy a joke." Mary Dyer attended meetings at Enfield (N.H.) where there were pipes to smoke, cider to drink, and melons, apples, and nuts to eat; and where the participants sang such "merry love songs" as

I love the brethren the brethren love me
Oh! how happy, how happy I be,
I love the sisters, the sisters love me,
Oh! how happy, how happy I be.
How pretty they look, how clever they feel,
And this we will sing when we love a good deal.

A former member of a Niskeyuna family recalled that two aged brethren, one a Whig and the other a Democrat before they joined the order, used to argue their political principles in these meetings; and that a young sister, on one occasion, raised the issue whether members would not be better Shakers if they were allowed to study instrumental music, languages, and fine literature. The aristocratic Mrs. Hall found the Believers at this community "a very conversible set of people" — a verdict later shared by Howells, who felt that the renunciation of marriage was "the sum of Shaker asceticism."

These social gatherings were nevertheless misinterpreted by the world: as Isaac Youngs put it, "advantage was taken by some apostates and evil minded persons . . . to construe this sacred order of union, [especially the placing of certain brethren with certain sisters] into a particular union or connection, as savoring of husband and wife." Eunice Chapman, for one, testified to seeing "the spiritual husbands, each with their spiritual wife," withdraw after meeting to their different apartments — observing to one of the sisters that there must be "general courtship throughout the house." Furnishing further grounds for detraction was a custom connected with the meeting, namely, that of assigning to each sister general "oversight over the habits and temporal needs" of the brother sitting opposite her — taking care of his clothes, looking after his washing and mending, providing new garments when they were needed, and so forth — in return for which the brethren "did needful favors for the sisters." Visitors sometimes noticed the tender solicitude of a brother toward a certain sister, or vice versa. Though such attention was a violation of the letter of the Separation Acts, it seems to have been accepted, quite naturally, as a justifiable expression of spiritual union.

A combination of factors — the system of orders and surveillance, communal opinion, the rites of confession and atonement, the force of principle, the union meeting, the freedom to withdraw from the society — fostered and enforced a relationship between the two sexes which one enthusiast called "more harmonic than anyone seriously believes attainable for the human race." As to its effectiveness, we have the empirical judgment of the student Macdonald:

> I have always found that those who spoke ill of the Shakers on this subject, to be ignorant, and low minded persons, who probably judged others by themselves, and who founded their opinion upon mere supposition. Those who have been most among them, and consequently the best Judges, have been compelled to believe, that the Shakers are generally speaking, sincere, both in the Belief and practice of abstinence from sexual coition. I have heard Individuals who have lived with them, for periods varying from thirty years, to a few months, all declare, that there was no such immorality among the Shakers, as had been attributed to them. In the vicinity of Union Village, O. I heard suspicions and suppositions, in abundance, and have no doubt the same surmises may be heard in the vicinity of any of their settlements. But I have never met with one individual who was a Witness to or could prove a Case of immoral conduct between the Sexes in any of the Shaker Communities. . . .
>
> It is quite true that sometimes, young Shakers in whom the tender passion is not entirely subdued, fall in love with each other, but these generally contrive to leave the Sect, and go to the "World" to get married and reside.

The "order of the day" left little room, indeed, for vain or idle thoughts. At the sounding of the bell or "shell," the Shakers arose early in the morning, between four o'clock and five in summer, between five and five-thirty in the winter. After kneeling together for a moment of quiet prayer, the occupants of each retiring room stripped the sheets and blankets from their narrow cots, laying them neatly over two chairs at the foot, on which the pillows had previously been placed. Fifteen minutes after rising, the rooms had been vacated, the brethren had gone to their morning chores, and the sisters were entering to close the windows, make the beds, and put the room in order. At breakfast time, six, six-thirty, or seven, the chamber work was finished, fires had been started in the dwelling rooms and shops, the cattle fed, the cows milked, and arrangements for the day's industry were all complete.

Before all meals — the early breakfast, the noon dinner, the six o'clock supper — brethren and sisters would assemble, each group by themselves, in appointed rooms, where for a ten or fifteen minute pause which was a kind of "broad grace," they quietly awaited the bell. Then, in two columns led by the elders and eldresses, respectively, and in the order in which they were to be seated, they proceeded to the dining hall. Taking their places behind their chairs or benches, the sexes at separate tables, they knelt in prayer at a sign from the lead, and after a meal eaten in monastic silence, knelt again before departing directly to their labors. . . .

A series of table monitors, emphasizing economy and good manners at meals, testifies to the concern with standards of behavior. An early monitor (undated manuscript) illustrates how detailed was the instruction:

> First, All should sit upright at the table.
>
> 2d The Elder should begin first, after which all may take hold regularly.
>
> 3d When you take a piece of bread, take a whole piece (if not too large) and when you cut meat, cut it square & equal, fat & lean, & take an equal proportion of bones — take it on your plate together with the sauce, whether it be cabbage, herbs, potatoes or turnips; and not be cutting small pieces in the platter and putting directly into your mouth.
>
> 4th When you have tea or coffee, and any kind of minced victuals or meat cut into mouthfuls, it may be proper with a knife or fork to eat it directly from the platter. . . .
>
> 8th Eat what you need before you rise from table, and not be picking & eating afterwards.
>
> 9th When you have done eating, clean your plate, knife & fork — lay your bones in a snug heap by the side of your plate — scrape up your crumbs — cross your knife & fork on your plate with the edge towards you.
>
> 10th When you reach a mug or pitcher to a person give the handle; and when you take hold of bread, biscuit, pies, etc. to cut or break, take hold of that part which you intend to eat yourself, and cut it square & equal — then you will not leave the print of your fingers for others to eat. . . .
>
> 12th If you are obliged to sneeze or cough, don't bespatter the victuals, make use of your handkerchief.
>
> 13th Clean your knife on your bread before you cut butter, & after cutting butter before you put it into apple sauce, etc. but never clean it on the edge of the platter etc.
>
> 14th Scratching the head, picking the nose or ears, belching, snifing the nose, drinking with the mouth full of victuals, or picking the teeth, are accounted ill manners at a table & must be left off.
>
> 15th And lastly, when you drink, never extend your under lip so far down that one would think the cup was agoing to be swallowed whole. Always wipe your mouth before & after you drink your bear (beer) or water at the table.
>
> Note — Children under the age of 12 or 14 years must have their pie cut for

them & laid by their dishes — Also, when they have bread & butter, suitable pieces must be properly spread & laid by their dishes. . . .

After the evening chores were done, at seven-thirty in summer and eight o'clock in winter, all repaired to their apartments for half an hour, known as "retiring-time," when, on the evenings devoted to family worship, the Shakers disposed themselves in ranks, sitting erect with hands folded "to labor for a true sense of their privilege in the Zion of God." If perchance one should drowse, it was the order to rise and bow four times, or shake, and then resume one's seat. At the end of the period, announced by the ringing of a small bell, brethren and sisters formed separate columns in the corridors, marched two abreast to the meeting-room, and, after bowing as they entered, formed ranks for worship.

Assemblies varied with the time and place. In the early years of the order, and often during revivals, "labouring" meetings were held nightly, and sometimes during the day. As the society expanded, however, evenings not devoted to union meetings or the regular religious service were given over to the practice of songs and exercises. Thus, at New Lebanon in the 'seventies, singing meetings were held on Tuesday and Friday, union meetings on Sunday and Wednesday, and "labouring" meetings on Thursday and Saturday. On Mondays, during this more liberal period, there was a general assembly in the dining hall, where the elder read letters from other communities, selections from the news of the week, or some appropriate book. At the conclusion of such gatherings, to which strangers were admitted on occasion, the family retired quietly to rest. The occupants of each room, after kneeling again in silent prayer, went to bed at a uniform hour — nine o'clock in winter and ten in summer.

Anyone watching such temperate people in the intervals between work and worship would have been impressed, above all else, by the tranquillity of their movements and behavior, as though the daily round was itself a service. No sign of tension or aggressiveness was apparent; speech was subdued; doors were opened and closed with care; all "walked softly." The dwelling, whose orderly, neatly furnished rooms were seldom occupied during the day, was also, in a true sense, a sanctuary. Many a visitor, like Hester Pool, was sensitive to that "indescribable air of purity" which pervaded everything, feeling with her "that this purity is a portion of the mental and moral as well as the physical atmosphere of the Shakerian home." Though all comings and goings followed the pattern of plainness, in the simplicity of domestic life there was an element of freedom, grace, and the contentment, or perhaps resignation, of those who had made peace with themselves and with the world.

The Children's Order was also carefully regulated. Boys and girls lived apart from each other and the rest of the family under "caretakers" responsible to the elders or eldresses. In the indenture agreements the trustees bound the society to provide them with "comfortable food and clothing," the common branches of learning, and training in such manual occupation or branch of business as shall be found best adapted to the "minor's genius and capacity." In return, the parent or guardian relinquished all rights over the child's upbringing. At maturity the youth was free to leave or remain.

In education emphasis was placed on character building and the useful arts. Though the early Believers, "being chiefly of the laboring classes and generally in low circumstances of life," were not in a condition to pay much attention to letter learning, Mother Ann strongly recommended religious and "literary" studies. Meacham advocated the kind of learning that would lead to order, union, peace, and good work — "works that are truly virtuous and useful to man, in this life." The idea that instruction should concentrate on developing good habits and useful talents was subsequently expanded by Seth Wells, the superintendent of the Shaker schools. Self-government, Wells believed, was the prerequisite of both moral and literary education. "When a man is able to govern himself, and subdue his evil propensities . . . he is then in a fair way to be benefitted by moral and religious instructions. . . ."

Nor was innocent recreation considered superfluous. The girls at Canterbury had gymnastic exercises and a flower garden; the boys played ball and marbles, went fishing, and had a small farm of their own. Picnics, sleigh rides, and nutting and berrying parties lent diversion to the ordinary routine. Elkins' frank account of his boyhood at Enfield is the record of a not uncolorful life, with interesting companions, mild paternal control, and normal healthful experiences in a beautiful countryside. Elder Briggs recalls that wood-chopping and maple-sugaring were gala times, like picnics, and mentions the diversions of fishing, swimming, and playing ball, the half-holidays once a week during warm weather, the refreshments during haying, which consisted of sweet buttermilk; lemon, peppermint, checkerberry, raspberry, and currant shrub; cake, cheese, and smoked herring. One who had been a young Shakeress at Niskeyuna remembers many happy days in the Children's Order there:

> Hiding beneath an arcade of the bridge which spanned the dear old creek, we would pull off shoes and stockings, and wade knee-deep in the cool, bright water. Then, loading our long palm-leaf Shaker bonnets with dandelions, which, grown to seed, looked like little white-capped Shakeresses, we would float them down the stream in a race, the boat which won being decorated with buttercups and violets. What mud-pies we made and baked in the sun! What fun we had secreting golden kernels of corn in clam-shells, and peeping from our hiding-place to see the chickens find them and peck them up, firmly believing that they "gave thanks" when they turned their bills up to heaven after sipping water. . . . We had no world's toys, but were just as contented

with our corn-cob dolls, clam-shell plates, acorn-top cups, and chicken-coops for baby houses.

From sources such as the above we suspect that Shaker life was not always as austere as its principles would have had it be; that the Believers, in their effort to extinguish natural affections, tried to do the impossible — particularly where children were concerned. We read of candy-making parties, culinary favors tendered by the "kitchen-sisters," humorous tolerance when children behaved "contrary to order," the attachments for favorite children, close friendships within the Children's Order. Human nature was constantly breaking up the artificial restrictions designed to subdue "carnal desire." It seems that the lot of Shaker youth compared favorably with that of the sons and daughters of farmers in the rural America of the period. . . .

The belief in progress, or "travel," found expression in the field of medicine as in education. Ann Lee's bias against physicians was shared by Joseph Meacham, who assured a doubter that "they that have my spirit have no occasion to go to world's doctors." In the early years Shakers were healed by faith or the laying on of hands. The "gift" against professionals was still held in 1813, when Mother Lucy's attitude to that effect was recorded; but Father Job Bishop, speaking "beautifully" on the same subject, qualified his stand by asserting that a surgeon might be called "in case of a broken bone or any very bad wound." About this time greater reliance was placed on regimen and simple medicines, with resort to shocking, bleeding, sweating, poulticing, and blistering. With the development of the herb industry in the 1820's, the Thomsonian medical practice, which relied on steam baths and herbal remedies and required little academic knowledge, came into increasing favor. Another step was taken in 1840, when messages prohibiting the use of strong drink, swine's flesh, and tobacco ushered in a reform which was more than temporary. In mid-century, largely through the influence of Elder Frederick Evans of New Lebanon, Grahamism and vegetarianism won converts in certain families. Proper diet, supplemented by the water treatment, simple massage, and hot herbal drinks in case of sickness, was the prevalent prescription late in the century. Faith in the "healing gift," however, persisted all this time, with many a cure allegedly effected by spirit touch and mental control.

As interpreted by Elder Evans, the science of health had a theological basis. To provide better food, clothing, and housing, a better distribution of heat, improved lighting, ventilation, and sanitation was the proper field of science. In the "new earth" the human body should be "the central object of influence and attraction," whose "salvation" was no less important than the "health" of the soul. Evans suggested eight main principles of dietetics:

1. Supply the family with at least one kind of course grain flour. Avoid cathartics.
2. Have the "sickly and weakly" cease using animal food, especially fats.
3. Keep the skin clean by regular bathing, with the water at such a temperature as to cause a warm, glowing reaction.
4. Keep room at a temperature not exceeding 60°.
5. Clothing — "regulated on the same principles as water and fire" — should be light, "a little less than you could possibly bear." The young should dispense with underclothes. "Sleep under as little clothing as possible."
6. Breathe pure air. Every room of the home should be of equal temperature. Ventilation of bedrooms important.
7. Thorough ventilation of beds and bedding.
8. "Be comfortable in mind and body."

While these views were the opinion of one person, a natural reformer, they were not unrepresentative of Shaker practice. The vent pipes over the lamps, the slots placed between the two sashes of every window, and the holes in the baseboards in the halls and under the radiators in the gathering rooms were additional evidences of a concern for fresh air. Baths, sinks, and water closets were well ventilated. Pure spring water was ingeniously piped for refrigeration. Temperate outdoor labor, regular hours, wholesome food, good clothing, comfort of mind, and the utmost cleanliness everywhere combined to promote the health of all. On the latter characteristic in particular, often contrasting favorably with conditions elsewhere, strangers were wont to remark from the earliest times. "Great importance is attached to cleanliness," Blackwood's correspondent reported in 1823; "this luxury they appear to enjoy in a truly enviable degree." "Visit them upon any day in the week," the historian of the town of Shirley wrote, "at any hour of the day, and when they are engaged in almost any employment, and you will scarcely ever find them in dirty dishabille. The shirts and pants and frocks of the men are rarely soiled, and the plain linen caps and kerchiefs of the women never." "Everything is . . . kept so delicately clean," remarked an English visitor in 1884, "that an air of refinement, not to say luxury, seems to pervade [the] bedchambers, in spite of their absolute simplicity."

Testimonies on the health of the Shakers are nevertheless conflicting. . . . With allowances made for prejudice, it is a matter of wonder, from the phrases used about the sisters, whether they were in health or out. They were called "a wretched-looking lot of creatures" (Fountain); "their pale faces . . . and flabby condition indicated . . . a low state of health" (George Combe); "the females and sedentary people . . . were occasionally indisposed" (Blackwood's correspondent); "the females . . . look remarkably pale and sallow" (Silliman); the women were "pallid, thin and withered" (Martineau); the sisters, with few exceptions, were "old, wizened, ascetic — perfect specimens of old maids" (Colonel A. M. Maxwell). The difference in the physical appearance of males and females was due, according to one mid-century author, to the "unaspiring, earthly" quality of the former, and the effect on such natures of a comfortable life, outdoor work, plenty of food, and an absence of anxieties. "The Shaker woman, by contrast, has a more melancholy lot. Love — 'the first necessity of woman's nature' — is dwarfed, in her case, to most unnatural ugliness. She must renounce the natural affections." On the other hand, Finch was struck with "the cheerfulness and contented looks" of the people in all the communities; Dixon remarked on "the rosy flesh" of the people of New Lebanon — "a tint but rarely seen in the United States"; and the usually reliable Nordhoff spoke of the "fresh fine complexion [which] most of the Shaker men and women have — particularly the latter."

If the Shaker way of life was detrimental in any way to physical well-being, certainly life was not shortened. The longevity of members of the sect has often been reported. In 1875 Nordhoff, making the first fact-finding tour of the communities, was impressed by the low rate of mortality: at Harvard, where the average age at death for a number of years was 60 to 68; at Union Village, where a large proportion of the members were over 70, and many over 90; at North Union, where many were past 80; at Pleasant Hill, where a considerable number lived past 90; and at Enfield (N.H.), Watervliet (N.Y.), and South Union, where the brethren and sisters often lived well over 75 years.

To support an argument on the "Longevity of Virgin Celibates," Elder Giles Avery advanced facts [selected?] that in five families at New Lebanon, during the period 1848–50, the average age of 29 members at death was $70\frac{1}{2}$ years; at Alfred, during an unspecified period, the average age of 200 members at death was $62\frac{3}{4}$ years (with 100 over 70, 37 between 80 and 90, and 13 between 90 and 97); at Watervliet (N.Y.), in the decade 1870–80, the average age of 39 members at death was 73 years; and at New Gloucester there were "at the present time" (*c*. 1880) 14 persons over 70 years of age, of whom seven were between 79 and 89 years old. Elder Evans estimated that life expectancy among the Believers was over a decade more than that of the world. . . .

When death occurred, complete simplicity marked the funeral. The coffin was pine, plainly lined, unpainted and unadorned. In the mind of the Believer, the life of the spirit was so real that death was but a way-mark in "travel," and the "trappings of grief" superfluous. Following the Quaker custom, the Shakers, led by the elders and eldresses of the family, devoted the main part of the service to personal tributes and memories. Songs were sung, and during one period of Shaker history, messages from the spirit were communicated by the instruments. The procession to the grave was not unlike the heavenly march of worship. Throughout the ritual the tone was one of reverence, strength, and inspiration.

Since followers of Mother Ann did not believe in physical resurrection, they thought of the living soul and not of the dead body. "He is not here," they testified at the burial service. Appropriate, therefore, were the simple slabs of stone, all alike and engraved only with initials, age, and date, which marked the resting place. Many advocated that even these be replaced by a mound of earth, or perhaps a shrub or tree, not as a memorial but rather as a contribution to earth's fertility and beauty.

Comparison of the living conditions of the early Shaker colonists with those prevailing a century or so later furnishes an index to the temporal progress of the society. In 1780 its possessions were limited to a few unpromising acres, a single cabin, the slim resources of John Hocknell. Eight years later the Believers at Niskeyuna were still poor. Money was scarce, and the community was not allowed to run into debt. According to the account of Jonathan Clark of Hancock:

> Our principle food was rice and milk, sometimes we went to the river to procure fish. . . . We had little, and sometimes no bread, butter or cheese, but upon this simple fare, we all subsisted during the Spring and Summer. . . . All our work was very laborious, and at the end, we looked more like skeletons, than working men. . . . Our breakfast consisted of a small bowl of porridge. Supper the same. Dinner, a small bit of cake about 2½ inches square which Aaron Wood cut up, and gave to us. One day Joseph Preston and another brother went to the River to catch Herring; and Joseph stated that he was so hungry, that he ate two *raw*, as soon as they came out of the water. . . . We had but little house room, and of course were obliged to lie upon the floor. . . . Fifteen of us lay upon the floor in one room; some had one blanket to cover them, while others had none. . . .

The "manner of dress and building" was in the same inferior state. "Those who first believed, in America," Youngs wrote, "adopted such dress as seemed the most suitable, of the common plain forms that prevailed among people at the time they lived in England"; and the form, fashion, and quality of garments were "extremely various." In form and manner of construction, buildings also were of poor quality and ill-adapted to the purpose for which they were needed.

In all departments, however, the Shakers, by the will to make everything uniform with the best, steadily raised their standard of living. During the nineteenth century the preparation of wholesome food was considered more and more important, and as a result the Shakers achieved a considerable reputation for their recipes and public meals. As for clothing, painstaking care came to be paid to the needs of age groups and occasions, to uniformity of color and material, to the marking and laundering of garments. Buildings, too, were constantly improved and their numbers increased to meet the expanding needs of the colony. In New Lebanon, for instance, from the few small farmhouses which the Shakers took over in the 1780's, the community grew until it had 125 buildings in 1839, and property, including 2,292 acres of land, valued at $68,225. Within the same period the original colony at Watervliet had grown to a community of over 2,500 acres, valued, with buildings, at $46,900. When Nordhoff made his survey in 1875, the home farms of the eighteen societies, taken by themselves, amounted to nearly 50,000 acres, to which figure must be added extensive outside holdings in mills, wood lots, and "outfarms" — one in Kentucky, owned by the Watervliet (N.Y.) society, as large as 30,000 acres — which were often operated by tenants.

Following the eight immigrants from England some seventeen thousand persons, at one time or another, were gathered into the society. To the Shakers this was a "great harvest" — the "blessed binders" had followed closely on the reapers, "severing all the worthless cockle till the work was done complete."

STUDY GUIDE

1. Explain the techniques the Shakers used in order to maintain celibacy. What explanation can you give for the skepticism about celibacy and the rumors of sexual excesses that often develop in the outside world with respect to convents, monasteries, and other celibate communities?

2. Describe the "order of the day" in a Shaker community and the religious life of the Shakers. Aside from separation of the sexes and the religious doctrines, what values and attitudes do you see among the Shakers that were not substantially different from those of many other rural, farm folks in the period?

3. Though some might consider the Shaker life as barren and harsh, Andrews suggests that most of the Shakers felt a sense of freedom, contentment, and peace. What evidence is there in the selection that Shakers really felt this way, and how can one explain such a disciplined, plain, celibate life bringing happiness? What parallels are there between the Shaker philosophy and other experiments in alternative life-styles that you know of (such as Henry Thoreau's experiment at Walden Pond)?

4. In terms of permanence and long-range influence upon American society, none of the other communitarian groups were any more successful than were the Shakers. What forces in American life and in the development of the American nation made it unlikely that these small-group experiments could successfully serve as a pattern for all of American society?

5. What do you see as the explanation for the development of so many communal groups in our own time? What evidence is there that such groups continue to have — on a reduced scale — the same problems that exist in the larger society?

BIBLIOGRAPHY

The historical literature on the Shakers and on other communitarian groups that flourished in the pre-Civil War years is both ample and interesting. A number of volumes can serve to introduce you to the entire range of communitarianism. You might begin with Arthur Bestor, Jr.'s prize-winning work, *Backwoods Utopias: The Sectarian and the Owenite Phases of Communitarian Socialism in America: 1663–1829* (Philadelphia, 1950), or with the same author's essay on "Patent-Office Models of the Good Society: Some Relationships Between Social Reform and Westward Expansion," *American Historical Review*, Vol. LVIII (1953), pp. 505–526. Additional surveys of the topic will be found in the following: Alice Felt Tyler, *Freedom's Ferment: Phases of American Social History to 1860* * (Minneapolis, Minn., 1944) — a description of almost all of the reform movements, communitarian and otherwise, of the period; Charles Nordhoff's older but still valuable volume, *The Communistic Societies of The United States* (New York, 1875; reprinted, 1960); Mark Holloway, *Heavens on Earth: Utopian Communities in America, 1680–1880* * (New York, 1951); and Everett Webber, *Escape to Utopia: The Communal Movement in America* (New York, 1959). More specific in focus is the volume from which the preceding selection was taken, Edward D. Andrews, *The People Called Shakers: A Search for the Perfect Society* * (New York, 1953). Andrews also wrote volumes on Shaker furniture and on their music and dance. Other works on the Shakers have been written by Marguerite Melcher, Francis D. Nichol, and Clara E. Sears.

There are biographies of Owen, Fourier, and many other communitarian leaders, and studies of most of the communities of the pre-Civil War period. Jane and William Pease describe communities founded to aid recently freed Negroes in their book *Black Utopia: Negro Communal Experiments in America* (Madison, Wis., 1963). Other works of merit include: Herbert W. Schneider and George Lawton, *A Prophet and a Pilgrim* * (New York, 1942); Maren L. Carden, *Oneida: Utopian Community to Modern Corporation* * (Baltimore, Md., 1969); and Lindsay Swift, *Brook Farm: Its Members, Scholars, and Visitors* (New York, 1961). It is not possible here to list the many works dealing with the post-Civil War period of utopianism or the broader aspects of utopian thought in American life. Three works that are essential in understanding these subjects are: Donald Egbert and Stow Persons, eds., *Socialism and American Life*, 2 vols. (Princeton, N.J., 1952); Helmut R. Niebuhr, *The Kingdom of God in America* * (Chicago, © 1937); and Robert S. Fogarty, *American Utopianism* * (Itasca, Ill., © 1972). The last of these is a collection of source material on utopian communities.

V PEOPLES AND SECTIONS

In our time, more than in any earlier period, the American people are a single people. They drive the same cars, use the same products, eat much the same food, and dress alike — whether they live in California or New England. With slight differences, their values and their popular culture — on the screen, on the airwaves, and in national magazines — are practically identical in Atlanta, Georgia and Minneapolis, Minnesota. The present homogeneity of American society tends to obscure the fact that differences among classes, nationalities, and sections played a prominent role in earlier American history.

The strong nationalistic sentiments of the first three decades of the nineteenth century faded rapidly after 1830. Always somewhat distinct in language, politics, and social life, North and South now saw their respective economic interests as being in conflict with each other. Both hoped for the support of what was rapidly emerging as a third distinct section, the trans-Appalachian West. Industrialization and urbanization were making the Northeast a region of constant change. In mining fields and factory towns, on canal and railroad projects, the strange tongues of several European nationalities could be heard. In contrast, the South was largely untouched by industrialism and the urban growth that would eventually characterize the entire country. Few immigrants went South, and slavery, with all its social as well as economic implications, swept westward from the south-Atlantic states into Mississippi, Alabama, and other newly opened cotton lands.

The West was less clearly defined than the North or South; indeed, what was West was ever-changing as the line of settlement passed from western New York to Ohio, Iowa, and beyond. What we now call the Midwest was a region of non-slave-holding farmers, many of them Scandinavian, German, and other immigrants who had come directly west from the port of entry. On the slavery issue, they were frequently in conflict with their border state neighbors in Kentucky and Missouri, but on such questions as government support of internal improvements and banking, they found they had much in common.

The first reading in this section describes the extraordinary politics, oratory, and folklore of the trans-Appalachian region. The second affords a graphic picture of slavery, the institution that was more important than any other factor in setting the South apart. The third and fourth readings deal with two groups of people who brought about significant changes in the population and the workforce of the North — the immigrants who arrived in such great numbers during this period, and the women who entered factories to operate the new machines.

Courtesy St. Louis Art Museum

"The County Election" by George Bingham, 1852. (Detail) Frontier politics were born in exuberance and drunken confusion.

THOMAS D. CLARK

Frontier America

.

Events in American political life during the past decade have placed severe strains on the democratic system in this country. Political assassination, violent demonstrations, and the dirty tricks and public corruption that were summed up in the word "Watergate" led many citizens of all ages and political beliefs to a sad sense of disillusionment and alienation. The integrity of elections was questioned, the basis of government policy seemed to be favoritism, and many wondered whether their participation in politics was essentially futile.

Most Americans had so fully accepted the superiority of democratic government that they had failed to recognize some of its difficulties and were hardly aware of some of the questions posed by critics. At the opening of the nineteenth century, Hugh Henry Brackenridge published a picaresque novel in which an illiterate buffoon, Teague O'Regan, personified the American equalitarian spirit. Brackenridge's biting portrayal of the average man and of the level of public discourse was actually written in the age of the Founding Fathers, whereas the mass entrance of the average man into political life is traditionally dated some decades later.

President James Monroe, the last of the "cocked hat and powdered wig" presidents, seemed something of a relic of an earlier, gentlemanly aristocracy. With the end of his administration, American politics took on an earthier tone, both in political rhetoric and in the assumptions as to who should participate in political life. Revisions in state constitutions broadened the suffrage by eliminating property qualifications, and though Tom, Dick, and Harry seem not to have rushed to the polls in great numbers, the possibility of their doing so was never far from the minds of office-seekers. Politicians now felt compelled to pretend to humble birth in a log cabin and to a level of intelligence and literacy not much above Brackenridge's Teague.

No region was so closely associated with the roughnecked, plain-spoken politics of the 1830s as the middlewestern states drained by the Ohio and Mississippi rivers. Out of this backwoods democracy came poker-playing Henry Clay, "Old Hickory" Jackson, and Davy Crockett. More interesting than the individual politicians of the West was the social milieu that gave rise to them, the electorate that chose them, and the political course they ran in gaining office. Thomas D. Clark writes of this region with considerable humor and a knack for finding colorful tall tales of the old South and Middle West. One must, however, look beneath the rhetoric, the boasting, and the yarns to discover the real life and politics of this area. The amiable exaggeration and humor in the following selection are amusing, but Clark's description also discloses some very serious problems of politics in a democracy.

"Rotation in office, and frequent election, salutary principles which disjoint the schemes of usurpation, and frustrate the systematic continuations of power," was the toast of a rampant frontiersman at a Washington's birthday celebration. This utterance was greeted with thunderous applause, lengthy swigging at the jug, and a sustained fire by the militia. "Rotation in office" and "frequent elections" were indeed "salutary principles" of the frontier. Western polls were storm centers of political activity. Fight after fight occurred during elections. Kentucky alone followed the time-honored precedent of Virginia and prolonged the delectable process of selecting public officials by keeping its polls open three days. By the time the Bluegrass State had endured a three-day bender its eyes were reddened for months to come.

Strangers visiting in Kentucky during elections were frightened out of their wits. Fortesque Cuming had to pass through Carlisle, where he said: "I counted above a hundred horses fastened under trees — I was induced to hasten past this place as the voters in that sterile part of the country did not appear quite peaceable and orderly as those in Paris. Some of them might have been moved by the spirit of liquor to challenge me to run a

From chapter 6 of *The Rampaging Frontier* by Thomas D. Clark. Reprinted by permission of the author.

race with them or to amuse the company with a game of rough and tumble, at both of which the backwoods Virginians are very dexterous." One would be led to doubt Cuming's statement of affairs in Kentucky during elections if it were not for the fact that other travelers, and, likewise, native observers, have left similar accounts.

Nothing could have provoked more excitement than a three-day election at which the voters made their choice known to the clerks viva voce. Cuming found the election in Lexington quiet. "It was the day of election for representatives in the legislature of the state. The voting was very simple. The county clerk sat within the bar of the courthouse, and the freeholders as they arrived gave their names, and the names of those voted for." This was at Lexington, a town of more refinement, but down the river James Flint contrasted conditions in Indiana and Kentucky. He said: "A few days ago I witnessed an election of a member of congress from the state of Indiana — members for the state assembly and county officers, and the voters for the township of Jeffersonville were taken by ballot in one day. No quarrels or disorder occurred. At Louisville in Kentucky the poll was kept open three days. The votes were given viva voce. I saw three fights in the course of an hour."

Usually the candidates sat inside the enclosure with the clerks of the elections, and when the voters appeared they announced their choice by turning to their favorite candidates, and with a patronizing smile said, "I vote for you, Sir," to which the candidates replied, "Thank You, Sir, and may God bless you, Sir."

Candidates were able to keep tab on their standing at the polls by the viva-voce method of voting, and they stimulated their constituents' choice by administering frequent and generous potations of the best bourbon which all the land of famous bourbon liquor could supply. Liquor barrels stood within easy reach of the polls, and ham-fisted bullies gulped down deep draughts and cast fighting epithets at less intemperate voters. Along with liquor which flowed as freely as mountain branch water there were other coveted commodities. Gingerbread, pawpaw, and trinket salesmen surrounded the polls. There were loafers, huckster women, "niggers," and horse jockeys all milling around the grounds. By nightfall they were all drunk and craving excitement. The candidates bought all the gingerbread available and sent the crowd home loaded to return the next day in even higher spirits. By the second day the election contests grew warm, and a two-day drunk began to tell on the nervous temperaments of the minions of democracy. Fights broke the tedium for election clerks, and even for the candidates who waited for each new crop of citizens to make up their minds. If by chance the candidates were running nose and nose down the homestretch on the third day, liquor flowed more freely, and each side lambasted the other with fiery vocal fusillades. Treats were passed out to all within reach, and voters were bullied, badgered and openly intimidated. Fighting ruffians tumbled to and fro before the clerk's stand and at many polls ears were bitten off, noses impaired and eyes gouged. Benjamin Drake in describing a third-day election fracas in Mason County, Kentucky, said the highly excited partisans of each of the candidates were shouting "Huzza, the Little Red," "Well done, Bald Eagle," "Go it, Captain," "Nail him, Coffin." The native son of Old Kentucky in this particular contest saw that his chances for success were becoming more uncertain with the passage of each hour. He bought two barrels of "stout" liquor, rolled them into the courtyard where he mounted one and proclaimed to the crowd that his father was a "pyore canebrake" pioneer, that he himself was a native son who had been rocked in a sugar trough and raised on "possum fat and hominy." He was a captain of the "melishy" and waded in muck and mire up to his belly for his country. He declared his opponent to be a "New Englander by birth, a college-learnt dandy schoolmaster, who carried his sheepskin in a tea cannister." To his gaping audience this "sugar-trough" scion flung the opprobrious denouncement that his opponent was a hawk-billed "blue belly." To top this thunderclap, he invited "all true sons of Ol'Kentuck to come to the trough and liquor!" This fiery brand of the Limestone bottoms leaped from his barrel-head platform, and knocked the ends out of his mellow prizes and ladled out the "spirit of democracy" by the gourdful to gasping "citizens." Shouts of "Huzza for old Kentuck" and "Down with the Yankees," filled the air. The opposition, undaunted by this eleventh-hour show of strength, answered the militia captain's free-handed generosity with "stones, clubs and brickbats [which] were hurled by the assailing party, and returned with equal violence; half-horse half-alligator encountered all Pottawattamie — a Mississippi snag was loosened from its moorings by a full-grown snapping turtle — the 'yaller flower of the desart' bruised the nose of 'Old Tecumseh,' 'Bill Corncracker' walked right into 'Yankee Doodle' and made the 'claret' run in torrents; in short, so hot waxed the patriotism of the belligerents, that many of them were trampled under foot, some were gouged, others horribly snake-poled and not a few knocked clear into a cocked hat."

George D. Prentice started an editorial fight in Kentucky which lasted until 1842. Prentice had witnessed an election in Frankfort which he described in detail in his "Letter of a Strolling Editor" to the *New England Weekly Review*. The editor of the Cincinnati *Advertiser* was the first to publish this letter in the West and it was later republished in the Louisville *Advertiser* under the exciting title of "Prick Me a Bull Calf Until He Roar." This letter paints a lusty picture of democracy at work in the West:

> I have just witnessed a strange thing — a Kentucky election — and I am disposed to give you an account of it [said Prentice]. An election in Kentucky lasts three days, and during that period whiskey and apple toddy flow through our cities and villages like the Euphrates through ancient Babylon. I must do Lexington the justice to say that matters were conducted here with tolerable propriety; but in Frankfort, a place which I had the curiosity to visit on the

last day of the election, Jacksonianism and drunkenness stalked triumphant — "an unclean pair of lubberly giants." A number of runners, each with a whiskey bottle poking its long neck from his pocket, were busily employed bribing voters, and each party kept half a dozen bullies under pay, genuine specimen of Kentucky alligatorism, to flog every poor fellow who should attempt to vote illegally. A half a hundred mortar would scarcely fill up the chinks of the skulls that were broken on that occasion. I barely escaped myself. One of the runners came up to me, and slapping me on the shoulder with his right hand, and a whiskey bottle with his left, asked me if I was a voter. "No," said I. "Ah, never mind," quoth the fellow, pulling a corncob out of the neck of the bottle, and shaking it up to the best advantage. "Jest take a swig at the cretur and toss in a vote for Old Hickory's boys — I'll fight for you, damne!" Here was a temptation to be sure; but after looking alternately at the bottle and the bullies who were standing ready with their sledgehammer fists to knock down all interlopers, my fears prevailed and I lost my whiskey. Shortly after this I witnessed a fight that would have done honor to Mendoza and Big Ben. A great ruffian-looking scoundrel, with arms like a pair of cables knotted at the ends, and a round black head that looked like a forty pound cannon shot, swaggered up to the polls and threw in his bit of paper, and was walking off in triumph. "Stop, friend," exclaimed one of the Salt River Roarers, stepping deliberately up to him, "Are you a voter?" "Yes, by God," replied he of the bullet head. "That's a lie," rejoined the Roarer, "and you must prepare yourself to go home an old man, for I'll be damned if I don't knock you into the middle of your ninety-ninth year." "Ay, ay," replied the other, "come on, then; I'll ride you to hell, whipped up with the sea sarpint!" They had now reached an open space, and the Salt River bully, shaking his fist a moment by way of feint, dropped his chin suddenly upon his bosom and pitched headforemost toward the stomach of his antagonist with the whole force of his gigantic frame. Bullet Head, however, was on his guard, and, dodging aside with the quickness of lightning to avoid the shock, gave the assailant a blow that sent him staggering against a whiskey table, where he fell to the ground amid the crash of bottles, mugs, and tumblers. Nothing daunted by this temporary discomfiture, the bully gathered himself up and with a single muttered curse renewed his place in front of his foe. Several blows were now given on both sides with tremendous effect, and in a few moments the Salt River boy, watching his opportunity, repeated his maneuver in which he had first been foiled. This time he was successful. His head was planted directly in his antagonist's stomach, who fell backward with such force that I had no expectation of his ever rising again. "Is the scoundrel done for?" inquired the temporary victor, walking up and looking down on his prostrate foe. Bullet Head spoke not, but with the bound of a wildcat leaped to his feet and grappled with his enemy. It was a trial of strength, and the combatants tugged and strained and foamed at the mouth, and twined like serpents around each other's bodies, till at length the strength of Bullet Head prevailed and his opponent lay struggling beneath him. "Gouge him!" exclaimed a dozen voices, and the topmost combatant seized his victim by the hair and was preparing to follow the advice that was thus shouted in his ear, when the prostrate man, roused by desperation and exerting a strength that seemed superhuman, caught his assailant by the throat with a grasp like that of fate. For a few moments the struggle seemed to cease, and then the face of the throttled man turned black, his tongue fell out of his mouth, and he rolled to the ground as senseless as a dead man. I turned away a confirmed believer in the doctrine of total depravity. . . .

There are extant many samples of the rantings of the "flat-top" stump speakers who sought public favor by their peculiar brand of persuasiveness. Some of these which remain may be fictitious, others perhaps are authentic recordings. Governor Ford has preserved the speech of Adolphus Frederick Hubbard who sought the governorship of Illinois over the opposition of Ninian Edwards. "Fellow Citizens," shouted the eloquent Adolphus, "I offer myself as a candidate before you, for the office of governor. I do not pretend to be a man of extraordinary talents; nor do I claim to be equal to Julius Caesar or Napoleon Bonaparte, nor yet to be as great a man as my opponent Governor Edwards. Nevertheless I think I can govern you pretty well. I do not think it will take an extraordinarily smart man to govern you; for to tell the truth, Fellow Citizens, I do not think you will be very hard to govern nohow." This speech had the virtue of being a very frank argument to the effect that the Suckers [citizens of Illinois] should elect just an "ordinary" man to the governorship.

In Arkansas voracious sons entranced their hearers with discourses, which neither the speakers nor the listeners could possibly understand; nevertheless they got right down to business. "Feller Citizens," began a slouchy, shock-haired mud turtle, "this are the day for the people of Wolf's Mouth, and I mought say, if I warn't modest, that our carnal entranchasemen (that's a hard word but I got through it!) depends on our heterogenous exertions! Bill Sculpin are our candidate, and Jack Dondee swears he is bound to shoot every man that don't vote for him! Feller Citizens — I'm going to sand my speech with quotations from Seizem the celibrated Latin cricket, when he addressed the Cathagenions and Rocky Mountain cods at the baittle of Cow Pens! Look out I'm comin — cock your rifles and be ready! Eat ye brute! As the immaculate feller said, when he got stabbed in the back in the House of Representatives!"

To this brash sanding of an Arkansas stump speech with the words of the "great Seizem" by the friend of Bill Sculpin, a raw specimen replied: "Feller Citizens, there arn't no one skeered in this crowd! I'm not afflicted like Charlie Culliver, with the disease called *E Plurubus Unum!* Tempt us fugit! by the concordat and evacuating nabob of Jerusalem! Old Jim Grime thought he'd frighten me with his Greek! But I can put in the big licks and pile on as much agony as he ever heard of! Poe stultus! Santa Parsima Block, Island Point, Judih Lex Taglinois! Historia Sacre! and fiducet et Broadaxe! What does the fellow think of himself now? He's a traveling synagogue; but can't catch me with his high-falutin words! Vote for Tom Cressy, he's a horse, and so am I! Ecco Signum! Abinito! De jure dum spire-Hurrah for Tom Cressy."

Whether this speech was ever uttered matters little here. It is representative of the kind of stuff that flowed (and still does, possibly without the sandings of Seizem) from breast-pounding politicians of the backwoods. . . .

Repartee in stump speaking was a very necessary part of the art of impressing an audience of voters. Although the Hoosiers and Suckers did not enjoy the privilege of fighting three days around their polls, they did take their elections seriously. A frontiersman in one election went to log rollings, barbecues and other public meetings as a dutiful and unostentatious citizen. He rolled logs, basted meat and did anything else he could to help along the good cause. His opponent was a dandified fellow who never offered his services at any time, nor to any cause, but he continually chided his uncouth native opponent for wearing borrowed shoes and for doing other things which he considered beneath the dignity of a seeker after public office. This humiliating chiding continued until the buckskin son happened to realize that his dandified tormenter's name was Jack Bass, and that by dropping the "B" in his surname he could turn the tables. Not only was Jack B'Ass laughed off the stump, but out of the country. . . .

No officers in the states' governments attracted more attention, or committed more asinine blunders than members of the general assemblies. One Fourth of July toastmaster, after speaking in stilted terms in which he bathed heroically and extravagantly every institution in the state from its cities to its "Fair," rendered in a tremulous voice: "Ohio *Legislature,* more deeds and fewer words." This sentiment did, or should have, prevailed throughout the West. Surely the toastmaster in Ohio did not have in mind, when he pleaded for action, that vigorous member of the Ohio House of Representatives who announced that he would whip the first three men who voted for a bill to amend the charter of the city of Cincinnati.

State general assemblies were the favorite "stomping" grounds for all eloquent sons who had more wind than brains. Some of the queerest specimens the backwoods could rake up were loaded onto flatboats, stagecoaches, or sent away on horseback to the state capitals to "make" laws. No state in the West could possibly exceed Kentucky in this respect. At least fifty volumes of legislative acts and journals stand today as open chapters revealing the devious ways of asserting democratic rights.

The sons of the Bluegrass became exceedingly wrought up over the foreign intimidation of Americans prior to the outbreak of the War of 1812. Leaders in the general assembly in 1807 laid all of the blame at England's feet. Henry Clay was active in this assault on Britain and actually took part in passing a law forbidding citation of certain English statutes. Clay, later, was placed in a humorous predicament because of this taboo of British laws. He found occasion, when appearing before the house of the assembly on a special occasion, to quote the common law of England. A bearded representative of the people jumped to his feet and shouted, "Mr. Speaker, I want to know, Sir, if what that gentleman said is true? Are we all living under Old English law?" The speaker explained that the English common law was recognized as a part of the law of the land. "Well, Sir," resumed the ardent buckskin patriot, "when I remember that our fathers, and some of us fit, bled and died to free us from the English law, I don't want to be under it any longer, and I make a motion that it be repealed right away." The motion was seconded, and it was with difficulty that the learned gentlemen at the foot of the great hill at Frankfort were spared the ordeal of making asses of themselves and their state by repealing a great body of fundamental law.

It might be that the editor of the *Monitor of Western America* was correct in part of his statement concerning the general history of the Kentucky legislature. He reported, "We are glad to find by the result of the election that the people of Kentucky prefer *men to horses* — human beings to brutes — as their representatives in the state legislature. A horse may neigh and snort, may be taught to follow his master, do as he is bid, and obey instructions; a horse may prance and kick, and do mischief, but rational beings only are worthy of a seat in the legislature, and we *do hope* in the *future* they will be sent there." This optimistic scribe might have employed his time more profitably hoping for the millennium. In the very year in which he proclaimed freedom from the tyranny of "equine" legislators a singularly fine crop of long-eared sons tried to tear up not only the state government, but likewise threatened an invasion into the national constitution through the famous "relief laws."

Legislators of the early western states were restless creatures. In Illinois the assembly had its ups and downs. Pending before that body in 1826 was the business of electing a state treasurer. The incumbent in the office was defeated, and before members of the house could vacate their seats he had knocked down and thrashed four of the largest and strongest of the people's representatives, and the others "broke and fled" from the house.

The Suckers had great trouble making up their minds what should be the law of the state. At every meeting of the legislature the laws were changed to suit the whims of that particular crop of legislators. It was said that it was indeed a fortunate thing that the Illinois assembly did not have power to rectify the scriptures for if it had it would have been certain "to alter and amend them, so that no one could tell what was or was not the law of the state." Perhaps the Sucker assemblymen should have adopted the suggestion of the Reverend Mr. Wiley and the Covenanters of Randolph County who complained that the Governor of Illinois was unbaptized and therefore was a heathen chief executive. They begged that the constitutional convention make Jesus Christ the head of the state, and the scriptures the rule of faith and practice.

Laws were transferred from Virginia and the other southern states, and from Kentucky many of them were spread throughout the western states without much fundamental change. One of the most disturbing bits of legislation ever passed in a western general assembly was the "scalp" or "bounty" law which permitted payment of rewards for wolf scalps. The original laws instructed magistrates to pay bounties for scalps with few or no questions asked, but soon more scalps were appearing than there were funds with which to pay rewards. In Kentucky the honorable gentlemen of the assembly discovered that scalpers were not killing bitch wolves, but harboring them for breeding purposes. In Clay County an ingenious evader of the law exercised a rare entrepreneurial ability by maintaining wolf pens where he caught bitches and kept them for breeding. With the scalps from his domesticated pups he was highly successful in euchering a sumptuous living out of the state treasury. When laws were passed forbidding payment for wolves under six months of age, the boys learned the fine art of stretching scalplocks from weanling pups to make them appear as old varmints.

More disputes and bickerings occurred over wolf scalps possibly than over the scalps which the Indians removed from the heads of early pioneers. Indiana and Illinois adopted scalp laws from Kentucky, and, apparently, a generous number of Kentucky tricksters were included in the deal because the Hoosiers and Suckers were continually wrangling over the dishonesty of bounty-seekers. Time and again they changed laws to prevent swindling, but only the disappearance of wolves saved the states from eventual bankruptcy, or at least from a generous run upon the treasury.

Wolves were more plentiful in Arkansas, and the scalp law was a lucrative source of income because many of the hillbillies wandered throughout the wooded sections of that state. The old Arkansas law permitted magistrates to issue certificates of payment upon the delivery of scalps, but as wolves grew scarce the bold hunters cut a single bounty into many strips, and cut larger scalps from sheepskins. When they appeared to take the oath that they held in their hands a wolf scalp they clutched the thin strip just tightly enough to evade the law. A "wolf bill" was proposed in the house in December, 1837, which would be more lenient on the riflers of the state treasury. This law had been passed by the senate and had come to the house where another important law, the real-estate bank bill, was pending. A long series of amendments were offered to both bills, and the good-natured Major Anthony proposed that the president of the real-estate bank sign all bounty certificates — since both involved the delicate frontier art of scalping the people. Since the president of the bank was the speaker of the house and was a man of extremely fine sensibilities, he took as personal any disparaging remarks about his pet bill. This suggestion of Major Anthony had a bit of sneer in it. The Speaker deserted the chair, reached for his bowie knife and made straight for the wisecracking member. Major Anthony staved off this vicious attack for a time with a chair and his bowie knife, but the Speaker being experienced in such delicate matters soon knocked Anthony's knife out of his hand, and thrust his blade to the hilt in the innocent member's breast.

Interfering with the sanctity of the people's rights in Arkansas was an extremely dangerous business, and the boys from the "big bottom" cherished with genuine affection their "wolf law."

Speakers of the house in some of the other states did not stab members for their frivolities on the floor, but surely a Hoosier one would have been justified in committing mayhem upon the Honorable Mr. Marvin of Hendricks County. Mr. Marvin, whose term was about to expire, and who was not accountable for legislative blunders back home, proceeded to "come the giraffe" over a bill to reduce the assessor's pay to one dollar and fifty cents a day. His ire was up, and he bellowed: "Mr. Speaker! I second the motion of the gentleman from Carroll, I do by God! I'm for paying men damned well for their services, and not for starving them until they are as lean and hungry as starved wolves. I'm not so infernal pussillanimous as some gentlemen who haven't no guts! I'll be damned if I don't oppose some gentlemen here who are cavorting on this question like stub-tailed dogs in high rye, or a young heifer in fly time. I'm fornenst such cussed stinginess, and for the proposition of the gentleman from Carroll, who for onst is right, but by God that is rarely the case, I must admit. I hope the committee of the whole will do their duty and not act the part of damned fools. I am now done, and would say to the house, go it, go it."

It was a far more docile member who appeared for his first term in the Missouri legislature. This honorable gentleman, who having been caught up by the scruff of the neck and instructed "to hit" for Jefferson City as a representative of the people, appeared at the statehouse and entered what he thought was the lower house. The members of this chamber, however, were cavorting somewhat after the manner of "stub-tailed dogs in high rye," and he ventured upstairs to the senate where he found proceedings under way in a less riotous manner. He presented his credentials to the president who in turn informed him that the room below was the house. The "green" member stood looking frightened for a moment and then replied in a timid voice, "Why I was in *that* room and thought it was a grocery [saloon]."

Often there was a bit of difficulty with public servants who took their oaths of office too seriously — or, at any rate, too literally. When the Missouri legislature was organized for the first time, an honest but indiscreet colonel was given the choice plum of doorkeeper. With uplifted right arm he swore sanctimoniously "to support the constitution and to keep the doors of the house open." Upon assuming the responsibility of guaranteeing the liberties of the people, the pompous colonel threw open the double doors, disregarding the coolness of the weather, and complaints from the legislators. To all requests "to shut the doors," the colonel replied that he had sworn to keep the doors of the house open, and keep them open he would as long as there was breath in his body. Finally this faithful public servant chose to resign his office rather than be a party to the raping of constitutional authority in the sovereign state of Missouri. Timothy Flint was in Missouri at the time the state government was organized, and he found a wild scramble for political positions. He thought all the evils of office-seeking in the eastern states seemed to be concentrated in this new commonwealth. When the assembly met, not only did the open doors cause confusion, but likewise the headless activities of the "gentlemen" who represented the people. A waggish member inscribed above the Speaker's chair, "Missouri, forgive them, they know not what they do."

Kentucky was most notorious of all western states for its verdant statesmen. There were a few Clays, Nicholases, Marshalls and Breckinridges. Other legislators were pale imitations. Eastern counties elected loud-mouthed "yahoos" who floated to the "outside," and to Frankfort on the Kentucky River. Roads were poor, and there were few or no public conveyances to transport the "statesmen" from the upcountry. One such "honorable representative," Mullins by name, floated into Frankfort on the famous old Kentucky River packet, the *Blue Wing*, and began "looking into the situation" at once. At court day back in his beloved county, following adjournment of the assembly, he gave an accounting of his lawmaking activities in a sonorous oration which fell a little short of the manner of Clay. "Feller Citizens!" saluted the redfaced Honorable Mullins, "when you elected me to the legislature I wished that I mought have the tallest pine growed in the mountings, so I mought strip the limbs from the same and make it into an enormous pen, and dip it in the waters of the Kaintuck River and write acrost the clouds, 'God bless the people of Estill County!'

"Arter you elected me I went down to Frankfort on the *Blue Wing* and as we wended our winding sinuosities amidst its labyrinthian meanderings, the birdlets, the batlets, and the owlets flew outen their secret hidin' places and cried out to me in loud voices: 'Sail on, Mullins, thou proud defender of thy country's liberties.'

"When I reached Frankfort, I went up into the legislatur hall and thar I spied many purty perlicues a-hangin on the ceiling to pay for which you had been shamefully robbed of by unjest taxation. When matters of small importance were before the body I lay like a bull pup a-baskin in the sunshine, with a blue-bottled fly a-ticklin of my nose; but when matters of great importance come up I riz from my seat, like the Numidian lion of the desert, shuck the dew drops from my mane, and gave three shrill shrieks for liberty." . . .

Legislators of the early West were tenderhearted individuals when a constituent approached them with a tale of woe and despair. They would get him a divorce from a wife who had been delivered of a mulatto baby, change his name, or slice off a nice chunk of public land and waive the fee. Poor widows, indigent orphans, and ailing and aged patriarchs were ever uppermost in the minds of the "servants of the people." Often legislators did foolish things for the "boys up the creek."

The representative from Monroe County, Kentucky, announced to a sympathetic assembly that Mrs. Chillian Carter, the wife of a loyal supporter, had been delivered of triplets. This unexpected stroke of generosity on the part of Mother Nature placed a serious burden on poor Chillian's shoulders,

but his friend, the gentleman from Monroe, proposed to aid him. He introduced a bill in the house which is a masterpiece of legislative drafting.
"Whereas, it is represented that Mrs. Carter, wife of Chillian Carter, of the
County of Monroe, had on the eighth day of the present month of January,
three children at one birth — one son and two daughters," and "For encouragement whereof," the general assembly of Kentucky authorized the
county court of Monroe to appropriate "one thousand acres of vacant and
unappropriated land lying in the state of Tennessee." A question arises at
this point as to whether the gentlemen of the Kentucky assembly were
adding chaos to confusion and frustration in the fruitful Chillian Carter's
household. Perhaps these statesmen-like gentlemen recalled the date of birth,
January 8, and believed that Tennesseans, remembering that this was the
anniversary of the great victory of their favorite son at Chalmette, would
overlook this rather bold violation of their sanctity as a sovereign state. . . .

"Phil" of Jefferson City, Missouri, contributed the following story of a
Missourian appearing before the state legislature with chickens for sale. If
what Timothy Flint saw in the Missouri assembly is a true account of what
went on there this yarn is not an unreasonable one. [He reports:]

> While the Legislature of Missouri was in session a few years ago a green fel-
> low from the country came to Jefferson to sell some chickens. He had about
> two dozen, all of which he had tied by the legs to a string, and this being
> divided equally, and thrown across his horse or his shoulder, formed his mode
> of conveyance, leaving the fowls with their heads hanging down, with little
> else of them visible except their naked legs, and a promiscuous pile of out-
> stretched wings and ruffled feathers. After several ineffectual efforts to dispose
> of his load, a wag, to whom he made an offer of sale, told him that he did not
> want chickens himself, but that perhaps he could sell them at that large, stone
> house over there (the capitol), that there was a man over there buying, on
> speculation, for the St. Louis market, and no doubt he could find a ready sale.
>
> The delighted countryman started when his informer stopped him.
>
> "Look here," says he, "when you get over there, go upstairs, and then turn
> to the left. The man stops in that large room. You will find him sitting up at
> the other end of the room, and now engaged with a number of fellows buying
> chickens. If a man at the door should stop you don't mind him. He has got
> chickens himself for sale, and tries to prevent other people from selling theirs.
> Don't mind him, but go right ahead."
>
> Following the directions, our friend soon found himself at the door of the
> Hall of Representatives. To open it and enter was the work of a moment.
> Taking from his shoulder the string of chickens and giving them a shake to
> freshen them, he commenced his journey toward the speaker's chair the
> fowls, in the meantime, loudly expressing, from the half-formed *crow* to the
> harsh *quaark,* their bodily presence, and their sense of bodily pain.
>
> "I say, Sir," — Here he had advanced about half down the aisle, when he
> was seized by Major Jackson, the doorkeeper, who happened to be returning
> from the clerk's desk.
>
> "What the devil are you doing here with these chickens; get out, Sir, get
> out," whispered the doorkeeper.

"No you don't, though, you can't come that game over me, you've got chickens yourself for sale, get out yourself, and let me sell mine. I say, Sir (in a louder tone to the Speaker), are you buying chickens here today? I've got some prime ones here."

And he held up his string and shook his fowls until their music made the walls echo.

"Let me go, Sir (to the doorkeeper), let me go, I say. Fine large chickens (to the Speaker), only six bits a dozen."

"Where's the Sergeant-at-Arms," roared the Speaker. "Take that man out."

"Now don't will you, I ain't hard to trade with, you let me go (to the door-keeper), you've sold your chickens, now let me have a chance. I say, Sir (to the Speaker in a louder tone), are you buying chickens too?" "Go ahead," "At him again," "That's right," whispered some of the opposition members, who could command gravity enough to speak. "At him again." "He'll buy them." "He only wants you to take less — at him again."

"I say, Sir (in a louder tone to the Speaker) — cuss your pictures let me go — fairplay — two to one ain't fair (to the Speaker and Sergeant-at-Arms), let me go: I say Sir, you up there (to the Speaker), you can have 'em for six bits: won't take a cent less. Take 'em home and eat 'em myself before I'll take — Drat your hides, don't shove so hard, will you! you'll hurt them chickens, and they have had a travel of it today, anyhow. I say you, Sir, up there —"

Here the voice was lost by the closing of the door. An adjournment was moved, and carried, and the members almost frantic with mirth, rushed out to find our friend in high altercation with the doorkeeper about the meanness of selling his own chickens and letting nobody else sell his adding that "if he could just see that man up there by himself he'd be bound they could make a trade and that no man could afford to raise chickens for less than six bits."

The members bought his fowls by a pony purse, and our friend left the capital, saying, as he went down the stairs:

"Well, this is the darndest roughest place for selling chickens that ever I come across, sure." . . .

STUDY GUIDE

1. Summarize the characteristics of voter behavior described by Clark. Which of them might have been found in such eastern cities as Boston or Philadelphia, and which were probably unique to the West? How do you explain the unique characteristics of western politics?

2. Explain the behavior of legislators in the assemblies in light of the period or the character of the region Clark writes about. Do public officials normally reflect the values and qualities of those who choose them? Support your answer with examples from recent American politics.

3. Some of the stump speeches quoted by Clark may be mythical, but he suggests they were representative of the political oratory of the backwoods. How do you explain the appeal that such extraordinary language had for the people of this region?

4. What in Clark's description of elections and law making in the assemblies tends to call into question the integrity of democratic government?

5. Crude as the politics of the 1830s was, it might seem a model of civic virtue and honesty compared to American political life in the last decade. Compare the two periods, and suggest how the following have influenced modern political life: rapid growth and increasing wealth of business, labor, and other groups; the size of government; the functions performed by government today; popular conceptions of morality. What arguments can you think of to support the position that American government and democracy are better in our time?

BIBLIOGRAPHY

In the period from 1830 to 1860, one of the most powerful forces in the United States was a new feeling of sectionalism — the feeling that Northerners, Southerners, and Westerners had unique characteristics and special interests apart from those of the nation as a whole. Much of the literature concerning this subject concentrates on a single section, but the older work of Frederick J. Turner, *The United States, 1830–1850: The Nation and Its Sections* * (New York, © 1935), is a general treatment of the role of sectionalism in American history. William R. Taylor, *Cavalier and Yankee: The Old South and the American National Character* * (New York, 1961) is an interesting comparative study. Many of the characteristics of the trans-Appalachian frontiersman studied by Clark were attributed to them in the accounts written by Charles Dickens and the many other European travelers who visited the United States in the early nineteenth century. Henry S. Commager, ed., *America in Perspective: The United States through Foreign Eyes* (New York, 1947) presents a good selection of their writings.

There are several good secondary works on the politics and social life of frontier America. Among many others, the following deserve mention: Thomas D. Clark, *Frontier America: The Story of the Western Movement* (New York, 1959); R. Carlyle Buley, *The Old Northwest: Pioneer Period, 1815–1840*, 2 vols. (Bloomington, Ind., 1951); Everett Dick, *The Dixie Frontier: A Social History of the Southern Frontier from the First Transmontane Beginnings to the Civil War* * (New York, 1948); and Arthur K. Moore, *The Frontier Mind: A Cultural Analysis of the Kentucky Frontiersman* * (Lexington, Ky., 1957).

The role of the frontier, especially the midwestern frontier of the 1830s, in democratizing American politics is still a subject of lively dispute. Studies have been made of particular elections and of individual states to try to determine the basis of Andrew Jackson's support. A different approach is used in the fascinating study by John W. Ward, *Andrew Jackson: Symbol for an Age* * (New York, 1955), which suggests that, whatever Andrew Jackson himself may have been, this man from Tennessee served as a symbol for Americans of the virtues of the frontier. There is no entirely satisfactory study of the grass-roots politics described by Clark.

In the last decade, historians have paid increasing attention to popular, or folk, culture in both early and modern American history. Today, Sears-Roebuck catalogs, comic books, and a host of other "pop" cultural materials are being collected by libraries. The tall tale, the folk song, and folklore have a longer history of recognition as valuable aids in understanding the culture and values of a civilization. In addition to the many special studies of frontier humor, Constance M. Rourke, *American Humor: A Study of the National Character* * (New York, 1931) is worth reading. Richard M. Dorson, *American Folklore* * (Chicago, 1959) is a brief introduction to that subject, and the same author's *America in Legend* (New York, 1974) is a fuller and more recent work.

A slave fills a basket with his pickings. The cotton gin will separate the seeds from the cotton fiber.

GERALD W. MULLIN

Life under Slavery

Colonial laws on slavery were established in the late seventeenth century, and the slave system was elaborated and widely extended in the eighteenth century. Despite the abolition of slavery in the North and the passage of state and federal laws against the foreign slave trade, on the eve of the American Civil War nearly four million black people lived as permanent, hereditary slaves. Forming the chief labor force from the tobacco fields of Virginia to the cotton fields of Mississippi, southern blacks were crucial to southern agriculture and to several other parts of the southern economy. As chattels, bought and sold like livestock, they were an important capital investment and an easily marketable property that could bring ready cash to the slaveowner.

But American slavery was much more than a key feature of southern economic life. Its influence was all-pervasive, affecting law, social class, sexual mores, and every other aspect of thought and feeling. Much of its impact upon southern society was owing to the fact that American slaves were black, rather than simply the fact that they were slaves. No one in the South entirely escaped the influence of slavery and racism, whether he was slave or slaveowner, free Negro or non-slave-holding white farmer. Wilbur J. Cash has written, "Negro entered into white man as profoundly as white man entered into Negro — subtly influencing every gesture, every word, every emotion and idea, every attitude."

In the South before 1860, life for a majority of blacks and whites alike was rural and agricultural. This does not mean that most people lived on large cotton plantations; the pre-Civil War South was a land of considerable diversity. Corn, sugar, tobacco, livestock, and other products accounted for a larger part of the southern economy than did cotton, and there were substantial differences between life on a large plantation and life on a small farm in the hill country. Disagreement remains concerning some aspects of slavery in the Old South, but historians have reached a reasonable consensus concerning the life of the slave. By the use of more representative records of several kinds and new approaches to the study of slavery, they have drawn a graphic portrait of the slave's family life, housing, food, legal status, rewards and punishments, his work both in the fields and in the cities, and his reaction to enslavement.

Gerald W. Mullin's *Flight and Rebellion* is a sensitive study of how the African people adapted to, and resisted, their enslavement. Mullin deals with slavery in Virginia at the end of the eighteenth century, but his description of the slave's condition is largely applicable to the South of 1830 or 1850. On one question — whether slaves were generally contented with their lot or fundamentally rebellious — his work may actually be more informative than later studies. For he writes of a period before the rise of the antislavery movement, with its tracts, newspapers, and underground railroad. In the eighteenth century, the slave community reached its own decision on slavery, and Mullin describes the various sorts of black resistance in Virginia.

The field slave "is called up in the morning at daybreak, scarcely allowed time to swallow three mouthfuls of homminy," wrote the English traveler J. F. D. Smyth. Brief notations like this in travelers' and plantation accounts and record books must suffice for data on the field slave's material condition. Although the records are sketchy, his diet, although probably adequate in bulk, was scarcely nourishing. "Homminy," Indian corn, was the slaves' staple food.

Random accounts of quantities of corn allotted suggest that provisions were sometimes based on the worker's productivity. During the Revolutionary War, "Councillor" Carter asked that "the stronger Shears [shares] men & women" be given one peck of corn per week, "the Remainder of the Black People they to have ¼ Peck per Week each." By 1787 Carter, who was one of the least oppressive slave masters, increased this slightly. He ordered 44 pecks of shelled Indian corn as two weeks' allowance for 26 slaves, less than a full peck per week per laborer. (One peck equals 14 lbs. of Indian corn.)

Meat was seldom given to slaves. Smyth said slaves ate hoecakes and little else; unless their master "be a man of humanity the slave eats a little fat, skimmed milk, and rusty bacon." La Rochefoucauld-Liancourt said that on large plantations the slave subsisted on corn and sometimes on buttermilk. They were given meat 6 times a year. Robert "Councillor" Carter estimated that the common allowance for wheat per hand per year was 15 bushels for those "negroes, who are not fed with animal food" (e.g., meat). These slaves only received meat on special occasions. Joseph Ball wrote his steward that slaves were to "have ffresh meat when they are sick, if the time of the year will allow it." The cuts were to be the least desirable, although not necessarily the least nutritious. When calves were slaughtered, Ball ordered him to give the field hands the "head and Pluck"; the "ffat backs, necks, and other Coarse pieces" of hogs were also to be reserved for the slaves. James Mercer directed his steward to give the slaves the innards of chickens unless he sold them to the local Negro chicken merchants.

Plantation slaves wore clothing usually cut from a heavy, coarse cloth of flax and tow originally manufactured in Osnabrück, Germany. Following the non-importation agreements of the late 1760's, coarse-textured cotton wool weave, "Virginia plains," "country linen," replaced "Osnabrugs." Unlike the colorful variety of many of the artisan's clothing, the notices for runaways after 1770 indicate that field laborers wore uniform pants and trousers. "They are well clothed in the usual manner for Negroes"; "clothed as usual" and "the usual winter clothing for corn field negroes" are representative descriptions from advertisements of that period.

Black women who worked on the quarter wore clothing of the same weight and texture as the men. They usually dressed in a loose-fitting smock or shift, often tied at the waist; a short waistcoat was fitted over this dress. A Dutch blanket used for a sleeping robe and shoes and stockings completed the plantation Negroes' clothing allowance.

Housing for slaves varied widely. But there are frequent references in travelers' accounts to clusters of slave cabins that looked like small villages, and, in plantation records, numerous directions from masters indicating a concern for warm, dry houses with floors, lofted roofs, and on occasion, fireplaces. Slave quarters, however, may have been a late development. Subscribers who used advertisements to sell plantations frequently mentioned "negro quarters," but usually only in those notices published in the last quarter of the century. The plantation's size, location, and wealth were not factors; nearly all had slave quarters. It is likely that the smaller planter's field hands may have slept in the lofts of barns, in tobacco houses, and other outbuildings before the war. Joseph Ball told his nephew that the slaves "must ly in the Tobacco house" while their quarters, 15 by 20 feet with fireplace and chimney, were "lathed & fitted." However, several planters, including George Washington, used a less substantial, pre-fab arrangement. These shacks were small, temporary, and were moved from quarter to quarter following the seasonal crop.

J. F. D. Smyth was forced to take shelter one evening in a "miserable shell" inhabited by six slaves and their overseer. Unlike many slaves' houses "it was not lathed nor plaistered, neither ceiled nor lofted above . . . one window, but no glass in it, not even a brick chimney, and, as it stood on blocks about a foot above the ground, the hogs lay constantly under the floor, which made it swarm with flies."

On the home plantations, "servants," like the crop hands, usually slept in their own quarters. A planter who moved to the valley in 1781 asked his steward to place the "house Servants for they have been more indulged than the rest" with the overseer and his family, "till Such Time as Warehouses can be provided for them." Slaves evidently rarely slept in the great house. A letter dated 1823, written to Dr. A. D. Galt of Williamsburg, mentioned that the writer's father could not find a house, "and the ones he has seen have not had separate quarters for the servants." They would then "have to stay in the basement or the garret rooms." This, she concluded, "[as] you know cannot be very agreeable to Virginians."

Some idea of a slave's yearly expenses is provided by James Madison's remark to a British visitor earlier in the nineteenth century. "Every negro earns annually, all expenses being deducted, about $257," wrote John Foster. "The expense of a negro including duty, board, clothing, and medicines, he [Madison] estimates from $12–$13."

The lean, spare character of the field slave's material condition was a function of his place in the servile work hierarchy. Most plantation slaves worked in the fields where their tasks were tedious, sometimes strenuous, and usually uninspiring. Although tobacco is a difficult and challenging crop, field laborers — especially the "new Negroes" — were forced into the most routine tasks of transplanting seedlings, weeding, suckering, and worming. Following the harvest their work days extended into the night, when they sorted, bundled, and pressed the tobacco into hogsheads for shipment.

The slave jobber's work assignments were not as routine as the field laborer's chores. Armistead was hired out by his master to "act as a jobber, viz. to cut firewood, go to [the] Mill, work in your garden, and occasionally to work in your Corn-field." Jobbers also mended stone and wood fences, patched and whitewashed the plantation's outbuildings, dug irrigation and drainage ditches, and the like. "Councillor" Carter hired John McKenney to "overlook" his jobbers in 1777. Their agreement read:

> the sd Jobbers to make a Crop of Corn Pumpkins, Irish Potatoes, at my plantation called Dickerson's Mill, that is, a full crop fr about 4 Shares — the sd Jobbers to raise Stone to build a tumbling Dam at Dickerson's Mill, they to make ye dirt Dam sufficient, there, and to do several Jobs at Nomony Hall in the course of this year.

McKenney's wages indicate that this type of work was not well paid: he was "to receive f[o]r his services at the rate of 25s/6 per month, [is] to find himself, Board, lodging, Washing &c."

But jobbers were scarcely better off than the field laborers, because they too did not travel outside the plantation. Nor did their menial tasks spur assimilation and a corresponding change in their view of slavery. Regardless of the specific nature of their tasks, the horizons and expectations of most plantation slaves were sharply limited by the plantation environment.

Their tiresome routines in the meager setting of reserve land, in meadow and woods, monotonous rows of tobacco, and temporary, ramshackle buildings, made the quarter a world of its own. But the isolation and work routines of the quarter provided slaves with a convenient means of expressing their unhappiness, so it was also a constant, nagging source of trouble for the planter. Blacks and whites alike knew that the plantation's efficiency and profitability could be seriously impaired simply by a "little leaning" on the slaves' part. "My people seem to be quite dead hearted, and either cannot or will not work"; "my people are all out of their senses for I cannot get one of them to do a thing as I would have it and as they do it even with their own time they have it to do again immediately." These words are Landon Carter's. A tough and competent man, Carter did not bend easily, but this note of resignation is heard early in his diary.

Accounts of the field slave's performance are rare, but one of the best can be found in Jack P. Greene's fine edition of Landon Carter's Diary which tells a dreary story of the crop laborers' quiet and persistently non-cooperative actions. Slaves reported ill every day but Sunday when there were no complaints because they considered this "a holy day"; men treading wheat slept while their "boys," left to do the job, "neglected" it; the "crop people," forced to stem tobacco in the evening hours, retaliated "under the guise of semi-darkness [by] throwing away a great deal of the saleable tob[acco]"; men whom Carter harassed about weeding a corn patch feigned stupidity and leveled thousands of hills of corn seedlings. Carter's slaves, in fact, were so rebellious that he came to question the profitability of slavery. "It is the same at all my plantations," he complained:

> Although I have many to work and fine land to be tended, I hardly make more than what cloaths them, finds them tools, and pays their Levies. Perhaps a few scrawney hogs may be got in the year to be fattened up here. If these things do not require the greatest caution and frugality in living I am certain nothing can do.

William Strickland, an Englishman who visited colonial America in 1800, concurred. As well as any traveler, he succinctly defined the character of the plantation slaves' rebelliousness in a letter to the Board of Trade:

> Any slave that I have seen at work, does not appear to perform half as much, as a labourer in England; nor does the business under which the master sits

down contented, appear to be half of what we require to be performed by one. . . . If to this be added the slovenly carelessness with which all business is performed by the slave, the great number of useless hands the slave owner is obliged to maintain, the total indifference to, and neglect, not to say the frequent wilful destruction, of whatever is not immediately committed to his case. . . . And also the universal inclination to pilfering shown by them, I cannot do otherwise than acquiesce in the received opinion of the country, that slave labor is much dearer than any other.

Lazy, wasteful, and indifferent work was a chronic problem on eighteenth-century plantations. Slaves understood that there was a great deal of time to waste, and little hope of improving their lot. "It will be better to have more eyes than one over such gangs," Landon Carter noted. Following another inspection he complained, "the old trade, take one hour from any job and it makes a day loss in work." Most plantation slaves desired challenging tasks, but once they had them, they dragged out the job as long as possible. Herdsman Johnny, charged with breaking up the quarter patch at Sabine Hall, "does not intend to finish," Carter wrote, "by contriving that all his lambs should get out of the yard that he may be trifling about after them."

Careful planters habitually spot-checked their slaves' productivity. Planters like Landon Carter and George Washington who demanded from their slaves punctiliousness, order, and a high output, were convenient and effective targets for the slaves' piddling laziness and wasteful procedures. A 1760 entry in Washington's diary noted that four of his sawyers hewed about 120 feet of timber in a day. Dissatisfied with this rate of production, and determined to apply gentle pressure, Washington stood and watched his men. They subsequently fell to work with such energy and enthusiasm that he concluded that one man could do in one day what four had previously accomplished in the same length of time.

How many seemingly routine plantation practices were actually concessions to the unreliability of slave labor? For years Landon Carter refused to introduce plows and carts onto his quarters since he felt that these technological innovations would only serve "to make Overseers and people extremely lazy . . . wherever they are in great abundance there is the least plantation work done."

Feigned illness was another remarkably simple but effective ruse. When a slave asked to "lay-in," his master often suspected he was faking, but could never be certain. Too many had stood helplessly by while a strange and lethal "distemper," or "ague," suddenly swept through their slave quarters and carried off numbers of workers. Plantation records are filled with notes on these epidemics: "The mortalities in ties in my families are increased. . . . The number of my dead is now fifteen working slaves. I thank God I can bear these things with a great deal of resignation," or "a grievous mortality of my familys hath swept away an abundance of my people"; and, "we kept the plantations on James River to try to make Crops, but there broke out a malignant fever amongst the Negroes & swept off most of the able Hands; this threw all into Confusion & there has been little or no thing made since."

Women who feigned illness were usually more effective than men. "As to Sall," James Mercer wrote his steward, "I believe her old complaint is mere deceit, if it is not attended with a fever it must be so unless it is owing to her monthly disorder & then can only last two days, and exercise is a necessary remedy." Washington complained of women who "will lay up a month, at the end of which no visible change in their countenance, nor the loss of an ounce of flesh, is discoverable; and their allowance of provision is going on as if nothing ailed them." Exasperated and uncertain about the health of a black woman, Betty Davis, he explained that "she has a disposition to be one of the most idle creatures on earth, and besides one of the most deceitful." When two of his slave women approached clutching their sides, Landon Carter told them to work or be whipped. He observed that they had no fever (the test of whether or not slaves were ill). "They worked very well with no grunting about pain." But Sarah, one of the women who had pretended to be pregnant for eleven months earlier in the year, soon ran off. When Wilmot used the same stratagem, Carter noted: "it cost me 12 months, before I broke her." This lesson was not satisfactory; for a third woman "fell into the same scheme," and "really carried it to a great length." So Carter whipped her severely; and she was "a good slave ever since only a cursed thief in making her Children milk Cows in the night."

Plantation slaves who "hid out" in the woods and fields as runaways represented a more serious breach of plantation security. They often returned to the quarter in the evening for food and shelter and were an invitation to others to follow their example. But truancy was also inward rebelliousness: it was sporadic, and it was directed toward the plantation or quarter. Unlike the real fugitives, truants had no intention of leaving the immediate neighborhood and attempting to permanently change their status. Truancy was so common that most planters either did not make it a matter of record or simply referred to it in a random manner in their correspondence. "King" Carter actually viewed it as part of his "outlandish" slaves' learning process: "Now that my new negro woman has tasted the hardships of the woods," he observed to an overseer, "she'll stay nearer to home where she can have her belly full." Planters accepted the fact that absenteeism, particularly in the evening hours, was scarcely controllable. In response to Landon Carter's complaint that his pet deer were straying in the Sabine Hall fields, John Tayloe wrote:

Dear Col

. . . Now give me leave to complain to you, That your Patroll do not do their duty, my people are rambleing about every night, . . . my man Billie was out, he says he rode no horse of Master & that he only was at Col. Carter's, by particular invitation, so that the Entertainment was last night at Sabine Hall, & may probably be at Mt Airy this night, if my discoverys do not disconcert the Plan, these things would not be so I think, if the Patrollers did the duty they are paid for.

Plantation slaves probably "rambled" to the "entertainment" in the neighborhood several nights of the week; as long as they reported for work the following day few efforts were made, or could be made, to curtail this practice.

Truants habitually remained very close to the quarter or plantation; but this did not make it much easier for the planter to recapture them. Evidently they were sufficiently clever (and the other plantation slaves were sufficiently secretive) to keep themselves in hiding until they decided to return on their own. Sarah ran off because Carter refused to let her "lie-in" as ill. She spent a week in the woods and ate during the evening hours while visiting the slave quarters. Simon, an ox-carter, also hid beneath the vigilant Carter's very nose. He "lurked" in Johnny's "inner room," and in the "Kitchen Vault."

The outlaw, a far more dangerous type of runaway, used his temporary freedom to inflict punishment on his tormentors. Outlawing a slave was a legal action, placing the runaway beyond the law, making him a public liability, and encouraging his destruction by any citizen. Those who killed outlaws did so without fear of legal prosecution; they also collected a fee from the public treasury and a reward from the slave's owner. The master's advertisements usually did not encourage the slave's preservation: George America was worth forty shillings if taken alive; five pounds if destroyed.

Some slaveowners only threatened to outlaw truants. Recognizing the effective communication between slaves who remained on the quarter and their "outlying" brother, masters used outlawry as a warning for slaves to come in or suffer the consequences. Many did not return, nor were they satisfied with merely "lurking" about and "tasting the hardships of the woods" until hunger brought them back to the quarter. Outlaws destroyed. The omnibus slave codes of the century (four were passed from 1705 to 1797) described these desperate, courageous and "incorrigible" slaves in language which changed only slightly during the ninety years:

> WHEREAS many times slaves run away and lie hid and lurking in swamps, woods, and other obscure places, killing hogs, and committing other injuries to the inhabitants . . . upon intelligence, two justices (*Quorum unus*) can issue a proclamation . . . if the slave does not immediately return, anyone whatsoever may kill or destroy such slaves by such ways and means as he . . . shall think fit. . . . If the slave is apprehended . . . it shall . . . be lawful for the county court, to order such punishment to the said slave, either by dismembering, or in any other way . . . as they in their discretion shall think fit, for the reclaiming any such incorrigible slave, and terrifying others from the like practices.

Newspaper advertisements provide a glimpse of why a few runaways were outlawed: John Smith outlawed Mann because he threatened to burn Smith's house; and John Tayloe's manager at the Occoquan Furnace reported that "Leamon's obstinacy in not delivering himself up when lurking a considerable time about the ironworks, and doing mischief, Induced me to have him outlawed; in which condition he now stands and remains." Other explanations were not as clear as these. Moses and his wife were "harboured" by some "ill disposed" persons in Williamsburg. His master advertised "such notorious offences are not to be borne with any degree of patience." Edward Cary's explanation for outlawing Ben and Alice was even more cryptic. Cary was the chairman of the House of Burgesses committee that reimbursed masters whose slaves were outlawed as public liabilities. "As neither of those slaves have been ill used at my hands, I have had them outlawed in this county and for their bodies without hurt, or a proper certificate of their death, a proper reward will be given."

Some potentially explosive outlaws stayed on the quarters and physically assaulted their overseers. One of Landon Carter's supervisors, Billy Beale, chastised a slave who was weeding a corn patch. Told that his work was "slovenly," the slave replied "a little impudently" and Beale was "obliged to give him a few licks with a switch across his Shoulders"; but the slave fought back, and he and Beale "had a fair box." Subsequently, the laborer was brought before his master; and Carter noted that "it seems nothing scared him." Direct confrontations such as these, between comparatively unassimilated slaves and whites, seem to have been rare; a few, however, are described in detail in the advertisements for runaways. Two fugitives, for example, a husband and wife, were recaptured by an overseer while crossing a field, and were "violently" taken from the overseer and set free by field workers. Another runaway, also a field hand, escaped by "cutting his Overseer in Several Pieces [places?] with a Knife." John Greenhow of Williamsburg lost a slave who "laid violent hands" on him; this man ran off with another field slave who had also beaten his overseer.

Murders, small and unplanned uprisings, and suicides are instances of rebelliousness that was clearly inward-directed in a psychological sense as well as directed against the confines of the plantation. A September 1800 newspaper story graphically illustrates how even the most calculating, courageous, and murderously violent action could be, in a fashion, internalized violence: for after this slave methodically stalked and killed his master he simply "went home."

Captain John Patteson, a tobacco inspector at Horsley's warehouse in Buckingham County, punished his slave for "some misdemeanor"; and from that time, the slave told the court, "he ever after meditated [Patteson's] destruction."

On the evening to which it was effected, my master directed me to set off home . . . and carry a hoe which we used at the place. . . . I concluded to waylay him. . . . after waiting a considerable time, I heard the trampling of horses' feet. . . . I got up and walked forwards — my master soon overtook me, and asked me (it being then dark) who I was: I answered Abram; he said he thought I had gone from town long enough to have been further advanced on the road; I said, I thought not; I spoke short to him, and did not care to irritate him — I walked on however; sometimes by the side of his horse, and sometimes before him. — In the course of our traveling an altercation ensued; I raised my hoe two different times to strike him, as the circumstance of the places suited my purpose, but was intimidated. . . . [W]hen I came to the fatal place, I turned to the side of the road; my master observed it, and stopped; I then turn'd suddenly round, lifted my hoe, and struck him across the breast; the stroke broke the handle of the hoe — he fell — I repeated my blows; the handle of the hoe broke a second time — I heard dogs bark, at a house which we passed, at a small distance; I was alarmed, and ran a little way, and stood behind a tree, 'till the barking ceased; in running, I stumbled and fell — I returned to finish the scene I began, and on my way picked up a stone, which I hurl'd at his head, face, &c. again and again and again, until I thought he was certainly dead — and then I went home.

The most violent reactions to slavery were small, unorganized uprisings. A newspaper account written in 1770 reported a battle between slaves and free men, which suddenly erupted during the Christmas holidays on a small plantation quarter in New Wales, Hanover County. The reporter's explanation for the uprising was a familiar one. "Treated with too much lenity," the plantation slaves became "insolent and unruly." When a young and inexperienced overseer tried to "chastise" one of them by beating him to the ground and whipping him the man picked himself up and "slash[ed] at the overseer with an axe." He missed, but a group of slaves jumped on the white and administered such a severe beating that the "ringleader," the slave whom the overseer had whipped, intervened and saved his life. The overseer ran off in search of reinforcements; and instead of fleeing or arming themselves, the slaves tied up two other whites and "whipped [them] till they were raw from neck to waistband." Twelve armed whites arrived, and the slaves retreated into a barn where they were soon joined by a large body of slaves, "some say forty, some fifty." The whites "tried to prevail by persuasion," but the slaves, "deaf to all, rushed upon them with a desperate fury, armed solely with clubs and staves." Two slaves were shot and killed, five others were wounded, and the remainder fled.

Some slaves took their own lives. The journals of the House of Burgesses contain 55 petitions from slaveowners who sought reimbursement from public funds for slaves who committed suicide. Most of these men were outlawed runaways who, since they feared trial and conviction for capital crimes, hanged or drowned themselves. Since few petitioners reported the circumstances of a slave's death, the journals are not too informative. But one suicide, William Lightfoot's Jasper, was also described in a runaway notice:

> [A] well set Negro Man Slave, much pitted with the Small-pox; he was lately brought from *New-York*, but was either born or lived in the *West-Indies*, by which he has acquired their peculiar Way of speaking, and, seems to frown when he talks; he carried with him different Sorts of Apparel.

If indeed Jasper was a suicide his decision to "dash his brains out against a rock" must have been sudden, for he took a change of clothing with him.

But the field slaves' rebelliousness was not typically violent, self-destructive, or even individualistic. In fact they were much more inclined to attack the plantation in a quietly cooperative and effective way than were the slave artisans. Pilferage was a particularly rewarding and often organized action. "I laughed at the care we experienced in Milk, butter, fat, sugar, plumbs, soap, Candles, etc." wrote Landon Carter. "Not one of these ennumerations lasted my family half the year. All gone, no body knows how . . . thievish servants . . . Butter merely vanishing." Washington estimated that his servants stole two glasses of wine to every one consumed by the planter's visitors. His slaves made a practice of stealing nearly everything they could lay their hands on. Washington had to keep his corn and meat houses locked; apples were picked early, and sheep and pigs carefully watched.

The following offhand comments in records and newspapers indicate that much of this pilferage was not simply to satisfy hunger or anger. "Tell ye overseers to keep the keys of the folk's Cornhouse or else they will sell it, and starve themselves"; "bacon to spare will allow me a preference with the Country People, or rather Nigroes who are the general Chicken merchants"; and, "papermills I believe will answer well there . . . and I am sure the Negroes would supply them with Rags enough for Trifles"; and Washington's order that all dogs belonging to slaves be hanged immediately, because they "aid[ed] them in their night robberies."

The slaves' traffic in stolen goods was extensive, relatively well organized, and carried on virtually with impunity. The problem was of such proportions that by the 1760's it led to several letters to newspaper editors and to a series of laws. "I suppose every family must have so sensibly felt this evil," noted one letter writer to the *Virginia Gazette*. He observed that in every part of the country, henhouses, dairies, barns, granaries, gardens, and even patches and fields were "robbed in every convenient moonshiny night." Another contributor noted that, in his travels about the country, he had heard "frequent and various complaints" of this "pernicious evil." There was "hardly a family that was not full of enjuries they had received from the numerous thefts of servants and slaves."

Many slaves were fences for stolen goods; they had licenses from "over-

tender" masters to sell produce. Whites, too, cooperated with the plantation slaves; they were referred to in the newspapers as "common proprietors
of orchards," "liquor fellers," and "idle scatter lopping people." One
writer made the interesting observation that some slaveowners, with "a
modest blush," were so ashamed to sell certain farm products that they gave
them to their slaves to dispose of. "Pray why is a fowl more disgraceful,"
he asked, "in the sale of it at market, than a pig, lamb, a mutton, a veal,
a cow or an ox?"

Additional evidence of organized thievery as an outgrowth of the plantation slaves' culture and community is preserved in the Richmond County
court records. Between 1710 and 1754 the justices tried and passed sentence
in 426 cases. In 1750, although blacks made up 45 per cent of the population and there were nearly twice as many black tithes (1,235) as white
(761), only 26 of these 426 actions involved slaves. (It should also be
remembered that all slave criminals — with the exception of insurrectionists
and murderers who were supposed to be tried by the General Court —
were tried by county justices.) Only two trials concerned serious crimes.
These were murder trials and both defendants were slave men. One was
convicted of stabbing a black woman to death; the other, who later died
in jail under very unusual circumstances, was charged with killing his
master's young daughter. After his death, the court ordered his body to
be quartered and displayed. Most slave crimes in this forty-four year period
were petty thefts of the kind described earlier; that is, the charge was
nearly always breaking and entering, and the slaves usually took a few
shillings' worth of cider, liquor, bacon, cloth, or hogs. One typical case
involved a slave who stole five sheets, a fishing line, and a bottle of brandy.
Nearly all of these robberies were committed by one person; but the largest
theft was conducted by a man and a woman. They took forty gallons
of rum and fifty pounds of sugar. Evidently these thefts were well organized;
the slaves usually selected such vulnerable targets as the homes of widows,
ministers, warehouses, and slave quarters. Only on one occasion did a
slave rob his master (who was Landon Carter!). The usual punishment
for these crimes was between ten and thirty-nine lashes. For more serious
crimes (including a conviction of perjury) slaves lost one or both ears.
For capital crimes, slaves were often allowed to plead benefit of clergy.

The plantation slaves' organized burglaries were similar to the rebellious
styles of the mobile, comparatively assimilated slaves. These crimes required
planning; they took the slaves outside the plantation, and evidently com-
pensated them with money and goods which could be exchanged for articles
they needed.

Most field slaves, however, never acquired sufficient literate and occupa-
tional skills to move away from the quarter and into the society beyond
it. Most were Africans and they remained "new Negroes" all of their lives.
There are, then, two possible aspects to the personal dimension of slave
life on the quarter. First, from an outsider's point of view, the quarter

was a stultifying experience which slowed and restricted the slave's rate of acculturation. Second, from the slave's point of view, life on the quarter was perhaps preferable to daily contact with his captors, because it allowed him to preserve some of his ways.

Household slavery entwined the lives of whites and blacks. In the household more than anywhere else, there were direct and personal encounters that intensified the meaning of slavery for slaves and free alike. For the black servant these situations were often harrowing experiences which threatened to expose a nature sharply divided between enervating fear and aggressive hostility. His inward styles of rebelliousness and such related neurotic symptoms as speech defects were often manifestations of a profound ambiguity about whites and his own "privileged" status. For the white master the intimate presence of so many blacks subtly influenced domestic affairs, particularly his behavior toward his wife and children. The roles developed in household slavery restricted the master's actions toward his servants too. Once a style of discipline and correct order had been established, the master's reactions were often determined by what the slaves had come to expect of him. Highly sensitive to the patriarch's role, servants were quick to exploit any weakness in his performance. If the master was insecure, so were his dependents; but they also kept him that way by their persistent and petty rebelliousness. Household slavery then was the epitome of Professor Tannenbaum's dynamic view of human relationships in slave societies in which slavery was "not merely for blacks, but for the whites [and] . . . Nothing escaped, nothing, and no one."

The greatly enlarged situational (or interpersonal) dimension of slavery in the household is fundamentally important for another reason. Our limited understanding of slave behavior is based almost exclusively on interpretations of these personal encounters. These interpretations, which argue that slaves became the characters they played for whites, that their masters' view of them as infants or Sambos became their self-view, must be used with extreme caution. The interpersonal encounter was only a fragment of slavery's reality for both whites and blacks. When slaves were among their own and using their own resources as fugitives and insurrectionists, it is abundantly clear that much of their true character was concealed or intentionally portrayed in a dissembling manner in the presence of whites.

STUDY GUIDE

1. Differences between black slaves and poor white farmers with respect to freedom are obvious. How would their lives compare with respect to the following: housing; the actual labor they performed; food; health and medical care?

2. What were the various kinds of violent resistance that slaves used to protest enslavement? What were the techniques of "quiet resistance" that they used?

3. How might the following factors have influenced the slave's choice of violent or passive resistance: the master or conditions on the plantation; the slave's personality and character; the slave code and attitudes of a particular region, such as South Carolina as compared to Virginia?

4. How did the household slave's relationship to whites differ from that of the field slave? What were the relative advantages and disadvantages of each position?

5. Though Mullin's selection focuses on the life of the slave, he mentions several times that the institution of slavery influenced every aspect of life in the South for both blacks and whites. How do you think black slavery might have influenced each of the following aspects of southern life: education of whites; relations between whites of different classes; the relative slowness of the South in industrial development; southern politics? Can you think of specific evidence to support your arguments on these points?

BIBLIOGRAPHY

Mullin's book is a study of slavery in eighteenth-century Virginia. While it reveals much about slave conditions and the slave's reaction to his enslavement that is equally applicable to the nineteenth century, there are many other studies of slavery in the period just before the American Civil War. An older southern historian, who had a patronizing view of the Negro and a rather rosy view of slavery, was Ulrich B. Phillips. Despite the limitations of his work, he was one of the first scholars to study slavery as a total system, rather than as only an economic or racial system. The most important of his works are: *American Negro Slavery* * (New York, 1918) and *Life and Labor in the Old South* * (Boston, 1929). The most interesting works of a general nature written since Phillips are Kenneth Stampp, *The Peculiar Institution: Slavery in the Ante-Bellum South* * (New York, 1956) and John W. Blassingame, *The Slave Community: Plantation Life in the Ante-Bellum South* * (New York, 1972). Virtually every major conclusion of earlier historians on the social and economic aspects of American slavery has been challenged in the highly controversial study by Robert William Fogel and Stanley L. Engerman, *Time on the Cross* * (Boston, 1974).

An issue of great interest is the influence of slavery upon the American black's personality and his reaction to slavery. In his work, *Slavery: A Problem in American Institutional and Intellectual Life* * 2nd edition (Chicago, 1968), Stanley M. Elkins compares the American slavery system with the Nazi concentration camp. Elkins believes that the slave identified with his oppressor, and he emphasizes the "Sambo" personality of the American black in studying the effects of slavery upon the black's psychology. Other scholars have argued that the Sambo role was merely a survival technique in a white

world, and Mullin and Blassingame suggest that there were different personality types. Benjamin A. Botkin, in *Lay My Burden Down: A Folk History of
Slavery* * (Chicago, © 1945), has edited a collection of reminiscences of ex-
slaves, which provides the slave's own perspective. Frank L. Owsley, *Plain
Folk of the Old South* * (Baton Rouge, La., 1949) gives a fair picture of the
life of poor whites, but the studies of slave life are generally better. Richard
C. Wade, *Slavery in the Cities: The South, 1820–1860* * (New York, 1964) is
a study of a sizable number of slaves who do not fit the plantation stereotype.

There are state studies of slavery, as well as many books on particular aspects of slavery, such as how profitable this system was. There is also a very
substantial literature on the antislavery crusade, including Dwight L. Dumond,
Antislavery: The Crusade for Freedom in America * (Ann Arbor, Mich., ©
1961) and Louis Filler, *The Crusade Against Slavery, 1830–1860* * (New York,
© 1960). John Hope Franklin, *From Slavery to Freedom: A History of American Negroes* * 3rd ed. (New York, 1967) is a general history of black Americans.

Smithsonian Collection of Business Americana

An immigrant transfer barge docked at Castle Garden offers transportation to the Erie Railroad, 1874.

CARL WITTKE

Nation of Immigrants

The extraordinary flow of people from Europe, Asia, and Africa
to the New World for more than three centuries constitutes the
largest migration of mankind ever experienced on this planet.
All of us here are descendants of immigrants — of Indians who
crossed the Bering land bridge from Asia, of early black and white
migrants who settled the British colonies, of German, French,
Italian, Russian, Hungarian, Chinese, or other immigrant ancestors
who poured into the United States in the nineteenth century. By
1930, the tide had waned, but by then the country's history could
not be understood without taking into account the impact upon
American civilization of the many races and nationalities that
had immigrated to the United States.

The most obvious question involved in the study of immigration history is why particular groups left their homelands to
come to a strange country. As Carl Wittke indicates in the following selection, there were some factors common to most groups
of Europeans, but in each country there were special influences
that promoted emigration at a particular time. A second question
is why certain nationalities settled in the areas they did and
tended to enter particular trades and occupations. Some remained largely in eastern cities as unskilled manual laborers,
while others went on to Minnesota or Wisconsin to enter farming. One of the striking characteristics of early-nineteenth-century
population movements was the extensive immigration to the
North and the very small number of immigrants who were attracted to the southern states. This pattern was determined by a
number of factors, including the greater industrialization taking

place in the North, the slave labor system of the Old South, and the different social attitudes in the two regions.

Many immigrant groups, even in the colonial period, faced substantial hardship and considerable animosity in establishing their roots in this land. In many ways, the difficulties increased during the nineteenth century, and even English-speaking groups such as the Irish found that adapting to the new culture posed serious problems. Most nationalities developed one or another sort of agency to assist them in preserving their heritage while adjusting to their new society; churches, schools, recreational associations, and other institutions served such purposes. Wittke describes the special problems faced by one such group, the Irish, a group that one might expect to have had fewer difficulties than some others.

Attitudes of immigrants toward their heritage have varied, as have attitudes of older Americans toward immigration policy and assimilation of new nationalities. For many years, much of our thought was dominated by the "melting pot" metaphor, which implied that the distinctive characteristics of each group should disappear into a new American nationality. In our time, there has been a resurgent interest in preserving the cultural heritage of various nationalities, and a suggestion that the melting pot theory should be replaced by a cultural pluralism that recognizes the integrity and contribution of different ethnic groups.

In the nineteenth century, and with increasing volume after 1830, the tide of emigration set in again from Europe. Wave after wave rolled over the cities and prairies of the New America. The Irish, the Germans, and the Scandinavians, in more or less sharply defined but overlapping streams, poured into the United States; and these major groups, together with several minor ones, constitute the "old emigration" from western and northern Europe, in contradistinction to the newer groups that came in the last quarter of the century from the south and east. Each deserves detailed treatment. In each case, specific causes, . . . operated to start the emigrant tide on its way across the Atlantic and to keep it flowing steadily for decades. Aside from the universal desire for adventure and greater opportunity, there were certain causes for emigration common to all these groups; and it must be remembered that much of the European emigration was artificially stimulated and encouraged by interests in America desirous, for one reason or another, of bringing in a larger population.

First of all, . . . the earlier population movements were influenced by the "America letters," "the literature of the unlettered" written home by those who had ventured out first and whose accounts of the New Canaan were eagerly awaited and devoured by those who had remained behind. Christopher Saur's "America letters" praising "the goodness I have heard and seen" were printed and reprinted many times in Germany during the latter half of the eighteenth century, in order to induce people to come to Pennsylvania. What the United States after 1776 symbolized to the liberty-loving, thwarted, and exploited Irishman can readily be imagined, especially when the glowing accounts that reached the Irish countryside assured the readers that "there is a great many ill conveniences here, but no empty bellies." In 1818, an enthusiastic reporter described the region around Wheeling in extravagant terms that must have been irresistible. He wrote:

> I believe I saw more peaches and apples rotting on the ground than would sink the British fleet. I was at many plantations in Ohio where they no more knew the number of their hogs than myself . . . . The poorest family has a cow or two and some sheep . . . good rye whiskey; apple and peach brandy, at 40 cents a gallon . . . . The poorest families adorn the table three times a day like a wedding dinner—tea, coffee, beef, fowls, pies, eggs, pickles, good bread; and their favorite beverage is whiskey or peach brandy. Say, is it so in England? . . .

. . . "There are no large estates," wrote one Swedish-American, "whose owners can take the last sheaf from their dependents and then turn them out to beg." Ministers and churches were said to be less worldly in America, and "there is ceaseless striving to spread the healing salvation of the Gospel." Hired men and maids ate at the same table with their employers and wore clothes of the same style. "Neither is my cap worn out," added another, "from lifting it in the presence of gentlemen." Small wonder that enthusiastic newcomers wrote: "We see things here that we could never describe, and you would never believe them if we did. I would not go back to Sweden if the whole country were presented to me." "It is no disgrace to work here," wrote a Swede in 1841. "Both the gentleman and the day laborer work. No epithets of degradation are applied to men of humble toil . . . . I do not agree . . . that in order to appreciate the blessings of monarchy, one must live in a democracy." . . .

Ship companies and organizations interested in land speculation did their part to keep the America fever burning at the proper temperature. Advertisements in American newspapers reveal a veritable flock of emigration agents; immigrant bankers dealing in remittances, steamship, and railroad tickets; and dealers in foreign exchange, each of whom had his special reasons for keeping the immigrant tide flowing in a steady, unbroken stream to the United States. Land agencies, with acreage for sale in Texas, Missouri, Wisconsin, and other parts of the West, advertised their bargains in newspapers published at the Eastern ports of arrival. . . .

In the middle of the last century, the Middle West needed population above everything else. To attract desirable immigrants was the overpowering ambition of practically every new state in this region. State after state began to enact legislation to encourage and stimulate migration to its borders. The attractions offered by favorable legislation and the persuasiveness of the agents of state immigration commissions were important factors in directing the immigrant tide into the Mississippi Valley.

By its constitution of 1850, Michigan gave the franchise to all newcomers who had declared their intention to become naturalized and who had resided in the state for two and a half years. Its immigration agency, established in 1848 and not abolished until 1885, issued attractive pamphlets in German, and its first immigration commissioner was instructed to spend half his time in New York and half in Stuttgart, Germany. Wisconsin had a special commissioner as early as 1851, and its board of immigration, created by legislative act in 1867, published pamphlets in seven different languages. From 1871 to 1875, 35,000 copies were printed for distribution in Europe. Other material was distributed in New York, in taverns and at the docks; and advertisements lauding Wisconsin's attractions were published in eight foreign newspapers, such as the London *Times,* the Tipperary *Free Press,* the *Baseler Zeitung,* and the *Leipziger Allgemeine Zeitung.* In 1880, Wisconsin issued 10,000 pocket maps of that state, with legends in English, Norwegian, and German. The Wisconsin Constitutional Convention of 1846 gave the franchise to immigrants after a declaration of their intention to become naturalized and one year's residence in the state. . . .

From 1860 to 1862, Iowa had a state commissioner of immigration, the German-born lieutenant governor, Nicholas J. Rusch, who maintained offices at 10 Battery Place, New York City. Later, an immigration board, similar to those in other states, was created. A handbook, *Iowa: The Home for Immigrants,* was prepared in English, German, Dutch, Danish, and Swedish; and agents were sent to Holland, England, and Germany to make propaganda for the state.

Steamship and railway companies [also] had a special interest in stimulating the immigrant traffic, for obvious reasons, but the latter had an additional objective in promoting the disposal of their railroad lands to actual settlers. In 1870, Jay Cooke, as the financial promoter of the Northern Pacific Railroad, employed Hans Mattson, who resigned his position as secretary of state of Minnesota to undertake the assignment, to go to Sweden to advertise the resources of the road and to draw up a plan for the disposal of its lands. J. J. Hill may have saved his road from financial disaster by promoting the settlement of Minnesota by Norwegian and

Swedish farmers, whose bumper crops quickly tripled the earnings of the railroad. Hill, in order to make the Red River Valley district more attractive to settlers, described it as an area "where the depth of the humus was equal to the height of a man." The Northern Pacific at St. Paul gave special passes to ministers of the Gospel, so that they might more frequently visit outlying immigrant settlements where no church had as yet been organized. When a trainload of Dunkards moved from Indiana to North Dakota, they went by special train, with streamers on the railroad cars advertising "the bread basket of America." The Atchison, Topeka, and Santa Fe Railroad, through its foreign immigration department, extended its activities to the Ural Mountains, bringing over 15,000 Russian-German Mennonites to Kansas. By 1883, they had settled along the route of the railroad in Kansas, with branch settlements in Oklahoma and Colorado. The Burlingame and Missouri Railroad also was active in attracting Mennonite settlers to the American West.

The sea voyage safely passed, the immigrant was likely to run afoul of the beasts of prey in human form who waited to pounce upon him on his arrival in New York, to exploit his ignorance of the English language, and his "greenness" about American conditions generally. New York was infested with "runners," who were paid by trucking firms, railroad ticket offices, and immigrant hotels and boarding houses for no other purpose than to compete with other runners and lead the unsuspecting immigrant into the clutches of the hotelkeeper or baggage agent. Runners were paid from $10 to $30 a week, or a certain percentage of the business they secured. Competition became extremely keen and, on many occasions, violent; for, in order to hold his job, a runner had to be a good "shoulder hitter" as well as a persuasive talker.

When a ship arrived, runners rushed to the gangplank and began fighting with other bullies over the immigrant's luggage, in order to get him to stop at a particular boarding house. These immigrant hotels and boarding houses were generally operated, not by native Americans, but by foreigners who congregated like vultures in the seaport towns to prey upon their own countrymen. In the worst of these houses, the immigrant was overcharged for everything, particularly for the storage of his baggage, which was then held as security until all bills had been paid. Occasionally, but not often, an immigrant runner's license was revoked for fraud. Usually, the law was indifferent to the plight of the stranger in a strange land. Occasionally, too, charges were lodged against runners and steamship, baggage, or railroad agents who had cheated unsuspecting immigrants out of hundreds of dollars or had collected sums of money as commissions for securing jobs that never materialized. The newspapers usually recorded that the culprit had "left for parts unknown," and that ended the case. An article in *The New York Times* for June 23, 1853, accurately described the arrival of an emigrant ship as follows:

Every one in the great City, who can make a living from the freshly arrived immigrants, is here. Runners, sharpers, pedlars, agents of boarding-houses, of forwarding offices, and worst of all, of the houses where many a simple emigrant girl, far from friends and home, comes to a sad end . . . .

Some immigrants hung around the German boarding houses in Greenwich Street, each day losing more of their savings. Others, Irish and Germans, settled down in the Eleventh Ward, to become peddlers and ragpickers and to succumb to the vice of intemperance. . . .

The ordinary prices by steamer and canal from New York to Albany and thence inland were reasonable enough, and the railroads tried to stop the selling of bogus tickets by swindlers in New York, but forwarding houses were hard to regulate and generally charged the immigrants higher rates, on one pretext or another, in order to divide the profits with their agents and runners. In the 1840's, the "official" table of prices was as follows:

New York to Albany	$ .75
New York to Buffalo	4.50
New York to Cleveland	7.00
New York to Detroit	8.00
New York to Milwaukee	14.50
New York to Chicago	14.50

Baggage up to 50 pounds was supposed to be transported free. Children under twelve paid half fare; those under two were carried free. A Norwegian immigrant, in 1847, was able to go from New York to Albany, up the Hudson, for $.50. To go by rail from Albany to Buffalo cost $12, but by way of the Erie Canal the rate was only $7.50, including meals, with a special price of $2 if immigrants brought their own food.

There apparently was little uniformity in the charges made. In 1844, a Norwegian immigrant went by steamer from New York to Albany, on a boat 290 feet long and with cabins on three decks, for $1.50. Nine hours were required to make the trip. The next year, a traveller who went by train from New York to Buffalo, in "wonderful closed wagons with windows," paid $3.50. The journey took several days, because in the dark nights "we stood still." To go from Albany to Buffalo in 1847 by canal boat required a day longer than by train, and the fare was $7.50, including meals. Some canal boats took longer to make the trip, furnished no food, and charged only two dollars.

Immigrant travel over this route, across New York and then into the West by way of the Great Lakes, was heavy. Immigrant trains were not distinguished for their accommodations and comforts. Often the cars marked "Immigrant Cars" were springless boxcars, with hard benches and no drinking water, and the immigrant passenger was expected to bring or buy his own food. Sometimes the coaches had absolutely no conveniences, not even seats, except for long boards running lengthwise along both sides of the cars, so that many had to sit or lie on the floor. Newspapers recorded the passage of long immigrant trains through Albany and Buffalo, trains with extra locomotives and long lines of cars, filled with Germans, Dutch, Swiss, or Scandinavians. In Chicago and other terminal points, runners for land companies, railroads, and state immigration commissioners met the incoming trains. In 1853, a resident of Chicago wrote: "One fourth of the persons you meet in Chicago cannot speak a word of English, and a good part of the remainder cannot speak it well. Germans, Irish and Norwegians seem to be as plenty as natives." The immigrants were so numerous in Milwaukee in 1842 that they were forced to lodge in the streets, while in Racine and Southport all tavern facilities were exhausted. In the 1850's, emigrant trains passed over the New York and Erie road at regular intervals, attracting much attention with their car windows trimmed with green vegetation and their passengers smoking long German pipes and singing German songs. . . .

The figures for the period of the Irish famine immigration mounted to startling totals: 92,484 in 1846, 196,224 in 1847, 173,744 in 1848, 204,771 in 1849, and 206,041 in 1850. The Census of 1850 reported 961,719 Irish in the United States; by 1860, the total had reached 1,611,304. These were to be found in greatest numbers in New York, Pennsylvania, Massachusetts, Illinois, Ohio, and New Jersey. The character of Irish immigration changed under the pressure of intolerable suffering and famine. The poor, small farmer, who had constituted the bulk of the migration up to 1835, who knew English, had sufficient energy to be proud of his independence, and was determined to rise, gave way to a new type — namely, the laborer, with little background aside from his potato patch, who was ignorant of the English language, and who was of a mercurial temperament, and likely to find life and progress in the United States very difficult.

Early in 1847, the roads to Irish ports were literally thronged with immigrant families. Sometimes strong men actually battled with each other at the ports of embarkation to secure passage on ships entirely inadequate to provide transportation for all who wished to go to America. The description of the ravages of the Irish famine tax the reader's imagination. Children and women were described as too weak to stand; the livestock had perished, people were eating carrion, and "the weekly returns of the dead were like the bulletin of a fierce campaign." Beggars crowded the roads and the city streets. People huddled half-naked in fireless and foodless hovels. Thousands crossed to Liverpool and demanded transportation to the United States on crowded and filthy emigrant ships whose resources were taxed to the utmost. . . .

The Irish temperament is noted for buoyancy, and hope sustained the voyagers across the Atlantic, but for many it vanished like the rainbow when the actual conditions of life in America had to be faced. Almost all Irish immigrants had to begin in the United States as unskilled laborers, and many got no farther. Year after year, the Irish Emigrant Society of New York advised immigrants to shun the cities of the Atlantic seaboard and to scatter throughout the United States, particularly into the West. "Thousands continually land entirely penniless and are at once in a state of destitution," the warning continued, "whereas such person should have at least five pounds on his arrival to enable him to prosecute his journey to the interior." The advice was sound, but thousands found it impossible to follow, for all their earthly possessions had been used up during the voyage. They arrived in the New Canaan with their pockets empty. The almshouses and hospitals were filled to overflowing, and beggars wandered aimlessly through the streets. Men and women accustomed to no other existence than eking out a living from the soil were suddenly left stranded in congested cities. They had no trade and no particular skills; some did not even know the language. They were destined to become the un-skilled, marginal workers of the America of the middle nineteenth century, with all that that implies. Many lurid accounts of Irish "shanty towns" are available to the historian of the Irish immigration. Some are descriptions obviously colored by a deep hatred for the newcomer, but there is enough in the comments of friendly critics to indicate that conditions were de-plorable, to say the least. Indeed, one who is familiar only with the Irish-Americans of the twentieth century may find it hard to credit the tales told about their ancestors of several generations ago.

The Irish, as a class, came to America with less means than many other immigrant groups. The majority were poverty-stricken. Having no money to proceed westward on their own account, they usually got out of the cities only when contractors for internal improvement projects recruited them in the labor markets of the East and transported them to the West and South. On their arrival in the port towns and larger cities, the Irish crowded the tenements, sometimes twenty or more families living in one house. These Irish tenements were hardly more than "human rookeries." What a difference it might have made, and what an excellent investment it might have turned out to be, had the government used its funds to transport the Irish into the West and helped them to become established as farmers on the public lands! There are many unnamed graves of Irish-men along the canal and railroad routes which they helped to build. In South Boston in 1850, the Irish slums were buildings from three to six stories high, with whole families living in one room, without light or ventilation, and even the cellars crowded with families. Saloons were the curse of the neighborhood, and police records abundantly reflected this unhealthy condition. The death rate among the children of the Irish poor was alarmingly high. Disease, particularly during cholera epidemics, always ravaged the immigrants living in hovels in the western and eastern sections of New York City worse than in other communities. Secret societies arose in the Irish shantytowns among Irish laborers with such names as "the Corkonians," "the Connaughtmen," and "the Far Downs," who engaged in bloody brawls and riots, which even the repeated denunciations of the Church authorities seemed powerless to stop. In some of the "better-class" tenement houses in New York, Negroes were preferred as tenants to the poor Irish and Germans. . . .

The Irish laborer in the middle nineteenth century frequently found himself in difficulties because of shameless exploitation and bad working conditions and because of the resentment harbored against him by native Americans who feared his competition, although apparently few Americans had any wish to do the heavy, dirty, unskilled labor that fell to the lot of the Irishman with his pick and shovel. Newspapers friendly to the Irish immigrant warned him to stay away from the canal and railroad construction projects, for "these railroads have been the ruin of thousands of our poor people" and their workers are treated "like slaves" by railroad contractors. Wages were low, usually $1 a day but often less; they were not clearly fixed and were paid partly in whiskey and "store pay," or merchandise, sold at high prices. Friends of the Irish urged them to form protective associations, with objectives somewhat like the trade unions, in order to stop competition, rivalries, and fights between warring gangs which drove wages down in their competition for the available jobs. Above all, the Irish were advised to go to the country to work on farms or squat upon government land in the West, to "do anything, in fact, in preference to railroading."

Irish longshoremen were employed at the docks in all the leading sea and lake ports. They bitterly resented the invasion of Negroes, who were often brought in expressly to depress the wage scale. Riots between Irish and Negro dock workers were not infrequent. It is this economic competition that helps to explain the strong hostility of the Irish toward the abolitionist movement and the New York draft riots during the Civil War. Workers on the Chesapeake Railroad and Ohio Canal were known as the Longfords and Corkonians. On some of the Ohio canals, Irish and German pick-and-shovel workers received only $.30 a day, with board, lodging, and a "jigger-full" of whiskey. Everywhere the Irish were doing the hard work, even in the South, where they were so badly treated at one time that Bishop England found it necessary to publish a warning in Irish newspapers advising Irish workers to avoid the South. Accidents, deaths, and injuries were numerous in road building and canal digging, and cave-ins occurred frequently in excavations for tunnels. Little tumbledown markers in tiny Catholic burying grounds along the route of these internal improvements still bear mute testimony to the hazards of pick-and-shovel work.

In the 1840's and 1850's, little "Dublins" sprang up in the factory towns of New England and in the Middle Atlantic states, for the Irish were invading the mill centers. The Irish population of Boston trebled in a decade. Often the mill population was the residue from the labor supply that had dug the canals or constructed the mill race. In Rhode Island, for example, the first Irish millworkers were recruited from those who had built the railroad between Providence and Boston, and the Woonsocket Irish Catholic settlement was due entirely to the construction of the Blackstone Canal. Irishmen went into the mill towns of Pawtucket and the "coal pits" between Fall River and Newport. At first, the competition of Irish labor was resented by other workers. Towns tried to restrict the sale of lots so as to keep out Catholic purchasers, and the sign "No Irish Need Apply" was posted in some of the factories. The children of the Irish were twitted and abused on the playground and in the schoolyards much as some Irish children later joined in making life uncomfortable for "dagos," "wops," and "kikes." But the economic urge was irrestible; and the Irish captured the mill towns, only to be in turn dispossessed in a later generation by Poles, Italians, French-Canadians, and Greeks, the products of the "new" immigration.

Irish workers had a bad reputation for rioting and brawling, and the newspapers of the middle of the last century are full of graphic accounts of their bloody battles. In 1853, for example, the eviction of an Irishman from a circus performance at Somerset, Ohio, for smoking a pipe, started a battle in which Irish railroad workers fought all night and into the next day. A company of militia had to be called from Zanesville to restore order. Feuds between groups of Irishmen hailing from different counties in Ireland led to frequent riots. On one occasion, in Indiana, 400 militia had to be called out to stop an impending assault by several hundred belligerent Irishmen from County Cork. A riot that broke out along the line of a projected Pacific railroad, in 1853, over the election of a foreman of a labor gang, would have had serious consequences but for the timely intervention of a Roman Catholic priest, who served as peacemaker.

After reading the many accounts of brawling and fighting among Irish workingmen that appear in the American newspapers, one becomes aware of the fact that not all the trouble was due to the Irishman's belligerent temperament, his love of the bottle, or his belief that contentiousness is the spice of life. Much of this rioting was the result of intolerable labor conditions. The brawls were often efforts, however misguided and unwise, to achieve an improvement in labor standards at a time when the labor movement had hardly begun. There were strikes for higher wages on internal improvement projects, many of which led to a display of force, particularly when contractors refused later to respect the agreements they had been forced to accept. In 1840, a serious riot broke out when the wages of Irish laborers on an aqueduct in New York City were cut from $1 to $.75 a day. There were similar disturbances, caused by wage reductions, on the Illinois Central, the Buffalo and State Railroad, the Steubenville and Indiana, and other lines.

The reign of terror instituted by the "Molly Maguires" in the anthracite coal regions of Pennsylvania is well known to students of American history and is usually described as one of the worst examples of mob rule and blackmail in the whole history of labor relations, for which Irish coal miners are held primarily responsible. Viewed from a longer perspective, the incident is but another illustration of the battle for better working conditions in the coal-producing areas, although the movement fell under the control of criminals and ended in a number of executions. The anthracite coal regions of Pennsylvania had a mushroom growth in the 1830's, with immigrant labor, poor housing facilities, and all the evils of company towns and company stores as natural concomitants of this rapid expansion. The region suffered from the evils of overdevelopment and frequent business slumps, which weighed especially heavily upon the Irish coal miners. Working conditions in the mines were terrible, with no safety requirements, inspection, or proper ventilation. From 1839 to 1848, wages were $1 or $1.25 a day for miners and $.82 for ordinary laborers. In 1869, a peak of $18.20 a week was reached, but by 1877 the wage had declined again to $9.80. "Breaker boys," aged 7 to 16, worked like slaves in the mines under mine bosses whose character left much to be desired. An editorial in *The Boston Pilot* exposed conditions in the coal mines — the inadequate pay, the "murderous neglect" of ventilation, the "rancid provisions" available at high prices in company stores, the explosions in the firedamp caverns in which Irish and Welsh miners were blown to pieces, and the "scandalous ungenerosity" subsequently shown by the operators toward their mutilated workmen — and concluded by denouncing some of the owners as men with "the conscience neither of Christian nor of Pagan."

Irish benevolent societies were formed to deal with some of these problems. The Ancient Order of Hibernians, a semisecret organization, became the backbone of the miners' unions. In a very long story of real class war, the responsibility for violence in the Pennsylvania coal fields seems to be pretty well divided. By 1860, the Molly Maguires terrorized the whole anthracite region, elected sheriffs and constables, and resorted to arson, blackmail, and murder. The organization was not finally broken up until 1875, when, because of the detective work of James McParlan, 19 were hanged after trials held in an atmosphere of great excitement and prejudice. The incident for a long time blackened the record of Irish-Americans, and many refused to see the industrial conditions which had provoked such criminal action. . . .

The United States has been known and ridiculed as a nation of "joiners." One reason may be the large immigrant element, which has had its special incentives in a new land to form benevolent, patriotic, and social organizations to keep alive the memories of a common origin. The Irish were no exception, and Irish societies of many kinds — such as the Hibernians, athletic clubs, and sodalities — exist in large numbers, generally closely connected with the Church and the Catholic hierarchy. . . .

For many years, fire fighting in the United States was in the hands of volunteer companies. The opportunity to become a "fire laddy" was irresistible for many Irishmen. These companies performed superhuman feats of strength and heroism. Each firehouse, especially in large cities like New York, also attracted a group that ran along to every fire, so that "running with the machine" eventually degenerated into a sport which attracted the hoodlums and gangs of the Bowery districts. The volunteer firemen of the 1840's and later decades appeared in brilliant uniforms and ponderous equipment of the comic opera variety. Much feasting and drinking seemed to be part of the routine of these organizations, and until the temperance movement made its inroads upon the profession, companies frequently had a steward, whose business it was to ladle out liquor to exhausted firemen from a barrel hauled along with the engine to each fire. . . .

How the Irish established themselves on the police force of the larger American cities needs no discussion. A study of the New York force in 1933 revealed that, out of a total of approximately 20,000 policemen, 2,309 were themselves foreign-born and 11,014 were of foreign-born parentage, representing 42 countries in all. Ireland led the list of foreign-born policemen with 1,533, and also the list of those of foreign-born parentage with 5,671.

Nearly all that has been said hitherto has concerned the Irish immigrant as a city dweller. It has been shown that most Irishmen began as unskilled laborers, working in construction gangs on the docks, in livery stables, in the streets, or, with the rise of industrial towns like Lowell and Paterson, in the mills — wherever brawn and not skill was the chief requirement. Many ended their days as unskilled workers in the cities and towns. But although it is true that the Irish immigrant is primarily a phenomenon of urban civilization in the United States, some did go into agriculture. Students of immigration have speculated on the reasons why a predominantly rural people should have shunned the land in their new home. Poverty, of course, made it impossible for large numbers to leave the port towns in which the immigrant ships happened to land them. Ignorance of improved American methods of farming was another reason, along with memories of bitter experiences on the land in Ireland. Irish gregariousness and the incentive of cash wages in the city were other factors. In some cases, the demoralizing effects of the saloon and political clubs in the cities operated to keep Irishmen from moving West. . . .

The importance of the Irish in the history of the Roman Catholic Church in the United States and the role of the Church in the life of Irish-

Americans are so generally recognized that the statement that the Catholic Church in America became essentially an immigrant church in the 1840's, and continued for decades to receive its strongest additions from abroad, will hardly be challenged by anyone familiar with the facts. There were Roman Catholics in America at the time of the Revolution, but they were under special disabilities in a number of the American colonies. The first great accession of Roman Catholics came from the purchase of Louisiana, which brought into the American Church about 100,000 communicants. Others came in with the annexations following the Mexican War, but none of these additions can be remotely compared in importance with the great flood of Irish who came across the Atlantic in the 1840's and later decades.

To the poor Irish immigrant, his Church was a part of home. It had always brought him consolation in time of trouble. In a new land it gave him a measure of dignity at a time when he was often made to feel that he was of a lower breed of humanity. It became the role of the Catholic Church to make law-abiding citizens from the hordes of newcomers, to provide parochial schools for the nurture of their religion, to dispense charity in many forms and to provide the counsel of priests for the crises an immigrant had to face in a new and strange environment.

Lay and clerical leaders have testified to the special mission of the Irish to preserve and spread Roman Catholicism in the United States. "What Ireland has done for the American Church, every Bishop, every priest can tell," wrote Maguire in 1867, in his book on *The Irish in America*. "There is scarcely an ecclesiastical seminary for English-speaking students," he added, "in which the great majority of those now preparing for the service of the sanctuary do not belong, if not by birth, at least by blood, to that historic land to which the grateful Church of past ages accorded the proud title — Insula Sanctorum." . . .

It has been estimated that there were 30,000 adherents of the Roman Catholic faith in the United States in 1790. By 1830, the Church claimed 600,000 and, by 1860, 4,500,000 members. Both figures are probably too large. The Metropolitan Catholic Almanac of 1852 listed 1,980,000 Catholics in the United States. By that time, there were Catholic newspapers in nine of the leading cities and Catholic publishing houses in Baltimore, Philadelphia, New York, and Boston. . . .

Devout Irishmen, of course, followed their clerical leaders in matters of religion and religious education. In politics, they learned to follow the ward boss. The latter's affiliations generally were more intimate with the saloon than with the Church, and saloons and fire houses were the centers from which ward-heelers carried on their activities. To an Irishman, politics proved to be the salt and breath of life, and Irishmen in America found it hard to resist the temptation to plunge at once, and deeply, into the American political stream. They learned the tricks of the political game from native American leaders, and then rapidly improved on their instruction. From the first, Irish allegiance was to the Democrats. The name itself had its allure. "Federalist" and "Whig" were names that had little significance for an immigrant who had come to the United States to enjoy freedom and democracy. Moreover, both Federalists and Whigs were suspected, with much truth, of a nativism that frowned upon the newcomer, seeking to protect American institutions from the inundations from abroad and opposed to the easy and quick naturalization of foreigners. Irishmen had little in common with the "Anglomen and monocrats" who supported Federalists and Whigs. Posing as friends of the poor, the Democrats, in the tradition of Jefferson and Jackson, opened their hearts to the immigrants and sought to win and hold their support by admitting them at once to the inner sanctuary and to the minor spoils of the American political system. Irishmen generally had an ingrained hatred for aristocracy and long-standing reasons to be "agin the government." By the year 1820, Tammany Hall was Irish. Tammany celebrations toasted Ireland's sons and their patron saint, St. Patrick, and Tammany used its charities to win and to hold the immigrant vote.

A regiment of well-drilled Irish voters, once organized in any of the larger port towns, was able to enlist new arrivals among the immigrants as soon as they landed. The Irish usually were more interested in local political issues than in national questions, but thorough organization in the local communities led to party solidarity on any issue that might arise. Needless to add, immigrants favored universal manhood suffrage, and the Democratic leaders championed what their supporters wanted. A deliberately cultivated Anglophobia helped to preserve Irish unity. Irish wit and adaptibility, a gift for oratory, a certain vivacity, and a warm, human quality that made them the best of good fellows at all times — especially in election campaigns — enabled the Irish to rise rapidly from ward heelers to city bosses, and to municipal, state and federal officials of high distinction.

The Irish added turbulence and excitement to political campaigns. They also contributed a new picturesqueness and dramatic quality to the methods of political campaigning and canvassing the vote of large masses of people. By building up strong political machines in the cities, they became, along with the Solid South, the one stable element that kept the Democratic party — then a minority group — alive after the Civil War and gave it its occasional chance for victory. Reformers have often overlooked the fact that the same political boss who bought votes, stuffed ballot boxes, and brazenly perpetrated naturalization frauds was also the warmhearted leader who got the immigrant his pushcart license, "fixed" arrests for petty violations of the law, and sent the poor their Christmas turkeys and coal in winter, paid their rent when the landlord threatened eviction, and sent flowers to their funerals. Indeed, some political bosses contended that they were public benefactors, for they took money out of the public till to help bring about a fairer distribution of the world's pleasures among the underprivileged. . . .

The Americanization of the Irish proceeded so rapidly, in spite of the alarmists of the 1850's and 1860's, that no detailed discussion of this process is necessary here. The Irish have become so much a part of present-day Americanism that it seems curious indeed to review the characteristics they brought with them several generations ago and to describe the reception they received from their American contemporaries. The Irishman is now so thoroughly Americanized that he is not averse to joining in denunciations of later immigrants whose ideas he considers dangerous to American institutions, apparently completely forgetful of the treatment his ancestors received 100 years ago. . . .

STUDY GUIDE

1. In this selection, Wittke mentions only a few of the common factors that operated in most countries to lead people to emigrate. Which ones does he mention, and what other common factors can you think of?

2. The selection is concerned only with pre-Civil War migration, which was mostly from northern and western Europe. Based on your own knowledge, indicate in what areas each of the following settled and what occupations they tended to enter: Germans, Scandinavians, Hungarians, Jews, Poles, Italians.

3. What special factors operated in Ireland to promote emigration? How do you explain the poor economic and social condition of the Irish once they arrived here?

4. In the final paragraph, Wittke suggests that there is not necessarily a positive relation between attitudes of tolerance toward other groups and a history of having been persecuted or discriminated against oneself. How can you explain this irony, which we know to be characteristic of many minority groups?

5. What factors in modern American economic life and in new social attitudes might make a cultural pluralism, in which various nationalities and races live in mutual respect and appreciation of their differences, more feasible in the United States today than in the early nineteenth century?

BIBLIOGRAPHY

The study of immigration as a significant theme in the American experience is a relatively recent phenomenon. In addition to the volume from which the preceding selection is taken, two older studies by Marcus Lee Hansen are well worth reading: *The Immigrant in American History* * (edited with a foreword by Arthur Schlesinger, Sr., Cambridge, Mass., 1940) and *The Atlantic Migration 1607–1860* * (edited with a foreword by Arthur Schlesinger, Sr., Cambridge,

Mass., 1945). More recent publications on this theme include a number of volumes by Oscar Handlin: his Pulitzer Prize-winning book, *The Uprooted: The Epic Story of the Great Migrations that Made the American People* * (Boston, 1951, revised, 1973); *Race and Nationality in American Life* (Boston, 1957), a series of essays on the immigration topic; and *Immigration as a Factor in American History* (Englewood Cliffs, N.J., 1959), a collection of primary documents relating to immigration and the author's informative commentary on them. A good, short survey of immigration as an aspect of American life — which includes a well-chosen bibliography — is Maldwyn Jones, *American Immigration* * (Chicago, 1960). Two specialized studies, tracing the migration of particular nationalities to our shores and their experiences, are Oscar Handlin, *Boston's Immigrants, 1790–1880: A Study in Acculturation* * (Cambridge, Mass., 1941, revised, 1959), which is especially strong on the coming and the adjustment of the Irish to that city, and Louis Wirth, *The Ghetto* * (Chicago, 1928), a classic study of the Eastern European Jewish response to Chicago. Two other migrations to our shores are examined in Rowland Toppan Berthoff, *British Immigrants in Industrial America, 1790–1950* (Cambridge, Mass., 1953) and Theodore Saloutos, *The Greeks in the United States* (Cambridge, Mass., 1964) — both excellent studies by American historians.

LOWELL OFFERING

August, 1845.

" Is Saul also among the prophets?"

A REPOSITORY

OF ORIGINAL ARTICLES, WRITTEN BY

"FACTORY GIRLS."

LOWELL: MISSES CURTIS & FARLEY.
BOSTON: JORDAN & WILEY, 121
Washington street.
1845.

This magazine was one of the many projects of the "Improvement Circles" organized by women in the Lowell Mills.

NORMAN J. WARE

The Industrial Worker

There are few developments in all of human history that are as important as the Industrial Revolution. The many changes in production, marketing, technology, business organization, and labor that comprised this revolution have created wealth, material goods, and services on a scale unimaginable to the people of any earlier society. Before the Industrial Revolution, the resources necessary to provide a reasonable standard of living for virtually the entire society simply did not exist, and most people were doomed to remain untrained, uneducated, and barely able to sustain life.

Yet industrialization had unfortunate social consequences as well as beneficial economic ones, and the history of labor, one of the key factors in industrial growth, was not necessarily characterized by steady improvement in either wages or conditions. A number of factors determined the condition of workers in a particular period. Among them were the available supply of labor, the skills necessary to a particular job, the type of industry in which one was employed, and the attitudes of courts and other governmental agencies toward labor and business. During much of our industrial history, the economic theory that considered labor a commodity whose value would fluctuate with supply and demand, just as the cost of raw materials or manufactured products might, dominated American thinking.

The first half of the nineteenth century is an especially interesting period in American labor history. During these years, industrialization — with substantial technological innovation and the introduction of the factory system of labor — proceeded quite rapidly. Yet there was a widespread ambivalence about the new machinery and the new spirit of industrial growth. There was also a well-established social philosophy as to the position of classes, the responsibilities of the employer, and the roles of men and women in the labor force and in the home. Such deep social beliefs are not easily discarded; only grudgingly were they modified to meet the demands of the new industrialism. However, one of the interesting facets of labor history during this period is the way in which some of the new capitalists attempted to reconcile the old social philosophy of the paternalistic employer and his responsibility for the worker with the factory system of labor and the introduction of women workers.

In his book *The Industrial Worker,* Norman Ware studies the period 1840 to 1860, when the controversy over the factory system and the issues of child and female labor were fully developed. He gives a graphic picture of the wages and conditions in the iron industry and the needle trades and describes the two different systems of factory labor that developed. As you read the selection, consider the difference of labor then and labor now with respect to standard of living, type of work, and union organization.

The problem of primary importance for the industrial worker of the forties and fifties is to be found in the changes in his status and standards of living. A rising money wage is no sign of improved standards. Increasing commodity wages constitute a better test, but if accompanied by losses in other respects of greater significance, conclusions drawn therefrom are of little value. Working conditions, hours, speed, or effort must all be taken into account before an approximation can be made to a true estimate of the worker's condition. But in the last analysis the status of the worker is not a physical but a mental one, and is affected as much by comparisons with past conditions and with the status of other groups in the community as by the facts in themselves. In other words, the problem of status is one of satisfactions, and satisfactions are relative.

The depressions of 1837–39 left one-third of the working population of New York City unemployed. [Horace] Greeley estimated that there were not less than ten thousand persons in the city "in utter and hopeless distress with no means of surviving the winter but those provided by charity." The same

From chapter 4 of *The Industrial Worker: 1840–1860* by Norman Ware. Reprinted by permission of Hart, Schaffner, and Marx.

was true, in a somewhat less pronounced degree, throughout the industrial districts. The New England mills were either closed down or running only part-time and undermanned. Between 1839 and 1843 wages generally fell from thirty to fifty per cent, and the improved business conditions of the latter year were not reflected in the wages of the workers. In 1844 the same amount of labor that had once produced for the mechanic and his family a comfortable subsistence was inadequate to maintain his standards, and his only alternative was increased effort or the reduction of his wants.

Pauperism was increasing. "Thirty years ago," said Evans, "the number of paupers in the whole United States was estimated at 29,166, or one in three hundred. The pauperism of New York City now amounts to 51,600, or one in every seven of the population." In New York State the proportion of the poor was said to be increasing and the wages of labor to be steadily declining.

The labor papers that sprang up in these years constantly complained that the condition of the worker was growing worse; that he was becoming more and more dependent on capital; that his resources were being curtailed and a new uncertainty had entered his life as to wages and employment.

In the iron industry, the wage per ton of ore produced was being constantly reduced. The following are the "prices" for certain kinds of work in the Pittsburgh district from 1837 to 1858:

Year	Boilers	Puddlers	Hammermen
1837	$7.00	$4.25	$1.25
1838	7.00	4.25	1.25
1839	6.50	4.00	—
1840	6.00	3.75	—
1841	5.50	3.75	—
1842	5.00	3.50	1.00
1845	6.00	4.00	—
1850	4.50	3.50	—
1858	3.00 to $4.00	1.90 to $2.50	—

After a steady decline of wages in the iron industry from 1837, a strike of the boilers occurred in February, 1842, as a result of notification of a further cut to five dollars a ton. The strike lasted until July, when the boilers resumed work at the reduced price. This price was continued until May, 1845, when a second strike occurred for the recovery of the one dollar a ton they had lost between 1840 and 1842. This lasted until August and resulted in the advance being granted. The new price, identical with that of 1840, lasted until 1850 when reductions were again proposed:

Puddlers	from $4.00	to $3.50 per ton
Boilers	from $6.00	to $4.50 per ton
Refiners	from $1.00	to $0.80 per ton
Scrappers	from $3.75	to $2.50 per ton
Heaters	from $1.37½	to $1.00 per ton . . .

The strike against these reductions had not been broken by February when some of the mills were started with imported labor. Riots broke out in which the puddlers took possession of one of the mills, in the face of the protest of some of their fellows and the pistol of the mayor. The wives of the workers were said to have been the most violent of the rioters. Some slight damage was done and arrests were made. But by the end of March the mills were fairly well filled with imported help working at the reduced rates. Many of the strikers left the city and those who remained returned to the mills in the summer. Of those who were arrested, three men were acquitted and two men and four women found guilty. The men were sentenced to pay fines of six and one-fourth cents and costs and imprisonment for eighteen months. The women were sentenced to pay fifty dollars each and costs and imprisonment for thirty days. On petition of the jury that convicted them and of a large number of citizens, they were pardoned and the fines remitted in August, 1850. . . .

No class of workers was better paid than those in the building trades. Where shoemakers, printers, hatters, cabinet-makers, and so on were getting $4, $5, and $6 a week, the carpenters, plasterers, and bricklayers were getting $10. But even this latter wage was inadequate to maintain the worker's family at anything like a decent comfort standard. In 1851 the carpenters of Philadelphia struck for an advance of twenty-five cents a day which would give them a wage of $10.50 a week. The [New York] *Tribune* published a week's budget for a family of five, as follows:

Budget for Family of Five for One Week

Barrel of flour, $5.00, will last eight weeks	$0.62½
Sugar, 4 lbs. at 8 cents a pound	.32
Butter, 2 lbs. at 31½ cents a pound	.62½ (*sic*)
Milk, two cents per day	.14
Butcher's meat, 2 lbs. beef per day at 10c per lb.	$1.40
Potatoes, ½ bushel	.50
Coffee and tea	.25
Candle light	.14
Fuel, 3 tons of coal per annum, $15.00; charcoal, chips, matches, etc., $5.00 per annum	.40
Salt, pepper, vinegar, starch, soap, soda, yeast, cheese, eggs	.40
Furniture and utensils, wear and tear	.25
Rent	3.00
Bed clothes	.20
Clothing	2.00
Newspapers	.12
Total	$10.37

"I ask," said Greeley, "have I made the working-man's comforts too high? Where is the money to pay for amusements, for ice-creams, his puddings, his trips on Sunday up or down the river in order to get some fresh air, to pay the doctor or apothecary, to pay for pew rent in the church, to purchase books, musical instruments?" . . .

There was not in our period, or probably in any other, a more helpless and degraded class of workers than the needlewomen of the cities. Their condition had earlier enlisted the efforts of Mathew Carey and others, without appreciable result. They were incapable of organizing themselves permanently because of the semi-industrial nature of their trade and the surplus of that sort of labor. What little organization was achieved among them depended rather on the spasmodic efforts of "humane persons" who interested themselves in their behalf.

From 1840 to 1860 a complete revolution occurred in the tailoring industry as a result of the introduction of ready-made clothing in common use. Until 1835 the only clothing kept for sale was "shop clothing" which was sold almost entirely to seamen. The wholesale manufacture of clothes began in New York in 1835, but went under in the panic of 1837. In 1840 the trade revived and offered employment, such as it was, to thousands of women. At first, much of this work was sent into the country to be made up, but it was gradually being brought into the "factories."

The sewing machine made its appearance in the clothing trade in the early fifties. At first the tailor was required to buy his own machine and, as those who had sufficient savings to do this were few, those who had not were compelled to pay the machine tailor for straight stitching. The machine tailor soon discovered that his investment was not a paying one. His earnings were no greater than before and his savings were gone. The profit of the machine went to the bosses; "they got their work quicker and it was done better." . . .

There were at this time four groups of needlewomen corresponding to the classes of work and the stages of advance toward the complete factory system of a later date. The journeymen dressmakers, who were employed by the week, often worked fourteen to sixteen hours a day, and were paid from $1.25 to $2.50 per week. The dressmakers who went into the homes of their customers were better paid, receiving 62½ cents, 75 cents, and $1 a day. Apprentices were usually paid nothing for the first six months and boarded themselves. They were frequently required to pay the employer $10 or $15 for the privilege of "learning," and, if they were unable to pay, they worked for a year without wages and boarded themselves. Instead of being taught the trade, the apprentices were usually kept at plain sewing, and at the end of the apprenticeship two-thirds or three-quarters of them were not trained dressmakers at all. The last group, and the lowest in the scale in every respect, were those who worked in their own homes, calling for their work and returning to the shop with it when finished. There were ten thousand of these women in New York City alone in 1854, and their wages, hours, and conditions of work were inconceivably bad. Widows in Cincinnati were supporting children by making shirts for ten cents each and pants for fifteen and seventeen cents. It was estimated that they could make nine shirts in a week, or ninety cents for a long week's work. In New York, in 1845, some of the needlewomen were being paid ten to eighteen cents a day for twelve to fourteen hours' work, while others, who were more proficient, were paid twenty-five cents a day. Work which had brought 97½ cents in 1844 was paid only 37½ cents in 1845. The average earnings of these women were $1.50 to $2 a week, though many of them could not earn more than $1.

> A great number of females are employed in making men's and boys' caps [said the *Tribune* reporter in 1845]. By constant labor, 15 to 18 hours a day, they can make from 14 to 25 cents. We are told by an old lady who has lived by this kind of work for a long time that when she begins at sunrise and works till midnight, she can earn 14 cents a day. . . .
>
> The manner in which these women live, the squalidness and unhealthy location and nature of their habitations, the impossibility of providing for any of the slightest recreations or moral or intellectual culture or of educating their children, can be easily imagined; but we assure the public that it would require an extremely active imagination to conceive the reality.

When the industrial worker and his friends protested that there was white slavery in the North as evil as the black slavery of the South, they were thinking of conditions of this sort. But the wages, hours, and homes of these women were not their only difficulties. It was a common occurrence for one of the seamstresses to carry back to her employer, after a week's work, a heavy bundle of clothing in her arms and find that it would not pass his examination. Many of the cheap "slop shops" required the women to pay a deposit of the full value of the material before it could be taken out. When work fell off and there was no more to be given out, this deposit was frequently retained by the employer. Needlewomen receiving only five cents for shirts, on which they were required to deposit the full value of the material, were said to have been paid at the rate of ninety-six cents on the dollar. In some cases only a part of the money due was paid, the woman being told to allow the remainder to stand over for later settlement. In this way many of the employers who professed to pay good wages reduced them to the level of the worst. Instances were known where fifty cents was paid on account and the remainder postponed week after week until the claimant became discouraged and gave up trying to collect. In the meantime she had to neglect her chances of getting other employment. One woman after seeking work for two days managed to get something that paid her sixty cents for the first week. When she returned the goods, she was given credit on the books to be settled when the amount was worth while. In another case, the girl delivering her work and asking for payment was kicked into the street and left without money to cross the ferry to her home. . . .

In New York, in 1853, prices were as low as they had been in 1845: summer vests were eighteen cents; pantaloons, twenty cents; light coats, eighteen cents. A twelve-hour day gave a return of about twenty-four cents, "provided [the goods] were not returned upon the hands of the worker." Shirts were made for four, five, seven, and eight cents apiece; three of them were a hard day's labor and brought the worker from twelve to twenty-four cents a day. "The average yearly income of these women at the best of the above prices, all doing full work the year round, amounts to ninety-one dollars!"

The beginnings of the "sweating system" are to be found here. The *Tribune's* reporter described it in 1853 as a "middle system." Near one of the streets running from the Bowery to the East River an old Irish woman was found with four girls working for her. Their pay consisted solely of their food for six days a week. Another woman had hired four "learners," two of whom received only board and lodging, while the other two were paid one dollar a week without their food.

The milliners of New York were [no?] better off than the sewing-women. As apprentices they received no pay or board for a year, and, in the better shops, had frequently to pay a bonus for the privilege of "learning." The hours were from ten to twelve, and at the end of the year they were turned out to find employment, and a new batch of apprentices was taken on. All through the period and in very many trades the apprenticeship system had become little more than a cheap method of getting the greater part of the work done. There was no attempt made to teach the full trade. One or two journeymen were sufficient as overseers to supply all the craft knowledge and skill required for the shop and the routine work was done by so-called "apprentices." The journeymen milliners working from sunrise to 9 P.M. could earn from $2.50 to $3 a week. Their board and washing cost at least $2. . . .

. . .

The new industrialism found its completest expression in the textile mills of New England, New York, and Pennsylvania. Here the New Power was most firmly established and the new discipline most intense. In the barracks-like mills by the swift rivers of the northern seaboard the Industrial Revolution reached completion, and the lesser status of the industrial worker was revealed. And there developed in the forties a remarkable controversy over the Factory System, originating, in part, in the political field and involving the tariff question, and, in part, in the feeling that the new industrialism was alien to and destructive of American ideals and standards.

The introduction of the cotton industry in Massachusetts at the beginning of the century was achieved under difficulties that arose, on the one hand, from the want of a labor force and, on the other, from the English control of the new machines and the technical knowledge required to set them in operation. A new labor force was available in the women and girls of New England, once their initial aversion to the factory discipline could be broken down. The degraded condition of the operatives of the English mill towns was notorious, and Americans, including the Boston capitalists intent on cotton manufacture, had no desire to reproduce those conditions here.

"The question . . . arose and was deeply considered," said Nathan Appleton, "whether this degradation was the result of the peculiar occupation or of other and distinct causes. . . ." The matter was decided in favor of the latter hypothesis, and the Boston capitalists who had interested themselves in cotton manufacture proceeded to make such arrangements as seemed good to them to attract the New England women into the mills and guard them from immoral influences as best they could.

This protection involved what is known as the "Waltham System" which was copied in the foundation of Lowell and came to be regarded as the perfection of what an industrial community should be. The basis of the Waltham system was the company boarding-house, where the girls were required to be in at 10 P.M. and generally to live under the somewhat fictitious supervision of the boarding-house keeper. Upon this basis was erected a puritanical paternalism originally intended for the welfare of the girls, but capable — in the hands of agents less high-principled than the early mill-owners — of being turned into a very effective and harmful despotism. In addition to the boarding-houses, the Waltham system involved the payment of wages in cash, the "moral police" or community censorship of morals, the requirement that the girls should attend church, discharge for immoral conduct, and a thorough understanding among the corporations as to wages, hours, and the "blacklist."

> I visited the corporate factory establishment of Waltham within a few miles of Boston [said Harriet Martineau in 1834]. The establishment is for spinning and weaving of cotton alone and the construction of the requisite machinery. Five hundred girls were employed at the time of my visit. The girls can earn two and sometimes three dollars a week besides their board. The little children earn one dollar a week. Most of the girls live in houses provided by the corporation. . . . When sisters come to the mill it is a common practice for them to bring their mother to keep house for them and some other companions, in a dwelling built by their own earnings. In this case they save enough out of their board to clothe themselves and have two or three dollars to spare. Some have thus cleared off mortgages from their fathers' farms; others have educated the hope of the family at college; and many are rapidly accumulating an independence. I saw a whole street of houses built with the earnings of the girls; some with piazzas and green venetian blinds, and all neat and sufficiently spacious.
>
> The factory people built the church which stands conspicuous on the green in the midst of the place. The minister's salary, eight hundred dollars last year, is raised by a tax on the pews. The corporation gave them a building for a Lyceum which they have furnished with a good library and where they have lectures every winter, the best that money can procure. The girls have, in many instances, private libraries of some value.
>
> The managers of the various factory establishments keep the wages as nearly equal as possible and then let the girls freely shift from one to another. . . . The people work about seventy hours a week on an average. . . . All look like well-dressed young ladies. The health is good, or rather it is no worse than elsewhere.

This picture is somewhat *couleur de rose* and naïve in its treatment of the compulsory tax for the upkeep of the church and the uniform wage and freedom of movement of the operatives. The only fault Miss Martineau found

with the mills was the overcrowding of the boarding-houses where girls sometimes slept three in a bed and six or more in a room. She must have been
misinformed as to the hours of labor which were nearer seventy-five than
seventy a week. . . .

In sharp contrast with the Waltham system there was found in the Middle
States, and especially in Rhode Island, what can be called the English system
of *laissez-faire*. This was the original method of cotton manufacture in New
England, having been established by Samuel Slater at Pawtucket before the
beginning of the century. The Rhode Island system, to be found also at Fall
River, Massachusetts, was not a conscious method at all, but simply a growth
along English lines with the material at hand. Instead of employing adults
almost exclusively, as in Massachusetts, whole families were employed, and
it is in this district that child labor was chiefly found. There was no attempt
made by Slater and those who followed him to guard the morals of the
operatives or to do anything for them within or without the mills. There
were no company boarding-houses, the operatives being allowed to find what
homes they could, and instead of cash wages being paid, factory stores were
established and store orders issued. The first mill opened by Slater was operated by seven boys and two girls between the ages of seven and eleven, and
some of the early mills recruited children from the almshouses and overseers
of the poor.

The contrast of the two systems is interesting because the scarcity of factory labor was probably as great in Rhode Island as in Massachusetts, which
suggests that the Waltham system was the result of the Puritan traditions of
the Boston capitalists, rather than the real necessities of the case, while the
presence of the company store in Rhode Island reveals it as less a convenience for the operatives than a means of exploitation by the companies. For
if the company store had been a real convenience to the operatives, as is
often assumed, it would probably have been found in Lowell rather than
Pawtucket, though the large percentage of single women at Lowell would
have reduced its trade. . . .

But the essential difference between Lowell and Rhode Island or Fall
River was the psychological one between paternalism and *laissez-faire*. General Oliver, who had been an agent at Lowell, visited Fall River in 1855 and
was greatly shocked by the attitude of the agents at the latter place.

> I inquired of the agent of a principal factory whether it was the custom of the
> manufacturers to do anything for the physical, intellectual, and moral wel-
> fare of their work-people. . . . "We never do," he said. "As for myself, I
> regard my work-people just as I regard my machinery. So long as they can do
> my work for what I choose to pay them, I keep them, getting out of them all
> I can. What they do or how they fare outside my walls I don't know, nor do
> I consider it my business to know. They must look out for themselves as I
> do for myself. When my machines get old and useless, I reject them and get
> new, and these people are part of my machinery."

A Holyoke manager found his hands "languorous" in the early morning because they had breakfasted. He tried working them without breakfast and got three thousand more yards of cloth a week made.

It would appear at first glance that there could be no comparison, from the standpoint of the operatives, between the two systems; that the puritanical paternalism of Lowell was infinitely superior to the callous indifference of Fall River. Nevertheless, two rather unexpected facts emerge to modify this opinion: the attack on the factory system by the intellectuals centered not on the evil conditions of Fall River, but on the relatively admirable conditions of Lowell; and the operatives' revolt began at the former rather than at the latter place. This would suggest, at least, that there were elements in the Lowell situation that were regarded as even more harmful than bad conditions, and that the Fall River system left the operatives greater initiative. It would be unwise to press these deductions too far because it is equally possible to say that the Fall River revolt was the result of exceptionally bad conditions and the attack on Lowell, the result of its proximity to Boston.

The Lowell factory system was being attacked in our period from two directions. The Battle of Books represented the opposition of the intellectuals and was directed chiefly against the alleged tendency to degrade the morals and health of the operative, while the attack of the operatives themselves was chiefly against the "tyranny" and "despotism" of the system, its increasing discipline and antirepublican nature.

> That the factory system contains in itself the elements of slavery, we think no sound reasoning can deny, and every day continues to add power to its incorporate sovereignty, while the sovereignty of the working people decreases in the same ratio.

Like other workers of the period, the factory operatives — men and women — felt that they were losing something of their dignity and independence, so that, from the point of view of the workers, much of the heated argument over factory conditions missed the point. The worker objected to his cage, whether it was gilded, as in Lowell, or rusty and unkempt, as in Fall River.

In the matter of discipline the Fall River system had advantages over that of Lowell. Once out of the Fall River mills, the worker was free, while in Lowell there was hardly an hour of the day or a relationship of any sort that was not covered by the regulations, written or understood, of the corporations. . . .

The factory controversy began with an editoral in the Boston *Daily Times* (Democrat) for Saturday, July 13, 1839, entitled "A Manufacturing Population." The interest of the *Times* in the matter was partly political. The Whigs had always contended that the factories gave easy, pleasurable, and remunerative employment to women and girls who would otherwise have been idle, and that the fears of the opponents of the system were unfounded. The *Times* undertook to show that the young girls are compelled to work in unhealthy confinement for too many hours every day; that their food is both unhealthy and scanty; that they are not allowed sufficient time to eat: . . . that they are crowded together in ill-ventilated apartments in the boarding-houses of the corporations, and that in consequence they become pale, feeble, and finally broken in constitution . . . and that hundreds of the vilest of the female sex throng to the manufactories with corruption in their manners and upon their tongues to breathe out the pestilence of the brothel in the boarding-places.

The *Times* objected to the fact that the girls were made to board at the company houses except when they had friends or relatives in Lowell; that they had to be in their rooms at ten o'clock; and that the price of their board was fixed by the corporations at $1.50 a week and deducted from their wages. It was claimed that the price of board was too low, that a decent table could not be maintained at the price when potatoes were selling for 75 cents to $1 a peck, flour was $9 to $12 a barrel, and beef 10 to 16 cents a pound. The girls were underfed and unhealthy-looking, except the newcomers from the country.

In the early days, the *Times* contended, conditions had been better. When the Merrimack Mill was started, besides the workmen employed from Europe the proprietors had to rely on such girls as they could obtain to attend the looms and spindles. These girls came in gradually from the surrounding country — daughters of farmers and mechanics, "generally poor, but of un-blemished reputation." Provisions were cheap, the food sufficient, and the girls seemed happy and healthy. They dressed well and preferred the mills as their own mistresses to being servants. Many of them saved money and went home, but others squandered their earnings and found themselves tied to the mills. But the supply was still inadequate and the corporations had to send men out to scour the country through New Hampshire, Vermont, and Canada. Thus the permanent mill population increased and their dependence upon the corporations. The labor turnover was tremendous, one hundred girls arriving and leaving every day for several weeks in the spring and fall, but always some remained behind to swell the factory population, unfitted to be wives and mothers, in slavish dependence on the mills.

When the corporations began to realize, said the *Times,* that this permanent factory population was increasing, they reduced wages by agreement. On the first occasion the girls "turned out," but new hands were found, and "there has been created and there is now growing up in Lowell a manufacturing population whose tendency in the scale of civilization, health, morals, and intellectuality, is manifestly downwards."

As to the morals of the girls, the *Times* quoted a Lowell physician to the effect that

there used to be in Lowell an association of young men called "The Old Line" who had an understanding with a great many of the factory girls and who used to introduce young men of their acquaintance, visitors to the place, to the girls for immoral purposes. Balls were held at various places attended mostly by these young men and girls, with some others who did not know the object of the association, and after the dancing was over the girls were taken to infamous places of resort in Lowell and the vicinity and were not returned to their homes until daylight.

Another medical practitioner in Lowell stated that, in one week, he had more than seventy persons apply to him for remedies for venereal diseases, most of whom were girls. Occupants of brothels in New York and Boston who had become diseased were also said to have entered the mills. The late deputy sheriff of Lowell had stated that he had found three houses to which these professional prostitutes were in the habit of bringing factory girls.

Dr. Elisha Bartlett of Lowell replied to the *Times* articles in the Lowell *Courier,* and this was later published as a pamphlet under the title "A Vindication of the Character and Condition of the Females Employed in the Lowell Mills against the charges contained in the Boston Times and Boston Quarterly Review." The editor of the *Courier* also replied, as did Harriet Farley, editor of the *Lowell Offering.*

As is frequently the case in controversies of this sort, the opponents were not talking about the same thing and never really came to grips. Bartlett insisted that the morals and health of the factory operatives were good, while the *Times* claimed that their morals and health were getting bad. Bartlett was thinking of a condition, often of a past condition, and the *Times* of a tendency. Neither was concerned with the problem that bothered the worker, the problem of social status and freedom. The mill girls had been, and the majority perhaps still were, what Bartlett claimed, but at the same time they were becoming more or less what the *Times* insisted they were: "a permanent factory population" of a more degraded sort than the New England mill girls of the twenties and thirties.

Dr. Bartlett dealt chiefly with health, morals, chances of marriage and wages, and his argument was followed quite closely by Miles and Scoresby in 1845. He made a statistical comparison between Lowell and Portsmouth, New Hampshire, . . . and declared that "the manufacturing population of this city is the healthiest portion of the population." He defended the morals of the factory girls, claiming that the mill overseers, the "moral police" of the corporations, and the censorship of the girls themselves kept the tone of the community high. He insisted even that the morals of the girls improved on coming from the country where all was not as pure as it looked.

As to wages, the average, clear of board, amounted to about two dollars per week. The number of depositors in the Lowell Savings Institution was 1976 and the amount of deposits $305,796.75. Of these depositors, 978 were factory girls. The amount of their deposits is not given, but it is estimated at not less than $100,000, while it was a common thing for a girl to have $500 in the bank. Bartlett claimed that the girls' chances of marriage were good and the boarding-house keepers quite able to make a living and supply satisfactory food if they managed properly.

The controversy was continued by a reply to Dr. Bartlett which appeared in the *Vox Populi* of Lowell in 1841. This was written by "A Citizen of Lowell" and was later published under the title "Corporations and Operatives: Being an exposition of the condition of factory operatives and a review of the 'Vindication' by Elisha Bartlett, M.D." The reply was an able discussion that left nothing of Bartlett's mortality and marriage statistics, but began in a demogogic vein that tended to obscure the value of the later argument. The Lowell "Citizen" charged the defenders of the factories with being paid "servants of interested aristocracies," a "pensioned press" and "bought priesthood." The question of the hours of employment, that later supplanted all others, was here first emphasized. It was claimed that the operatives had only fifteen minutes in which to eat their meals when time was deducted for going to and from the boarding-houses. The price allowed for board had been $1.25 until 1836, when it had been raised to $1.37½ because the boarding-house keepers had been unable to live. There it remained until 1841, when it was again reduced to $1.25. The boarding-houses were overrun with vermin. The hours in the mills were nearly thirteen a day and not less than twelve and one-half of actual toil. But this was to reckon only the time actually in the mills, and even this was not correct because some corporations cheated the operatives by starting before the ringing of the bell. Reckoning the time stolen and the time occupied in preparing for meals, eating, and going to and fro, the operatives were engaged fifteen hours out of the twenty-four.

Not only were the hours long, but they were getting longer. The corporations were adding to them "year after year, week after week, minute by minute," until they ran fifteen minutes a day longer in 1841 than twelve years before. "I do not believe," said the "Citizen of Lowell," "that there is upon the face of the earth any large class of persons who labor incessantly for so many hours each day as do the factory operatives of New England." . . .

STUDY GUIDE

1. How did each of the following contribute to the debased condition of labor described by Ware: technological changes such as new, heavier machinery; machinery that required less skill to operate; a labor surplus; social attitudes toward labor?

2. In terms of potential labor force and the type of labor involved, why were the needle trades more susceptible to exploitative labor conditions than some other industries?

3. What were the differences between the Waltham and the Fall River or Rhode Island systems of factory labor? Which of them seems more exploitative and which more paternalistic? In what ways did the less paternalistic system have advantages from the worker's point of view?

4. In another country or another period, the expansion of the available labor force by the introduction of women, children, and immigrants might not have resulted in a general degradation of the position of all labor. What, in the position of labor in the early nineteenth century or in the general state of the Industrial Revolution at that time, might account for the fact that such degradation did happen in the United States?

5. What similarities and differences are there in the lot of the worker in the early nineteenth century and in the present with respect to: his ability to bargain to improve his position; the training necessary for his job; his mobility; his relationship to his employer; his security?

BIBLIOGRAPHY

While Ware's book is one of the best specialized works ever published on American factory labor, it is limited to the two decades before the Civil War. Also, there are many other aspects of the Industrial Revolution in the United States that merit attention, which were not within the scope of Ware's study. Carl Bridenbaugh, *The Colonial Craftsman* * (New York, 1950) is an interesting study of labor in the pre-industrial period. Two of several works that elaborate on the topics of which Ware writes are Caroline F. Ware, *The Early New England Cotton Manufacture: A Study in Industrial Beginnings* (Boston and New York, 1931) and Hannah Josephson, *Golden Threads: New England's Mill Girls and Magnates* (New York, 1949).

There are a number of one-volume surveys of American labor history that carry the story beyond the Civil War. Henry Pelling, *American Labor* * (Chicago, 1960) is a very brief introduction. Foster R. Dulles, *Labor in America: A History* * (New York, 1949) and Joseph G. Rayback, *A History of American Labor* * (New York, 1959) are longer works.

Some decades ago, the Industrial Revolution was seen as largely due to the efforts of great business leaders and the technological developments of inventors, with relatively little attention given to labor and other factors. One book which provides a readable survey of the many factors — from transportation and technology to business leadership and labor — that contributed to the Industrial Revolution is Thomas C. Cochran and William Miller, *The Age of Enterprise: A Social History of Industrial America* * (New York, 1942). An extremely interesting survey of technology, emphasizing the social environment of inventions, is Roger Burlingame, *March of the Iron Men: A Social History of Union through Invention* * (New York, 1938). There are biographies of Samuel Slater, Samuel F. B. Morse, and other important figures in the development of American technology, but two of the best are about Eli Whitney: Jeannette Mirsky and Allan Nevins, *The World of Eli Whitney* (New York, 1952) and Constance Green, *Eli Whitney and the Birth of American Technology* * (Boston, 1956).

VI EXPANSION AND CONFLICT

In the Treaty of Paris of 1783, the boundaries of the United States had been set at the Mississippi River on the west and along the 31st parallel on the south. By 1853, the country had added the huge Louisiana Purchase, acquired Florida from Spain, and swept westward over Texas, California, and Oregon into every square mile of territory that was to make up the continental United States. This breath-taking acquisition of territory had involved American intrigue in Florida, revolution in Texas, a blustering threat of force in Oregon, and full-scale war against Mexico. Generally, however, the American people were in advance of their government. Land — to settle on or speculate in — rather than gold, was the chief lure that drew Americans westward into lands beyond the borders of their own country.

The acquisition of millions of acres of land beyond the Mississippi was one of the crucial factors in accentuating the sectional conflict that had begun in the 1830s. During the 1850s, the morality of slavery was the overriding issue in the minds of abolitionists. But for most of the people of North and South alike a matter of more immediate concern was whether or not slavery would expand into the western territories. The slogan of the Free Soil Party embodied the several aspects of sectional conflict: "Free Soil, Free Speech, Free Labor, and Free Men." The concern of this northern political party that labor and soil in the West be free points up the economic division of North and South. But the other parts of the slogan — free speech and free men — suggest that the country was also divided by psychological and social differences.

By 1861, many national social institutions, including the major religious denominations, had broken apart along sectional lines. And by that time, many thousands of Southerners saw the triumph of the northern Republican Party in the 1860 election as not simply a political defeat but a threat to all southern institutions and to the southern way of life.

The first reading in this section describes the travails of the pioneer, who, as he went westward with his few belongings in his wagon, took with him into the wilderness American traditions and social institutions in law, religion, government, and other fields. As Americans moved into the Southwest, they encountered a Spanish-speaking people with a different religion, culture, and attitude toward slavery. The hostilities that arose from this encounter are described in the second reading. The third selection gives us a sense of the feelings of average men who were turned into soldiers to fight those who had been their fellow countrymen. American society had been torn asunder, and the reweaving of the disparate threads into a new social fabric was to prove a long and trying process.

Goldminers in California, 1852. The hope of striking it rich lured thousands to brave the trail west.

EVERETT DICK

The Way West

Few movements in all of our history have captured the imagination as has the settlement of the great American West. The image of the sturdy pioneer, plodding beside his lumbering covered wagon, fighting off Indian attacks, fording swift streams, and finally looking out upon the blue Pacific has become enshrined in American folklore and on Hollywood celluloid. There is much in all of this that is sheer myth, but there is also much that is true.

The earliest opening of some American frontiers was accomplished by lone trappers and hunters who, because the game was there or because they weren't comfortable in more settled communities, turned their paths westward. Though such men served as guides and added to the scant geographical knowledge of nineteenth-century America, they were relatively unimportant in western settlement. Even in the case of the fur trade, the single hunter was rapidly supplanted by the business organization, and it was John Jacob Astor's Pacific Fur Company that led thousands of other Americans to dream of the Oregon country.

In fact, settlement of the West in large numbers required careful planning, substantial equipment and supplies, organization, and community effort. Whether seeking gold in California, land in Oregon, or a religious Eden in Utah, the pioneers usually went west in a group. Leaders were chosen, supplies carefully assembled, and laws of the trail set down. While pioneer life was that of an organized community, rather than that of the lone scout, this does not mean that the stories of struggle and hardship are entirely mythical.

Americans today are still a migratory people, and until very recently California was the chief lodestar. But as we speed on interstate highways alongside the Platte River or fly over the Rocky Mountains in jet comfort, we have little idea of life on the trail in 1848. For this we must turn to the diaries of the men and women who made the long trek, who gave birth to infants on the wooden beds of wagons and pushed on the next day, and who buried children and parents in unmarked graves to which they would never return.

Professor Everett Dick has written a shelf of books on American frontiers from the opening of the Southwest to the "Sod House Frontier" of the northern plains. His book *Vanguards of the Frontier* describes the opening of the Far West. The following selection on the pioneer journey to Oregon and California treats transportation, food, hardship, desolation, and other aspects of social life in a migratory community beyond established institutions.

The overland trail which frayed out like a rope at its eastern end, with starting-points at the various Missouri River towns from Kansas City, as it is now called, north to the mouth of the Platte, was bound into a unit near Fort Kearney, Nebraska, and ran along the Platte to the mountains in Wyoming. In the western part of that State and in Idaho it again divided, one branch leading to Oregon and the other to California.

The first travelers over the eastern end of this highway were the trappers and fur-traders who, in order to avoid the hostile Indians on the Missouri River, struck directly across the prairie with their goods for the rendezvous. Captain William L. Sublette was the first to use wheeled vehicles on this route in 1830.

In 1841 the first band of emigrants set out from the Missouri border for California and Oregon, and by 1843 the so-called Oregon Trail had become well enough established that more than a thousand moved over it in the early years. Joel Palmer, who traveled up the trail in 1845, tells us that a large body of three thousand emigrants paused for organization on Big Soldier Creek in Kansas. According to the arrangements, two chief officers were to be elected, a pilot to act as guide and a captain. That year one candidate offered to guide the party for five hundred dollars in advance. Another offered to do the work for half that amount with a small sum down and the balance at Vancouver. The latter candidate was elected. A host of

Everett Dick, *Vanguards of the Frontier* (New York: D. Appleton-Century Co., 1941) chapter 10. Reprinted by permission of the author.

lesser officers were also elected — lieutenants, judges, sergeants, and so forth. But a number of disappointed candidates were unwilling to abide by the will of the majority and manifested such a spirit of insubordination that it was mutually agreed to break the group into three companies with separate officers, though the chief officers elected in the first place were to continue to hold the supreme offices. An attempt was then made to collect enough money to ensure the wages of the pilot. Only about one hundred and ninety dollars of the sum promised could be obtained. Some refused to pay, and others had no money. Each of the three companies took its turn in leading the train for a day. Henry Howe records that in 1846 a company of 288, which organized on May 12, had split twice, making three divisions, by June 2.

When he left behind the restraint of civilization and entered a pathless prairie which knew no law or order, the worst side of man's nature revealed itself. In time of sickness men sometimes deserted their companies, leaving them to die; or at the period of a stampede they disregarded their solemn promise to aid their fellow-travelers in time of distress and drove off, leaving them with insufficient animals to pull their wagons. In the many disputes which arose, hard words were often followed by bloodshed. In some instances perpetrators of capital crime were haled before a hastily summoned people's court, given a brief, though fair, trial, sentenced, and summarily executed.

Jesse Applegate, who led a band of emigrants to Oregon in 1843, described the government drawn up by his organization. A council composed of the ablest and most respected fathers of the migration exercised legislative and judicial authority. As a rule the council was called into session on the days when the group did not travel. On one occasion he recorded a special session called to deal with a dispute which did not admit of delay. In this instance the controversy related to a young man who had agreed to do a man's work on the journey for his board and bed.

When such a dispute was to be settled, the council resolved itself into a high court from which there was no appeal. The offending and the aggrieved parties appeared before the body. Witnesses were examined, and the parties represented themselves or had home legal talent to represent them. When these proceedings were over, the judges, without being in any way cramped by technicalities, decided the case according to its merits. Justice was thus efficiently and promptly administered without any monetary cost. Judgment executed largely by public opinion was not always carried out, however, due to division among a party with resultant splits.

According to one traveler, the camp was aroused at sunrise by the sound of a bugle. After breakfast the cattle were caught up and there was a scene of hurry and confusion, with oxen bellowing and men and women hastening here and there about the final preparations to break camp. On the trail a train of fifty wagons and one hundred and fifty people with numbers of loose stock would string out a mile. At noon the travelers stopped for an hour's "nooning." The pilot, by considering the terrain and estimating the speed of the wagons and the walk of his horse, was able to go ahead and locate a camp-site at the proper distance. Proceeding with a band of "pioneers," he prepared the road and selected a campground perhaps an hour in advance of the main column. When the caravan arrived, the path-breakers had little wells dug and other preparations made for the night camp. A day's travel amounted to about twelve to fifteen miles. In 1846, when the travelers had gone approximately one hundred miles, they were overtaken by an express from the frontier post-office bringing the last papers and letters they expected from the States until they reached the Pacific.

In good weather life on the emigrant trail was often pleasant. The camp with its huge covered wagons, white tents, and blazing camp-fires lighting up the prairie presented a charming picture. Children played about, and here and there groups of men and women gathered around the fires, talk-ing, laughing, and singing as night settled down. Often the travelers stopped over Sunday. For the most part the time was spent in hunting, fishing, wash-ing clothes, baking, and ironing, although a minister often held meetings and the more religious could have spiritual food. Those not so inclined obliged the worshipers by ceasing their fiddling. Some played cards, read novels, or in other ways amused themselves.

Nevertheless the continual travel day after day bore heavily on the women — the eternal grind with its dust, dirt, and lack of finer con-veniences that women appreciate. Such things as baths and toilet facilities were almost unknown. Childbirth in the rough surroundings was hard, indeed, without the care so much valued under the circumstances. On June 26, 1851, a company from Peoria, Illinois, stopped a few hours at North Skunk River while Mrs. Jeemes Taylor gave birth to a fine baby. Her husband, upon proudly viewing the heir, inquired: "Do you feel able to go on, Sally?" "Oh, yes, Jeemes, I feel pretty pert. I reckon you'd better hitch up the steers." And with this brief pause for hospitalization the proud husband hooked up and the onward march to Oregon was resumed.

All of the fundamental procedures of life in the old home continued. There were social good times, love-making, marriage, birth, and death. One traveler recorded that in one camp a wedding took place, and at an-other a mile and a half distant a boy was buried by torch-light, while at a third in close proximity a child was born. In less than a month after the first party left civilization in 1841, a romance had developed to such a point that Elder Joseph Williams felt constrained to marry the couple on the Platte River, as he said, "without law or license, for we were a long way from the United States." . . .

The natural flow of population westward to Oregon and California had gone its tranquil way for nearly a decade when the discovery of gold at Sutter's mill near Sacramento inoculated the country with the most virulent case of gold fever it has ever had. As a consequence the little rivulet of humanity trickling westward each season became a mighty torrent from the Missouri River to California. With this new development the tempo of travel was speeded up, and men strained every nerve as they pushed resolutely forward to the land of promise, anxious to reach the rainbow's end before someone else had removed the pot of gold.

During the winter of 1848–49 the eastern states literally seethed with excitement over the possibility of riches for every person who could reach California. Men sat around the stoves in the general stores talking and dreaming of the wealth to be had for the trip. Meetings were held in lodge halls, and organizations were formed for mutual aid in making the long, dangerous journey. The excitement spread like a contagious disease, and man after man announced to neighbors and friends that he had decided to go west.

Of the many companies formed to travel to the gold-fields the Jefferson County, Virginia, Mining Company was a typical example. Eighty men joined the company, contributing $300 each, which was the customary sum paid by members of such organizations. Each man was given a rubber sack with the company's marker on it in which to carry his clothing. The company left Charleston on March 3, 1849. The Granite State Mining Company, numbering twenty-nine members paying the same fees as the Jefferson County Company, made arrangements to travel to California with the Mount Washington Company. As the names indicate, both of these were from New England. Companies from the East often went west by train and boat to the Missouri River and obtained special rates by buying a block ticket for the entire group. Those who did this, for the most part, arrived at Independence or St. Joseph by river steamboat in April or May. Many unattached emigrants joined in the mad rush, however, and from the Great Lakes region of the Old Northwest, companies, little groups, and individuals drove their covered wagons across Iowa and waited patiently to cross the Missouri River by the ferry-boat at Council Bluffs. One company spent a month and four days in crossing Iowa. The rush of business was so great that the ferry, working at full speed, was days behind when Sarah Royce and her husband arrived. A snow-white city of covered wagons congregated and waited turns. As the wagons arrived, each was given a number, and while waiting for their numbers to be called, the emigrants amused themselves by visiting each other's camps and whiling away the time as best they could.

On reaching the west side of the Missouri, various individuals and small groups proceeded to organize into a traveling company of their own. Resolutions were adopted and officers elected. The following set of resolutions, drawn up on the west bank of the Missouri on May 6, 1850, is representative of hundreds during the gold-rush of 1849 and the decade of the fifties:

> Whereas we are about to leave the frontier, and travel over Indian Territory, exposed to their treachery, and knowing their long and abiding hatred of the

whites; also many other privations to meet with. We consider it necessary to form ourselves into a Company for the purpose of protecting each other and our property, during our journey to California.

Therefore Resolved, That there shall be one selected from the Company, suitable and capable to act as Captain or Leader.

Resolved, That we, as men pledge ourselves to assist each other through all the misfortunes that may befall us on our long and dangerous journey.

Resolved, That the Christian Sabbath shall be observed, except when absolutely necessary to travel.

Resolved, That there shall be a sufficient guard appointed each night regularly, by the Captain.

Resolved, That in case of a member's dying, the Company shall give him a decent burial.

As a rule, companies which started with optimism and the best of resolutions began to disintegrate before many days. Disagreements over one thing or another caused division after division. One of the most fruitful sources of dissension was the provision for resting on Sunday. In their anxiety to reach the gold-fields a large portion of the group was likely to be determined to travel on the day of rest. Often the more pious travelers felt obliged on this account to part company with their less particular associates. In the absence of the restraint imposed by formal government, men were prone to give vent to unbridled anger, and frequently quarrels between individuals resulted in a company's dividing into two partisan groups. It seems unlikely that many of the organizations that left the East remained intact until California was reached.

Apparently the physical rigors of the journey, added to the mental strain, wore on the nerves until even trival matters appeared of great consequence, causing the destruction of friendships or business contracts. Even the women felt the urge to break through the conventionalities and let the more savage qualities of their nature assert themselves when the coffee-pot began to leak and the daily routine grew unbearably monotonous.

One man and his wife had such a violent quarrel that they cut their wagon in two, made a cart of each part, and equally divided their team, each taking a yoke of oxen. Out there on the Plains, without judge, jury, lawyer, or fees, they had a divorce.

Two men who had prepared an outfit together in Independence frequently quarreled over the traveling and camping arrangements. At Chimney Rock one of the company suggested that they fight it out and be done with it. The mere suggestion was enough. Each drew his knife, and they closed in fierce and deadly combat. In a short time one fell and expired almost immediately. The other, fainting from loss of blood, was carried to the shade, where he died within an hour. At set of sun, with the grim irony of fate, they were laid side by side in the same unhallowed grave, never more to disagree.

With the first rush of gold-hunters the towns along the Missouri River experienced a tremendous boom. St. Joseph, Independence, and Council Bluffs, which had been mere villages, became outfitting towns, doubling and trebling in business and population overnight. Even St. Louis profited enormously by this large increase in business. As soon as the Missouri River was open to navigation in the middle of February, 1849, the adventurers began to stream into St. Joseph from all of the more northerly states. The landing was a scene of the greatest animation. The town was packed so full of people that tents were pitched around the outskirts and on the west side of the river in such numbers that it seemed the city was besieged by an army. Every house lot became a stable and brought in money for the owner. Prices rose by jumps. Corn, formerly fifteen cents a bushel, rose to a dollar. Ham, which before had brought from three to seven cents a pound, sold for twelve cents, and butter rose from eight to twenty-five cents. Oftentimes bread could not be had at any price. The most extravagant dreams of riches engrossed the emigrants, and they were anxious to be on their way. They had visions of returning with fifty thousand dollars, and there went up from around the camp-fires the popular song of the Forty-niners sung to the tune of "Oh! Susanna":

> Oh, California, that's the land for me,
> I'm bound for California with a washbowl on my knee.

The outfitting towns showed enterprise and in a few weeks were ready to cater to the needs of the overland travelers. There quickly appeared on the shelves every conceivable kind of goods which either bore the brand "California" or were offered especially for use of the traveler. Under an advertisement head of "For California" was described a large variety of meats hermetically sealed in cans and guaranteed to keep for five years in any climate. "California bacon" was packed in boxes or small bales and was a marked improvement over ordinary salt pork of the time. So unexpected was the avalanche of buying that the shelves of St. Joseph mercantile houses were emptied, and the proprietors had hastily to replenish their stocks from the stores lower down the river to tide them over. In 1849 the Phoenix Mutual Life Insurance Company was organized at St. Louis primarily to insure going to California. The premiums were calculated at the regular life rates with an extra charge of $2\frac{1}{2}$ per cent of the principal amount insured on account of the hazardous nature of the undertaking.

At Independence in 1850 every state in the Union except Delaware and Texas was represented by a delegation of emigrants to California. Many of the adventurers brought a part or all of their equipment with them on the steamboat, putting only the finishing touches on their outfitting at the Missouri River points of departure. Many bought live stock at these points, however. The standard equipment consisted of a covered wagon pulled by oxen, horses, or mules. In front the white-duck top had flaps, and in the rear there was a "pucker string" drawing the top taut. A sheet-iron cooking stove hung on the rear of the wagon, although in some cases this spot was occupied by a keg of whisky, a sheet-iron gold-washer, or other mining equipment. The interior of the wagon was loaded with provisions and bedding. Some overland travelers carried tents for sleeping purposes while others slept in the wagons. Many wagon covers had names on them, such as "Badgers," "Hoosiers," "From Suckerdom," "From Pike County, Missouri," "Ho! for California — if you get there before me, say I'm coming," "Pilgrim's Progress — Traveling Edition," "Rough and Ready," and "Gold Hunter." The Jefferson County, Virginia, Company took two wagons with sheet-iron beds fashioned into boats. When the train arrived at a stream that could not be forded, these boats were used to ferry the goods of the whole party across. Some companies felt it more desirable to adopt the pack-train mode of travel. It was argued that such equipment would enable a group to travel fast and light, without the hindrance of heavy wagon traffic, and thus reach the gold-mines quickly.

The Mount Washington Mining Company of Boston and vicinity required its mess to undergo a rigid physical examination. They took a doctor along as a member of the company, and an old spring wagon was rigged up for an ambulance. They used a pack-train, and although they did not leave the Missouri River until June 10, which was considered dangerously late, they made good progress, arriving in California about October 1. With the company well mounted, one man rode the bell-mare, and the pack-mules followed. . . .

Almost every kind of team or vehicle was to be seen on the road. Among the more unconventional modes of travel were numbered push-carts, wheelbarrows, and even hikers. One man with a push-cart hauling his meager supplies stayed one night with a company. The next morning he was invited to swing his cart on the back of a wagon and ride with them. He declined, saying he could make better time on foot. . . .

The migration of 1849 was a deluge which all but swamped the ferries. H. Egan wrote under date of May 31, 1849:

> Eight miles east of the head of Grand Island; today we have passed where the St. Joseph and Independence road intersect this road; there is one continual string of wagons as far as the eye can extend, both before and behind us; . . . This evening there are twenty-nine camps in sight, numbering from fifteen to forty wagons in a company.

Another traveler, who spent a day in camp guarding the oxen and watching the mass of humanity pass by, confided to his diary:

> I did not realize until today how great was the tide of emigration. The trains passed our camp like the flow of a river, and I suppose the line extends from Iowa to the Rocky Mountains.

Still another traveler wrote: "It would appear from the sight before us — that the nation was disgorging itself and sending off its whole inhabitance."

It is estimated that the lead-mining area of southwestern Wisconsin lost a quarter of its population. Property in the region declined in value to a fraction of what it had been, such was the rage for disposing of it and going to the gold-fields. By a check on the ferries and Fort Kearney and Fort Laramie records, it has been estimated that eight thousand wagons, eighty thousand draft animals, and between twenty-five and thirty thousand people passed over the trail in 1849.

As this endless white-topped column rolled slowly along, a multitude of horses carrying riders pranced by, and crowds of men moved forward on foot. In truth, the whole array looked like a mighty army on the march. The migration of 1850 was even larger, however.

The year 1849 and the early fifties were cursed by an epidemic of the Asiatic cholera. It apparently was brought to New Orleans by boat and thence up the Missouri River. The disease took a heavy toll of the travelers. Many deaths occurred on the river steamers, and near the river deaths were numerous. Farther out on the Plains there were fewer cases, and the scourge ceased by the time the Rocky Mountains were reached. Young people often died within a few hours. Old people would live as long as five or six days. From forty to fifty per cent of the victims died. One man in 1849 wrote: "Almost every camp-ground is converted into a burial-ground, and at many places twelve or fifteen graves may be seen in a row."

So great was the fear of the dire disease that sometimes the victims were deserted. In one instance a mess of eight men was stricken. They had two wagons and a good outfit and had been associated with a large company. When the cholera appeared, their fair-weather friends were frightened away. A passer-by found two in their graves, three sick, one watching them, and two watching the teams. Little time was spent in obsequies. One man passed about noon an encampment where there were three men. One lay sick inside a tent where he could look out upon his companions digging his grave. About four o'clock the two men in their spring wagon drove past the observer. Their companion in the meantime had died and been buried.

When the dread death struck, a feeling of gloomy foreboding pervaded the camp. The natural feeling was: Who will be next? If a death occurred in the night, the long, weary hours dragged on until daylight came, when the sorrowful survivors sewed the body of their companion in his sheet or blanket and lowered it into the grave which was dug a short distance from the trail. Then came the work of cleansing the wagon, washing the bed-clothes, and sunning everything.

The end-gate of a wagon was shaped into a headboard, and the immigrant's name and the date of his death were burned in or smeared on it with tar axle lubricant. Soon there was a path running out diagonally from the trail to the grave and another from the grave to the trail. These were made by people who walked out to see who was buried there. A woman buried at South Pass had been remembered in a more elaborate way than most of the departed. Her friends built a pen of cottonwood poles around her grave and placed her rocking-chair, which bore her name, to mark the spot. William Lobenstein in 1851 passed the grave of an emigrant on which lay a live dog, a faithful servant howling out the token of his sympathy for the one resting beneath the sod.

A traveler who went out in the early dawn to catch his horse noticed something sticking out of the grass. Upon investigation he discovered a newly-made grave with this inscription on the headboard:

Our only child
Little Mary

Somewhere in the multitude ahead were the empty arms and grief-stricken heart of a mother who mourned a precious loved one sleeping on the lonely prairie.

Granville Stuart said that in 1852 his party drove as fast as they could in order to get through the terrible region of death, where they were seldom out of the sight of graves. One day they met a young woman with her four children from two to seven years of age. Her husband had died three days before, and she was trying to return to her relatives in Illinois. When sickness or an accident occurred, a doctor could often be found among the traveling neighborhoods. Gilbert Cole mentioned seeing a covered wagon with a doctor's shingle on the side.

In the years 1849 and 1850 a large number of adventurers became discouraged and returned to their homes. The fear that the route would be depastured by the great multitude with its numberless head of live stock, the dread of Indian attacks, the horror of the cholera, and plain homesickness, often induced by the terror occasioned by death, caused many to obliterate the golden air-castles that had lured them from their homes. Some who had traveled two hundred miles west of the Missouri River turned back, saying they had seen enough of "the elephant." J. H. Benson wrote in his diary on May 13, 1849:

A few minutes ago a man came into camp on horseback going back home. He had been over 100 miles out from here. He assigned no reason except he was homesick. Some of the boys told him he would go home and go to plowing corn. He said he was not particular about what he did so long as he got home.

One man mentioned buying a horse from a pilgrim who, having traveled seven hundred miles, had "seen the elephant and eaten his ears" and was on his way back home.

By 1850 a number of streams had been bridged or furnished with ferries by the Mormons or others. In 1849 a man from New Orleans stopped at the North Platte River and established a crude ferry consisting of three canoes lashed together. It would transport one wagon at a time. Each company furnished its own rope, performed all the labor, and paid five dollars per wagon for the use of the catamaran. Its owner, an enterprising man, sent his family on with the promise of overtaking them, and he remained there coining money with his business.

The most dreaded crossing on the entire trip was that of the South Platte near where it unites with the North Platte. One traveler mentioned that on the morning before the crossing there was little joking. "Once started, never stop," was the solemn admonition. Two men cut willow sticks, and, wading across the river, stuck them into the sandy bottom to mark the ford. The first hoofs and wheels to strike the water, he said, sounded dirge-like. Every man except the drivers waded alongside the horses to give assistance if need be. Scarcely a word was spoken during the entire crossing, which occupied twenty-five minutes. In describing the ordeal he said that

> the nervous strain had been terrible, and at no time in our journey had we been so nearly taxed to the utmost. One man dug out a demijohn of brandy from his traps and treated all hands, remarking that "the success of that undertaking merits something extraordinary."

The trains moving westward were really traveling neighborhoods. Members got acquainted with one another, visiting on the road by day and around the camp-fires at night, much as they had visited neighbors in the old home. They spent the evenings pleasantly talking of the road over which they had just passed and conjecturing what it would be like on the morrow. There were good story-tellers, good singers, and in almost every company was a wag who cracked jokes to the merriment of the whole company. There was seldom a company without a fiddle, and nightly the musicians sat on a wagon tongue fiddling. Often the women from other trains came to visit and gathered about the fire, seated on water-kegs. "Old Dan Tucker" and "The Arkansas Traveler" were two favorite tunes. Often the young people gathered on the prairie grass under the starry skies and tripped it "on the light fantastic toe" with as much hilarity as though in a luxurious ballroom. . . .

In spite of these relaxations, the pilgrims lived a narrow, circumscribed life. Their thoughts, hopes, fears, and anxieties all centered about the train, the health of the company, grass and water for the stock, fuel for cooking, and the dread of Indians. Their lives scarcely extended beyond the moving cloud of dust that enveloped them on their westward way. Day in and day out the monotonous tramp continued with scarcely a break.

Many of the men in their eastern homes had been well dressed and clean shaven with well-groomed hair. After a few weeks on the trail their uncombed locks, unshaven faces, and ragged clothes identified them as having changed from a civilized to a semicivilized status. Unwashed, sunburnt, and clothed in old, greasy buckskin coats, the treasure-seekers portrayed a different world. Women riders had discarded their silks, satins, laces, flounces, and pantalets for riding-habits made of dark-brown denim that protected them somewhat from the sun and wind. Mounting their ponies, they often rode far ahead of their own train or several miles back, visiting and learning the caravan's news.

The outstanding error of the gold-hunters of the year 1849 was that of overloading. Great quantities of goods, tents, provisions, and mining tools and equipment of all kinds were packed into the wagons or on animal-back to be wearily dragged or carried across the Plains and over the mountains.

By the time the pilgrims reached Grand Island, they were beginning to seek ways of lightening their loads. One traveler noticed an advertisement at Fort Kearney offering one hundred pounds each of flour, bacon, and dried beef for fifty cents a hundred. The next day he saw two feather beds that had been thrown away, and meat and beans were strewn along the trail. On June 1, 1849, an emigrant wrote in his diary: "This was a day of scenes of abandoned property; items too tedious to mention; stoves, blacksmith tools, wagons, cooking utensils, provisions of every kind were strung along the road." For the next month the travelers found quantities of discarded goods. All the camp-grounds near Fort Laramie were literally covered with wagon irons, clothing, beans, bacon, pork, and provisions of almost every kind left by the advance emigrants in an effort to increase their speed. Some buried lead and marked the place, hoping to have someone recover it later. One company ruthlessly cut a foot off the length of each of its wagons and piled the excess provisions along the road. Crowbars, miners' washing machinery, log chains, and even rifles, revolvers, and expensive guns were broken and thrown away. As a rule provisions were rendered useless by the ones who abandoned them. Sugar had turpentine poured on it; flour was emptied and scattered on the ground, and clothes were torn to pieces. There were a few exceptions where foodstuffs were left in good order with instructions to the finder to help himself.

Parties traveling ahead often wrote messages to friends on buffalo skulls and shoulder-blades or even on human skulls. Such notices gave information about advance trains or contained a personal note. Everyone read the bone messages scattered along the way, and sometimes a postscript was added. Besides thousands of these bone letters, sometimes news for the public was left on a prominent spot. A notice on a board read: "Look at this — look at this! The water here is poison, and we have lost six cattle. Do not let your cattle drink on this bottom." A company, on camping along a shallow stream bordered with timber, found posted on a tree:

Notice — we camped here on the tenth day of May. Jim Lider went up the creek to hunt deer and never came back. We found his dead body two miles up the creek after two days' hunt, his scalp, clothes, gun all gone. The Pawnees did it. Look out for the red devils.

Water was sometimes hard to find. On the whole, later comers fared better in this respect than earlier travelers, for they used the wells which had been dug in the sand or in a slough and had filled with water. The old reliable diet was bacon, beans, and coffee. This was supplemented by bologna and crackers in the early part of the journey and by game and fish as opportunity came to procure them. Flapjacks and bread cooked in a Dutch oven supplied the breadstuffs. Wild onions, currants, strawberries, gooseberries, and plums gave a welcome addition of fresh "stuff" to the diet otherwise wholly lacking in green food.

Considerable difficulty was caused by the oxen's becoming sorefooted. Sometimes the animals had to be abandoned or butchered. Sometimes rough boots were made and fitted over the hooves. This device allowed the hoof to be treated with grease and tar and protected it from sand and sharp stones. In 1852, near the mountains in Wyoming where shoes became a necessity, a man sat by the road with a bushel basket of horseshoe nails, selling them for $12\frac{1}{2}$ cents each. One traveler recorded his anger at this holdup but forthwith paid ten dollars in gold for eighty nails. . . .

[The] last major gold-rush within the continental United States (aside from Alaska) bore many of the characteristics of the former ones. Companies formed in the East for mutual protection. The New England Black Hills Company of Springfield, Massachusetts, found that the entire expenses for equipment and fare to Yankton were $246.24. This stampede had few of the hardships incident to the grueling journey of 1849. In the quarter of a century since the California gold-rush, transportation had so improved that the gold-seeker could ride most of the way by train or steamer and stage-coach. And yet some of the attributes of the former excitement held sway. First, there was the feverish anxiety to reach the "diggin's." Again, people converged upon the district in every sort of conveyance with mining tools and merchandise stocks. One Eastern company purchased a steamboat in which to travel to Yankton. Again there was a rush out of the region when gold was not found in the plentiful quantities expected. Over three hundred left for Sidney in one day, according to the *Deadwood Pioneer,* which could be relied upon not to exaggerate an item that was by no means complimentary to the region.

The discovery of gold led to the establishment of permanent systems of transportation and communication — the stage-coach, Pony Express, telegraph, and the railroad — opening a new era on the northern plains and mountains and leading to the coming of the permanent homemaker, the farmer, and the town-builder.

STUDY GUIDE

1. An established government in a settled community normally has a substantial body of law and formal institutions such as a bureaucracy, courts, and a legislature to govern the society. How did the pioneers handle law-making, the meting out of justice, and the administration of the migrant party?

2. Many of the parties began with considerable organization and high hopes. What conditions contributed to the individual quarrels and disintegration of parties along the trail? In this respect, consider the impact of the break from established laws in the older states, the isolation they endured, and the particular problems encountered on the trail.

3. Consider the preparations for a journey from Independence, Missouri, to Oregon or California. What would be essential in terms of food, clothing, housing, transportation, medicine, and tools? What mistakes in planning seem to have been most common?

4. For some states entry into the Union depended on special circumstances, such as whether or not slavery would be allowed. But, in general, the date of admission indicates that the area had become fairly well populated with a settled society. Explain why California (1850), Oregon (1859), Nevada (1864), and Colorado (1876) were developed to the point of statehood well before the Dakotas, Montana, Washington, Idaho, and Wyoming, which were admitted in 1889–1890.

5. In the great migration described by Dick, the discovery of gold was especially important. Yet many millions of people stayed home in the settled communities of the East, and many went to Texas, Oregon, and other areas rather than to California. In social and psychological terms, rather than in terms of gold and land, how do you explain the motivation of the people who left their homes and went west?

BIBLIOGRAPHY

In his many volumes on the frontier, Professor Dick discusses virtually every aspect of life in the American West. Two of his books that are available in paperback editions are *The Dixie Frontier* * (New York, 1948) and *Tales of the Frontier: From Lewis and Clark to the Last Roundup* * (Lincoln, Neb., 1964). The first historian to call attention to the great significance of the frontier in American history was Frederick Jackson Turner, whose ideas are discussed in the bibliography following the selection by Henry Adams, "America in 1800." Most college libraries will have at least some of his stimulating essays; see especially his book *The Frontier in American History* * (New York, © 1920). Various aspects of the "Turner thesis" have been elaborated or subjected to severe criticism over the decades since he wrote. A number of essays on the subject have been collected in Ray A. Billington, ed., *The Frontier Thesis: Valid Interpretation of American History?* * (New York, © 1966).

Ray Allen Billington, a student of Turner, carried forward his teacher's work in a number of studies, especially *Westward Expansion: A History of the American Frontier* 3rd ed. (New York, 1967). The deep symbolic and psychological significance of the West for Americans is set forth in Henry Nash Smith, *Virgin Land: The American West as Symbol and Myth* * (Cambridge, Mass., 1950). There are special studies of the mining frontier, the cattle frontier, and of particular groups such as the Mormons. The following books are especially interesting: Rodman W. Paul, *Mining Frontiers of the Far West, 1848–1880* * (New York, 1963); Wallace Stegner, *The Gathering of Zion: The Story of the Mormon Trail* * (New York, 1964); and George R. Stewart, *Ordeal by Hunger: The Story of the Donner Party* * rev. ed. (Boston, 1960), which tells the story of a party, stranded in the mountains, that resorted to cannibalism. Daniel J. Boorstin, in his book *The Americans: The National Experience* * (New York, 1965), argues persuasively that community cooperation, rather than individual effort, was the key to western settlement.

"Rackensakers on the Rampage, American Atrocities on Mexicans" by Samuel Chamberlain, 1874. (Detail)

CAREY McWILLIAMS

The Expansionist Urge

Though nationalism is relatively new in the history of mankind, it has certainly been widespread during the past two centuries. In our own country, it has influenced such diverse fields as foreign policy, architecture, immigration policy, literature, and religion. Frequently it has been an important force in harnessing American public opinion to support war efforts and to hate the enemy. In the fifty years from 1803 to 1853, the United States acquired Florida and the lands between the Mississippi River and the Pacific Ocean that constituted the forty-eight United States. An American nationalism, under the guise of "Manifest Destiny," provided the rationalization for much of this expansion. Coupled with an assumption of Anglo-Saxon superiority, nationalism sometimes promoted an invidious and ruthless treatment of other peoples that is not always characteristic of mere economic imperialism.

In his book *North from Mexico*, Carey McWilliams treats the long history of antagonism between the Spanish- and the English-speaking peoples of the Southwest. He considers the Mexican-American War of 1845 to 1848 as but one incident in their conflict, which began during the Texas Revolution and has continued into the present. It is, of course, a most important incident both for the hatreds it engendered and for what it tells us about nineteenth-century nationalism. The shape of nationalism may vary in different countries and at different times, but when racial hostility forms a part of it, the manifestations can be remarkably similar — whether directed against "greasers" in the Southwest, "dirty Japs" in World War II, or "gooks" in Southeast Asia.

The second part of the selection discusses language, and in

it McWilliams uses speech to illustrate some of the mutual contributions that the people of Spanish and Anglo-American backgrounds have made to each other's culture. He might equally well have used politics, law, social life, or architecture. In any event, writing in 1949, he was optimistic about the development of a common culture in the Spanish-American borderlands. As things have turned out, his prediction comes a lot closer to the mark than most people might have imagined at the time he wrote. Mexican-Americans have indeed asserted themselves and made an impact upon American society as a whole. In the vineyards and lettuce fields of California, César Chávez presented a charismatic image and a distinctive labor philosophy that had not been seen among American labor leaders for a great many years. An unusual number of books by and about Mexican-Americans is being published each year. Spanish influences have been widely felt upon American architecture and interior design; and in American politics the days of "not counting Mexicans" are long past. Hopefully, by studying the development of hostilities between various races and ethnic groups, we can learn something both about ourselves and about others that will help us build a better society for future generations.

When asked how many notches he had on his gun, King Fisher, the famous Texas gunman, once replied: "Thirty-seven — not counting Mexicans." This casual phrase, with its drawling understatement, epitomizes a large chapter in Anglo-Hispano relations in the Southwest. People fail to count the non-essential, the things and persons that exist only on sufferance; whose life tenure is easily revocable. The notion that Mexicans are interlopers who are never to be counted in any reckoning dies but slowly in the Southwest. To this day Mexicans do not figure in the social calculations of those who rule the border states. As I write these lines, the Mexican consul-general in Los Angeles has just entered a vigorous protest against the insulting behavior of custom inspectors at the municipal airport.

A majority of the present-day residents of the Southwest are not familiar with the malignant conflict of cultures which has raged in the borderlands for more than a century. Blinded by cultural myths, they have failed to correlate the major events in a pattern of conflict which has prevailed from Brownsville to Los Angeles since 1846. Once this correlation is made, it

From chapters 6 and 16 of *North from Mexico: The Spanish-Speaking People of the United States* by Carey McWilliams. Published by J. B. Lippincott Co., 1949. Reprinted by permission of the author.

becomes quite apparent that the Mexican-American War was merely an incident in a conflict which arose some years before and survived long after
the Treaty of Guadalupe Hidalgo. It is only within the framework of this
age-old conflict that it is possible to understand the pattern of Anglo-
Hispano cultural relations in the Southwest today. In summarizing the
history of this conflict, one necessarily starts with Texas, for there the
first blood was shed.

In Texas the Spanish-Mexican settlements were directly in the path of
Anglo-American expansion. Unlike the rest of the borderlands, Texas was
not separated from the centers of Anglo-American population by mountain ranges and desert wastes; geographically it invited invasion. In a series
of belts or strips, its rich, alluvial plains stretched from the plateaus to the
gulf. The rivers that marked these belts could be crossed, at all seasons,
at almost any point, without much trouble. On the other hand, between
the most southerly settlements in Texas and those in Mexico, there was,
as Dr. Samuel Harman Lowrie has pointed out, "a great expanse of semi-
arid land which at that time served as a more or less natural, though temporary barrier to the effective extension of Mexican influence and control."
Texas was 1,200 miles removed from its capital, Mexico City.

By 1834 the Anglo-Americans outnumbered the Mexicans in Texas: thirty
thousand to five thousand. Most of the Mexicans were concentrated in the
old Spanish towns or along the border, while the Anglo-Americans were to
be found on the farms and ranches. Mexican townspeople had few opportunities for acculturation for they saw very little of the Anglo-Americans.
From the outset, moreover, relations between the two peoples were clouded
by the fear of war. The Anglo-Americans bore the brunt of Mexico's hostile
distrust of the United States and were, in turn, encouraged to take an un-
friendly attitude toward the natives by the unconcealed, aggressive designs
of the jingoes in Washington.

As might have been expected, each group formed a highly unfavorable
initial impression of the other. To the early American settlers, the Mexicans were lazy, shiftless, jealous, cowardly, bigoted, superstitious, backward, and immoral. To the Mexicans, on the other hand, the Texans were
"los diablos Tejanos": arrogant, overbearing, aggressive, conniving, rude,
unreliable, and dishonest. The first Mexican ambassador to the United States
had complained in 1882 of the "haughtiness of these republicans who will
not allow themselves to look upon us as equals but merely as inferiors."
Still another Mexican official had charged that the Americans in Texas
considered themselves "superior to the rest of mankind, and look upon
their republic as the only establishment upon earth founded upon a grand
and solid basis." Full of brag, bluster, and spreadeagle chauvinism, the
Americans of the 1800's were hardly the most tactful ambassadors of good-
will. The truth of the matter is that the border residents were not a credit
to either group.

Under the most favorable circumstances, a reconciliation of the two cultures would have been difficult. The language barrier was, of course, a constant source of misunderstanding; neither group could communicate, for all practical purposes, with the other. The Mexicans knew almost nothing of local self-government, while the Americans, it was said, travelled with "their political constitutions in their pockets" and were forever "demanding their rights." Although tolerant of peonage, the Mexicans were strongly opposed to slavery. The Anglo-Americans, most of whom were from the Southern states, were vigorously pro-slavery. The Anglo-Americans were Protestants; the Mexicans were Catholic. Speaking of a Mexican, a Protestant missionary is said to have remarked: "He was a Catholic, but clean and honest." Both groups lacked familiarity with the existing Mexican laws, for there was no settled government in Texas. Anglo-Americans found it extremely difficult to respect the laws of Mexico in the absence of law-interpreting and law-enforcing agencies. Thus it was, as Dr. Lowrie writes, that "cultural differences gave rise to misconceptions and misunderstandings, misunderstandings to distrust, distrust to antagonism, and antagonism on a very considerable number of points made open conflict inevitable."

The first Anglo-Americans literally fought their way into Texas. While most of these early filibustering expeditions were defeated, they succeeded in laying waste to the country east and north of San Antonio. Both Mexicans and Americans were killed by these invading private armies. No sooner had the Mexicans driven out the filibusters, than the Comanches raided the entire stretch of country between the Nueces and the Rio Grande. According to one observer, the whole region was "depopulated, great numbers of stock were driven off, and the people took refuge in the towns on the Rio Grande." Preoccupied with revolutionary events in Spain and Mexico, the government could give little attention to the Texas settlements. After 1821, however, a measure of protection was provided against the devastating raids of the Comanches, and many of the settlers moved back across the Rio Grande.

With the Texas Revolution came the embittering memories, for the Texans, of the slaughter of Anglo-Americans at the Alamo and Goliad; and, for the Mexicans, of the humiliating rout and massacre at San Jacinto. Prior bitternesses were now intensified a thousandfold. "Towards the Mexicans remaining within the limits of the Republic," writes Dr. Garrison, "the feeling of the Texans was scarcely better than towards the Indians." Memories dating from this period still poison relationships between Anglos and Hispanos in Texas. Some years ago a district judge told of how, as a child, he had heard an old man give an eye-witness account of the slaughter at the Alamo. "I never see a Mexican," he confessed, "without thinking of that," José Vasconcellos, the well-known Mexican educator and philosopher, tells in his autobiography of how these same memories poisoned his boyhood in Eagle Pass. After the Texas Revolution, as Erna Fergusson has pointed out, "Texans could not get it out of their heads that their manifest destiny was to kill Mexicans and take over Mexico."

Throughout the decade of the Texas Republic (1836–1846), the shooting was continued in "the Spanish country" south of the Nueces. Murder was matched by murder; raids by Texans were countered by raids from Mexico. Since a peace treaty was never negotiated, no boundaries could be fixed. Texas claimed to the Rio Grande, while Mexico insisted that its boundary rested on the Nueces. In the bloody zone between the two rivers an uninterrupted guerrilla warfare continued throughout the life of the Texas Republic. In 1839 General Don Antonio Canales launched a revolution on Texas soil against Santa Anna and raised the banner of the Republic of Rio Grande. Of the 600 men who rallied to his standard, 180 were Texans. Awakening to the fact that Texans were using his insurrection as a cover for an attack on Mexico, General Canales finally surrendered but not until his troops had fought several engagements along the border. At the head of a raiding party of five hundred men, General Vásquez captured San Antonio in 1842 and held it for two days. These are but two of many similar episodes that occurred during the hectic life of the new republic.

Throughout the period of this border warfare, the Texas-Mexicans were caught between opposing forces. "When the Americans have gone there," explained a delegate at the Texas constitutional convention, "they have preyed upon the Mexicans; they have been necessarily compelled by force or otherwise to give up such property as they had. So vice versa, when the Mexicans have come in, they have been necessarily compelled to furnish them the means of support. . . . Since 1837 they [the Texas-Mexicans] have been preyed upon by their own countrymen as well as by ours." The Texans constantly suspected the Mexicans of inciting the Indians against them, and every Indian raid provoked retaliation against the *Tejanos*. The Mexicans naturally regarded the Texas Revolution as American-inspired and the prelude to the conquest of Mexico.

However, all Mexicans were not equally affected by this complex warfare. A sizable number of the upper-class settlers quickly became identified with the Texans. These Texanized Mexicans or "the good Mexicans" were called *Tejanos* and were invariably of the *rico* class. Two of the fifty signers of the Texas Declaration of Independence were native Mexicans and a third, born in Mexico, became the first vice-president of the republic. At a later date, Captain Refugio Benavides commanded a company of Texas-Mexicans which operated along the border against Mexican raiders and marauders.

Provoked by the annexation of Texas in 1846, the Mexican-American War represented the culmination of three decades of cultural conflict in Texas. To the Mexicans, every incident in Texas from the filibustering raids to the Revolution of 1836 was regarded, in retrospect, as part of a deliberately planned scheme of conquest. To the Anglo-Americans, the war was "inevitable" having been provoked, in their eyes, by the stupidity and backwardness of the Mexican officials. Not only did Mexico forfeit an empire to the United States, but, ironically, none of the signers of the Treaty of Guadalupe Hidalgo realized that, nine days before the treaty was signed, gold had been discovered in California. That they had unknowingly ceded to the United States territories unbelievably rich in gold and silver — the hope of finding which had lured Coronado and De Oñate into the Southwest — must have added to the Mexicans' sense of bitterness and defeat.

Furthermore, the way in which the United States fought the Mexican-American War added greatly to the heritage of hatred. A large part of our invading army was made up of volunteers who, by all accounts, were a disgrace to the American flag. General Winfield Scott readily admitted that they had "committed atrocities to make Heaven weep and every American of Christian morals blush for his country. Murder, robbery and rape of mothers and daughters in the presence of tied-up males of the families have been common all along the Rio Grande." Lieutenant George C. Meade, of later Civil War fame, said that the volunteers were "driving husbands out of houses and raping their wives. . . . They will fight as gallantly as any men, but they are a set of Goths and Vandals without discipline, making us a terror to innocent people."

How bitterly these outrages were resented is shown by a passage which Lloyd Lewis has culled from one of the Mexican newspapers of the period: "the horde of banditti, of drunkards, of fornicators . . . vandals vomited from hell, monsters who bid defiance to the laws of nature . . . shameless, daring, ignorant, ragged, bad-smelling, long-bearded men with hats turned up at the brim, thirsty with the desire to appropriate our riches and our beautiful damsels." The year 1844 had seen the rise of a Native American Party in the states, and much anti-Catholic feeling found expression during the war. Mexicans charged that the volunteers had desecrated their churches, "sleeping in the niches devoted to the sacred dead . . . drinking out of holy vessels." Two hundred and fifty American troops, mostly of Catholic background, deserted and joined the Mexican army to form the San Patricio battalion. The barbarous manner in which eighty of these deserters were executed in San Angel, a suburb of Mexico City, was long cited by the Mexicans as further proof of Yankee cruelty.

Nothing was more galling to the Mexican officials who negotiated the treaty that the fact that they were compelled to assign, as it were, a large number of their countrymen to the Yankees. With great bitterness they protested that it was "not permissible to sell, as a flock of sheep, those deserving Mexicans." For many years after 1846, the Spanish-Americans left in the United States were known in Mexico as "our brothers who were sold." As late as 1943 maps were still used in Mexican schools which designated the old Spanish borderlands as "territory temporarily in the hands of the United States." It is to the great credit of the Mexican negotiators that the treaty contained the most explicit guarantees to protect the rights of these people, provisions for which they were more deeply concerned than they were over boundaries or indemnities. It should never be forgotten that, with the exception of the Indians, Mexicans are the only minority in the United States who were annexed by conquest; the only minority, Indians again excepted, whose rights were specifically safeguarded by treaty provision.

Just as the end of the Texas Revolution did not terminate hostilities in Texas, so the Treaty of Guadalupe Hidalgo failed to bring peace to the borderlands. Under the terms of the treaty, it became the obligation of the United States to police 180,000 Indians living in the territories which we acquired from Mexico. This obligation the United States failed to discharge for many years. Taking advantage of the confusion which prevailed, the Indians launched fierce raids on both Anglo and Hispano settlements, conducted marauding expeditions deep in Mexican territory, and cunningly exploited the hatred that had been engendered between Anglo and Hispano. The Anglos promptly attributed these raids to Mexican duplicity and instigation; the Hispanos as promptly charged them up to the malice or carelessness of the Americans. Hard-pressed on all sides, the Indians had come to live off the plunder seized in these raids which, with the confusion and demoralization which prevailed in Mexico, were conducted on a larger scale than ever before. It was not until about 1880 that the United States finally managed to bring the Indians of the Southwest under close police surveillance.

Nor were Indians the only troublemakers in the post-war decades. Between 1848 and 1853, various American filibustering expeditions violated Mexican territory in Sonora, Lower California, and at various points along the border. When word of the discovery of gold reached the Eastern states, swarms of emigrant gold-seekers passed along the southern routes to California, often travelling in Mexican territory without passports, and not infrequently helping themselves to Mexican food and livestock en route.

In 1850 José M. Carvajal organized a revolution in Mexico, sponsored by American merchants, which aimed at converting the State of Tamaulipas into the Sierra Madre Republic. Carvajal was a Texan by birth who had been educated in Kentucky and Virginia. Backed by Richard King and Mifflin Kennedy, two of the great cattle-barons of south Texas, the Carvajal revolution was supported by bands of armed Texans who crossed the Rio Grande. The American ambassador reported that these raids, in which as many as five hundred Texans participated, had "awakened a feeling of intense prejudice against everything connected with American interest."

The fateful strip of territory between the Nueces and the Rio Grande once again became the home of numerous outlaw bands who preyed indiscriminately upon both Mexican and American settlers. In the face of these staggering blows — filibustering expeditions, Indian raids, revolution, war, and constant guerrilla fighting, — the Mexicans in Texas constantly retreated, and their retreat, of course, gave rise to the notion that their conquerors were pursuing a mandate of destiny. Major Emery, writing in 1859, said that the "white race" was "exterminating or crushing out the inferior race"; and an American soldier wrote home that "the Mexican, like the poor Indian, is doomed to retire before the more enterprising Anglo-Americans.". . .

· · ·

But today the ineluctable facts of geography and history dictate a somewhat different conclusion. Mexico is not France or Italy or Poland: it is geographically a part of the Southwest. Residing in the Mexican states immediately south of the border are approximately 2,500,000 Spanish-speaking people; in the American border states approximately the same number of Spanish-speaking reside. Essentially these are one people, occupying a single cultural province, for the Spanish-speaking minority north of the border (a majority in some areas) has always drawn, and will continue to draw, support, sustenance, and re-enforcements from south of the border. Our Spanish-speaking minority is not, therefore, a detached fragment but an integral part of a much larger population unit to which it is bound by close geographic and historical ties. Furthermore, Hispanic influences in the United States have a strong anchor in New Mexico where these influences are actually older, and perhaps more deeply rooted, than in the Mexican border states.

The Spanish-speaking and the Indians of the Southwest have the highest birth rates of any ethnic groups in the region. Infant mortality rates are declining, for both groups, throughout the borderlands: between 1929 and 1944 the rate decreased in New Mexico from 145.5 infant deaths per 1,000 live births to 89.1. With high birth rates and rapidly declining infant mortality rates, the Spanish-speaking element will retain its position relative to Anglo-Americans for many years to come, barring unforseeable contingencies.

These facts alone would indicate that the Hispanic minority cannot be regarded as merely another immigrant group in the United States destined for ultimate absorption. In this instance, however, demographical considerations are fortified by the facts of geography and the implications of history. While Spanish cultural influences have retreated in portions of the Southwest, they have never been eclipsed. "Whether they will or not," wrote J. P. Widney in the 1880's, "their future [that is, the future of Anglos and Hispanos] is one and together, and I think neither type of race will destroy the other. They will merge." With the Spanish-speaking element having been re-enforced by a million or more immigrants in the last forty years, virtually all of whom have remained in the Southwest, some type of cultural fusion or merger must result. In fact, a surprising degree of fusion has already taken place.

The development of speech and language patterns not only mirrors the relationships between Anglos and Hispanos in the Southwest but is the best gauge of the degree of cultural fusion that has occurred. Needless to say, I discuss this highly complex subject not as a linguist, nor in terms of its linguistic interest, but rather to indicate what has actually happened to the two cultures in the region and to trace a relationship. For the attitude of a minority toward language and speech has an important bearing on the direction that the process of acculturation is likely to take.

The language pattern in the Southwest has, of course, a number of variable factors. It varies in relation to the numerical proportion between the two groups in any one place; the age of the community; whether it is rural or urban; the degree of isolation; the history of social relations in the community; and many other factors. Quite apart from these variations, however, there is a larger aspect to the language pattern which can be considered from three points of view: Spanish borrowings from American-English speech; Anglo-American borrowings from the Spanish; and the development in both groups of a kind of jargon which is more "Southwestern" than Spanish or English.

In 1917 Dr. Aurelion M. Espiñosa listed some three hundred words of Anglo-American origin which have been incorporated into the Spanish language as spoken in New Mexico after first being Hispanized. Most of these words had been borrowed from necessity rather than choice, for they related, in the main, to commodities, practices, things, and concepts for which there was no Spanish equivalent (at least not in the Spanish spoken in New Mexico). Many of them had to do with commercial, industrial, and political practices unknown to the Spanish population prior to the American conquest as shown by the fact that more than fifty per cent of the terms had been incorporated after 1880. In large measure the adopted words had to do with "work terms" related to the new jobs which New Mexicans had acquired; others related to slang expressions used in American sports. Obviously most of this borrowing was based on strictly utilitarian considerations.

In another study of word-borrowing, Dr. Manuel Gamio listed the following among many terms that had been hispanicized: picnic, laundry, ties (railroad ties), matches, stockyards (*estoque yardas*), groceries, lunch, tickets, depot, time-check, truck, truck-driver, biscuit, omelette, bootlegger, taxes, ice cream, board and boarder, boss, automobile, sweater, jumper, sheriff, etc. In still another list, Dr. Harold W. Bentley added: home run (*jonronero*); scraper (*escrepa*); plug (*ploga*); puncture (*ponchar*); jack (*llaqui*); and such expressions as *"vamos flat"* — to have a flat tire (literally, "we go flat"). Generally, the Spanish-speaking people have borrowed from necessity rather than choice and have shown either resistance or indifference to other types of borrowings. Still the number of such borrowings, from necessity or otherwise, has been substantial and would probably be much greater today than when these studies were made. . . .

Anglo-American borrowings from Spanish have also been dictated by necessity, in many cases, but from other motives as well. One important grouping of borrowed words has to do with things and practices for which there was no English equivalent, as in the cattle industry, the mining industry, and in the pack-train business. . . . But, in addition to these borrowings-by-necessity, there is a long list of Spanish words which have apparently been taken over for local color, humorous effect, and, above all, for their appropriateness in an arid environment. In his *Dictionary of Spanish Terms in English* (1932), Dr. Bentley lists some four hundred words which have been incorporated in the English spoken in the Southwest. Actually the list is much longer than linguists such as H. L. Mencken and George Philip Krapp have indicated, for they have not been looking in the right quarter, namely, the Southwest.

Considering that we had just fought a war against Mexico, it is indeed remarkable that so few Spanish place-names were changed after 1846. In addition to the names of rivers and mountains, Dr. Bentley states that there are two thousand or more cities and towns in the United States with Spanish names: four hundred or more in California; two hundred and fifty in Texas and New Mexico; and a hundred or more in both Colorado and Arizona. In Colorado the name of the state and the names of nineteen counties are Spanish. Spanish place-names also appear, with less frequency, in such states as Nevada, Wyoming, Utah, Oregon, Montana, and Idaho; in fact, they appear in every state in the union. Often the original Spanish has been Anglicized, as in Waco, California (originally Hueco); and, in many cases, Spanish and English terms have combined, as in Buena Park, Altaville, and Minaview. There are eight "Mesas," four "Bonanzas," and thirteen "El Dorados" in the United States. Many of the Spanish place-names outside the Southwest refer to the names of battles or of events related to the Mexican-American War.

In the Southwest most of the Spanish place-names were preserved — in my opinion — because of their extraordinary appropriateness and beauty. The Spanish named places with the uncannily descriptive accuracy of poets. For example, who could improve on "Sangre de Cristo" for the name of the great range of mountains in northern New Mexico? The very persistence with which resident Spanish-speaking people kept calling mountains, rivers, and towns by their Spanish names must, also, have been a factor. In Southern California, virtually all the Spanish place-names were retained; but many of the street names, in places such as Santa Barbara, San Diego, and Los Angeles, were changed or Anglicized after 1846.

Long familiar with an arid environment, the Spanish gave vivid and accurate names to the novel features of the Southwestern landscape. "The *acequia madre* ("mother ditch") of every village," writes T. M. Pearce, "has almost a personality of its own. It becomes the most intimate friend of every inhabitant of the place. With dancing and ceremony, the *acequias* are opened in the spring . . . with scrupulous care the *acequias* are scraped and strengthened in the villages and towns." To call these life-giving main canals "ditches" would have been to minimize their importance in this environment.

And so it is with many similar expressions, relating to the natural environment of the Southwest, which were retained and incorporated into Anglo-American speech. The list is a long one indeed and includes such words as: *malpais, mesa, vega, cumbre, bosque, sierra, pozo, hondo, loma, bajada, ciénaga, piloncillo, potrero, arroyo, laguna, barranca, cañon, llano, brasada, chaparral, canada,* and many others. "The Southwest," writes Pearce, "with its peculiar brilliance of day and quick shadows of nightfall, with its hard-baked earth and sudden water gushes, with its thirsty sands at the very edge of soggy river bottoms, cannot be described in terms of Shakespeare's Stratford." For example, an *arroyo* is *not* a gully. As Pearce points out, "it is a bare rent in the side of Mother Earth where only yellow jaws yawn until a cloudburst in the mountains miles away sends the lashing torrents hurtling through it to crush and engulf everything caught in its maw." The word *malpais* means more than "badlands": it refers to the lava ridges or serrated volcanic ash "dumps" to be found in the Southwest. It is quite impossible to convey the peculiar significance of *ciénaga,* as used in the Southwest, by some such expression as "marshy place," for the latter does not carry the connotation of an encompassing aridity. Thus *vega* is not just "meadow"; *bosque* is more than "a clump or grove"; and *sierra* carries overtones of meaning not suggested by "saw-toothed range." . . .

From the contact between the British and Spanish navies came such words as armada, cask, cork, and cargo. And then there is, of course, a long list of words, Spanish in origin, which have become fully "naturalized": vigilante, filibuster, avocado, barbecue, cockroach, corral, creole, tobacco, cannibal, vanilla, hammock, tornado, alfalfa, canary, cigar, maroon, Negro, palaver, paragon, parasol, sherry, soda, canoe, banana, alligator, cocoa, sassafras; as well as many words that came by way of South America: alpaca, armadillo, chinchilla, cocaine, condor, cougar, jaguar, llama, and tapioca.

Spanish borrowings from American speech have naturally been most numerous in the speech area along the Rio Grande and immediately south of the border; while American borrowings have been most common throughout the old Spanish borderlands area. Many southwestern words and idioms are Spanish in origin: jerky, hackamore, buckaroo, mustang, stampede, lariat, fandango, hoosegow, wrangler, desperado, vamoose, hombre, adios, agua, bandido. In this area, the corruption of Spanish has been paralleled by the cultivation of what J. Frank Dobie calls "sagebrush" or "bull-pen" Spanish. Most of the borrowings, on both sides, have been by ear for neither group has been a serious student of the language of the other. In the isolation of the region, each group borrowed from the other so that today part of the vocabulary of the Southwest is bilingual in origin. A kind of Spanish is still spoken in the range country along the border where, according to Doris K. Seibold, fully half the cowmen are bilingual. Most of the Mexicans born in the region since 1900 are, of course, bilingual. Cowboy talk is so thoroughly bilingual that, in a single issue of *Lariat,* a popular "western" or "cowboy" magazine, Dr. Bentley found 376 Spanish words or words of Spanish origin. Most authors who have written about the Southwest have felt compelled to include a glossary of Spanish terms in common use. . . .

Throughout the Southwest the imprint of Spain and Mexico is indelible; not as Spanish or Mexican influence per se but as modified by contact with Indian and Anglo-American culture. The three influences are woven into nearly every aspect of the economy, the speech, the architecture, the institutions, and the customs of the people. For the people of the Southwest share a mixed cultural heritage in which the mixtures, rather than the pure strains, have survived. In a Navajo rug, an adobe house, or an irrigated farm, one may find elements of the three cultures inextricably interwoven and fused. The rug may be of Indian design, woven by Indian hands, and colored by native dyes; but the loom may be Spanish or Mexican and the wool probably came from some New Mexican's herd or it may have been purchased from an American mail-order catalogue. The rug, however, is most likely to be owned by an Anglo-American. The irrigated farm may lie within a district irrigated by water from some huge dam or reservoir built by American engineers, but the fields will be tilled by Mexicans, using a knowledge of irrigation which, in part, was acquired from Indians.

"Three types of domestic architecture," writes Ruth Laughlin, "have come down to us in their chronological order — the Pueblo, the Mexican, and the American-Spanish. They are seldom found absolutely true to type for the needs of men have overlapped since the days of the first Americans. In each we find resemblances to the others, like the faces of mothers and daughters." Where these elements have been mixed, as in the domestic architecture of New Mexico, they have attained the most enduring expression. Where the Indian element has been lacking, as in the so-called "Spanish-Colonial" architecture seen in Florida and Southern California, the fusion has been least successful. Even the public buildings of the Southwest tend more and more to derive from Indian and Spanish-Mexican sources with the Anglo-Americans showing great ingenuity in adapting these forms to modern uses. In short, this mixed heritage belongs to all the people of the Southwest, not to any one group or to the combination of any two.

Of paramount importance to the future of this culture is the role that the coming generation of Mexican-Americans will play. The region has yet to experience the impact of the first articulate generation of persons of Mexican descent. In another generation, Mexican-Americans will be found in all walks of life — in the arts, the professions, in the colleges and universities — and in significant numbers. In the past, Mexicans have been a more or less anonymous, voiceless, expressionless minority. There has yet to be written, for example, a novel of Southwestern experience by an American-born person of Mexican descent or a significant autobiography by a native-born Mexican. The moment the group begins to achieve this type of expression, a new chapter will be written in the history of the Southwest. For as the Spanish-speaking attain cultural maturity, as they achieve real self-expression, they will exert a profound influence on the culture of the region, and Spanish-Mexican influences that have remained dormant these many years will be revived and infused with new meaning and vigor. . . .

STUDY GUIDE

1. Some of the other reading in your course may explain the economic and political aspects of the war with Mexico. Summarize the social and cultural factors that McWilliams suggests contributed to Mexican-American antagonisms.

2. During the same period, in a somewhat similar situation (the Democratic Party slogan was "Fifty-Four Forty or Fight"), the United States settled a dispute over the Oregon country without war. Was this peaceful settlement possible because of differences in geography and patterns of settlement compared to Texas, differences in the economic interests involved, diplomatic factors, or perhaps because of an absence of racial and cultural antagonism between the British-Canadians and Americans?

3. In the selection McWilliams uses language to illustrate the reciprocal cultural contributions of Mexican-Americans and Anglo-Americans. Suggest some ways in which the two peoples have influenced each other in other areas, such as style of living, politics, social attitudes, architecture, and music.

4. Evaluate McWilliams's contention that a distinctive and viable "Spanish-American" culture can be developed in the borderlands, in light of modern communications, transportation, and technology, which seem to be breaking down cultural distinctions and creating a homogenized America.

5. How do you explain the relatively rapid disappearance of hatred against the Japanese following World War II or the North Vietnamese following our war in Southeast Asia, as compared to the long-standing hostility against Mexicans? Do you think that proximity is more important than racial differences, or are there other diplomatic, economic, or political factors involved?

BIBLIOGRAPHY

As mentioned earlier, there have been many recent books by and about Mexican-Americans, especially on the Chicano movement of the 1970s. Not many works of historical interest have appeared, and the best works on the Mexican-American War are older studies. The fullest of them are two books by

Justin H. Smith: *The Annexation of Texas* (New York, 1911) and *The War with Mexico,* 2 vols. (New York, 1919). Three shorter treatments are Alfred H. Bill, *Rehearsal for Conflict: The War with Mexico, 1846–1848* (New York, 1947); Robert S. Henry, *The Story of the Mexican War* (Indianapolis, Ind., 1950); and Otis A. Singletary, *The Mexican War* * (Chicago, 1960). Bill's book treats the Mexican War as a dress rehearsal of North and South for the great conflict of 1861–1865. An older, well-written study by an American literary man is Bernard De Voto, *The Year of Decision: 1846* * (Boston, 1943). All of these writings deal with the political and military aspects of American expansion to the virtual exclusion of the social and psychological factors. More pertinent to the social aspects of the subject is Leonard Pitt, *The Decline of the Californios: A Social History of the Spanish-Speaking Californians, 1846–1890* * (Berkeley and Los Angeles, 1966).

There have been a number of outstanding studies of the diplomatic maneuvering between Britain and the United States over the possession of Oregon and of the intellectual justification for American expansion. Frederick Merk wrote on both of these subjects in *The Oregon Question: Essays in Anglo-American Diplomacy and Politics* (Cambridge, Mass., 1967) and *Manifest Destiny and Mission in American History: A Reinterpretation* * (New York, 1963). The fullest study of the ideas behind our expansion in the early nineteenth century is Albert K. Weinberg, *Manifest Destiny: A Study of Nationalist Expansionism in American History* (Baltimore, 1935). Norman A. Graebner, *Empire on the Pacific: A Study in American Continental Expansion* (New York, 1955) is a more recent work on the subject. For firsthand accounts of the war, see George W. Smith and Charles Judah, eds., *Chronicle of the Gringos: The U.S. Army in the Mexican War, 1846–1848, Accounts of Eyewitnesses and Combatants* (Albuquerque, N.M., 1968). Nationalism has been reflected in many fields other than politics and diplomacy; the literary and intellectual aspects of American nationalism are treated in Benjamin T. Spencer, *The Quest for Nationality: An American Literary Campaign* (Syracuse, N.Y., 1957).

Top, a young Confederate soldier.
Bottom, his Union enemy.

BELL I. WILEY

Life in Wartime

The selections in this volume have illustrated the exceptional variety of American life in different parts of the country from the founding of the British settlements to the American Civil War. The editors hope that you have received some impression of the actual working conditions in early American factories, of the life of Indians and slaves, of education, family life, and social reform. The selections from Wallace Brown on the American Loyalists in the revolutionary period and Carey McWilliams on Mexican-American relations touched upon certain aspects of two of our wars. The final selection, from Bell I. Wiley's *The Life of Johnny Reb*, describes the life of soldiers under fire and behind the lines during the American Civil War.

In the twentieth century, there is little about war that is glamorous or chivalric. Those who fought in World War II, the Korean War, or the long war in Southeast Asia know the full import of General William T. Sherman's phrase, "War is hell." Massive bombings of civilian areas, atomic weaponry, napalm, massacres, and pushbutton slaughter have made a grim mockery of wartime heroism. The American Civil War has been described as the first modern war — partly because of tactical and logistic innovations and partly because of the astounding casualties, the use of scorched earth policies, and a number of other grim forecasts of the future.

Yet, there are common elements in nearly all wars — elements that connect the Civil War and our modern warfare with the so-called gentlemanly wars of the seventeenth and eighteenth centuries. Death, cruelty, callousness, cowardice, and bravery are a part of the human condition in wartime, and they know no spe-

cial period. Equally common are the hatreds engendered in time
of war, the boredom of army life, the loneliness for home and
family, and the compassion for the enemy that Wiley describes.
Such emotions might be found in any war in any country, but
the sectional split of the United States that led brother to fight
brother gave life in wartime a very special poignancy.

It was a hot July day in 1862. A Confederate soldier of twenty-three years
sat beneath a tree on a hill near Richmond guarding a group of Yankees
captured during the recent Seven Days' fighting. Ordinarily this Reb —
whose name must remain in the realm of the unknown because of the in-
completeness of his records — was a buoyant, zestful character, but on this
particular day he was morose and inconsolable. He had just read a list of
the casualties of Mechanicsville, Gaines's Mill, Frayser's Farm, and Malvern
Hill. Included among the dead were a number of boys with whom he had
frolicked during days of peace. But now they were gone.

As he mused over the loss of his comrades this young soldier laid aside his
gun, drew from his pocket the small leather-bound diary that his sweetheart
had given him when he left for camp, and began to write:

July 10, 1862 . . . May God avenge us of our infernal enemies — and if I ever
forgive them it is more than I Expect. "Forgive your Enemies" is the Divine
precept — a hard one to obey — How can one forgive such enemies as we are
contending against? Despoiling us of our property, driving us from our
homes & friends and slaying our best citizens on the field are hard crimes to
forgive — At any rate let me have a chance to retaliate & *then* I can forgive
with a better grace. I hope to see many such epithets as this:

> The Yankee host with blood-stained hands
> Came Southward to divide our lands
> This narrow & contracted spot
> Is all this Yankee scoundrel got

So May it be.

Most soldiers in the Rebel Army had feelings toward the Yankees very
much like those expressed by this unidentified Virginian. There were some
who excelled him in the pungency with which they recorded their antipathy.
"I hope that we may slay them like wheat before the sythe," wrote a North

Carolinian to his homefolk; "I certainly love to live to hate the base usurping vandals, if it is a Sin to hate them, then I am guilty of the unpardonable one."

A Mississippi private who had heard that his homefolk were being despoiled by the invaders blurted out, "I intend to fight them as long as I live and after this war stops. . . . I intend to kill Every one that crosses my path."

Not a few Rebs got so worked up over Yankee meanness that they swore to perpetuate hatred of the foe in generations to come. Typical of this group was the Georgian who wrote his wife in the spring of 1862:

> Teach my children to hate them with that bitter hatred that will never permit them to meet under any circumstances without seeking to destroy each other. I know the breach is now wide & deep between us & the Yankees let it widen & deepen until all Yankees or no Yankees are to live in the South.

Hatred of Southern soldiers for those of the North was due to a variety of reasons. In their letters and diaries very few of the rank and file mention violation of states' rights as a cause of their antipathy. While most of them had heard small-fry politicians denounce the Lincoln government on this score, it is doubtful whether many of them either understood or cared about the constitutional issues at stake. The threat to slavery was resented rather widely, not so much as an unwarranted deprivation of property rights, but as a wedge for "nigger equality."

Common soldiers hated the men in blue primarily because they thought them to be an unsavory sort of people who came from a low and vulgar background. It is amazing how many Rebs commented on the crudity and obscenity of letters found on the battlefields addressed to Union soldiers. One Confederate who read a number of letters found in the Atlanta area in 1864 wrote to his wife, "I would send you a sample of them, but I am ashamed they are so vulgar. . . . I do not believe God will ever suffer us to be subjugated by such a motly crew of infidels." . . .

The Federals were also thought to be a bunch of thieves, having little regard for the rights of private property, particularly if that property happened to belong to Southerners. The robbery and despoliation that accompanied Union invasion was, indeed, one of the greatest of all causes of hatred. A Mississippi soldier whose home had been visited by raiders wrote to his mother as his regiment headed Northward on the Gettysburg campaign:

> I can fight so much Harder since I have got a gruge against them it is my Honest wish that my Rifle may Draw tears from many a Northern Mother and Sighs from Many a Father before this thing is over.

Rebs liked to point out the superior regard of their own army for civilian rights. Whenever they invaded the Northern or border country, they were amused at the fear of brigandage manifested by the inhabitants along the way. "Poor fools," remarked a soldier marching with Bragg through Kentucky in 1862, "the Yankees treated them so badly, they thought we would do the same. They soon found out that there is a great difference. The Yankee army is filled up with the scum of creation and ours with the best blood of the grand old Southland."

This Reb's observation gives a clue to an impression that was widely prevalent in the Southern ranks and accepted by them as a partial explanation of the low character of Union soldiery; namely, that the majority of the Federals were recruited from the lowbred immigrant class which swelled the population of the East and the Midwest. It was pointed out repeatedly in home letters that prisoners encountered by the correspondents could not speak the English language. There can be no doubt that a particularly strong prejudice against foreigners in the South increased hatred of the Yankee soldiery. The comment of a sergeant of Bragg's army is typical of a general attitude. "Quite a number of Northern bums, called U.S. soldiers passed our camps," he wrote; "most of them were imported from Germany." . . .

The concept of heartlessness or brutality swelled considerably the hatred springing up in the hearts of the soldiers of the South. Atrocity stories circulating through the camps told of the bayoneting and shooting of Rebels after they were captured; of helpless Confederate wounded having throats slashed and tongues cut out; of gray-clads shot in the act of ministering to suffering Federals lying between the lines; of Yankees using poisoned bullets; and of the denuding and abuse by Northerners of defenseless Southern women in areas of invasion.

Warriors of all ages have been quick to resent affronts to women. The South, with its chivalric traditions, was unusually touchy on this score. It was this oversensitiveness that caused the Northern general B. F. Butler to be so thoroughly despised. For his alleged thievery the General was derided as "Spoon" Butler, but it was his notorious Order No. 28, in which he threatened to regard as harlots some New Orleans ladies who were "acting up" under his rule, that gave him the sobriquet of "Beast." . . .

Hatred for Sherman, Sheridan and other generals was hardly less than that for Butler. Lincoln was likewise regarded as low and brutish, so much so in fact that even intelligent soldiers regarded his demise as a blessing, as witness the entry of April 19, 1865, in the diary of Private R. W. Waldrop: "Everything in mourning today for old Abe who ought to have been killed four years ago." The attitude of the man in the ranks toward those of the North, both high and low, was aptly if not accurately summed up by the Virginian who wrote his mother that "the Yankee horde have forgotten the laws of war & have not natural honour and chivalry enough to suggest them on the conduct they enforce. . . . They are like ferocious monkeys which I believe the Spanish proverb makes the most cruel, wicked, and capricious of tyrants."

Another factor which contributed to Johnny Reb's loathing of the Yankees was the conviction that the men in blue were lacking in courage. This belief had a powerful hold on Southerners before hostilities began; it gained wider currency after the battle of Bull Run, and continued to flourish till the end of the war. Occasionally a soldier's letter or an officer's report of a battle conceded gallantry to the foe. After Missionary Ridge, for instance, Lieutenant James Hall wrote to his father that the scaling of the heights by the Federals "was a sublime spectacle and I could not withhold my admiration."

In similar vein wrote Captain B. E. Stiles after an encounter on the Virginia front in 1862. "It is all stuff saying that the Yankees are cowards," he concluded. "They fought as boldly as men ever fought and they fight well every time I'v been in front of them," was the testimony of still another officer after Second Manassas. But complimentary expressions such as these are amazing for their rarity.

Derogatory sentiments on the other hand were often recorded. "I saw a house full of Yankee prisoners," wrote a Texan in 1861; "they were large hardy looking men, but as you know they lack the courage."

A short time later an Alabamian boasted to his brother, "We whip them everytime We meet, no matter how great their Numbers, or how few ours. The infernal Scoundrels cant stand the Bayonet — they Scamper like a herd of cattle." A year and a half later this Reb held his antagonists in the same low esteem. "I hope it won't be long," he wrote then, "untill fighting Jo Hooker will be able to advance . . . with his army of white livers and give us a chance to enrich some of the poor land of old Virginia with their corrupt Bodyes." But, on second thought he retracted the statement attributing fertilizing qualities to Federal remains, recalling that a farmer whose property included a portion of the Manassas battlefield had told him that "one Yankee body will kill an acre of land whereas a Southerner's bones will enrich it for all time to come." . . .

Antipathy toward ordinary Yankees was deep and pervasive, but it was mild in comparison with the hatred which most Rebs felt for Negroes who wore the blue. All in all some 200,000 Negroes were taken into Federal ranks during the war. These colored soldiers did not get to do their full share of fighting, but they did figure prominently in a few engagements, including Port Hudson, Fort Pillow, Brice's Cross Roads and the Crater. The mere thought of a Negro in uniform was enough to arouse the ire of the average Reb; he was wont to see in the arming of the blacks the fruition of oft-repeated Yankee efforts to incite slave insurrections and to establish racial equality. Anticipation of conflict with former slaves brought savage delight to his soul. And when white and black met on the field of battle the results were terrible.

Negroes were taken prisoners in several engagements, but if the wishes of the private soldiers who fought them had prevailed, no quarter would have been granted. Most of the Rebs felt as the Mississippian who wrote his mother: "I hope I may never see a Negro Soldier," he said, "or I cannot be . . . a Christian Soldier."

On more than one occasion Negro troops were slain after they were captured. Following the Crater affair a Reb wrote his homefolk that all the colored prisoners "would have ben killed had it not been for gen Mahone who beg our men to Spare them." One of his comrades killed several, he continued; Mahone "told him for God's sake stop." The man replied, "Well gen let me kill one more," whereupon, according to the correspondent, "he deliberately took out his pocket knife and cut one's Throat."

But the War of Secession was not all hatred. Many Rebs whose anger flashed to white heat in battle became indulgent and generous toward the foe when fighting subsided. Others felt little or no hate for the men in blue, even while they were pinning writhing bodies to the earth with their bayonets. To these latter, fighting Yankees was regarded more or less in the light of a regular chore — disagreeable, indeed, but unavoidable.

The war of the sixties has been called a "polite war," and in a sense the designation is apt. The conflict followed generally the pattern of a series of battles. Men of the opposing armies when not actually engaged in a shooting fray were wont to observe niceties that in twentieth-century warfare would be regarded as absurd. And even during combat there were occasional exchanges of courtesy. The conduct of the war in its entirety had something of the flavor of a medieval tournament.

The chivalric concept manifested itself at the very outset of the war. When Beauregard's aides were conferring with Major Robert Anderson in April 1861 on the eve of Sumter's bombardment, one of the Union officers complained jokingly to A. R. Chisolm that the garrison's supply of cigars was woefully short. The Rebel officers said nothing, but when they returned to the Fort for further conference a short time later they brought to the Yankee garrison not only a generous supply of cigars but several cases of claret as well. Before the night was over, these same Rebs gave the order to the batteries to open fire on the Fort — an order calculated to reduce the bastion to utter ruin.

This Fort Sumter incident was but the precursor of thousands of acts of mutual kindness. In many instances the motive was sympathy for an unfortunate antagonist. A Rebel cavalry company while on a scouting expedition in the fall of 1861 surprised a group of Yanks and took several prisoners, including a lieutenant in his late 'teens. The leader of the Confederates wrote his wife the next day that he could have killed "the handsome little fellow," but that he had not the heart to shoot him when he saw his beardless face. So he pulled his youthful prize up behind and as they rode along they "got to be quite good friends." When this officer overtook his company he found to his surprise that the other prisoners had likewise captivated their captors, for "every rascally Yankee was mounted and my men on foot." And thus they proceeded to camp.

During the second battle of Bull Run in 1862, W. F. Jenkins, a seventeen-year-old private of the Twelfth Georgia Regiment, was severely wounded.

At nightfall two of his comrades came to take him to the field hospital. As they struggled along through the darkness, they were halted with the query, "Who are you?"

"We are two men of the Twelfth Georgia, carrying a wounded comrade to the hospital," they replied.

"Don't you know you are in the Union lines?" asked the sentry.

"No," answered one of the Rebs.

"You are. Go to your right," said the Federal.

"Man, you've got a heart in you," said the second Reb as the little party turned to the right and headed for the Confederate lines.

In other instances Federals were the recipients of kindnesses. At Vicksburg, at Fredericksburg and at Cold Harbor, Yankee wounded who cried piteously for water as they lay between the lines were given succor by Rebs who dared to run a gantlet of fire to fulfill errands of mercy. During the engagement at Kenesaw Mountain in June 1864 a copse which sheltered some wounded Federals caught fire, threatening the helpless soldiers who lay there. Colonel W. H. Martin, of the First Arkansas Regiment, immediately jumped to the parapet, waved his handkerchief and cried out to the enemy, "We won't fire a gun until you get them away." Shooting on both sides ceased instantly, and the wounded men were removed from danger. At the end of the brief truce a Federal major gave his own fine pistols to Colonel Martin in appreciation of the humane action. . . .

In Virginia in 1862, and in Mississippi the next year, informal truces were called to give soldiers opportunity to pick the luscious blackberries ripening on the no man's land that lay between the lines.

Occasionally the spirit of mutual helpfulness was carried to amusing extremes. During the Georgia campaign of 1864 Rebel soldiers on picket, lacking digging implements to make rifle pits, were forced to beg spades of Yankee vedettes opposite them; and the Yanks were graciously accommodating. This politeness had a parallel on the Virginia front, but with the men in gray filling the role of lenders. . . .

The spirit of friendliness that sprinkled Yankee-Rebel relations had no more eloquent expression than the musical fetes in which the two armies occasionally participated. Sometimes Federal bands played for the Rebels, as at Fredericksburg during the war's second winter when a crack group of Union musicians posted on the Northern bank of the Rappahannock staged a concert unique in the annals of war. The program began with a medley of Northern airs — patriotic tunes and war songs. This was well enough for the listeners in blue, but not to the complete liking of that part of the audience stationed on the Southern bank.

"Now give us some of ours," shouted Confederates across the river.

Without hesitation the band swung into the tunes of "Dixie," "My Maryland" and the "Bonnie Blue Flag." This brought forth a lusty and prolonged cheer from the Southerners. Finally the music swelled into the tender strains of "Home, Sweet Home," and the countryside reverberated with the cheers of thousands of men on both sides of the stream.

At other times bands of the opposite armies participated in unpremeditated joint concerts. At Murfreesboro, for instance, on the night before the great battle, a Federal band began just before tattoo to play "Yankee Doodle," "Hail Columbia" and other tunes popular in Northern camps. After a little while the Union musicians yielded to the Rebel band which played a group of Southern favorites. These voluntary exchanges had continued for some time when one of the bands struck up "Home, Sweet Home." Immediately the other band joined in, and in a few moments the tune was picked up by a multitude of voices of both camps. For the brief period that the countryside reverberated with the notes of Payne's cherished song the animosities of war were lost in nostalgic reveries, and the fading away of the final notes found tears on the cheeks of scores of veterans who on the morrow were to walk unflinchingly into the maelstrom of battle.

The element of competition was occasionally introduced into these informal concerts. A Confederate band would run through a tune. Then a Federal band would attempt to give a better rendition of the same piece. In these contests — forerunners of present-day "battles of bands" — the Yankees usually came off with the honors.

In the absence of bands the joint fetes often took vocal form. Men on opposite sides of rivers bordering the Confederacy on several occasions united in the singing of "Home, Sweet Home." When in less mellow mood, their efforts were inclined to greater levity. In January 1863, for instance, Lieutenant W. J. Kincheloe of the Forty-ninth Virginia regiment wrote to his father: "We are on one side of the Rappahannock, the Enemy on the other. . . . Our boys will sing a Southern song, the Yankees will reply by singing the same tune to Yankee words." The lieutenant's observation is substantiated by the fact that several Civil War songs had both Yankee and Rebel versions.

One co-operative venture on the Rapidan was of a religious character. Private Goodwin of a Southern regiment, following the example of many of his fellow soldiers, "got religion" during the war, and a group of about fifty of his comrades escorted him down to the river's edge to be baptized. The procession attracted the attention of the Federals, and a considerable number of them came ambling down to the opposite bank to view the proceedings. Presently the Confederates launched into the hymn, "There is a Fountain Filled with Blood." This was a tune familiar to soldiers of both armies, and many of the Yanks joined in the song. Private Goodwin was duly dipped to the satisfaction of all.

This religious collaboration had an unhappy counterpart in interarmy gambling and drinking. There was a little island out in the middle of the Rappahannock where soldiers from both banks were wont to meet now and then to drown their woes in a draught of liquor. Gaming between pickets, and between other troops, was rather frequent. A Rebel officer making an unexpected tour of inspection one night on the Petersburg lines was shocked to find a considerable stretch of the trenches devoid of men. On close inquiry he discovered that the absentees were, by previous arrangement, in the Federal ditches playing cards.

Joint swimming parties were sometimes indulged in by troops stationed along rivers. These were apt to be accompanied by a great deal of "ducking" and banter. In fact, in whatever circumstances Rebs and Yanks came into proximity, there was usually not a little of "smart talk" or "jawing."

The boys in blue would sometimes shout across a Virginia river to inquire how "old Jeff" was getting along. The Rebs would retort by inviting the Yanks to come to Richmond and see, reminding them of several previous unsuccessful efforts to reach the Confederate capital. At Vicksburg the Federals would yell out, "Haven't you Johnnies got a new general — General Starvation?" The men inside the works would come back with the queries, "Have you Yanks all got nigger wives yet? How do you like them?" Before Atlanta the Federals would cry out from their trenches, "What is Confederate money worth?" or "How much do you ask for your slaves?" From the Rebel ditches would come the taunt, "What niggers command your brigade?" or "Have the niggers improved the Yankee breed any?"

A Yank who placed himself in a vulnerable position by shouting to a bedraggled Reb, "Hant you got no better clothes than those?" received the pungent answer from Private Tom Martin: "You are a set of damned fools — do you suppose we put on our good clothes to go out to kill damned dogs?"

On yet another occasion a Federal holding confab with an antagonist between the picket lines said sentimentally, "Why can't this war stop? I love you like a brother." The Reb's reply, in the words of a comrade, was: "You can say more for me than I can say for you for I haven't a dambed bit of love for you."

Good-natured raillery might be provoked by the most unexpected occurrences. One morning early in 1865 a large hawk came flying along over the lines before Petersburg. Soldiers from both sides immediately forgot their potshooting at each other and opened fire on the bird. It became bewildered by the cross fusillade and lit in a tall poplar tree halfway between the trenches. When finally it was shot down, both Yanks and Rebs let out a tremendous whoop, each side claiming the honors of marksmanship and demanding possession of the prize.

By far the most common form of fraternizing was the exchange of small articles of various sorts by men of the opposing camps. Throughout the war, in all portions of the armies, traffic flourished, and this despite the efforts of superior officers to put a stop to it. The usual method of procedure was for the men to meet at some intermediate point between the lines and there to swap tobacco for coffee, peanuts for pocketknives, pipes for stationery, and Southern for Northern newspapers. A Mississippian wrote his sister in 1864 from Petersburg, "We read each other's Papers in 15 minutes after the News Boys bring them from the Office."

These barter sessions were frequently the occasion of mutual cussing of "bombproof" generals, or grousing over troubles — which were very much the same in both armies — of talk about home affairs, of display, with polite comment, of daguerreotypes of sweethearts, and of expression of hope for a speedy end to the war. Now and then the parley would end with a generous snort of "tanglefoot," drawn perforce from the Yankee canteen. In more than one instance the participants in these get-togethers were members of the same family — brothers, or father and son, drawn to different allegiance by the fortunes of war.

Serious-minded Rebs were sometimes conscience-stricken as a result of these interminglings. A Mississippian who wrote his family of "our boys and the Yankees mixing up and talking together on friendly terms," remarked apologetically, "I threw an old dirty Yank a piece of Tobacco and He threw me a little sack of Coffee — I did not have any chat for them."

A Tar Heel who had trafficked recently with the Feds confided to his father:

> I tell you the Yankees assembled around me like a parcel of buserdes [buzzards] would around a lot of dead horses I chatted [with] them about ½ hour and left I tell you I dident feel rite no way.

Rebs and Yanks separated by narrow rivers developed an ingenious device for carrying on trade. Little boats, some two or three feet long, were made of bark or of scrap lumber, fitted with sails, loaded with coffee, tobacco and papers, and the sails set in such fashion as to carry the craft to the opposite shore. The recipients of the cargo on the other side would in turn load the vessel with items of exchange and head it back to the port of origin. A soldier in Lee's army records the fact that on pleasant days during the spring of 1862 the waters of the Rappahannock near Fredericksburg "were fairly dotted with the fairy fleet."

During the war's last winter, pickets facing each other along the lines before Petersburg, when denied the privilege of trade and communication, resorted to the expedient of tying small articles and messages to grapeshot or shell fragments and tossing them over to the rifle pits of their opponents. In this way they "flanked" the interdiction laid down by superiors.

Now and then a couple of Rebs would go over and spend the night in the Yankee camps, returning just before daylight. In such instances the Yanks might give expression to their good will by filling the haversacks of the parting visitors with coffee and other delicacies rarely seen by men in gray. Rebs likewise played host on occasion. A Delaware lieutenant who made a "hollering" acquaintance with a group of Confederates on picket was invited by them to a party behind the Southern lines. The Rebs called for their guest in a boat, outfitted him with civilian clothing, escorted him to the dance, introduced him to the country girls as a new recruit, and before dawn deposited him safely back on the Federal side of the river.

It would be easy to exaggerate the significance of the fraternizing that dotted the Confederate war. Hatred and fighting far outweighed friendliness and intermingling. But the latter always existed in such proportions as to worry high officers. The fact that the men on both sides spoke for the most part the same language, plus the fact that many had mutual acquaintances or relatives, tended to draw them together. This, coupled with curiosity, war-weariness in both camps, failure to comprehend clearly the issues of the conflict, and the desire to trade, made it increasingly difficult to maintain a definite line of demarcation between the two camps. In the last months of the war, as defeat became more and more apparent, Rebs who went out to swap or to parley with the Yankees failed in increasing numbers to return to their side of the lines.

This inescapable urge of blue and gray to intermingle and to exchange niceties suggests that — grim war though it was — the internecine struggle of the sixties was not only in some aspect a chivalric war but that it was in many respects a crazy and a needless war as well. There is some point, at least, to the observation made by a Reb after a conference on a log with a Yankee vedette. "We talked the matter over," he said, "and could have settled the war in thirty minutes had it been left to us."

STUDY GUIDE

1. In the opening of the selection, Wiley describes the hatred of some southern soldiers for the Yankee enemy. What reasons does he give for this hatred? What role might the following factors have played in the soldiers' letters: impressing the folks back home; bolstering their own morale; providing a psychological defense for participating in the horrors of war?

2. Aside from the denunciation of Yankees, the letters that Wiley quotes reveal an extraordinary boasting about the virtues of the South. Find instances in the selection that illustrate the Southerner's conception of women, chivalry, bravery and so forth. In what ways is there a disparity between their words and their actions?

3. Wiley notes that the Civil War has been called a "polite war," in contrast to twentieth-century wars. What evidence does he give to support this characterization? Does this evidence consist primarily of individual acts of kindness and compassion, or does the official policy of the two armies in conducting the war also reflect humaneness?

4. Consider the following aspects of warfare, and indicate how wars in our time differ from the Civil War in each respect: treatment of civilian populations; individual atrocities; personal confrontations of infantry soldiers

in battle and in picket-line duty; how soldiers are killed; the degree of personal responsibility and concern that higher officers feel for their armies.

5. Compare the feelings described by Wiley with the animosities that are described by Carey McWilliams in the selection on the Mexican War, "The Expansionist Urge." What differences and similarities can you find in the relations of enemy forces in the two wars? For example, is the hatred expressed by southern soldiers for Northerners quite the same as that of Anglo-Americans for Mexicans, as described by McWilliams? What accounts for the differences?

BIBLIOGRAPHY

There are more books and articles on the American Civil War than on any other aspect of American history. Much of this material deals with the causes of the war and the military campaigns; to discover some of this literature, you can examine James G. Randall and David Donald, *The Civil War and Reconstruction* 2nd ed. (Boston, 1961) and Thomas J. Pressly, *Americans Interpret Their Civil War* * (Princeton, N.J., 1954). A good many other aspects of army life are treated in Wiley's *Johnny Reb* and its companion volume by the same author, *The Life of Billy Yank: The Common Soldier of the Union* (Indianapolis, Ind., 1952). The attitudes of contemporaries toward the war are described in Henry S. Commager, ed., *The Blue and the Gray: The Story of the Civil War as Told by Participants,* 2 vols. (Indianapolis, Ind., 1950). Among the many general treatments of the war, the best are: Allan Nevins, *The War for the Union,* 3 vols. (New York, 1959–1971); Bruce Catton, *This Hallowed Ground: The Story of the Union Side of the Civil War* * (Garden City, N.Y., 1956); and a three-volume series by Catton, of which the best volume is *A Stillness at Appomattox* * (Garden City, N.Y., © 1953). George W. Smith and Charles Judah, eds., *Life in the North during the Civil War: A Source History* (Albuquerque, N.M., 1966) is a collection of writings from the period of the Civil War that will give you an idea of life behind the lines. One of the best secondary works on the same subject, but limited to the capital, is Margaret Leech, *Reveille in Washington, 1860–1865* * (New York, © 1941). Conditions there, of course, were considerably different from life in the Confederate capital, which is studied in Alfred H. Bill, *The Beleaguered City: Richmond, 1861–1865* (New York, 1946).

For a number of reasons, there are more good works on social conditions in the Confederacy than on wartime life in the North. A general work on the Confederacy, with several chapters on economic and social conditions, is E. Merton Coulter, *The Confederate States of America, 1861–1865* (Baton Rouge, La., 1950). Charles W. Ramsdell, *Behind the Lines in the Southern Confederacy* (Baton Rouge, La., 1944) is an excellent work more strictly confined to the home front, while Mary E. Massey, *Ersatz in the Confederacy* (Columbia, S.C., 1952) is a fascinating study of the substitutes that were used for food, clothing, and other necessities of life.

Bell I. Wiley also has works on southern whites and blacks in the Confederacy: *The Plain People of the Confederacy* (Baton Rouge, La., 1943) and *Southern Negroes, 1861–1865* * (New Haven, Conn., 1938). The latter work should be read in conjunction with the study on Negroes in the North by Benjamin Quarles, *The Negro in the Civil War* * (Boston, 1953). Chapters 7 and 8 of Quarles's book give an interesting picture of the reaction of blacks to emancipation.

10991

000243